The Qualitative
Research Experience

DEBORAH K. PADGETT, EDITOR
New York University

THOMSON
™
BROOKS/COLE

Australia • Canada • Mexico • Singapore • Spain
United Kingdom • United States

THOMSON
BROOKS/COLE

Executive Editor: Lisa Gebo
Assistant Editor: Alma Dea Michelena
Editorial Assistant: Sheila Walsh
Marketing Manager: Caroline Concilla
Marketing Assistant: Mary Ho
Advertising Project Manager: Tami Strang
Technology Project Manager: Barry Connolly
Editorial Production Manager: Edward Wade

Print/Media Buyer: Judy Inouye
Permissions Editor: Kiely Sexton
Production Service and Composition: UG / GGS
  Information Services, Inc.
Copy Editor: Jennifer D'Inzeo
Cover Designer: Andrew Ogus
Printer: Webcom

Printed in Canada
1 2 3 4 5 6 7   07 06 05 04 03

For more information about our products, contact us at
Thomson Learning Academic Resource Center
1-800-423-0563

For permission to use material from this text, contact us by
Phone: 1-800-730-2214 **Fax:** 1-800-730-2215
Web: http://www.thomsonrights.com

Library of Congress Control Number:
2003107276

ISBN 0-534-60165-0

Wadsworth/Thomson Learning
10 Davis Drive
Belmont, CA 94002-3098
USA

Asia
Thomson Learning
5 Shenton Way # 01-01
UIC Building
Singapore 068808

Australia/New Zealand
Thomson Learning
102 Dodds Street
SouthBank, Victoria 3006
Australia

Canada
Nelson
1120 Birchmount Road
Toronto, Ontario M1K 5G4
Canada

Europe/Middle East/Africa
Thomson Learning
High Holborn House
50/51 Bedford Row
London WC1R 4LR
United Kingdom

Latin America
Thomson Learning
Seneca, 53
Colonia Polanco
11560 Mexico D.F.
Mexico

Spain/Portugal
Paraninfo
Calle/Magallanes, 25
28015 Madrid, Spain

Contents

5   MIXED METHODS IN A DISSERTATION STUDY   119
by Deborah Gioia

9   THE ROLE OF THE MENTORING RELATIONSHIP IN QUALITATIVE RESEARCH   211
by Ida Roldan and R. Dennis Shelby

10   PEER DEBRIEFING AND SUPPORT GROUPS: FORMATION, CARE, AND MAINTENANCE   225
by Deborah K. Padgett, Reji Mathew, and Susan Conte

CODA: A FEW OBSERVATIONS FOR STUDENTS   316
by Deborah K. Padgett

Preface

Enthusiasm for qualitative methods is reaching an all-time high these days. It is now commonplace to hear a program officer from the National Institutes of Health plead for rigorous qualitative research proposals and to see qualitative studies published in the most prestigious medical and scientific journals. In social work, the proportion of qualitative methods dissertations tripled in between 1982 and 1992 (Brun, 1997) and the pace has undoubtedly picked up since.

The bandwagon has become even more crowded with the arrival of experienced quantitative researchers who have decided that qualitative methods can take them to places they could not have previously gone. When a leading research methodologist such as Thomas Cook states that "qualitative researchers have won the qualitative-quantitative debate" (quoted in Patton, 2002, p. 585), he is referring to this dramatic upsurge in popularity, a phenomenon that is gratifying and invigorating.

Meanwhile, the qualitative methods family has become more diversified and sophisticated than ever before. Although a child of the social sciences, qualitative research has had its most rapid growth in applied fields such as education, nursing, medicine, business, and social work. The addition of these practice-based professions and a blurring of genres with the arts and humanities (Denzin & Lincoln, 2000, p. 15) has brought an intellectual flowering of approaches and styles that almost defies description.

Qualitative studies are arrayed along multiple continua based upon epistemology, methodology, mode of presentation, and audience. Qualitative researchers may consider themselves (or be labeled as) postpositivists, neorealists, constructivists, constructionists, poststructuralists, critical theorists, interpretivists, feminists, queer theorists, or some combination thereof. Philosophical traditions range from pragmatism to phenomenology to postmodernism.

Qualitative researchers engage in ethnography, grounded theory, case studies, life histories, narrative analyses, and participatory action research. Some are committed to theory building; others value rich description; still others work almost entirely within the arenas of evaluation, policy, and practice. Although some epistemologies and approaches match up better than others, any given qualitative study may incorporate several elements from this menu of varied options.

The concerned (or skeptical) observer may think that this bewildering array points to: (1) a lack of consensus on standards of excellence in qualitative research and (2) the futility of establishing *any* standards, consensual or otherwise. Although few would argue about the first point, fewer still would agree with the second. Thus, most qualitative researchers hold to a position that some studies are better than others and that some form of criteria are necessary to judge their merit.

This, of course, begs the question: whose criteria? Imagine trying to get two college instructors—one in the arts and the other in the sciences—to agree on joint standards of excellence and you get a sense of the discourse taking place within the qualitative methods family. Should we judge a qualitative study by its methodological rigor or by its performative resonance?

No longer do researchers (quantitative *or* qualitative) insist that knowledge is infallible and value free. But points of difference come from what frames of reference are useful when judging qualitative studies. If we are unwilling to accept either of the two extreme positions (a single set of standards should be applicable for all studies versus every study should have its own idiosyncratic standards), we are left with the task of agreeing to disagree and moving on to explicate what standards we will use (and why) and make every effort that our studies adhere to them. Otherwise, we risk lapsing into a state of intellectual nihilism.

The standards problem recedes somewhat if we accept that standards of some kind are needed (no matter how localized or temporary these may be), but the problem of implementation still remains. Here is where this book enters the picture.

Although the contributions to this book represent diverse voices and inflections, a common purpose unites them: a desire to bolster the supportive structures of qualitative research. Prescriptions for a healthy environment for qualitative inquiry tend to be broadly defined and infrastructural—coursework supplemented by hands-on training and mentoring opportunities. But resources and personnel with expertise are, unfortunately, in short supply.

The juxtaposition of booming popularity with weak infrastructure supports presents a dangerous opportunity for qualitative researchers. The opportunity comes from having a greater impact on knowledge development that comes from gaining a wider, more appreciative audience. The danger comes from being spread too thin, leading to qualitative studies that are unimaginative, conceptually impoverished, and methodologically weak. This book is designed to assist in filling the gap left by these shortages.

There are literally dozens of textbooks on qualitative methods, so why add one more? Existing texts in qualitative methods tend to be either general introductory books or works devoted to particular advanced topics. There are many examples of the former, and I confess to contributing my own general text for social work researchers a few years ago (Padgett, 1998). Advanced texts can be roughly categorized as books on *specific methods* (e.g., narrative analysis, grounded theory, evaluation) or *skills and techniques* (e.g., data analysis, writing the report, using computer software).

There are, of course, exceptions to this dichotomy between general and advanced. But the landscape of publishing in qualitative methods offers few books such as the one you are now holding. Permit me to explain further.

This volume complements and expands upon existing texts by offering a comprehensive package, including (1) exemplary qualitative studies representing six of the leading approaches in qualitative research (grounded theory, narrative, ethnography, case studies, mixed methods, and evaluation) followed by essays in which the authors reflect on their behind the scenes experiences while conducting the research and (2) topical chapters on critical methodological issues in qualitative research.

In the genre of modeling exemplary research, the classic is Patricia Golden's *The Research Experience* (1972), a collection written by leading sociologists in which they offered personal essays about how the studies (mostly quantitative) were conceived and carried out. Golden's book was the inspiration and the template for Part I of this volume. Thus, the exemplary studies featured in Part I focus less on the rules of the game than on how those rules get applied in the field. The personal essays following each study allow the authors—all researchers who have successfully published and disseminated their work—to reflect upon their experiences and role model the qualitative research experience for readers.

The chapters in Part II cover up-to-date methodological issues and topics that are either given short shrift in the literature on qualitative methods (e.g., cross-linguistic interviewing and data analysis) or are too important to leave out (e.g., ethical issues). Each chapter offers an in-depth examination of a particular topic to enhance skills and supportive structures in qualitative research.

This book has another distinguishing feature: it is targeted to the largest and fastest growing audience of would-be qualitative researchers—students and experienced quantitative researchers in the practicing professions. Much has been written about the natural fit between qualitative methods and the various worlds of practice: nursing, education, social work, and medicine. An enormous sigh of relief seems to have emanated from these professions when qualitative methods were first introduced over the past few decades.

It is not difficult to see why—the allure of qualitative research is unmistakable. The messiness of the human condition has often overwhelmed the best intentions of quantitative researchers seeking to operationalize and measure phenomena that were deeply subjective (e.g., physical pain), sensitive (e.g., sexual abuse), or both (e.g., psychotic delusions and hallucinations). In the fields of nursing and education, the trickle of interest has since grown into a veritable river of research appearing in books and journals. For social work, straddling the macro (analyses of poverty and social welfare policies) and the micro (direct practice with individuals and families) made the embrace of qualitative methods a bit more hesitant, but the romance has intensified dramatically in recent years.

As with any such compendium, this book involved making choices of inclusion and exclusion. I confess to having vigorously exercised my prerogative as editor (including the shameless inclusion of four chapters in which I am sole or co-author). I accept full responsibility for the book's overall contours and areas of emphasis. For example, the contributions to this volume are all rooted in social work (although their relevance extends to the social sciences and human services professions in general). Every attempt was made to balance topics with populations of interest, with special emphasis placed on cross-cultural diversity.

The reader will also notice that this volume is book ended with chapters that reflect an editorial point of view best summed up as pragmatism. My pragmatic standpoint comes from a personal and professional journey that began with a doctorate in urban anthropology, took a quantitative turn with post-doctoral training in public health and epidemiology and, finally, landed me (comfortably) in the practice-based profession of social work. As will be discussed in the Introduction, postmodernism and social constructivism are appealing on many levels—the eloquence and passion of their proponents has been (and will be) a powerful force in shaping qualitative inquiry. But the reality principle inherent in practice-based (and practice-relevant) research makes the postmodernist revolution a tough sell outside of academia.

Espousing pragmatism might be seen as selling out to the hegemony of positivism and quantitative methods. I prefer to think instead of the two levels that we practice-based researchers are sandwiched between—the powerful (and unforgiving) world of research funding and policymaking and the local worlds of our targeted populations, programs, and services. My experience with the former has included private foundations, the Centers for Disease Control, various branches of the National Institutes of Health, and lobbying efforts in Congress (on behalf of social work research funding). My experience with the latter has included work with Bosnian refugees and medically underserved Latina and African-American women as well as advocacy and research with a paradigm-shifting agency that provides supported housing and services for homeless mentally ill persons in New York City (Pathways to Housing, Inc.). This work, along with many fruitful (and occasionally fractious) discussions with colleagues and students, has led me to pragmatic philosophy.

The other esteemed contributors to this volume do not necessarily share in this epistemological stance (nor should they have to)—we are a diverse lot. We also represented various stages of academic development when conducting our studies—including a masters student (Barr), doctoral students (Conte,

Mathew, and Roldan), junior faculty (Floersch, Gioia, Lukens, Överlien, Shibusawa, and Waldrop), and senior faculty (Drisko, Hydén, Oktay, Padgett, and Sands). We have all moved on to new studies and endeavors but we still have vivid memories (not to mention notes and journal entries) that capture those heady days when our studies were being carried out.

This book represents—in all of its glory and grittiness—the lived experience of performing qualitative research. We know that qualitative research never follows a straight and narrow path. It zigzags, banks around curves, takes forks in the road, and even makes U-turns. But it should not be an impenetrable maze and we need not end up on the road to nowhere. This book is not a road map but it could be a valuable companion for your journey. We hope that you will agree.

ACKNOWLEDGMENTS

This book was made possible by the many helpful and invigorating discussions I have had over the years with colleagues and students, including my fellow attendees at the annual conference of the Society for Social Work and Research (SSWR). I am deeply grateful to every one of the contributors for being so generous (and timely) in their work and for putting up with my editorial style. My thanks to Steve Rutter for linking me to Patricia Golden's seminal work. I would like to thank the following individuals who reviewed this book in its manuscript form: Dona Kenneally, University of South Dakota; John A. Casey, California State University, Bakersfield; Jeff Schrenzel, Western New England College; Vicki Gardine Williams, Tennessee State University; Christine Gringeri, University of Utah; Vicki Vandiver, Portland State University; Craig LeCroy, Arizona State University. Last but not least, Ms. Franchesca Davila was invaluable in helping to prepare the manuscript for submission.

REFERENCES

Brun, C. (1997). The process and implications of doing qualitative research: An analysis of 54 doctoral dissertations. *Journal of Sociology and Social Welfare*, 24, 95–112.

Denzin, N. K., & Lincoln, Y. S. (Eds.) (2000). *Handbook of qualitative research* (2nd ed.). Thousand Oaks, CA: Sage.

Golden, P. (Ed.) (1972). *The research experience*. New York: Columbia University Press.

Padgett, D. K. (1998). *Qualitative methods in social work research*. Thousand Oaks, CA: Sage.

Patton, M. Q. (2002). *Qualitative research and evaluation methods* (3rd ed.). Thousand Oaks, CA: Sage.

About the Editor

D r. Padgett, a professor at the New York University School of Social Work, received her doctorate in urban anthropology in 1979 and completed postdoctoral programs in mental health services research at Columbia University School of Public Health from 1985 to 1986 and at Duke University Department of Psychiatry from 1994 to 1995. She is the author of *Qualitative Methods in Social Work Research: Challenges and Rewards*, a leading textbook in social work (Sage, 1998), editor of *The Handbook of Ethnicity, Aging, and Mental Health* (Greenwood Press, 1995), and coauthor of *Program Evaluation*, 3rd edition (Wadsworth, 2001).

Dr. Padgett has also published extensively on the health/mental health needs and service use of older women, underserved ethnic groups, and the homeless. She has been co-principal investigator on four NIH-funded grants and national co-director of the Screening Adherence Follow-up (SAFe) project funded by the Centers for Disease Control and Prevention from 1997 to 2002. Her current interests include cancer screening and follow-up care for medically underserved women, qualitative studies of the "process" of care for psychiatrically disabled homeless adults, and pragmatic philosophy as a basis for qualitative and mixed-methods research.

Dr. Padgett has served on the editorial boards of The Gerontologist, The Journal of Gerontology: Psychological Science, Social Work, Social Work Research, Research on Social Work Practice, and The Journal of Behavioral Health Services and Research. She has been an active member of the board of directors of the Society for Social Work and Research (SSWR) since 1998 and was recently elected to serve as president of SSWR from 2004 to 2006. She is also a founding member of the National Program Committee of the John A. Hartford Foundation Geriatric Social Work Faculty Scholars Program.

Introduction

Finding a Middle Ground in Qualitative Research

DEBORAH K. PADGETT

SCIENCE, TECHNOLOGY, AND THE NEED FOR QUALITATIVE RESEARCH: A PARABLE

Faith in the scientific method has been the rock-solid foundation of technological advances in aviation, medicine, and engineering that transformed the twentieth century. With the advent of the Space Age and the computer era in the 1960s, our love affair with technology became solidified for decades to come. Postmodern criticism of this seeming reverence for science has had no visible effect on the continued investment of billions of dollars in research and development by government and industry in the search for new technologies (and profits).

But this boundless enthusiasm for science and technology has been tempered by recent events. Similar to what has happened in the field of medicine (where each day seems to bring a new media report of a studies debunking the benefits of sacred cows such as hormone replacement therapy), the pendulum has started to swing back as new questions emerge from unexpected places.

A tragic example comes from the aftermath of the terrorist attacks on the World Trade Center on September 11, 2001—a day of horror that thousands of downtown New Yorkers witnessed firsthand (including this author) and that the rest of the city and the world experienced in real time through nonstop media reporting. Among the disturbing sequelae of September 11 was an awareness of the limits of technology and information management (the latter defined as the science of connecting people in the know with people who need to know). In a newspaper article entitled "Too Much Information, Not Enough Knowledge" *New York Times* journalist John Schwartz wrote about the complete breakdown of information systems and emergency management on the morning of September 11 (Schwartz, 2002). On the one hand, technology provided unprecedented access to information—cell phone calls enabled flight attendants to alert the airlines about the hijackings and gave passengers on the airplanes a way to find out what was happening and communicate with their families. Satellite technology sent live broadcasts of the Twin Towers' collapse beaming to televisions around the world.

But technology failed in helping firefighters save workers trapped on the upper floors of the Twin Towers—the towers' elevators as well as satellite, radio, and telephone communications were disabled by the explosions. Fire and police department commanders lacked common radio frequencies and were forced to communicate by sending messengers running through the falling debris. Even the old standby Emergency Broadcast System was nowhere to be found.

Basic information sharing became impossible with this massive communications breakdown and hundreds of civilians and firefighters probably lost their lives needlessly (Dwyer, Flynn, & Fessenden, 2002). The significance of human factors emerged from another technological limitation in the wake of September 11—the loss of massive amounts of computer-stored data. Computer backup systems in World Trade Center offices were disabled because they were either destroyed or rendered inaccessible (many of the backup computer staff had perished and taken with them their passwords). Stymied but desperate, the office workers sat down and talked about their departed colleagues' lives—their spouses', children's, and pet's names, favorite vacation spots, and other personal information. In this way, they were able to come up with the passwords and gain access to retrieve valuable data (Kelly & Stark, 2002).

These brief anecdotes are not intended to question the fundamental importance of technology. Indeed, a convincing argument for greater reliance on technology could be made by citing tragedies caused by human error (surgeons and air traffic controllers come readily to mind). Nor can we fault scientific inquiry for being saddled with unrealistic expectations that are not met (or capable of being met). Seeds of doubt come from within science itself, thanks in large part to philosopher Karl Popper's influential thesis that science should be predicated upon skepticism, or "falsifiability," rather than conclusive proof (it takes only one black swan to disprove the hypothesis that all swans are white). To paraphrase writer Adam Gopnik (2002), Popper believed that science is more about quarrelling than proof.

The idea that such back-and-forth arguing produced incremental (and inevitable) growth in scientific understanding was challenged by Thomas Kuhn in *The Structure of Scientific Revolutions* (1970). Kuhn asserted that scientific inquiry was not a gradual accretion of new and improved knowledge but was instead a conservative, risk-averse enterprise in which scientists embraced new theories only after a critical mass of countervailing evidence had been accumulated and the old theory was no longer weight bearing. Kuhn's ideas about paradigm shifts in no way precluded appreciation of science or technology, but they did help to demystify what was assumed to be an ineffable process of scientific discovery carried out by detached, impartial scientists.

THE BOOM IN QUALITATIVE RESEARCH

The intellectual ferment of the 1980s and 1990s produced a contrarian tendency within the humanities and social sciences that was a healthy counterpoint to the seemingly unassailable truth that science and technology had all of the answers and that quantitative methods and measurements were the superior route to finding these answers.[1] What is noteworthy of late is that discussions of the limits of science and technology are entering public discourse from outside of the academy, for example, from journalists and public officials concerned with safety. Although it may seem a stretch to say that such discussions lend added support for qualitative research, they surely help by opening the door to new ways of thinking about knowledge-building related to human factors. If science and technology do not have all of the answers, who or what does? More to the point, do we really need answers—or better questions?

Qualitative research offers an approach that is both complementary to, and transcendent of, conventional scientific inquiry. Its reach has extended far beyond the social sciences to a variety of professional fields including business, education, nursing, medicine, and social work. Qualitative research is not technophobic (witness the rapid growth in sales of computer software for qualitative data analysis), but its central tenets of flexibility, naturalism, and immersion situate the researcher in a very different place from his or her quantitative colleagues. In short, qualitative methods can direct our attention away from the blind pursuit of answers toward thinking about the questions.

Along the way, qualitative methods have diversified, encompassing the ancient traditions of ethnography and grounded theory as well as the later addition of phenomenological and narrative studies, the latter tugging qualitative inquiry ever closer to the humanities and the arts. (See, for example, chapters on anthropological poetics and performance ethnography in the Denzin and Lincoln reader on qualitative methods [2000]). In social work, several books have emerged over the past decade (Padgett, 1998a; Rissman, 1994; Shaw & Gould, 2001; Sherman & Reid, 1994; Tutty, Rothery & Grinnell, 1996) and the journal *Qualitative Social Work* debuted in 2001. Not surprisingly, these works feature the same diversity and tensions that characterize the paradigm debates going on elsewhere.

Much of the diversity in qualitative methods hinges on the degree of interpretive latitude exercised by the researcher. This is usually a reflection of the researcher's epistemological stance and of where the study is located (and for whom). Qualitative researchers housed in the liberal arts and sciences generally have greater freedom to be creative and to take intellectual risks whether they choose to do so or not. For those of us in the practice-based professions (in or outside of academia), the need for relevance means that we channel our efforts toward studies that build knowledge for improving practice.

Still, there are commonalities that transverse disciplinary and other boundaries. Qualitative researchers work from the bottom up and close up, not top down or far away. Our data are collected in vivo without the protective distance afforded by a laboratory or an interview room. Seeking depth and texture, we prefer to ask "how," not "why" or "what"(Becker, 1998).

Of course, some quantitative designs also provide grass-roots views (e.g., household surveys) and many a qualitative study has become unhinged from its context and floated off into the realm of biased speculation. Quantitative researchers themselves are the first to admit that their methods are difficult to apply to dynamic situations and to the nuances of human relationships (turning them into variables and inserting interaction terms into multivariate regression equations is a proximal undertaking at best). When our "subjects"[2] are heterogeneous in gender, age, ethnicity, social class, and sexual orientation, the complexities become ever greater and more elusive.

Quantitative data are collected in bits, stored in bytes, and interpreted via statistical analyses where hypotheses are tested by aggregating (and reaggregating) the data. Qualitative knowledge is based not on decontextualized bits of information, but on weaving back and forth between local context and conceptualization. Only humans are sentient beings who can connect the dots.

The lesson of September 11 in this "true story parable" is that technology and scientific inquiry are necessary, but never sufficient. Qualitative methods invite us to assume a perspective that is open to interstitial meaning, to see both the overarching contours and the hidden crevices. When it comes to human factors, we qualitative researchers have the market cornered.

PRAGMATISM AND
PRACTICE-BASED RESEARCH

The paradigm debates of the late twentieth century pivoted on an attempt to develop and reify a dichotomy: quantitative methods were equated with positivist/empiricist epistemologies and qualitative methods were synonymous with interpretivist/postmodern epistemologies[3] (House, 1994; Lincoln & Guba, 1985; Tashakkori & Teddlie, 1998). The first part of this equation is reasonable enough (although it glosses over significant changes in postpositivist thinking in recent decades), but the second has proven to be problematic for a number of reasons, all interrelated.

First, the leading approaches in qualitative research (e.g., grounded theory and ethnography) predate social constructivism and have maintained their independence and viability without becoming part of the new epistemologies.[4] A number of qualitative researchers have criticized postmodern-influenced paradigm purism (Hammersley, 1995; Lofland & Lofland, 1995; Patton, 2002; Snow & Morrill, 1995) and many more have gone about their work without it. Second, such an assumption fuses epistemology and methods needlessly. Qualitative methods have been ecumenical in their application, adopted by postpositivists as well as antipositivists (the same cannot be said of quantitative methods because postmodernist epistemology is largely defined by its opposition to them). Finally, this fusion overlooks tremendous methodological diversity—the distance between a randomized clinical trial and a survey questionnaire can be greater than the distance between two interview studies, one quantitative and the other qualitative.

Self-consciousness about epistemology has been a driving force for social constructivists seeking to gather the multiple forms of qualitative inquiry under the big tent of nonpositivist thinking. (Interestingly, researchers in the hard sciences rarely see the need for such self-conscious elucidation). Qualitative researchers in practice-based professions are expected to declare allegiance to a paradigm and deploy it in studies relevant to the nitty-gritty world of practice. Although some social work researchers have adopted social constructivism (Dean, 1993; Rodwell, 1998) and postmodernism (Chambon & Irving, 1994), the vast majority conducting qualitative research (at least in the United States) are not overtly paradigmatic in their approach.

Doubts about the necessity of such declarations have led some qualitative researchers to turn to the philosophy of pragmatism (Howe, 1988; Patton, 2002; Reichardt & Rallis, 1994; Tashakkori & Teddlie, 1998). Pragmatic philosophy grew out of the writings of C.S. Peirce, John Dewey, William James, and Richard Rorty—all sharing a common concern with modern philosophy's futile quest to define *Truth* and *Reality* (Menand, 2001). Its adoption by qualitative researchers was based on a few basic tenets (Tashakkori & Teddlie, 1998):

- There is no need to establish metaphysical truth; all existing knowledge is fallible.
- All inquiry is value-laden and all "facts" are theory-laden.
- Any given set of data or "facts" can be subject to a variety of interpretations.
- Quantitative and qualitative methods are both concerned with collecting empirical data—the differences lie in how those data are collected, analyzed, and interpreted and in standards for rigor.
- The choice of quantitative or qualitative methods should be driven by the topic, not by allegiance to a paradigm.

Its roots intertwined with early twentieth-century thinking about social reform, pragmatism deeply influenced the founders of professional social work (Jane Addams and Mary Richmond, among others) who were contemporaries of John Dewey and William James (Menand, 2001). Closely identified with America, pragmatism has generally been viewed with disdain in Europe (Tashakkori & Teddlie, 1998).

By the 1980s, the paradigm wars heated up considerably when postmodernism and constructivism left the relative safety of the humanities and philosophy for the rougher, more contested terrain of the social sciences. We need not add to the reams of print devoted to this turn of events except to note that a standoff has ensued. At the polar ends of the debate, zealous advocates cling to irreconcilable convictions. In the vast middle ground, multiple discourses flow back and forth, a fluid mix of ideas and ideologies propelled by articulate, passionate proponents. This situation is tailor made for pragmatism.

One observation is pertinent at this point: regardless of the position taken, the paradigm debates originated in academia and have largely remained there. Thus, the main actors in this drama have been faculty members who communicate with one another via publications and lively exchanges at scholarly conferences. However, academicians in professional schools are obliged to pursue scholarly knowledge production *and* stay grounded in practical applications of extant knowledge.

This poses an enduring challenge—how to succeed where teaching and scholarly publications are the markers of success and remain true to the outside world where the needs and interests of practitioners and service consumers are paramount. Some practice-based researchers work in institutions where education and practice are blended (e.g., medical schools in teaching hospitals), but most of us are accustomed to shifting locations (and roles) from the classroom to the agency (not to mention the computer laboratory and the interminable call to yet another faculty or committee meeting). Juggling so many competing priorities can make a person dizzy.

Unlike anthropology and sociology (with their long traditions of qualitative research), the paradigm debates reached the practice-based professions at roughly the same time as did qualitative methods. Not surprisingly, early advocates often held joint degrees in a social science discipline and their field of practice. Anthropologists such as the Harry Wolcott (in education), Arthur Kleinman (in medicine), and Madeleine Leininger (in nursing) were tremendously influential in introducing qualitative methods and making the connection to practice.

Exemplifying innovative qualitative research is one thing—shaping the methodology itself is quite another. In the latter category, a few names stand out: Barney Glaser and Anselm Strauss in sociology (later joined by Norman Denzin), Michael Agar and Clifford Geertz in anthropology, Michael Q. Patton in evaluation, and Egon Guba and Yvonna Lincoln in education.

It is difficult to overestimate the impact of Lincoln and Guba in giving a voice to the opposition to postpositivism in the social sciences. Their formulation of naturalistic inquiry (1985) attracted adherents across a number of disciplines. Harnessing the energy of antipositivist sentiments in the 1970s and 1980s, Lincoln and Guba offered an integrated approach to inquiry rooted in constructivist epistemology. Eschewing traditional concerns with reliability and validity, they offered alternative criteria such as *credibility* and *trustworthiness* and made a convincing argument that naturalistic inquiry could chart its own way.

Going much further, Denzin and Lincoln's massive *Handbook of Qualitative Research* (2000) merged the constructivist legacy with radical postmodernism and placed the combination at the end of a linear continuum of historic moments leading away from the dark ages of positivism toward an Enlightenment of the Seventh Moment. (The second edition of the *Handbook* proved to be more adamant in this regard than the first, which was published in 1994.)

To paraphrase Martyn Hammersley (1995), news of this triumph has not yet reached the masses of researchers in the social and behavioral sciences.

A pragmatic center still holds and pragmatic philosophy has been the de facto backdrop for a host of qualitative studies in medicine, nursing, education, and social work. By nature reluctant to take strong paradigmatic stands, pragmatic qualitative researchers move comfortably within and among various discourses whether postpositivist, interpretivist, feminist, or constructivist. This non-committal nature might be seen as a disadvantage where ideologies divide and rule, but it can also be a welcome safeguard against partisanship. In effect, pragmatic philosophy counters a hazardous byproduct of constructivism—relativism. This endgame of constructivist thinking yields a form of know-nothing nihilism in which all knowledge—no matter how repugnant or absurd—is accorded equal value.[5] Pragmatism offers a way out of this maze without losing sight of what matters the most: allowing qualitative methods to showcase their strengths without ideological imperatives attached.

KNOWLEDGE FROM WHERE AND FOR WHOM? METHODOLOGY MATTERS . . .

Knowledge derived from research (quantitative or qualitative) constitutes only part of what we know about the world (and a small part at that). Personal and professional experience is often the preferred source of information guiding our day-to-day understanding of how the world works. *Practice wisdom* describes the reliance on insights derived from working with patients and clients as well as the theories that emerge from these observations and reflections (Reid, 1994, p. 474).

The much-discussed practice–research divide has been attributed to practitioners' reliance on practice wisdom to the exclusion of empirical evidence generated by scientific methods. Although the focus is usually on decision making in face-to-face encounters, the disconnect between research and praxis can also occur at the organizational or systems level (Gillespie & Murty, 1994). September 11 offers an example of this. In the disaster's aftermath, the Red Cross and other relief organizations operated from a premise of chaos—both interpersonal and intrapsychic—even though this contradicted findings from decades of disaster research as well as what actually occurred on that day (Padgett, 2002; Tierney, 2001). Despite the enormity of the disaster, survivors' resilient responses illustrated what researchers have maintained for some time: the primary sources of chaos after a community disaster are not located in individual actions or psyches but in the organizations designed to help them (Flynn & Dwyer, 2002; Quarantelli, 1985).

There are many other examples of policies and practices that defy empirical evidence—their persistence attests to the power of knowledge that is accessible and proximal to professionals' day-to-day experiences. The wealth of these experiences and the self-reflection they engender are essential aspects of the practitioner's role. However, practice wisdom accumulates without the benefit of the checks and balances of rigorously applied research methods.

As such, it suffers from a tendency toward overgeneralization, that is, a case or cases become a theory that is in turn supported by selective identification of confirming cases (Reid, 1994). Thus reified, the theory becomes its own self-fulfilling prophecy as additional cases are viewed through its lens and presented as further (highly selective) evidence of the theory's explanatory power.

The threshold of what constitutes research is not often elucidated and the term is used in a variety of ways (e.g., some of us say we do *research* on which bank offers the highest interest rates). But if we are focusing on knowledge building within (and across) disciplines, we can reasonably differentiate case vignettes (the sine qua non of clinical theory dating back to Freud) from systematic inquiry that has breadth (quantitative) or depth (qualitative)—or both. Whereas *scholarship* encompasses many types of intellectual pursuits, *empirical research* is distinguished by a reliance upon systematic, transparent methods in which biases are confronted through pursuit of disconfirmation and findings are verified in some way.

This does not mean that research is immune to criticism (nor should it be)—a study always emerges from the predispositions and prejudices of its investigators. The differences lie in how rigor is defined and pursued. Whereas quantitative studies are steeped in methodological controls, qualitative researchers must create their own safeguards against bias—the merit of a study depends on how successfully and vigorously this is done.

Denzin and Lincoln (2000) refer to the qualitative researcher as a *bricoleur*, a term introduced by French anthropologist Claude Levi-Strauss to refer to a do-it-yourselfer and multi-tasker who can sort through many sources of information to come up with a new formulation (or *bricolage*). Successful qualitative researchers are *bricoleurs*, but they are not simply assemblers, indiscriminately taking whatever comes their way and patch-working it together.

The pragmatic acceptance of multiple ways of knowing still requires the ability to critically weigh their merits, that is, methodology still matters. Put another way, knowledge generated by systematic, empirical research has greater value than knowledge accumulated through nonsystematic, ad hoc means. This statement does not privilege quantitative or qualitative methods—different strategies for verification are available depending on the various methods and approaches selected. It does, however, elevate rigorous research over nonrigorous research.

THE ART OF RESEARCH
AND THE SCIENCE OF PRACTICE

The much-bemoaned divide between research and practice is usually depicted in adversarial terms, with one side occupied by stubborn practitioners unwilling or unable to embrace empirical research and the other side composed of brittle researchers who are all science and no artistry. (Interestingly, these characterizations sideline the stakeholders who have the most to gain or lose in resolving differences: service consumers—more on this topic in Chapter 15.) Although never as polarized as depicted, the gap has nevertheless begun to show signs of shrinking.

In clinical practice, the Cochrane and Campbell collaborations strengthened the ethos of evidence-based practice by disseminating findings from systematic reviews of controlled trials of medical and behavioral science interventions ranging from back pain to sexually transmitted diseases to psychological debriefing (see www.cochrane.org and campbell.gse.upenn.edu/). Not intended to displace compassion and caring in health care, these reviews establish standards for treatment that enhance practitioners' decision making. They also empower consumers by providing user-friendly information (www.cochraneconsumer.org). Dominated by research from Europe and the United States, reports from Cochrane-sponsored studies appear regularly in the news media and sometimes cause a stir (as in the case of the Danish researchers whose findings questioned the efficacy of mammography—a controversy discussed further in Chapter 13).

As practice edges closer to incorporating what is known from extant research, science and medicine have moved toward greater appreciation of the nonquantifiable aspects of human beliefs and behaviors. Eloquent physician-writers such as Lewis Thomas and Oliver Sacks paved the way with books brimming with anecdotes and insights exploring the mysteries of the human animal. But the difference has been most striking in the leading medical and scientific journals (Devers, Sofaer, & Rundall, 1999; Giacomini & Cook, 2000; Green & Britten, 1998; Pope & Mays, 1995; Weaver, et al., 1996) where quantitative studies had always reigned supreme.

Only time will tell if these converging trends will intensify or stall out. In the meantime, it is reassuring to see scientists openly receptive to qualitative thinking and practitioners drawing on scientific evidence—however temporary—of what works.

CAUGHT (UP) IN THE MIDDLE: QUALITATIVE METHODS AND THE RESEARCH–PRACTICE DIVIDE

The allure of qualitative methods was entirely understandable given their compatibility with the ever-changing, messy world of practice (an undeniable attribute highlighted throughout this introductory chapter). Not just the product of pull, this affinity also grew out of a push impulse (disenchantment with the dominance and distance of quantitative methods). Antipathy toward scientific methods helped propel advocates away from positivism, but it also short-circuited a realistic appraisal of what the embrace implied. Thus, a "superficially persuasive argument" (Shaw & Gould, 2001, p. 42) emboldened some practice-based researchers to appeal to practitioners to join in a "natural" alliance against the dominance of positivism.

Along the way, the amorphous and unpredictable aspects of qualitative inquiry were either ignored or (by some) celebrated and the mode of data collection most familiar to practitioners (in-depth interviewing) was assigned the lead role with barely a nod to ethnography (a less accessible approach). Thus, a basic qualitative methods text in social work focused exclusively on interviewing (Tutty, Rothery, & Grinnell, 1996) and the use of grounded theory (an interview-dominant approach) was characterized as "sliding a hand into a well-made glove" for practitioners (Gilgun, 1994, p. 115).

In-depth interviewing clearly resonates with practitioners who are experts at listening empathetically. Interviewing skills—in contrast to participant observation—are readily transferable to qualitative inquiry (Fortune, 1994). By the same token, modes of qualitative inquiry such as narrative approaches have also been used in therapeutic encounters (Epston & White, 1990; Fish, 1996; Mishler, 1984; Sarbin, 1986).

No matter how skilled or sensitive, interviewing alone lacks the density and texture that come from incorporating observational data and/or use of documents. And interviewing skills become useful only when embedded within a framework that allows for inductively derived meaning making. Even the interview-driven approaches such as grounded theory, phenomenology, or narrative analysis involve going deeper and weaving in other sources of information to create a synthesis, or whole, that is greater than the sum of its parts.

What was missing in the romantic haze surrounding qualitative methods was a candid discussion of what their successful deployment required, that is, the practice-friendly proximity of qualitative methods belied a deeply labor-intensive and time-consuming dimension. Without such an expenditure of effort—a delicate balancing act of engagement and distance—qualitative studies produce findings that are shallow and obvious, exactly what quantitative critics delight in pointing out.

The headlong rush toward qualitative methods as the answer to practitioners' disaffection with research was not in itself a problem (although it was a bit oversold). The problem lay in the promise that these methods could be readily adopted by practitioners seeking to evaluate themselves at the same time as they were delivering services (Fook, 2001; Gilgun, 1994; Heineman Pieper, 1994; Lang, 1994). This "premise of simultaneity" was put forth as the solution to the practice–research divide. It was as if all those terrible dark days of being exhorted to adopt single-system designs and to decipher statistics and the Byzantine world of experimentation could be put behind us. At last, we could naturalistically serve clients and study them (and ourselves) at the same time!

Schon's groundbreaking work on the "reflective practitioner" (1983) provided an eloquent vocabulary for advocates seeking an alternative to number-crunching methods of evaluation. In his oft-quoted topographical metaphor, Schon distinguished the "high hard ground" of empirical research findings with the "swampy lowlands" where practitioners deal with real human concerns (p. 42). Such contrasts—hard versus soft, flexible versus rigid, caring about numbers versus people—have been the enduring features of a harsh landscape dominated by overseers wearing white lab coats, spouting numbers, and waving the twin whips of reliability and validity over a poor benighted citizenry. (To be fair, some advocates acknowledged the pitfalls of "reflective practitioner research" and of the gap between talking and doing (Fook, 2001; Scott, 2002; Shaw & Gould, 2001), but these drawbacks quickly fade into obscurity when contemplating the dreaded quantitative alternative.)

Going one significant step further, other advocates of reflective practice have celebrated a marriage of action and reflection brokered by postmodernist thinking (Denzin & Lincoln, 2000; Jarvis, 1999). Dissatisfied with Schon's hermetic perspective (Ixer, 1999) and concerned that reflexivity could produce endless self-absorption, they proposed an emancipatory agenda commensurate with an emphasis upon social justice. Now, practitioners could really do it all—serve clients, reflexively conduct research on their practice, and engage with clients to advocate for social change.

Although attractive, such a utopian vision strains credulity. In the first place, reflexivity in the service of practice improvement and advocacy is not necessarily research (nor should it be). Second, adding an expectation that practitioners engage in action research can only compound the problems attendant with simultaneously doing practice and research.[6] It is hard to imagine how direct services would not suffer given this burden of representation placed on overworked professionals.

Social work practitioners can become researchers, whether mainstream or activist. As such, they may conduct studies of practice or they may become partners with respondents to engage in research devoted to social action.[7] All of these activities can (and should) be undertaken in collaboration with clients, practitioners, and other stakeholders. But the vast majority of practitioners will stick with their chosen avocation—working in the trenches helping clients and communities.

This is a tall order in and of itself these days. Expected to bridge the micro and macro—attending to individuals in need and addressing the larger socio-economic context that visits poverty and discrimination upon them—social workers deal with society's most troubled and outcast. Although direct practice is more immediate and accessible (not to mention remunerative) compared to advocacy, working with communities in need and pursuing social justice are also fundamental tenets of social work.

Let us not forget that the vast majority of social work researchers are also practitioners (or are least former practitioners). Obviously, the same is not true of practitioners (nor should it be). The implication that researchers are from an alien planet (Quantoidia?) comes from understandable frustration with the distancing demands of quantitative research. Yet the counterargument that qualitative researchers are from the same planet as practitioners (Qualtopia?) is more wishful thinking than reality.

Practitioners who wish to become researchers (quantitative or qualitative) must undergo education and training to be credible in that role. Otherwise, their studies risk being dismissed as weak and anecdotal, lacking in breadth or depth. (As discussed earlier, we lower the threshold of what constitutes research at our own peril.) Practitioners have distinct and obvious advantages as researchers.

There are also disadvantages to practitioners studying their own—just as there are advantages to being an outsider (Margaret Mead, Erving Goffman, and Elliott Liebow come readily to mind). But the risks are worth taking, especially because practice-based professions deserve to have home-grown scholars who possess a deep understanding of the field as well as expertise in research methods.

To recapitulate an earlier argument, it is one thing for practitioners to conduct research in their own backyard and quite another for them to study their own work even as they are doing it (Hammersley, 1993). Studies of practice are crucial, but research in practice risks a disservice to both enterprises, weakening the research and compromising service delivery (Padgett, 1998b)—professional codes of ethics discourage dual relationships for a reason.

Practitioners seeking to evaluate their own work have a choice between single-system designs (from the quantitative menu) and reflective practice (from the nonquantitative menu). Although clearly useful as a means to improve one's practice, such reflexivity, if taken out into the world, must undergo the same scrutiny as any research findings (where qualitative or quantitative standards apply).

Although touted as such, reflective practice need not be considered incompatible with evidence-based practice knowledge coming from outside of the immediate practice context. (I prefer to view this as coming from *outside* rather than *above*, although the latter characterization has gained favor at least since Schon's metaphoric allusions were offered.) For example, a practitioner can use evidence-based practice findings to help in deciding what works and deploy reflexivity to evaluate its application in particular situations. Day-to-day practice and decision making must be the arena for carrying out empirical research, but they should not be weighed down by a research agenda attached to every encounter. Anecdotes and aggregates can coexist on different planes and complement each other.

To paraphrase one noted social scientist, "you can't generalize from the local, but you can't generalize without it" (quoted in Kotkin, 2002, p. B11). In this context, reflective self-evaluation is, at best, very weak research (and needlessly characterized as research at all). This does not take away from its power as a means for improving practice from the inside. When critically insightful, reflexivity enhances practice wisdom and stimulates new and important ideas that deepen understanding. Nevertheless, its conclusions rest upon a vaguely defined, ad hoc mode of inquiry. If we place our faith in it to the exclusion of objective research, the specter of marginalization—the bane of social work research in an increasingly competitive and interdisciplinary world—looms large.

One final caveat: labeling self-evaluation as research has ethical implications because clients are being recruited into a non–service-related endeavor

(Padgett, 1998b). As such, it automatically triggers scrutiny by Institutional Review Boards (IRBs) established to protect human subjects. Smaller agencies and clinics rarely have IRBs, but most large institutions do, and all researchers in the United States with academic positions must submit their research protocols for IRB review.

This is where intent is pivotal. If the practitioner–researcher evaluates strictly for personal use, IRB review is not required. But if he has any intention of disseminating his findings (a prerequisite for knowledge building), then the threshold of research is crossed with all that that implies.

What if one's intentions change midcourse? This is truly risky. The self-evaluating practitioner cannot expect freely given (voluntary) consent in the midst of treatment (or service delivery) because this has the taint of coercion no matter how well intentioned or sensitively put. If formal consent is not procured, and if no IRB oversight is available, she or he could still run into trouble later if asked by a conference planner or journal editor how "subjects" were recruited and consented into the study.

SUMMARY AND CONCLUSION

This Introduction began with a celebration of the explosive growth of interest in qualitative methods and ended on a cautionary note replete with conundrums and caveats. I (pragmatically) attempted to find a middle ground in the contested domain of qualitative inquiry by noting recent trends that present challenges and opportunities. First, the recent explosion of interest in qualitative methods has coincided with (and was accelerated by) a parallel trend—decreasing faith in science and technology, the latter exemplified by the parable of the September 11 attacks and their aftermath. Put simply, qualitative methods can go where quantitative methods cannot. I hasten to add that this is not a zero-sum game where an increase in one has to come at the expense of the other—quantitative methods have lost little ground as the dominant force in research (at least in the United States)—the pie just seems to be getting larger.

Second, there are indications that the divide between research and practice is closing, but a few caveats accompanied this observation. It was argued that philosophical pragmatism (epistemological agnosticism?) runs through much of qualitative research even as some of its leading spokespersons have intensified their call for postmodernism and social constructivism (e.g., Denzin & Lincoln, 2000). Indeed, this error of conflating qualitative methods with social constructivism has been compounded by heralding them as the answer to our concerns that research be meaningful and socially responsible.

We practice-based researchers are accustomed to paradigm wars within academia as well as skirmishes on the front lines occasioned by competing demands for rigor and relevance. Indeed, a perennial challenge confronts the practice professions as they seek to build knowledge that is situated in practice but also transcendent of it. Researchers in education, medicine, nursing, and social work—whether trained solely in their profession or in another discipline—want to generate findings with implications for practice. Some of these findings may be derived from randomized trials of interventions, others may come from quantitative surveys (e.g., needs assessments), and still others may come from ethnography, narrative analysis, and grounded theory. Each of these approaches has strengths and limitations and every study needs the critical scrutiny appropriate for its particular methodology.

The areas of fuzziness lie in role clarification (who does what, when, and why) and in recognizing the need to value rigorous methods regardless of their paradigmatic provenance. We can acknowledge hard-won expertise (in practice or research) without privileging one kind over the other (and without resorting to a lowest-common-denominator approach requiring everyone to do everything).

In the meantime, we need not deny the importance of brief case studies as well as other forms of knowledge—practice wisdom, personal experience, ad hoc observation, introspection, and reflection—in searching for new insights and in the production of scholarship in the truest sense of its meaning.

The stage is finally set for what lies ahead. In the spirit of editorial pragmatism, the contributors to this volume were not asked to state their epistemological stance or to endorse the ideas and opinions I have inscribed here and elsewhere. This book is about unity of purpose (strengthening the infrastructures of qualitative research) but diversity in its pursuit. If we "let a thousand flowers bloom," our spirited exchange just might create a lovely bouquet.

ENDNOTES

1. This discussion elides the question of whether qualitative methods could also be viewed as *scientific* and *empirical*, even though these terms have traditionally been reserved for quantitative methods. For the sake of clarity and argument, I will abide by the prevalent view that *science* implies quantitative methods and that relatively few qualitative researchers feel a need to adopt this label. However, I would argue that qualitative research is empirical, that is, based on systematic observation by a researcher engaged in a reality that is *external* (not imaginary), whether it is the product of *objectivity* (no matter how flawed) or is mutually created by the researcher and his or her participants. This stance is somewhat dismissively referred to as *neorealism* by constructivists (see Lincoln & Guba, 2000).

Systematic empirical-ness is what sets research apart from speculation and fabrication—a study's lack of rigor implies inadequate attention to standards of quality, however those are defined. These terms and their definitions are distinct from *empiricism* and *scientism*, both of which have acquired negative connotations as referring to an overemphasis on objective data at the expense of interpretation on the one hand and to unquestioning faith in science on the other (Garfinkel, 1967).

2. Because qualitative researchers reject the dehumanizing implications of the term *subject*, we use various substitutes: *respondents, informants participants,* and *partners,* among others.

3. Terminological confusion and differing definitions are particularly rampant in discussions of epistemology and methodology in qualitative research. By the 1980s, ways of knowing associated with qualitative inquiry were roughly classified into three streams of thought—postpositivist,

interpretivist, and postmodern/critical (LeCompte, 1990). *Postpositivism* was viewed as "positivism with a human face," a move away from scientism with its rigid, deterministic views of a single objective reality toward acceptance of the value-laden, social context of inquiry. *Interpretivism,* with roots in phenomenology and hermeneutics, focuses on narratives and meaning in human experience. Its counterpart in linguistics, *poststructuralism,* treats language as ever changing and unreliable as a representation of some external reality. *Postmodernism-critical theories* are defined by a commitment to social criticism and political change and were heavily influenced by the dense, almost impenetrable, theorizing of French scholars (e.g., Derrida, Foucault, and Lyotard; Skrtic, 1990). They are also described as *antifoundationalism.* To make matters more complicated, some critical theorists (particularly feminists) reject postmodernism for its navel gazing. To LeCompte's three broad categories can be added the less philosophically rooted approach of *participatory* or *action research,* which involves activating an emancipatory agenda as well as espousing it.

In developing and refining their naturalistic paradigm, Yvonna Lincoln and Egon Guba corralled the various nonpositivist approaches under a common constructivist rubric, asserting that all share a concern with " . . . subjective and intersubjective social knowledge and the active construction and cocreation of such knowledge by human agents . . . " (2000, p. 176). I have chosen to use *social constructivism* throughout this book as the best single descriptor of these multiple strands of qualitative inquiry united in opposition to positivism and wedded to notions of multiple realities and relativism. This term should be distinguished from its confusing counterpart *social constructionism,* which usually refers to the subset of qualitative studies that focus on language, narratives, and discourse. Although complete agreement and clarification elude us, further discussion of definitions can also be found in Denzin and Lincoln (2000, p. 24).

4. It should be noted that some grounded theorists (Charmaz, 2000) and ethnographers (Tedlock, 2000) have joined in the constructivist and postmodern movements.

5. Along these lines, French poststructuralist Lyotard asserted, "in truth, there is no such thing as a lie, except as measured by the standard of the desire for truth, but this desire is not truer than any other desire" (quoted in Dews, 1987, p. 210).

6. I have elsewhere offered opinions on how qualitative research is different from practice (Padgett, 1998b), a stand that drew immediate rebuttals from American colleagues (Bein & Allen, 1999; Heineman Pieper & Tyson, 1999) that did not seem to address my original concerns (Padgett, 1999). I was taken to task for the same position a few years later, this time by colleagues in Great Britain and Australia (Fook, 2001; Shaw & Gould, 2001). These responses were part of a much larger argument—which sometimes appears to be a groundswell abroad—that qualitative methods and "reflective practice" stand together as the answer to practitioners' yearning for research that is not quantitative and values practice wisdom (Scott, 2002).

Although flattered that anyone had read my work, much less took the time to disagree with it, I continue to be puzzled by the need to conflate *practitioner reflexivity* with *research* in any meaningful sense of the latter term. Contrary to mistaken impressions of my stance as averring that ". . . practitioners are ill-equipped to be researchers" (Fook, 2001, p. 130), I believe that they make the best researchers. Still, these arguments and exchanges have served a useful purpose for me by underscoring how the research–practice divide—and qualitative methods—can become contested domains within the larger debates on epistemology in the academy. As I noted earlier (Padgett, 1999), practitioners and researchers are often the first to tell me that they agree with opposition to a "premise of simultaneity." Citing the dangers inherent in such a dual relationship, they ask, "Why is this even an issue?" One wonders how much exhortations to pursue naturalistic research in practice actually appeal to their intended audience (practitioners) and to the ultimate beneficiaries (service consumers).

7. Nye (1994) and Sheppard and colleagues (2000) offer empirical studies of practice using a traditional approach of discourse analysis (Nye) and a more recent innovation involving "think aloud" protocols from cognitive psychology combined with grounded theory (Sheppard, et al.). Both offer illuminating glimpses into the processes of social work practice. Although there are many, one example of an action-oriented study is Lather and Smithies' *Troubling the Angels* (1997), which featured the voices of women participating in an AIDS support group with the authors.

REFERENCES

Becker, H. S. (1998). Tricks of the trade: How to think about your research while you're doing it. Chicago: University of Chicago Press.

Bein, A., & Allen, K. (1999). Hand into glove? It fits better than you think. *Social Work, 44,* 274–7.

Chambon, A., & Irving, A. (1994). *Essays on postmodernism in social work.* Toronto: Canadian Scholars' Press.

Charmaz, K. (2000). Grounded theory: Objectivist and constructivist methods. In N. K. Denzin & Y. S. Lincoln (Eds.), *Handbook of qualitative research* (2nd ed., pp. 509–36). Thousand Oaks, CA: Sage.

Dean, R. G. (1993). Constructivism: An approach to clinical practice. *Smith College Studies in Social Work, 63,* 127–46.

Denzin, N. K., & Lincoln, Y. S. (Eds.). (2000). *Handbook of qualitative research* (2nd ed.). Thousand Oaks, CA: Sage.

Devers, K. J., Sofaer, S., & Rundall, T. G. (Eds.). (1999). Qualitative methods in health services research. *Health Services Research, 34,* Special Supplement Issue, December.

Dews. (1987). Logics of disintegration: Post-structuralist thought and the claims of critical theory. London: Verso Press.

Dwyer, J., Flynn, K., & Fessenden, F. (2002, July 7). September 11 exposed deadly flaws in rescue plan. *The New York Times.*

Epston, D., & White, M. (1990). *Narrative means to therapeutic ends.* New York: Norton.

Fish, B. (1996). Clinical implications of attachment narratives. *Clinical Social Work Journal, 24,* 239–53.

Flynn, K., & Dwyer, J. (2002, January 30). Firefighting inquiry: Before the towers fell, fire department fought chaos. *The New York Times.*

Fook, J. (2001). Identifying expert social work: Qualitative practitioner research. In I. Shaw & N. Gould (Eds.), *Qualitative research in social work* (pp. 116–32). London: Sage.

Fortune, A. (1994). Commentary: Ethnography in social work. In E. Sherman & W. J. Reid (Eds.), *Qualitative research in social work* (pp. 63–70). New York: Columbia University Press.

Garfinkel, H. (1967). *Studies in ethnomethodology.* Englewood Cliffs, NJ: Prentice-Hall.

Giacomini, M. K., & Cook, D. J. (2000). Qualitative research in health care: What are the results and how do they help me care for my patients? *Journal of the American Medical Association, 284,* 478–82.

Gilgun, J. (1994). Hand into glove: The grounded theory approach and social work practice research. In E. Sherman & W. J. Reid (Eds.), *Qualitative research in social work* (pp. 115–25). New York: Columbia University Press.

Gillespie, D. F., & Murty, S. A. (1994). Cracks in a postdisaster service delivery network. *American Journal of Community Psychology, 22,* 639–60.

Gopnik, A. (2002, April 1). The porcupine: A pilgrimage to Popper. *The New Yorker*, pp. 88–93.

Green, J., & Britten, N. (1998). Qualitative research and evidence based medicine. *British Medical Journal, 316*, 1230–2.

Hammersley, M. (1993). On the teacher as researcher. *Educational Action Research, 1*, 425–45.

Hammersley, M. (1995). *The politics of social research*. London: Sage.

Heineman Pieper, M. (1994). Science not scientism: The robustness of naturalistic clinical research. In E. Sherman and W. J. Reid (Eds.), *Qualitative research in social work* (pp. 71–88). New York: Columbia University Press.

Heineman Pieper, M., & Tyson, K. (1999). Response to Padgett's "Does the glove really fit?" *Social Work, 44*, 278–9.

House, E. R. (1994). Integrating the quantitative and qualitative. In C. S. Reichardt & S. F. Rallis (Eds.), *The qualitative-quantitative debate: New perspectives* (pp. 13–22). San Francisco: Jossey-Bass.

Howe, K. R. (1988). Against the quantitative-qualitative incompatibility thesis or dogmas die hard. *Educational Researcher, 17*, 10–16.

Ixer, G. (1999). There is no such thing as reflection. *British Journal of Social Work, 29*, 513–28.

Jarvis, P. (1999). *The practitioner-researcher*. San Francisco: Jossey-Bass.

Kelly, J., & Stark, D. (2002, May). Crisis, recovery and innovation: Learning from September 11. Working Papers, Center on Organizational Innovation. Retrieved November 18, 2002 from URL: http://www.coi.columbia.edu/pdf/kelly_stark_cri.pdf.

Kotkin, S. (2002, September 7). A world war among professors: A clash between number crunchers and specialists in a single region. *The New York Times*, pp. B9, B11.

Kuhn. (1970). *The structure of scientific revolutions*. Chicago: University of Chicago Press.

Lather, P., & Smithies, C. (1997). *Troubling the angels: Women living with HIV/AIDS*. Boulder, CO: Westview Press.

LeCompte, M. D. (1990). Emergent paradigms: How new? How necessary? In E. G. Guba (Ed.), *The paradigm dialog* (pp. 227–45). Newbury Park, CA: Sage.

Lincoln, Y. S., & Guba, E. G. (1985). *Naturalistic inquiry*. Beverly Hills, CA: Sage.

Lofland, J., & Lofland, L. (1995). *Analyzing social settings*. Belmont, CA: Wadsworth.

Menand, L. (2001). *The metaphysical club: A story of ideas in America*. New York: Farrar, Straus, & Giroux.

Mishler, E. G. (1984). *The discourse of medicine: Dialectics of medical interviews*. Norwood, NJ: Ablex.

Morse, J. M., Barrett, M., Mayan, M., Olson, K., & Spiers, J. (2002). Verification strategies for establishing reliability and validity in qualitative research. *International Journal of Qualitative Methods, 1*, Article 2. Retrieved October 5, 2002 from URL: http://www.ualberta.ca/~ijqm/.

Nye, C. (1994). Discourse analysis methods and clinical research: A single-case study. In E. Sherman & W. J. Reid (Eds.), *Qualitative research in social work* (pp. 216–27). New York: Columbia University Press.

Padgett, D. K. (1998a). *Qualitative methods in social work research: Challenges and rewards*. Thousand Oaks, CA: Sage.

Padgett, D. K. (1998b). Does the glove really fit? Qualitative research and clinical social work practice. *Social Work, 43*, 373–381.

Padgett, D. K. (1999). The research-practice debate in a qualitative research context. *Social Work, 44*, 280–82.

Padgett, D. K. (2002). Social work research in the aftermath of September 11: A view from Ground Zero. *Social Work Research, 26*, 185–92.

Patton, M. Q. (2002). *Qualitative research and evaluation methods* (3rd ed.). Thousand Oaks, CA: Sage.

Pope, C., & Mays, N. (1995). Reaching the parts other methods cannot reach: An introduction to qualitative methods in health and health services research. *British Medical Journal, 311*, 42–5.

Quarantelli, E. L. (1985). An assessment of conflicting views on mental health: The consequences of traumatic events. In C. R. Figley (Ed.), *Trauma and its wake: The study and treatment of post-traumatic stress disorder* (pp. 173–218). New York: Brunner-Mazel.

Reichardt, C. S., & Rallis, S. F. (1994). Qualitative and quantitative inquiries are not incompatible: A call for a new partnership. In C. S. Reichardt & S. F. Rallis (Eds.), *The qualitative-quantitative debate: New perspectives* (pp. 85–92). San Francisco: Jossey-Bass.

Reid, W. J. (1994). Reframing the episte-mological debate. In E. Sherman & W. J. Reid (Eds.), *Qualitative research in social work* (pp. 464–81). New York: Columbia University Press.

Rissman, C. K. (Ed.). (1994). *Qualitative studies in social work research.* Thousand Oaks, CA: Sage.

Rodwell, M. K. (1998). *Social work con-structivist research.* New York: Garland.

Sarbin, T. R., (Ed.). (1986). *Narrative psychology: The storied nature of human conduct.* New York: Praeger.

Schon, D. (1983). *The reflective practitioner: How professionals think in action.* New York: Basic Books.

Schwartz, J. (2002, June 9). Too much information, not enough knowledge. *The New York Times,* p. 5.

Scott, D. (2002). Adding meaning to measurement: The value of qualitative methods in practice research. *British Journal of Social Work, 32*, 923–30.

Shaw, I., & Gould, N. (2001). *Qualitative research in social work.* London: Sage.

Sheppard, M., Newstead, S., Di Caccavo, A., & Ryan, K. (2000). Reflexivity and the development of process knowledge in social work: A classification and empirical study. *British Journal of Social Work, 30*, 465–88.

Sherman, E., & Reid, W. J. (Eds.). (1994). *Qualitative research in social work.* New York: Columbia University Press.

Skrtic, T. (1990). Social accommodation: Toward a dialogical discourse in educational inquiry. In E. G. Guba (Ed.), *The paradigm dialog* (pp. 125–35). Newbury Park, CA: Sage.

Snow, D., & Morrill, C. (1995). Ironies, puzzles, and contradictions in Denzin and Lincoln's vision of qualitative research. *Journal of Contemporary Ethnography, 22*, 358–62.

Tashakkori, A. & Teddlie, C. (1998). *Mixed methodology.* Thousand Oaks, CA: Sage.

Tedlock, B. (2000). Ethnography and ethnographic representation. In N. K. Denzin & Y. S. Lincoln (Eds.), *Handbook of qualitative research* (2nd ed., pp. 455–86). Thousand Oaks, CA: Sage.

Tierney, K. J. (2001). Strength of a city: A disaster research perspective on the World Trade Center attack. Social Science Research Council. Retrieved December 3, 2002 from URL: http://www.ssrc.org/sept11/essays/tierney.

Tutty, L. M., Rothery, M., & Grinnell, R. M. (1996). *Qualitative research for social workers.* Boston: Allyn & Bacon.

Tyson, K. (1994). Heuristic guidelines for naturalistic qualitative evaluations of child treatment. In E. Sherman and W. J. Reid (Eds.), *Qualitative research in social work* (pp. 89–114). New York: Columbia University Press.

Weaver, T., Renton, A., Tyrer, P., & Ritchie, J. (1996). Combining qualita-tive studies with randomized con-trolled trials is often useful (letter). *British Medical Journal, 313*, 629.

PART I

Exemplars

What actually happens during a qualitative study is rarely reflected in the polished product that emerges. This lack of transparency comes partly from ethnographic traditions in which field research was shrouded in mystery, but it also stems from the flexible, nonlinear nature of qualitative research. Some fear that to peer into the "black box" of qualitative methods will reveal a process somewhat like making sausage—better to just enjoy the outcome than think too much about the ingredients!

I would prefer adapting a more felicitous metaphor from the field of architecture. Although reversing the building process by working inductively, qualitative researchers take their data and design a conceptual framework that is weight bearing, embracing the broadest possible expanse of information before them. To stretch this metaphor a bit further, we want a sturdy, lasting structure, not a gossamer creation that cannot withstand scrutiny and skepticism.

This is rarely neat and tidy. The intensity and unpredictability of doing a qualitative study—gaining rapport, recruiting participants, collecting and interpreting data—ensures that there will be new challenges every step of the way. But we believe that getting there is a big part of the journey and that students can benefit from seeing the finished building as well as detailed notes on its construction.

DEFINING AN EXEMPLARY
QUALITATIVE STUDY (AND RESEARCHER)

Defining excellence is still an "eye of the beholder" issue in qualitative research because standards vary. However, I came across a list of qualities in a book entitled *Doing Exemplary Research* (Frost & Stablein, 1992) that comes as close as any to capturing what separates the exemplars from the "less-thans." In a commentary on what made a qualitative study conducted by Connie Gersick (1988) exemplary, Janice Beyer offered the following:

1. The study appears to spring from genuine curiosity.

2. It both acknowledges and questions existing theory.

3. It seeks new insights from immersion in the phenomena in question.

4. It uses research methods flexibly and imaginatively, as a tool serving the questions pursued.

5. It is an unstinting effort; the author's curiosity drove her to do whatever it took to arrive at a credible answer to her question (Beyer, 1992, p. 65).

Gersick's study in the field of organizational management was focused on presenting an innovative model to explain how teams function in the workplace. According to Beyer, Gersick's insight and dedication are what made the study rise to exemplar level. Indeed, one is struck by how much the above list reflects qualities of the researcher as well as the study—not surprising because in qualitative research the two are inextricable.

The chapters in Part I were selected as exemplars of specific types of qualitative approaches. Each chapter has two parts, the first a straightforward description of the study (similar to a journal article format) and the second a more free-form essay describing the real experience of doing the study (both professionally and personally).

In Chapter 1, Julianne Oktay offers a grounded theory study of the experiences of adult daughters whose mothers had breast cancer. Julie affectingly traces her personal and professional trajectory while conducting the study, that is, getting funding, finding respondents, and dealing with the inevitable bumps in the road. Chapter 2, by Roberta (Bobbie) Sands, also originated from personal interest, but reverses the mother–daughter vantage point by focusing on the stories of Jewish mothers experiencing a generation gap when their daughters become deeply religious. Bobbie employed narrative analysis with "rigor and relevance" in a collaborative study that brought feminist researchers together from several countries.

In Chapter 3, Jerry Floersch uses ethnography to take us into the world of a case management program for the seriously mentally ill. Developing the concept of *practice ethnography*, he draws upon multiple sources of data—field notes, case records, and interviews—to reveal the different meanings case managers ascribe to clients and their needs. Using a similar degree of immersion, Jim Drisko (Chapter 4) conducted intensive case studies of two family preservation programs. Jim describes the complex interactions of staff and at-risk families and also reflects on what was happening behind the scenes. The use of ethnography and case study methods are ideal for the agencies featured in Chapters 3 and 4, because such sites represent situated cultures where dynamic interaction is the norm.

The salience of doing research in agencies (practice-based research) carries forward in Chapters 5 and 6, with one noteworthy difference: the authors were carrying out their studies as students engaged in thesis research. In Chapter 5, Deborah Gioia relates how her practice experience with persons diagnosed with schizophrenia led to a doctoral dissertation exploring the meaning of work after the onset of serious mental illness. Deborah offers several helpful insights based on her journey from student to scholar. Finally, Amy Barr (Chapter 6) reports the findings of a qualitative evaluation of an innovative housing program for the homeless mentally ill—findings that enhance considerably our understanding of how such programs have an impact. Amy also traces her own experiences as a masters-level student and social worker who has been deeply moved by the suffering she witnessed in this population.

The authors in Part I all share a combination of insight and perseverance that sets exemplary qualitative studies apart. Frost and Stablein (1992) offer a vivid metaphoric description of the courage it takes to do qualitative research:

> Those who fish in the murky waters of 'real' phenomena without the security of a nomological net take risks. Having spent much time and energy, they may return empty-handed. When they do return with new insights, they are met by skeptical colleagues who have heard too many fish stories/anecdotes or the uncomprehending stares of those who haven't 'been there.' (1992, p. 51)

These days, most of us encounter less skepticism and incomprehension than before. Let us hope that our fishing expeditions bring prize-winning catches.

REFERENCES

Beyer, J. M. (1992). Researchers are not cats: They can survive and succeed by being curious. In P. J. Frost & R. E. Stablein (Eds.), *Doing exemplary research* (pp. 65–72). Newbury Park, CA: Sage.

Frost, P. J. & Stablein, R. E. (Eds.). (1992). Doing exemplary research. Newbury Park, CA: Sage.

Gersick, C. (1988). Time and transition in work teams: Toward a new model of group development. *Academy of Management Journal, 31,* 9–41.

1

Grounded Theory

JULIANNE S. OKTAY

A. Experiences of Women Whose Mothers Had Breast Cancer

Despite extensive research, breast cancer remains a major killer of American women, with approximately 185,000 diagnosed each year and 45,000 dying. The discovery (in 1994) of mutations in two genes (*BRCA1* and *BRCA2*) opened up new hopes for identification of at-risk women and eventual prevention or treatment. Although the genetic form of breast cancer applies to only a small proportion of the breast cancers diagnosed (5–10%), daughters in families that carry these mutations have a higher-than-normal probability (Offit, 1998; Strewing, Hartge, & Wacholder, 1997).

Counseling for women who are at risk, before and after genetic testing for breast cancer, is a fairly recent field (Schneider & Marnane, 1997). This counseling needs to go beyond the providing of information and facilitating decision making. The fact that most of the women defined as high risk have a first-degree relative who had breast cancer means that these women enter risk counseling with a history of serious illness and, in many cases, death of a close relative (Weil, 2000). To counsel such women effectively, this previous life experience has to be taken into consideration. One subset of such women is of special interest: daughters whose mothers had breast cancer. The experience of having a parent of the same sex with a serious illness, and especially losing a parent of the same sex to a gender-related illness, is especially traumatic. Adults who lose a parent when they are young often have long-term psychological consequences (Berlinsky & Biller, 1982; Gray, 1987; Wolfenstein, 1966). However, little research has been done on these daughters, and consequently, little is known about their needs. A qualitative study was designed to gain a better understanding of the experiences of women whose mothers had early breast cancer—those most likely to carry genetic mutations. This chapter describes the study and summarizes the findings with respect to those women whose mothers died.

METHODS

Recruitment

Forty-three women were recruited into the study through referrals from health professionals and advocacy group members, newspaper advertisements, and by way of a recruiting brochure. After screening for eligibility, women were matched to one of four interviewers by race, age, and religion. Two women dropped out before the first interview, leaving 41 women in the study. The average age was 33, with an age range from 19 to 52 years. More than 25% of the respondents were African American. There was a fairly equal distribution by age at mother's diagnosis. This paper is based on the 26 women (63%) whose mothers died.

Interviewing

Interviews took place in the women's homes, lasting from 1 to 2 hours. A basic interview outline was used to guide the interviews. Women were interviewed up to three times, with team discussions between interviews. The third interview was primarily confirmatory. All interviews were audiotaped. Most women were interviewed three times. Some participants were lost to the study or came in too late to complete all three interviews. In all, 103 interviews were conducted.

Coding and Analysis

Grounded theory is a methodology for developing a theory that is derived inductively; that is, it is developed out of the data (Glaser & Strauss, 1967; Strauss & Corbin, 1990). There are several important components of a grounded theory study. One of these is the notion of *constant comparison,* which means the ideas that constitute the theory are developed and refined throughout the project. As concepts are formed, they are compared to new data and refined until a point of saturation is reached. Another concept used in grounded theory research is *theoretical sampling.* This means that the characteristics of the sample are determined as the study progresses and new cases are sought on the basis of theoretical development. For example, in the daughters study, one of the important variables was the age of the daughter. To explore this variable, we needed to have cases of women who were children or adolescents at the time of mother's illness or death. As the study progressed, we stopped taking new cases who had been late adolescents or young adults at mother's diagnosis and sought out additional cases who were younger.

Audiotapes were transcribed as soon as possible after the interview and reviewed for errors by the interviewer. After open (marginal) coding, an analytical "tree" was developed using the NUD★IST software program (Gahan & Hannibal, 1998). As new data were coded, the conceptual framework was revised based on constant comparisons between the coding scheme and the data. Analysis moved to identification of concepts and categories and to identification of larger themes over time. A major variable in our analysis was the age of the daughter at time of mother's illness and death. Many of the code or analysis categories were determined by the daughter's age. Coded sections of the transcriptions were created for four age groups and broad themes were developed for each age group. Late in the study, a basic model was developed for women whose mother's died. Five questionnaires developed from the model, one on the basic model (for all ages) and one for each age group (children, early adolescents, late adolescents, and young adults), were sent to the respondents.

Trustworthiness

This study employed several devices to reduce bias (Guba, 1981; Padgett, 1998). We interviewed our respondents three times, over a period of $1\frac{1}{2}$–2 years (prolonged engagement). We came to know the interviewees fairly well and gave them opportunities to bring up information and ideas that they may not have raised with only one interview. It was common for women to remember information between the first and second interview (they may have been recalling information about events that occurred long ago, they often said that the interview got them thinking and talking to relatives to clarify their impressions). Also, we called everyone during the week following each interview. One respondent mentioned during the phone call that she had been sexually abused as an adolescent, something she had not mentioned in the interview. Triangulation was also used to increase validity. Our study had four interviewers, and all four read transcripts and interview summaries to identify possible themes and areas for further exploration. Therefore, no one researcher was able to allow preexisting ideas to define the direction of the study. Also, by using a questionnaire at the end of the study, we had confirmation of the qualitative results with a quantitative method.

Peer debriefing provided outside oversight throughout the project. To prepare for the first interviews, the research team had a day-long session with our peer debriefer where each of the four interviewers talked about relationships with mothers and previous experience with illness in the family. This helped provide external validation for developing ideas. Other forms of external validation occurred when we shared our emerging model with the Advisory Board at twice-yearly meetings, and when we gave presentations on the project to varied audiences. These meetings and presentations also provided validation for emerging ideas and alerted us to important issues that we had not examined. Member checking was probably the single most important devise we used to ensure trustworthiness. We routinely asked our respondents for their feedback in the interviews, the questionnaires, and a focus group that was held at the end of the project. In the final interview session, the questionnaires were discussed. Reaction to the model was noted, with particular emphasis on identifying things the women disagreed with or areas that were missing from the model.

Throughout the project, the principal investigator kept a journal, recording ideas, problems, and progress of the study. The journal and the record of the "nodes" developed in the NUD*IST program made it possible to trace the emergence and development of ideas, creating an audit trail.

RESULTS

We identified four major areas that contribute to the experience of women whose mothers died from breast cancer: Family Background, Characteristics of Illness and Treatment, Short-Term Impact (composed of Family Changes after Mother's Death and Grieving), and Long-Term Impact. Each of these areas has been put into subcategories and will be discussed.

Family Background

Family background was an important factor in shaping the experience of all women whose mothers had breast cancer. The most important component of family background was the daughter's age. Because our study focused on women who were under age 50 at the time of diagnosis, daughters ranged in age (at mother's diagnosis) from 1 year to the early 30s. The daughter's age influenced many basic components of the experience, including what information was shared with her, what role she played in the illness, and how profoundly she was affected by family changes if her mother died. Age became an organizing concept for the entire model. Each of the other variables will be examined in terms of the four age groups we identified: children (10 and under), young adolescents, older adolescents, and young adults.

The daughter's age interacted with her birth-order position and the gender of her siblings. If the daughter was an only child, she tended to bear more of the burden of mother's illness. If she was the oldest daughter, regardless of her age, she also tended to carry more responsibility and often took over mothering roles with her younger siblings. Younger daughters often took cues from their older siblings on how to behave and what to feel and think. Some women who had sisters found great comfort in sharing with them. Sisters often went through the experience together, and if mother died, mourned together. As adults, the sisters may share memories and stories of mother and may participate together in mourning rituals. Women who had brothers did not generally find the same comfort in these relationships. When a younger daughter's sister had already left home at the time of mother's illness, it was especially difficult, because the younger sister was not used to carrying heavy responsibilities in the family.

In addition to the daughter's age and birth order, communication emerged as an important characteristic of the family. Many of the women in our study identified a "lack of open communication" as a problem in their families even before their mother's illness. Families who had a history of keeping secrets were likely to handle mother's diagnosis with secrecy. A history of secrecy created an atmosphere that made it difficult to share information and feelings. In these cases, daughters experienced feelings of foreboding and even extreme fear. They never felt certain that they had been told all the information and suspected that things were going on without their knowledge. Closely related to family communication style is whether the family had experienced problems in the past, such as death of a parent (father), separation or divorce, chaotic lifestyle, a history of alcoholism or drug abuse, sexual abuse of children, or mental illness. The nature of past family problems made it more difficult for daughters to successfully resolve their loss, often resulting in complicated mourning.

In sum, whether the daughter was a child, an adolescent, or a young adult, whether she had siblings, and whether these were older or younger, brothers or sisters, made a big difference in how she experienced her mother's illness. Another important factor was the communication style in the family, which was usually well established before the illness. This was often related to the existence of prior family problems. Families with problems that had been handled with secrecy in the past were likely to handle breast cancer in the same way. The nature of these problems, and how they impacted the relationships in the family, affected the daughters' experiences.

On our questionnaire, family background factors were given a high level of importance by our respondents. Ninety-two percent of those whose mothers died rated Daughter's Age as Very Important or Somewhat Important. For Birth Order and Gender of Siblings, the figure was 96%. Family Communication Style was identified as important by 92% of those whose mothers died. The category Prior Family Problems had less support, with 86% of those whose mothers died rating it as an important factor. This was because some women felt that their families did not have prior family problems, and so rated it as Not Applicable to their case. The high ratings given to these components of the model suggest that they have validity.

Experience During Mother's Illness and Treatment

A second factor of daughters' experience when mother died from breast cancer was the experience of the illness and the treatments mother received. This area has three components: Illness Characteristics and Treatments, Communication With Daughter During Illness, and Family Dynamics During Illness. Again, age of the daughter tempered each of these areas.

The daughters' experiences with the illness itself was mostly determined by the treatments mothers had. Many mothers in our study underwent mastectomies. For the daughters, the first impact of this was the hospitalization. For younger daughters, this may have been the first time that mother was away from home, and so it was frightening. However, hospitalization was not nearly as traumatic as was seeing mother's mastectomy scar. Some of the mothers in our study underwent radical mastectomies and were left with major scarring and deformity of the chest wall. Often, these women covered themselves, not allowing their daughters to see their scars. Daughters reported that it was painful for them to be closed out of mother's room or bathroom for the first time. In some cases, when mothers had prostheses, very young daughters played with them. In contrast, older daughters often helped mothers find attractive clothes and prostheses.

The other treatment that was especially traumatic for daughters was chemotherapy. Chemotherapy can result in loss of hair and seeing mother without hair made the illness real; it made mother look sick, and she acted sick. Older daughters often helped their mothers to get to chemotherapy appointments and helped them shop for wigs. If mother was too weak or sick to perform household tasks, daughters took on chores such as cooking, doing laundry, and supervising siblings. One daughter remembers making milkshakes for her mother only to watch her vomit them up later.

Communication about the illness with the daughter was of primary importance to daughters. Daughters who were not told or who were told half-truths often felt isolated and alone with their fears. They sensed that something was wrong, but could not seek reassurance or comfort. They realized that this was something that was not talked about. The most stressful situation for daughters were those cases (hopefully no longer occurring) where mother herself was not told that she had breast cancer or that her cancer had metastasized. In these cases, the daughter knew that mother was dying, but had to maintain a fiction that she was getting better. This was extremely stressful for the daughters, who not only could not talk openly about their feelings, but had to try to hide them from their mothers. Those whose mothers were able to talk openly, to share information and feelings, felt that breast cancer was something that could be understood and fought. Their mothers were able to help them with their feelings, even if it meant preparing them for her death.

Because symptoms of breast cancer are not visible, it is not difficult for women to hide their diagnosis. The first awareness a young daughter may have that there is a problem is if she senses mother's fear, or if there is a disruption in routine, for example, when mother goes into the hospital. Some daughters talked about seeing mother or father crying, often for the first time. Young adult daughters were likely to be told and, if so, they were able to play supportive roles in the diagnostic process, perhaps by accompanying mother to the biopsy and by being there when the doctor reported the results of diagnostic tests.

The family dynamics during the illness were also very important for the daughters. The illness may have exacerbated prior family conflicts—intensifying conflicts between the parents, dysfunctional communication patterns, or dysfunctional behaviors (e.g., substance abuse)—making the illness experience more difficult. In other families, the illness may have increased family cohesion, open communication, and open expression of love.

The questionnaire sent to women at the end of the study showed strong support for the Illness Factors identified in the study in daughters whose mothers died. Seventy-four percent of those whose mothers died rated Illness Characteristics and Treatments as important. For Communication With Daughter, 87% of those whose mothers died agreed that this was important. The nature of Family Dynamics During Illness was identified as important by 78% of those whose mothers died.

Daughter's Experiences Following Mother's Death

Family Changes. Most women whose mothers died of breast cancer had to adapt to a changed family situation. In addition to losing mothers, some lost fathers (emotionally), homes, maternal relatives, and pets. Although fathers (when available) were in positions to play important roles, most were not able to help their daughters grieve for their mothers. Instead, fathers tended to withdraw from their daughters, physically and emotionally. Perhaps the fathers were absorbed with their own grief and panicked by their sudden family responsibilities. Some fathers made things worse for their daughters by inappropriate reactions to their losses. For example, one father threw out all of mother's things, only days after the funeral. Another father refused to speak to his daughter about mother or mother's illness (it wasn't until years later that this daughter learned the cause of her mother's death).

Many fathers remarried, especially those with young children, sometimes within months of mother's death. Daughters typically rejected their new stepmothers (the few exceptions in our study involved stepmothers who were known to the daughters before mother died). Daughters often felt that their fathers chose their stepmothers over them and they felt doubly abandoned. Some reacted with anger ("It was war!"), whereas others sought to escape. Younger daughters often found refuge in a surrogate family, usually the family of a friend, and teenagers escaped into organized activities or to the streets. Young adult daughters were more likely to seek out new relationships, some marrying soon after mother's death. Many daughters' stories had the familiar ring of the Cinderella story. There was a father who was aloof or weak, unable or unwilling to protect the daughter from the wicked stepmother. Sometimes, a prince would come to save Cinderella. Even the Fairy Godmother applied because many daughters describe their mother as a benevolent figure who watched over them and came to their aid in times of trouble.

Daughters also experienced changes in sibling relationships following mother's death. These changes depended on the family configuration discussed earlier. If the daughter was the oldest of the siblings or the oldest daughter, she may have tried to take on some of mother's roles, "mothering" her younger siblings. If the siblings accepted her mothering, it may have proved to be a satisfying yet burdensome role. In one case, the oldest of three daughters was given a station wagon for her first car; she had been hoping for something sportier! In some cases, the mothering gestures were rejected, leaving the daughter feeling like a failure, helpless to prevent the family from falling apart.

Younger sisters also experienced profound family changes. One younger sister felt abandoned by her older sister, because her expectation for mothering was not met. In another case, the youngest sister was in high school and two older sisters had already left home. This young woman felt completely unprepared for the responsibilities thrust on her while her mother was ill. In the final questionnaire, daughters rated Relationships With Siblings as important in 83% of the cases, second only to Relationships With Stepmothers (85%).

Grieving. There is extensive literature about grief, and especially about grief as experienced by children. In the past it was believed that children are not able to grieve (Freud, 1917). We too found that the "young adult" women were the only ones able to benefit from traditional grieving activities such as funerals, viewings, and religious ceremonies. Families did not know how to support daughters, to help them to grieve, or even how to talk about mother, her illness, and her death. One daughter used the metaphor of "the elephant in the living room" to describe her family life after mother's death. To this day, almost 40 years later, it is as if she never had a mother. Our youngest respondent, aged 3 when mother died, did not attend the funeral, did not understand what happened to her mother, and felt only a strong and pervasive anxiety that her mother had done something very bad.

One daughter, about 10 years old, did not tell her teachers that her mother had died, and for years after, they would threaten her with, "If you don't (behave), I'm going to tell your mother!" In some homes, mother became like a "dirty secret"—as if her whole existence was contaminated by the fact that she died.

In contrast, older daughters were often able to shape ceremonies in ways that were meaningful to them. One woman, who was in her early 30s, chose all of the music for mother's funeral, picked out her mother's favorite flowers, chose the dress mother would wear, and ultimately made the decision to take her mother's rings off before burial. All of these activities were extremely meaningful to her and helped her with her grief.

Long-Term Impact. Many women in our study felt that their mother's death affected them more than anything else in their lives. The most common outcome in daughters whose mothers died was a change in priorities or philosophy of life. Women whose mothers died see life in a different way. They are more likely to recognize that life is short, that things do not last, and that they do not have control. As a result, many of them live their lives fully every moment. One woman tells us that she says "I love you" to her children whenever they leave the house, always being sure to let everyone know her feelings. She does not want to leave something so important to later, knowing there may not be a later. Others keep themselves very busy and active, feeling that if they want to accomplish something, they had better do it now. Still others talked about changes in priorities, putting more emphasis on relationships and less on external accomplishment.

The second most common outcome was independence, acknowledged in three quarters of the women in our sample whose mothers died. This is especially true in the women who were young when mother died. These women often had to raise themselves and they learned to be highly self-sufficient, both emotionally and physically. Some women find that this independence interferes with adult relationships, because they tend to take pride in not needing others. These women seem to have developed a protective shell, which helped them to survive as little children alone in the world, but which may now interfere with intimate relationships, where shared vulnerability can bring greater closeness.

Somewhat less common (64%) was the perception that experiencing the early death of a mother had left them more compassionate than other women. Some of the daughters now work in the health care field, and attribute their understanding and empathy for others experiencing illness to their experience with their mothers. Approximately half of the women in our sample reported that they have low self-esteem attributed to their mother's death. One explained that mothers provide unconditional love, something that cannot be replaced. Some daughters experienced abusive relationships and attributed this to their lack of self-esteem.

Another common problem was Difficulty at Life Transitions. Many of the women (52%) indicated that times when mothers would normally play a significant role in their lives were especially difficult for them. Weddings were almost universally mentioned as difficult times. Childbirth was another time when they felt the loss of their mother. Even common occasions, like graduations, special birthdays, holidays, and Mother's Days were experienced with some sadness and an awareness of difference. Some women used these occasions to acknowledge their mothers by including a special token or gesture to represent their mother's presence. For example, one woman includes yellow roses, mother's favorite flower, in all such special occasions. The sadness felt at these occasions varies, depending on the occasion itself, and how long it has been since mother's death. Generally, the first and the biggest occasions are the most difficult.

Over one third (37%) of the women in our sample whose mothers died indicated that they suffered from depression. Some women had serious depressions, often triggered by the occasions mentioned. Others had milder forms, some chronic, and some more occasional. What is important is that these women attributed these depressions to their mother's deaths.

Less common (about 20%) was the identification of being "stuck," or unable to move into expected adult roles. Some women indicated that they had put off getting married or having children. In some cases, this stemmed from a belief that they themselves will get breast cancer and die young. Others said that they did not know how to be a mother themselves because they did not have a mother as a model or to guide them. One woman, whose mother died at age 32, was interviewed after her 33rd birthday. She said she hadn't realized that she had been expecting her life to end, but now that she had passed her 32nd year, she felt that she had a whole new lease on life. She was thinking for the first time about what she wanted to do with the rest of her life!

CONCLUSIONS

This research provides a picture of the experiences of women whose mothers had breast cancer. Results show that women whose mothers died of breast cancer have many issues of unresolved grief as well as family problems that resulted from the changes that occurred in the family following the death. Specific problems vary depending on the daughter's age and birth order/gender position in the family, and are likely to be greater if the daughter is younger. However, even women who were young adults (over age 23) were likely to experience profound grief over the loss of their mother, many years after her death. Also, family problems, especially around stepmothers, fathers, and siblings, stemming from the period following mother's death, were common.

This population is important because, as genetic services for those at risk of developing breast cancer become available, these women are likely to make up a sizeable proportion of the potential clients. The results of this study have implications for the development of genetic services for this population. An understanding of the experiences of women whose mothers had breast cancer should be part of the training of social workers and genetic counselors. Finally, the results can be used to guide breast-cancer advocates and professionals who work with and on behalf of women with breast cancer and their families to prevent future problems in the daughters of these women.

B. The Personal and Professional Experiences of Doing a Grounded Theory Project

BEGINNINGS

I was born . . . no, just kidding. But one of the characteristics of any qualitative research is looking inward, and in this project, there has been a lot of that, much more than I expected when I began (probably one thing that attracted me to qualitative research was the opportunity to combine the personal and the professional). When I was "coming of age," intellectually and politically, the phrase "the personal is the political" was hot. It was a heady time to be a woman, and one thing we tried to do was to look at the political context of what were previously defined as personal issues. Today, with so many years of deconstruction behind us, this hardly seems revolutionary, but even so, it was a bit scary to bring the personal side of my own life into the open. There is still in me a voice that fears my work will be devalued if it is seen as springing from personal issues rather than things defined in a dispassionate, scientific way.

This project grew out of an earlier project, which grew out of a friendship. I had been long interested in the psychosocial aspects of health and health care. Some of this may have been chance, because my research interests started out in international development, and not long after getting my doctorate, I got a job at Johns Hopkins in an innovative program to train a "new kind of health practitioner." This threw me into an environment of health care, and of course, sickness, disability, and death. But the year before I got that job, I had started having joint pain that was eventually diagnosed as rheumatoid arthritis— at Johns Hopkins! So I already had a personal experience on the other side of the health care divide (as a patient), and it was a life-transforming experience for me. At the time, I was a firm believer in a strong separation between the personal and the professional, and I struggled to keep this personal experience out of my work (in retrospect, this was clearly misguided, impossible, and unnecessary, but I was trained to be an "objective" social scientist. I believed that doing research in an area of personal experience would lead to poor-quality research, that bringing in my life experience would bias my work, and that my work would be devalued, and perhaps ridiculed, were I to make this connection explicit. I was young, and concerned about my reputation in what was then a very quantitative, male-dominated environment).

DISCOVERING QUALITATIVE RESEARCH

By the late 1980s, things were different. I had tenure. I felt much more confident and comfortable, willing to take risks, and ready to do something I truly wanted to do, not just what I felt would advance me professionally. I had published a number of quantitative papers in good journals. At this time, Carolyn Walter came to the University of Maryland, where I worked, and ended up in an office down the hall from mine. Carolyn's dissertation had been qualitative, on women's life course development and motherhood. I found myself envying her ability to combine her work and her life. We started having wonderful conversations about illness and women's life course development that moved easily from our personal lives to theories to research and back. I shared my concerns about how my arthritis had affected my children (and my relationships with them). We decided to work together, combining our expertise, in part because we were excited about the idea, and in part because we liked each other.

We decided to do a qualitative research project on breast cancer. Carolyn had a friend who was dying of breast cancer at the time, who provided many of the examples that sparked our interest in the topic. I didn't want to study women with rheumatoid arthritis. It seemed like it would be like studying myself and I wanted some distance. (More on this later.) The result was that we ended up doing a project on breast cancer in the life course and reported the results in a book of that name (Oktay & Walter, 1991). It was my first experience with qualitative research and I loved doing it! I was energized by the excitement of generating ideas, and exploring literature as the project progressed (this in contrast to quantitative research, where I had tended to use literature to build a case for doing the project that was defined largely by practical considerations, such as the availability of a population to study, instruments that met the necessary standards, and so on. It was a backward process, even though it sounded like a forward process in the articles that I wrote on these studies). In contrast, the development of ideas in qualitative research felt truly open, uncharted, and free. It could go in any direction, and it allowed me to bring in my own life experience, things I had read (including fiction, poetry, plays, and films), as well as the professional literature. I loved it and quickly lost interest in doing quantitative research again (this does not mean that I don't value it or see a need for it, but I just found the qualitative took me to places I wanted to go, and involved me in doing things I loved doing. I wanted more!).

I decided to get further training in qualitative methods, because this first project was done with only Carolyn to guide me. I took several courses then available in the Nursing School at University of Maryland, and I also did a lot of reading. I have also participated in the listserv of several qualitative research groups, and this has helped me to keep up with current ideas. Attending conferences and reading journals also helped. I developed a course in qualitative methods for the doctoral students in the social work doctoral program, and have been teaching this every year since 1994. This has been a wonderful experience, and working with the students as they are introduced to qualitative methods and struggle to develop qualitative projects has helped me to better understand the strengths and the limits of this methodology.

THE DAUGHTER'S PROJECT

As we finished up the book, I looked for ideas for follow-up work. One idea that kept coming back was related to the family issues surrounding breast cancer. Each chapter in the book ended up with a theme about children and a theme about mothers. When asked to identify what surprised me about our findings, I identified the themes about relationships with mothers. I had expected that women would be concerned about the implications of the illness for their children, but was surprised about the intensity of their relationships with their mothers, and how these relationships were reflected in (and changed by) the breast cancer experience. At around this time, I saw an RFP (Request for Proposals) indicating that the National Breast Cancer Action Plan had been successful in convincing the National Institutes of Health (NIH) to devote some of their enormous research funds to the projects that would further the goals of the action plan.

I was on sabbatical at the time, and had the time to work intensely on a grant proposal. Fortunately, the review committees for the proposals included members of the National Breast Cancer Coalition—that is, breast cancer activists. I believe that my proposal was successful because of the influence of the activists, although of course, I have no proof of this. In any case, the grant was funded, and I became one of the few social work researchers to obtain federal funding for a qualitative study! This was a heady moment. I was excited and at the same time, scared to death. I wanted to crawl under my bed and hide, fearing that I wouldn't be able to pull it off successfully. I found myself thinking about how the grant money ($150,000 per year for 2 years; not a large grant by NIH standards) represented a lot of money in ordinary people terms, and to my mind, it represented a trust in me. I wasn't sure I could deliver.

Somehow, I managed to hide these fears and insecurities, and move forward with the research.

By this time, Carolyn had moved on, both physically (she no longer worked at the University of Maryland), and in her personal life. I still wanted to involve her in the research, though, and happily, she agreed to serve as a peer debriefer. She could be a kind of advisor to the project staff, and we could have some of our wonderful talks as the project progressed. Due to the grant funding, I would be in a position to pay her for these activities (Lovely!).

Team Building

The first step was to assemble a team. I had asked Susan McFeaters, then a graduate student in the doctoral program, to serve as project manager. I hardly knew Susan at the time, but she was one of the only doctoral students who had an interest and a background in health care. Susan had worked as a clinical social worker in pediatric HIV before entering the doctoral program. She was a natural to work on the project. Susan brought strong clinical skills as well as a background in family therapy. This background proved invaluable. Susan also had excellent organizational skills, which was a good thing for me because I tend to be scattered, last minute, and always losing important things. Susan helped in all aspects of the project, including recruiting women into the study, keeping track of all information, organizing the team meetings, interviewing, coding, and retrieving coded information for analysis. She stayed on the project through the data gathering and initial analysis stages. At that point, she was ready to move on to work on her own dissertation. The team also included Julia Rauch, a colleague from Maryland who had a long background in social work in public health. Julia and I had worked together over the years in the Health Specialization in the MSW program, and grown to appreciate each other's strengths. Michelle Jones, who was then a doctoral student in our program, completed the team.

The grant proposal required the inclusion of an advisory board, so the grant application had needed what are called Letters of Support from potential members. I was calling people I hardly knew, or didn't know at all, and asking them to serve on this (at that point) imaginary advisory board for an imaginary project. Amazingly, people agreed to do it, and so the very first thing we did once the grant was approved was to get the board together for a meeting. The board meeting would become an important organizing device for the project. We held two each year, and used them to make progress reports, discuss our findings, and get advice and help. The first task for the project was to find respondents, and I asked the advisory board members for help. The board was made up of a combination of people—some involved professionally (physicians, nurses, social workers), some as breast cancer advocates, and some who were both. I developed an interview guide and we shared it with the board. We also made up a preliminary list of eligibility criteria. One of my criteria was that the women be able to discuss their experience without becoming emotionally overwhelmed. I was thinking about the fine line between

qualitative interviewing and therapy, and not wanting to get into sticky situations where the line would be too easy to cross. But the board members questioned this, and felt that we would be excluding an important part of the
experience. This challenged me to think more about what I wanted to exclude and why (perhaps I was just uncomfortable with emotion, and wanted
to avoid it?). I eventually decided that I would screen out those with very recent experiences. However, I was still wary of having a lot of people who
were agreeing to participate in the study as a way of getting therapy. (This is a
problem in this kind of study, compared to traditional, anthropological field
work, where the researcher picks the informants. Here, I had to rely on referrals from others and volunteers.)

Finding Informants

One of the characteristics of the grounded theory method is *theoretical sampling*, in which the researcher uses the developing theory to guide sampling
decisions. At first, I was just looking for anyone who would volunteer. I feared
that I wouldn't find anyone, and . . . the fact that the study was funded made
me more anxious about that than I would otherwise have been. Of course, we
had to go through the University Institutional Review Board (IRB), which
meant that our recruiting letter had to follow the standard format used in any
type of research—risks, benefits, confidentiality, right to withdraw, and an ob-
tuse statement of lack of liability written by the University lawyers. We distributed this ridiculous letter to the board members as a recruiting tool, and
got a furious call shortly after that from a potential respondent. This woman
was so angry at the language in the letter that she refused to participate. I decided to develop a different recruiting brochure that was much more user
friendly. After that, I only sent out the IRB-approved recruitment letter after
someone had called in response to the brochure (a number of other practical
details were worked out during this period, such as getting a telephone line
with a message from the "Daughters" project, as we started to call it infor-
mally, getting a brief questionnaire for Susan to use on telephone calls from
possible volunteers, setting up a database for project participants where we
could record essential information, like names, telephone numbers, and dates
of contact).

Enhancing Team Sensitivity

Early in the project, our peer debriefer, Carolyn, came down to meet with
the study team before we began any interviewing. I had budgeted four meetings with Carolyn for each year of the study, and I decided to ask her to do a
self-exploration type of session with the team before we began. My idea was
that we are all daughters ourselves, and some of us (Julie and I) were also
mothers. Because the study would deal with mother–daughter issues, it would
be important for us to have some self-understanding of our own issues in
this area, so as to be able to guard against our own issues taking over our

interviews or interpretations. Carolyn is an expert clinician, and the way she led the session reflected her strong clinical experience. She began by asking, in a warm, reassuring voice, for each of us to share our own view of our relationship with our mother. We also were asked to reflect on illness experiences in our families. I began and talked about how my mother and I had a "strained" relationship that I thought was typical of other women my age. I described my mother as a very strong, competent woman. We got along well, with weekly phone chats, but there was a strain because she never fully approved of my lifestyle (working mother). I always felt that she was not very warm or nurturing to me, preferring my two brothers, just because they were boys, and my younger sister, who conformed to her ideas of what a girl/woman should be. (As I am writing this now, I find it hard to even reconstruct these feelings, because my mother has since become very frail and increasingly forgetful, to the point that she is no longer in charge of even the most basic aspects of her own life. I find myself wondering what it was that used to bother me about my mother.) I think I told this story with a somewhat humorous tone, the kind one uses when talking with women friends about mothers, with some eye rolling and bemused camaraderie. I expected similar stories from the others, and was surprised and chagrined to hear their stories. Susan talked movingly about her father's death from cancer and how she felt that talking with respondents in our study would rekindle her feelings of sadness and loss. (Over the course of the study, Susan would experience other losses in her life. Having this early sharing helped us all to be in touch with Susan's pain, and to help support her in these losses.) Then, Michelle talked about her mother's experience with a brain tumor that was life threatening, but was now in remission. Michelle presented this story without much emotion and as "something that happened in the past." We sensed her need to see her mother as cured, and did not push her about her mother's prognosis. This stance turned out to be common in daughters whose mother's survived, and our early practice understanding Michelle's experience helped us to see the importance of denial in daughters whose mothers had been through a life-threatening experience like breast cancer.

The final speaker was Julia, a midlife woman with many adversities behind her, who also had a strong clinical background. Julia does not show her vulnerabilities, and in spite of working together for many years, I was not aware of her early family life. In this session, Julia shared, with great pain, her mother's mental illness when she was a young child and her early death. She ended up becoming overcome, having to leave the room. Julia's story helped to sensitize me to the long-term impact of a problematic experience with mother in early childhood, and the tendency to bury the pain from this experience and "truck along" in life. We did find many respondents who had never talked with anyone (even husbands) about their mother's death. Julia's sharing helped us to be prepared for lots of buried pain in women who are on the surface very successful, powerful, and in control. After the sharing, we discussed how the experiences in our lives might affect our interviewing. We each identified things and situations that we might need to avoid and biases that we might bring to the study. We vowed to help each other to avoid these in our own areas of blindness. Carolyn and I discussed the "team" strengths and weaknesses after the meeting. As the project progressed, I was able to address these weaknesses through biweekly team meetings and sharing our transcriptions. As a result, we were able to identify our interviewing weaknesses and mistakes, and identify good interviewing techniques from each other. All of us improved our interviewing skills through the process of the team meetings.

Shaky Beginnings

Before long, we had our first referral! A woman responded to an announcement placed on an internet discussion board by one of the board members. Her mother was diagnosed several years ago, and she met our screening criteria. Susan sent me her name and phone number, and I called and set up an appointment for the first interview.

Case #1 turned out to be a failure and never ended up on the final report. I went down to her office for the interview, prepared with newly purchased tape recorder, extra tapes, batteries, Kleenex, consent forms, and a list of referrals. She wasn't there. I drove back home, discouraged and frustrated. Perhaps this study was going to be more difficult than I had thought. Eventually, I had a long and intense interview with this woman; however, she did not respond to my follow-up call and did not continue in the study. The first interview raised a number of difficult issues and reinforced my conviction that some daughters are too close to the experience and too emotional to be good informants. She was in denial about the seriousness of mother's illness, and was having a hard time with the negative emotions she felt. Although the interview contained some good material, and highlighted the power and complexity of mother–daughter relationships, it also reinforced my concerns about screening women who had not attained some distance from the experience. Given the way she dropped out of the study, I did not feel comfortable using case #1, consent form or no.

By the time this experience was behind me, we had had several other referrals, and Susan and Julia had each had an interview. My next case (#4) turned out to be a delightful interview, long and meaty. There was also denial here, and a strong religiosity, but this respondent remained an eager participant throughout the study, and did not leave me feeling that she needed therapy. Case #4's mother had passed away about 5 years before the interview, and although the respondent cried, she was not overwhelmed with emotion. The problem lay in the way we defined the time needed to eligibility; since in case #1, there was adequate time since diagnosis, but the cancer had since recurred, and the daughter was actually living through a case that would eventually be classified as "mother died" and not "mother survived." This also pointed out a weakness in our simplistic idea of having half in each of these two categories; whereas the "mother died" category is clear-cut, women who report that "mother survived" on the screening interview are always in a position where mother's status could change.

Transcription Woes

Another early problem was with the recordings and transcriptions. Julia had a series of mishaps with the equipment, and her first interview ended up with nothing on the tape! This was extremely frustrating. She wrote up summary notes, but these did not provide any material that could be used in the analysis. After this happened a second time, Julia started asking her cases to come to her office for the interviews so that she could be sure that the equipment would work! After these early tape failures, we became much more careful to check and recheck the equipment, test the recording in the interview setting, and generally to be hyperaware that if something did not get recorded, "it didn't happen" as far as the study was concerned. Fortunately, this type of malfunction of the recorder only happened two other times—once to Susan and once to me. Susan did the interview again, and . . . because mine was the third interview and was primarily validating, I made due with a summary.

Getting "Good Informants"

About 6 months after recruitment had begun, I began to worry about whether we would get enough cases. The cases known to the advisory board had already entered the study, and new cases were entering slowly. I was getting a slow stream of new cases by distributing the brochure to places like the annual symposium of the local Komen foundation, the Race for the Cure, women's health conferences in the area, and a women's health booth in the hospital, but the study design needed to recruit the majority of the sample in the first 9 months of the study so that second and third interviews could be scheduled. I decided to put an advertisement in the local *City Paper*, a free weekly paper that has a large section that recruits volunteers for various medical research projects. This was something I had never done before and waited eagerly for a response. To my surprise, we got about 20 calls in the next few days. The population who responded to the advertisement was quite different from the women we had been interviewing through our health professional and advocate contacts. These women were more likely to have a mother who survived and to be motivated to participate because of the possibility of payment (we offered $25 per interview). There was one case that was very disorganized and, reading her transcript, I worried for the safety of the interviewer (we did not return for another interview). I also suspected that her mother had not really had breast cancer. Another case was also suspicious, because the daughter could not provide any details, although she said she had been a young adult at the time. She practically earned her living by volunteering for medical research studies. However, some of the interviews we got from the advertisement were good ones, and provided us access to women from a lower socioeconomic background than we were getting from more traditional techniques. We did not repeat the advertisement, and by the time we had completed interviewing the eligible women we recruited this way, we felt we were close enough to our required number to return to the more legitimate theoretical sampling strategy.

Our first cases were mostly women whose mothers had died of breast cancer when they were in their late teens or young adults. When the study proposal was developed, I indicated that the sample would include women whose mothers died and those whose mothers survived (50/50 split), women who were children, adolescents, young adults, and adults when mother was diagnosed, and racially varied (25% African American). The theoretical sampling concept used in grounded theory methodology suggests that the sampling strategy be based on the developing theoretical model. In our case, we kept our original idea of looking at difference by age at diagnosis, as the experience of women who were different ages at mother's diagnosis had clearly different experiences. We also worked to include 25% African American women, although this did not come out of our theory. We did hold several discussions on this, trying to identify racial differences, but it turned out that our African American sample was very disparate. We had a wide range of social classes (a much wider range than we had for White women), and the experiences of very poor African American women were very different from women from very well-educated, well-off families. The inclusion of a substantial number of African American women helped the study by providing diversity in family types. The "Cinderella" model was a powerful one, and there was a temptation to make this the main theme of the study. However, the Cinderella model did not fit for the African American women. I believe this is because the family was structured differently from the normative nuclear family more common among Whites. This meant that for most of the African American women, the loss of mother did not have the same familial implications as for White women. The inclusion of the African American women helped me avoid overgeneralizing a model that was appealing, but not universal.

We continued throughout the study to recruit women who were children or adolescents, and stopped accepting women who were over 18 at mother's diagnosis. By the end of the study, we were still trying to find an African American woman who was a child at the time of mother's illness. Amazingly, at one of the late advisory board meetings, one of the African American advisory board members suddenly remembered that he had a niece that would qualify (his brother's wife had died from breast cancer).

What To Do With the Women
Whose Mothers Survived?

The third sampling criteria—half mothers who died and half mothers who survived—was abandoned as the study progressed. The interviews with the women whose mothers died were meaningful and rich, whereas the interviews with the women whose mothers survived were often brief and superficial. Most daughters whose mothers survived presented the experience of mother's diagnosis and treatment as a minor event in their lives. This surprised me because of my earlier experience interviewing women with breast cancer. I knew that for all of these women, no matter how early the cancer was detected or how minimal the treatment, being diagnosed with breast cancer was a major life event. You would not know this by talking to the daughters! This group of daughters continued to puzzle me throughout the study. I could not develop a model that encompassed both groups of daughters, as their experiences were so different (except during the illness phase). In comparison to those whose mothers died, leaving them with life-long after effects, those whose mothers survived reverted to a more "normal" mother–daughter relationship, not unlike the one I described with my own mother in the early team meeting.

I decided after trying to balance the two experiences to weight the study toward those women whose mothers died and to limit the number of cases where mother survived. The group (Mother Survived) was also problematic for me in the analysis. I developed a "model" for the experience of women whose mothers died, but did not have anything comparable for those whose mothers survived. I speculated that the mothers who survived had protected their daughters from their own fears and had presented a very optimistic picture of their illness. This protection was something I was able to discuss with the women whose mother died, but not with those whose mothers survived, because it goes lockstep with the daughter's denial. It may have been more interesting to interview the mothers about this, but . . . That would be a different study.

At the end of the study, I felt it would be insensitive to include the two groups of women in the same debriefing session. I decided to hold two sessions. The session of women whose mothers died was well attended and intense. The women were very interested in the study, and eager to meet one another and to share. Some talked about having an ongoing support group. The session for the women whose mothers survived had only two women attend (several canceled at the last minute). The discussion focused on problems they were having with their mothers. One woman complained that her mother wanted her to have a child, and kept sending her "hints" like copies of newspaper articles on topics like "Having a baby in your thirties, even if you are not married." The other complained about how her mother criticizes her for being overweight. Both women presented (like Michelle in the early peer debriefing session) as feeling that mother was cured, and they were focused on their own lives. Their interest in the study results was minimal, and one even said that she was only there because her mother wanted her to go.

Analysis

The development of the major themes for women whose mothers died was fairly clear and straightforward from early in the study. Because Age of Daughter was identified in the original study, I sought to identify women who experienced mother's death from breast cancer across a range of ages, and then as interviews came in, sought to identify important concepts and themes within each of these age groups. In grounded theory, you start theorizing as you go along, and we did this initially in team discussions after each interview. We identified tentative themes for each case by pulling out the most salient issues for each woman. When we started using the NUD*IST program, we coded each case at a node for age and at another node for whether mother survived. The substantive categories of the NUD*IST scheme were Family Background,

Illness Experience, How Illness Affected Respondent, How Illness Affected Family, Issues of Risk (discussed in interview only if respondent brought it up), and Long-Term Impact. Over the course of the study, the tree holding the coding scheme evolved. Usually because as I coded marginally, if something didn't fit easily into an existing category, a new category was added. Sometimes, an existing category was divided into two (or more) parts.

When I wrote the questionnaire, developed the reports to the advisory board and to the two respondent groups, and wrote the final report for the National Cancer Institute (NCI), I used the NUD*IST outline. Only one category was dropped as a result of the questionnaire. I had a category on Family Status including Social Class and Race in the section on Family Background. This probably reflects my sociology background, where it is a given that social status is always a major variable. But the women responded negatively to its inclusion, indicating strongly that they felt that this was not an important factor in their experience, and that they had much more in common with other women who had a mother die, regardless of social class or race, than they had with other women of similar class or racial background. I decided to remove this category from the model. All other categories remained in the model. At this time, I knew that age was a critical variable, especially for the women whose mothers died, but I didn't have a clear model or theory to describe it.

Once the basic model was developed, I started writing my book. I began by developing case studies for the chapters that would deal with women whose mothers died. One very exciting moment was when I made a matrix of the themes that developed in each of the four chapters. I realized that even though I developed themes for each age group out of the case materials, without forcing conformity to the general outline I developed for the entire project (discussed in Part A), that the basic outline held up fairly well (a copy of the concept grid can be found on pages 46 and 47). For example, under Experience of Illness, I had four general categories: Illness and Treatment, Communication, Family Dynamics, and Role Shifts (the first three were in the earlier model, and the last was added). For children, I had themes on the Effects of Illness, Communication, and Family Dynamics. For young adolescents, I had something on Illness and Treatment, and something on Role Shifts. For late adolescents, I had Family Dynamics and Role Shifts. For young adults, all four themes were represented. I knew that I wanted the themes to flow from the case materials and did not want to force things. If they didn't fit, then I felt it was better to have a messy scheme, than to have a scheme that was neat but not valid. So it was exciting to see that the themes fit reasonably well with the basic outline. I was comfortable with the level of messiness.

Getting It Out the Door

After turning in the final report to NCI, I developed a book proposal and circulated it to various publishers. I was disappointed to get very little response, because I was convinced that the material I had was strong and important. I think I hit a bad moment in the publishing industry, when many firms were going under, and others were deciding not to take risks. Textbooks were being published and well-known authors who had had strong sellers in the past. I got an interested response from one publisher, but when they gave the proposal to their marketing person, he or she said there was no other book on the market like it, so they couldn't estimate how many it would sell. They turned it down! I was very discouraged. I did think about hiring an agent, to market the book to trade publishers. I read a couple of advice books for authors on finding agents, and was appalled when I read things like, "No one wants to read a sad book. Be uplifting." And "No one wants to read a complex book. Include a simple list of 'what to do' items in each chapter or section." I decided that although I wanted to have a best-selling book, I didn't want it so badly that I would distort the message of the women I had interviewed! Ultimately, I gratefully accepted an offer from Haworth Press.

The lack of enthusiastic response from publishers left me less confident about the value of what I was doing. Writing a book is a major, time-consuming process. I wondered if I had the energy to complete it. Shortly after that, my dean asked me to become the director of our doctoral program. I put the book on the proverbial back burner. Fortunately, I had a sabbatical coming up, and I used the 6 months to pick up the book project. I completed drafts for the four chapters on women whose mothers died, but still had much work to do. Unfortunately, the sabbatical was over. I returned to work, and was again immediately immersed in the doctoral program. Fortunately, academic jobs have summers off, and I am committed to finishing the book this summer!

Mother and Daughter, Redux

The summer before my sabbatical, my 85-year-old mother became ill. She was, for the first time, unable to take care of things herself. She was forgetting and I had to go out and get her into surgery for an infection. I realized that she couldn't remember what medicines to take, and she was having trouble with normal life activities like driving, shopping, doing bills, and caring for the house. My father had retired only the previous year (at age 90), and he was also increasingly frail. A couple of months later, he had a stroke, and came home after rehabilitation with many problems. So began my life as a caregiver. My husband and I have been going to my parents' home once a month for the past 3 years and doing almost daily tasks in between to keep them going in their beloved home. The experience has changed my view of the bereaved daughters in my study. I remember once coming up to mother's bedroom to find her in a deep sleep—motionless and unresponsive. I was immediately flooded with emotion, seeing her lying there so small, so helpless. *Was she dead?* Then she woke, and refreshed herself, and those feelings receded. But I experienced such a sudden shift—from seeing her as a strong and powerful force (to push against?), to seeing her as weak and needing my help. I felt a wave of terror seeing her like this. I was suddenly a little girl, feeling abandoned! And

I was in my mid-50s at the time, much older and more experienced than the women in my study had been when their mothers had become ill.

The other side of the equation has also changed. When I started this project, I was the mother of two young women who were exploring their worlds in exciting (and for me, too dangerous) ways. The older was a modern dancer living in a scary neighborhood in New York. The younger was sailing around the world. I felt a mixture of pride and fear for them. Now, my older daughter is married and I have a grandson, 6 months old! I became the sandwich generation in the last year, adding visits to my daughter and grandson to those to my parents! All of this has affected my work on this project in many ways. I find that I reinterpret the stories of my informants as my own experience with a life that feels out of control expands. And in a more fundamental way, I have less time to get "into the cave" as Lillian Rubin puts it so well (2000). Even when I am alone in my cubicle, I find my mind going round and round . . . *Remember to order the groceries for Mom and Dad! Remember to call the doctor about the prescriptions! Did my daughter take the baby in for his shots this month?* I am on call. Every time the phone rings, I jump. *What now? Is Dad in the hospital again? Do I need to go out there? Should I go to New York and help my daughter buy a crib?* We went to the beach this winter for a week of "quiet reflection." Dad got a urinary tract infection and was hospitalized on day 2 of the trip. Every day, I called, talked to the doctors, talked to him, tried to decide—could I stay or did I need to be there? Finally, I went. Although I was determined to complete my book before fall 2002, I realized that I was not in control of my time. Like women everywhere, I tried to balance family responsibilities (and joys) and work. At the same time, I was juggling new roles and responsibilities, and trying to find a balance between the personal and the professional parts of my life.

So the life cycle goes on. For women, I think this is such a central thing. It is so hard to be productive! I am always torn—wanting to be with loved ones, and wanting to be alone at the same time. Feeling guilty either way! The longer the project goes on, the more it gets entwined with my own life. Whatever illusion I had at the start of the project, that I would have some distance because my mother did not have breast cancer, seems to have dissolved. I am a woman, a mother, and a daughter. These facts both help and hinder me as I struggle to complete this work!

ACKNOWLEDGMENTS

Heartfelt thanks are due to the women who so freely shared their stories with us, and to my team, Susan McFeaters, Julia Rauch, and Michelle Jones, whose interviews provided such rich data. Thanks too to the Advisory Board of the Daughters Project who gave generously of their time and energy, and to the National Cancer Institute and the National Breast Cancer Coalition, whose advocacy led to the support of this type of unconventional research.

REFERENCES

Berlinsky, E. B., & Biller, H. B. (1982). *Parental death and psychological development*. Lexington, MA: DC Heath.

Freud, S. (1917). *Mourning and melancholia. Standard Edition*, vol. XIV, 243–72.

Gahan, C., & Hannibal, M. (1998). *Doing qualitative research using QSR NUD★IST*. Thousand Oaks, CA: Sage.

Glaser, B., & Strauss, A. (1967). *The discovery of grounded theory*. Chicago: Aldine.

Gray, R. E. (1987). Adolescent response to the death of a parent. *Journal of Youth & Adolescence, 16*, 511–25.

Guba, E. G. (1981). Criteria for assessing the trustworthiness of naturalistic inquiries. *Educational Resources Information Center Annual Review Paper, 29*, 75–91.

Offit, K. (1998). *Clinical cancer genetics: Risk counseling and management*. New York: John Wiley & Sons.

Oktay, J. S., & Walter, C. A. (1991). *Breast cancer in the life course: Women's experiences*. New York: Sage.

Padgett, D. K. (1998). *Qualitative methods in social work research*. Thousand Oaks, Calif: Sage.

Rubin, L. B. (2000). *Tangled lives*. Boston: Beacon.

Schneider, K. A., & Marnane, D. (1997). Cancer risk counseling: How is it different? *Journal of Genetic Counseling, 6*, 97–109.

Strauss, A., & Corbin, J. (1990). *Basics of qualitative research: Grounded theory procedures and techniques*. Newbury Park, CA: Sage.

Strewing, J., Hartge, P., & Wacholder, S. (1997). The risk of cancer associated with specific mutations of BRCA1 and BRCA2 among Ashkenazi Jews. *New England Journal of Medicine, 336*, 1401–8.

Weil, J. (2000). *Psychosocial genetic counseling*. New York: Oxford University Press.

Wolfenstein, M. (1966). How is mourning possible? *Psychoanalytic Study of the Child, 21*, 93–123.

CONCEPT GRID OF CODES

	Experience of Illness	Experience After Death	Long-Term Impact
	1. Illness and treatment 2. Communication 3. Family dynamics 4. Role shifts/daughter's role	1. Family changes (fathers, stepmothers, siblings) 2. Grieving and social support	1. Ongoing grieving 2. Change in personality 3. Change in philosophy of life
Children	1. Effects of illness/treatments 2. Lack of communication 3. Family dynamics—independence	1. Family changes—Stepfamily adjustment (Cinderella) 2. Survival 3. Lack of grieving	1. Grieving as adults 2. Lack of information 3. Major effect on personality (low self-esteem, sleep problems, strong and independent)
Adolescents	1. Illness/treatment—Focus on the body (body deterioration) 2. Role shifts—Conflict between need to separate (developmental) and illness requirements	1. Family changes—Relationship with father (too distant, too close) 2. Grieving—Fathers can't help daughters with grief 3. Grieving and social support—Peer group influence	1. Ongoing grieving—Grieving, anger, fear of loss of control, anger at God 2. Personality changes—Body image issues (fear of breast development, fear of breast cancer), eating disorders 3. Intimacy issues, problems
Late Adolescents	1. Role shifts—"Little Women" theme 2. Family dynamics—Relationship with mother—"role reversal"	1. Family changes—Fathers (rejection, loss of home) Oedipus? 2. Grieving and social support—Unresolved grief (loneliness, isolation, seeking mother surrogates)	1. Chronic grieving (depression) 2. Loss of support of mother in adult life

	Experience of Illness	Experience After Death	Long-Term Impact
Young Adults	1. Communication— Open communication or mutual protection 2. Role shifts— Balancing adult roles with caregiving 3. Role shifts— Expanded caregiving 4. Family dynamics— Adult relationship with mother	1. Family changes— Controlling relationship with stepmother 2. Taking on mother's roles— Caregiving for grandparents 3. Active grieving	1. Constructive memorials, activism 2. "Big cry"— Unending bonds. 3. Changing priorities (family, career, philosophy of life)

2

Narrative Analysis
A Feminist Approach

ROBERTA G. SANDS

A. The Family Context of Within-Religion Conversion

The study referred to in this chapter concerns families in which an adult daughter diverged from the moderate or cultural form of Judaism in which she was raised and became "reborn" as strictly Orthodox. This development obligates her to scrupulous adherence to religious laws and practices that were either overlooked or observed less fully in her family of origin. The research explores the family context of such a conversion within Judaism through the eyes of mothers and daughters. Specifically, the study inquires into the impact of this change in a daughter's religious intensity on the family of origin and ways in which families adapt to and cope with the new situation. I have been working on this study in concert with a team of women researchers who have been exploring this phenomenon in Israel, the United States, South Africa, and Holland. Our first study, of mothers and daughters from South Africa, found that mothers became increasingly ambivalent about their daughters' religiosity over time but that both mothers and daughters made strong efforts to maintain a close family relationship (Roer-Strier & Sands, 2001). The second study, of mothers who live in the United States and daughters who immigrated to Israel, found that most of the families tried to maintain close ties despite their own misgivings, but over time the mothers were more troubled about their children's living at a distance than the religious discrepancy (Sands & Roer-Strier, 2001). A few of the families included in the study differed from the others with respect to the closeness between the mother and daughter or some other facet of family solidarity. Narrative analytic methods such as those described in this chapter offer a way one can obtain an in-depth look at such "negative cases" (Padgett, 1998). This chapter presents a narrative analysis of an interview that I conducted with "Sylvia," the American mother of "Betty," who lives in Israel. At the time I met Sylvia, she was 77 years old and living with her husband, "Bill," in an apartment in a suburban community. She had not seen her religious daughter for 3 years, but she and Bill were planning to visit her in a few months. During the course of the interview, Sylvia recounted her own family life history and how she viewed Betty, which are the foci of my analysis. This section begins with discussions of the narrative and feminist research and is followed by a description of methods. Then it presents the analysis using illustrations from the transcribed interview with Sylvia.

THE NARRATIVE

Over the last few decades the boundaries between the humanities and social sciences have become blurred (Geertz, 1983). The narrative, which had traditionally been associated with literary studies, is now integral to qualitative social science research. Today, qualitative researchers regard written and oral stories, anecdotes, and life histories as data that comprise the whole or part of the data corpus used in their research projects. Generally qualitative researchers in the social sciences view these stories as constructions created through interpersonal, sociocultural, and historical processes. Stories or narratives *constitute*, rather than reflect, some aspect of a socially constructed reality (cf. Riessman, 1993). One expression of this narrative turn has been an exploration of the way in which the self is constructed in the act of storytelling. Several authors have described the process by which the self becomes organized in oral discourse (Cohler, 1991; Linde, 1993; Rosenwald & Ochberg, 1992; Schafer, 1992). From a postmodern feminist perspective, this self is not a fixed entity but is continually changing, context dependent, and multiple (Sands, 1996). Narratives may reveal different selves or facets of the self over the course of narrating an event (Wortham, 2001). Clinical social workers and other psychotherapists have noted that psychotherapy entails a telling and subsequent "restorying" of clients' lives (Laird, 1989). The clinician participates in this process by co-constructing stories. Narrative therapy is predicated on the idea that storying is a collaborative process in which the therapist listens attentively, asks questions, identifies oppressive stories and how they are interpreted, externalizes the problem, and opens up space for the production of new stories (Freedman & Combs, 1996; Kelley, 1996; White & Epston, 1990). Feminist researchers, too, have been attracted to the narrative. Stories are close to the everyday "lived experience" of women, whose knowledge is frequently submerged in favor of masculinist narratives. Narrating provides an opportunity for women to discover and hear their own voices and achieve insight that is a precondition for their changing themselves. Rissman (1992), for example, presented a narrative of a divorcing woman who changed her definition of herself from a victim of marital rape to a survivor. In her study, Jack (1991) showed how women moved in and out of depression depending on their ability to speak in their own voices.

FEMINIST RESEARCH

The feminist approach to narrative analysis used in this chapter was informed by literature on feminist research methodology. There are many genres of feminist research, including interview research, oral history, ethnography, survey research, and action research (Reinharz, 1992), suggesting that a feminist orientation is dependent on factors other than method. Some scholars insist that it encompass "feminist standpoint" epistemology, which takes women's experience in the everyday world as problematic (DeVault, 1999; Smith, 1987). Accordingly, the researcher shows how women's narratives are related to a presupposed, tacitly understood social organization around gender differences (Smith, 1987). Fonow and Cook (1991) have characterized feminist research methodology as reflexive, activist, attentive to emotions, and concerned with everyday life. A more recent review of "feminisms" and qualitative research indicates a growing diversity, complexity, and tension in the field (Olesen, 2000). I concur that there is no one feminist approach. Here I am viewing research as feminist on the basis of its concern with women's experiences as gendered subjects, incorporation of collaborative processes, and attention to voices, and will interpret findings from a feminist standpoint. Reflexivity, which is integral to qualitative and feminist research, will be addressed in Part B.

Research about women's experiences as *gendered subjects* is concerned with their efforts to understand and meet challenges related to their status as women. The challenges include, but are not limited to, pregnancy, sexual harassment, caregiving, parenthood, obtaining gynecologic care, and abusive relationships. Bell (1999), for example, explored women's knowledge, power, and resistance in their narratives of their experiences with diagnosis and treatment for reproductive problems and cancer as a consequence of their mothers' having taken diethylstilbestrol (DES). Two feminist qualitative researchers have explored the rationales and pathways of Jewish women who have joined highly gender-differentiated Orthodox Jewish communities (Davidman, 1991; Kaufman, 1985, 1991). Our study extends previous research on women who have become Orthodox by examining the family context and eliciting the perspectives of both the religious women and their mothers. The interview analyzed here highlights a mother's experience managing parenthood, work, and caregiving. Another characteristic of feminist research is that it is *collaborative*. To the extent possible, feminist research reduces the hierarchy between the researcher and the researched, "making space" for participants "to narrate their stories as they desire" (Bloom, 1998, p. 18). For our study, interviewers used an interview protocol that imposed some limits on participants' space. Most of us, however, diverged from the structure to allow participants to tell their stories. The narrative analysis presented examines the interaction between the interviewer and participant and how they collaborated. Feminist research is also sensitive to *voices*, those that are expressed and those that may be submerged. The focus on voice begins when the interviewer listens actively for hesitations, self-interruptions, meta-statements, self-criticism, and pauses, cues that suggest that the participant is struggling with the discrepancy between her own voice and moral discourses about what women should think, feel, or do (Anderson & Jack, 1991; DeVault, 1999). Transcriptions that show her hesitations, pauses, and self-interruptions convey the participant's process of finding her own voice. Another way of attending to voices is to examine the ways in which the narrator portrays herself and others. This chapter will analyze the narrator's "voicing" of characters in her stories and how she positions herself in relation to these voices.

METHODS

Data Collection

Our principal method of data collection has been the interview. In addition we conducted a focus group, consulted historical and demographic sources about Jewish communities in each national context, and read published personal narratives of men and women who have become Orthodox. With respect to the interviews, we have been conducting separate individual interviews with mothers and daughters, usually in person at the participant's home. The interviews have taken from 45 minutes to $2\frac{1}{2}$ hours over one or two sittings or telephone conversations. Our interview guide consists of open-ended questions that explore religiosity in the family over four generations; the daughter's spiritual journey; and the ways in which family members have reacted to, coped with, and adapted to the daughter's religious change. Methods used in our South African study are described in Roer-Strier and Sands (2001). For the study of American mothers and their religious daughters in Israel, we interviewed 17 mothers and 14 of their daughters. Two daughters refused to be interviewed and one mother (Sylvia) asked that we not contact her daughter. Sylvia was concerned that our interviewing Betty might disrupt what she considered a fragile mother–daughter relationship. We recruited our sample through networks of Orthodox research team members and a parents' organization in the United States. Two team members conducted the interviews in Israel; two in the United States.

Data Preparation

Sylvia's interview, like the other interviews in this study, was initially transcribed by someone else. According to Ochs (1979), transcription is a selective process that is guided by the researcher's theoretical goals. As a feminist researcher, I am interested in the interaction between the interviewer and the participant and thus want this reflected in the transcription. Furthermore, I wish to capture the nuances of the participant's speech, for these, as mentioned, provide evidence of a struggle to find one's own voice. I want to consider but not foreground aspects of the message besides words, because these can help me to interpret the meaning of the verbal communication. I asked the transcriber to type the words of both the interviewer and the interviewee in the form of a dialogue and to add anything else she heard (e.g., coughs, sighs, noises). I suggested that she insert sounds after typing a first draft. After the transcriber returned the tapes, I listened to them several times with the transcription in front of me. I made corrections here and there, knowing that one can never get a completely accurate transcription (Cameron, 2001). For the transcription of Sylvia's interview, I divided the lines into *message units*, minimal chunks of text that are identified by nonverbal and prosodic *contextualization cues* that signal how the message is to be interpreted (Gumperz, 1982). I listened for pauses, a lowering of the voice, and changes in the rhythm of speech to guide me in deciding where lines end and begin. The following excerpt shows how the beginning of this interview was transcribed following repeated listening. Transcription symbols, such as underlining where the participant emphasized a syllable, word, or set of words, are described on pages 72–73 of this chapter. Line numbers help reference where selections fit within the interview. "I" denotes the interviewer/author.

> **I:** Okay, um, I'd like to start out by asking you some questions about your family over a few generations religiously religi*osity*
>
> **Sylvia:** Are you interested in my husband's side of the family?
>
> **I:** I'm going to focus <u>more on yours</u>, but I may ask um ah-ah I think I may ask about his also.

Aside from the goal of obtaining a good transcript, I found it sensitizing to listen to the tape along the lines suggested by Brown and Gilligan (1992) in their "Listener's Guide" (Chapter 2). These authors suggest that the researcher listen to a taped interview at least four times, each iteration having a different focus. Initially one listens for the story, the events, and the contexts surrounding them. Next one listens for the *I* of the speaker in relation to oneself, so that the listener can connect emotionally with her. During the third and fourth listenings, one attends to the way the speaker talks about relationships from her own perspective and that of others. The narrator may describe experiences of authentic relationships, but her voice is also infused with voices of society and culture that restrain, silence, and introduce moral imperatives that she may accept, grapple with, or resist. The listener—who is empathetic, self-reflective, and responsive—attends to the impact of race, gender, and class on the speaker's views of herself and relationships (Brown & Gilligan, 1992). In listening to Sylvia, I also attended to what she said and how she talked about the bearing of age and religion on her life and the significance of religion to her family.

FINDINGS

There are many models of narrative analysis (Cortazzi, 1993; Mishler, 1995; Rissman, 1993) and none that I know of that is expressly feminist. Because I was interested in women's experiences, their voices, and their collaboration with the interviewer, I used analytic approaches that would illuminate these particular dimensions, and I interpreted the data from a feminist standpoint. I engaged in three types of analysis—topics and structure, voices, and the interaction between the interviewer and the participant. I will describe each of these analytic methods prior to presenting illustrative findings.

Topical and Structural Analysis

After Sylvia's interview was transcribed, listened to, corrected, broken into message units, and read numerous times, I divided the transcript into sections based on major topics and identified subtopics under each heading. The major topics and transcript lines were as follows:

Lines	Topic
1–6	Introduction
7–105	Sylvia's grandparents (maternal and paternal)
106–285	Sylvia's family of origin
286–390	Sylvia's husband's family of origin
391–448	Courtship and marriage
449–1253	Family of procreation (children, including religious daughter and her religious journey) and relations with extended family
1254–1679	Family response to religious daughter, coping, and adaptation; wrap-up of interview

The list of topics and subtopics served as a map of the transcript. In addition to developing this map, I reviewed the transcript to identify questions and their answers. This helped me to understand the flow of the interview and how later responses circled back to earlier questions. Next I identified stories in the transcript. The structural components that go into a minimal definition of a story include interrelated events, a setting, action aimed at attaining a goal, and an outcome (Stein & Policastro, 1984). Labov (1972, 1982; Labov & Waltzky, 1967) identified six elements, each having its own function, that comprise a fully formed oral narrative. The *abstract*, which is optional, is a summary of the substance or point of the narrative. *Orientation* sets the scene with respect to persons, place, time, and the initial situation. *Complicating action* is composed of clauses describing a sequence of events in temporal order. The *evaluation* elucidates the point of the narrative, that is, its meaning from the perspective of the narrator. The *resolution* refers to the outcome, which can coincide with the evaluation. Some narratives conclude with a *coda*, which signals the end of the story and returns to the present. Labov's framework helped me to identify the stories and their structural components. I also used cues from Sylvia's talk that she was about to tell a story (e.g., "Oh, I must tell you this") or end it (e.g., "So that was very sad"). Sometimes I signaled the end with the word *okay*. This process revealed that Sylvia had interjected stories within her responses to my questions and sometimes continued her stories ("and then") in response to later questions. I found that her stories were not discrete entities that fit neatly into Labov's model, but rather were spread out, repeated, and linked to other stories, and formed episodes of a larger story. To enhance my understanding of the stories and how they fit together, I reduced each episode to a *core narrative* or *skeleton plot* (Mishler, 1986) and constructed a sequence of episodes that built on each other. Like Mishler (1986) and Bell (1988), I excluded evaluation as a separate category within the skeleton plots, because evaluation pervades narratives (Labov, 1972). I diverged from Labov's definition of complicating action as past events by including contextual elements, such as descriptions of personalities, that seemed integral to the story or set of stories. Thus, I have renamed complicating action *complications*. Sylvia's Family Story presents a reconstructed, reduced version of Sylvia's narration of four interlocking life experiences. For the most part, the reconstructed text incorporates Sylvia's words. For the story to flow smoothly, I added sentences that filled narrative gaps on unnumbered lines and eliminated interviewer questions and comments. Large intervals between numbered lines indicate that the interview diverged from this story and later returned. I included a preamble describing Sylvia's mother's family because this sets the stage for subsequent episodes. We learn here that this was an immigrant family that came to the United States after having lost two children in pogroms. Sylvia remembers her grandparents as loving her, the only grandchild, but said that the family was not loving. She alludes to personality problems and conflicts between her grandparents and among their daughters. The first episode describes Sylvia's experiences growing up with two parents who were devoted to her but at odds with each other. Her father had been married previously, became widowed, and married Sylvia's mother, a woman 20 years younger than he and close in age to his three children. These three children lived next door to Sylvia's family and worked with their father. The tension between Sylvia's mother and the three grown children complicated Sylvia's parents' marriage. The Great Depression provides a historical backdrop through which to understand the conflict in the family. Sylvia's parents separate following her marriage, after which her father admitted being unhappy throughout his marriage. Sylvia expresses sadness over her parents' unhappiness and the feeling of being caught between two good parents.

The next episode occurs 4 years after Sylvia and Bill married, when they return home from living out of town, now with a 6-week-old baby ("Lennie"). Because of economic necessity, they move in with Bill's parents. This situation was complicated by the mother-in-law's overbearing personality and her interference, although helpful, with Sylvia's parenting. The resolution came when Bill and she gathered sufficient financial resources to move into their own home, where they lived for 40 years. The story does not, however, stop after the couple gains independence. Soon afterward, Sylvia's mother calls from Florida asking her daughter to allow her to move in with them. Because of what Sylvia attributes to her own inability to say "no," she agreed. Complications include her mother's help, her difficult personality, her mother's not getting along with two of the children but helping with one, and problems on holidays, with her mother feeling hurt, which in turn hurt Sylvia. The resolution was that her mother moved out and Sylvia's family continued helping her.

In the fourth episode, Sylvia describes the difficult years in which she and her husband were caring for their older parents while at the same time Sylvia was caring for her children, completing her education, and working. She felt torn among the people for whom she was responsible and frustrated that she could not give everyone the attention that he or she needed. She gives an example of what we would call *multitasking*: leaving work during her lunch hour to prepare her mother-in-law's medicines and then returning to work. She explains that, with her husband's help, she did what needed to be done.

Reduction of the stories to core narratives made visible themes that recurred across episodes. In the preamble, we learn that Sylvia was a loved only grandchild whose grandparents' family was beset with conflict and personality problems. We see this pattern repeated in the family in which Sylvia was raised, where she was her parents' only and loved child but there was conflict between her parents and between her mother and her father's sons. In both Episodes 2 and 3, Sylvia is in the grips of a woman who is helpful but interfering. Each of these women, like members of Sylvia's grandparents' family, was described as having a difficult personality. The only viable solution in both cases was separation.

In the fourth episode, we learn that Sylvia's status as the loved only child became a burden when she was older and became her parents' caregiver. Reading this set of episodes from a feminist standpoint, one sees Sylvia assuming traditional gender roles while suffering from feelings of guilt, helplessness, obligation, and powerlessness. The people who helped her (her mother-in-law and mother) undermined her as a parent, but Sylvia silenced her objections. Sylvia was simultaneously caring for her children, preparing for a career, and assuming caregiving responsibilities for her parents and in-laws. Although her husband "helped," she was the primary caregiver. She seems to have accepted the social expectation that women are to be responsive to the needs of others as a moral imperative. This analysis helps us to understand the stories that constituted Sylvia's experiences and the atmosphere in which Betty grew up. Nevertheless, it does not tell us much about Betty or the relationship between mother and daughter. To better understand Sylvia, Betty, and others in the family, we turn to the next analysis.

Analyzing Voices

The analysis of voices calls for attention to voicing, positioning, and ventriloquation (Wortham, 2001). *Voicing* is accomplished when a narrator constructs characters who resemble, sound like, and behave like recognizable social types. The narrator's word choice, tone of voice, and a variety of rhetorical devices index (point to) presupposed, culturally shared knowledge of these types (Wortham, 2001). When voicing others, the narrator situates or positions various voices (or character types) in relation to each other. Furthermore, the narrator positions herself in relation to these voices; that is, she indicates the type of person she is. The Russian literary theorist, Bakhtin (1984), called the narrator's speaking through others *double voicing* and the adoption of a social position for herself or himself in relation to the voices that have been created *ventriloquation*. Bakhtin's (1981) writings also sensitize one to the multiple potential meanings in language which evoke ideology, social phenomena, and historical processes. During her interview, Sylvia referred to and described many individuals whose lives intersected hers. Among these are her grandparents, each of her parents, her stepbrothers, her husband, her mother-in-law, each of her children, her son-in-law, her grandchildren, and Betty's husband's parents. Here I will focus on the ways in which Sylvia voiced Betty, the daughter who later became Orthodox, and Betty's husband, "Eli," who is integral to Betty's current life. This is how Sylvia described Betty as a child:

> Betty was the cutest, <u>adorable</u> little girl [I: Uh huh, uh huh] <u>perfect</u> little girl. [I: Uh huh] She was sweet, and pretty, and smart, she was <u>everything</u>. [I: Uh huh] But [voice gets lower] she didn't turn out to be a happy kid [I: Hmmm] and I tried [crying]. You see Janet, the youngest, was very open, and cute, she was the baby [I: Uh huh] and our oldest son, who used to love to play with Betty, but over the years kind of went towards the little one [I: Oh] and he used to take her out on sleds. Well, Betty was afraid to go on a sled. She didn't want to go on a sled, and uh, he used to fool around with Janet and, somehow or other, Betty <u>just didn't fit in</u>. [I: Oh.] And, I used to, you know, talking about it more, but it just didn't seem to work out. [I: Hmm, huh] Even though I observed it, and Bill and I used to try and work it out, you know [I: Uh huh] Betty wasn't what Lennie wanted in a sister [I: Oh.] but Janet was.

In this passage, Sylvia voices Betty as a model child who had "everything" positive going for her but had difficulty fitting into the family. The expression "just didn't fit in" has echoes of the word "misfit" and, along with allusions to Betty's being fearful, not joining her siblings, and not turning out to be happy, suggests that Betty had psychological and social difficulties. The excerpt also reminds us of Sylvia's depiction of her father as "not happy" during his marriage and her aunts' and mother's personality difficulties. Sylvia voices herself and her husband as concerned parents who tried to work things out within the family. Sylvia reflects on why Betty was unhappy:

> but, you know, part of it, I'm sure, was the, was the environment, but also with Betty, partly being maybe [voice shaking] the middle child, or maybe being the kind of person she was, maybe it wasn't anything. I don't know, because she had <u>every advantage</u> [voice shaking] that they all had. You know, she had <u>good health</u> [half laughing] [I: Right] she was <u>beautiful</u>, like a fairy princess, beautiful [I: Hah] but she's never had, as far as I'm concerned, [slowly] <u>inner peace</u>.

Sylvia's words show her drawing from her cultural knowledge of the debate between nature and nurture for understanding of Betty's unhappiness. The environmental issue (nurture) appears to be the turmoil that Sylvia's mother and mother-in-law produced within the family. An alternative explanation (nature) lies in Betty's personality make-up. Another hypothesis is that Betty's situation as a middle child put her at risk of developing a *middle child complex*, the perception of being insignificant because one is neither the privileged older child nor the beloved baby. Interestingly, Sylvia referred to Betty seven times in the transcript as her "middle child" and spoke at length about trying unsuccessfully to compensate for Betty's middle position. Here we are reminded of Sylvia's position in the middle of two good parents. In discussing Betty's adolescence, Sylvia said that, in contrast with her siblings, Betty did not have many friends and "it just went on kinda that way." When Sylvia suggested during one of Betty's visits home from college that she get counseling, Betty refused, but after she dropped out of graduate school after a few weeks, Betty took her mother's suggestion and, Sylvia said, "I think it helped her." Nevertheless, Sylvia describes Betty the young adult as vulnerable, lacking confidence, and not knowing how to handle men. Thus, when Betty started to become religious, her parents thought, "If that makes her feel good, we're glad." Betty's involvement in Orthodox Judaism came about through contacts she made with people from a Jewish religious outreach organization she came in contact with through her job on a college campus in the early 1970s. During this period, young people were feeling the effects of the earlier civil rights, counterculture, and various social and political movements. Like other ethnic groups, a sector of Jewish youth began to reclaim its ethnic identity, even if this meant returning to tradition (Danzger, 1989). Betty's parents, who were unaffiliated with a synagogue but defined themselves as culturally Jewish, were accepting of Betty's growing interest in Judaism. When Betty became kosher, Sylvia bought special foods for occasions when Betty came over for dinner. Sylvia said:

> I was very willing, you know, to do all those, I was anxious for her to come. [I: Uh huh] And we'd, she'd come, and we'd pick her up and take her back, and all, but she would think nothing of going out to the East Side and calling us up and asking us to come out and get her. [I: Uh huh] Well, you know, we were taking care of three sick, parents, and I was working [I: Uh huh] and uh, that was, <u>not easy</u> for us. [I: Uh huh] And, she got <u>very</u>, kind of <u>expected</u> us to do a lot for her physically.

Here Sylvia voices herself and her husband as accommodating and caring parents, and Betty, who was in her 20s at the time, as a dependent, demanding, and insensitive child. After bemoaning the fact that her daughter's religious journey resulted in Betty's living far away, Sylvia mentions that when she had surgery 2 years previously, Betty did not visit. She attributed Betty's absence to personal circumstances, but clearly Sylvia was disappointed:

> first of all, she's got three little kids, the one is big now, [I: Huh] and uh, where would she stay, you know I uh? And who would take care of the children? [I: Uh huh] It's, it's just a very we'd have to finance everything for her [I: Uh huh] so uh, it makes, it <u>hurts me</u>.

Here Sylvia voices Betty, a 47-year-old mother, as still dependent on her parents and incapable of making the arrangements that would allow her to be there for Sylvia during her hour of need. Sylvia is critical of Eli, the American, college-educated man whom Betty married about 20 years previously. According to Sylvia, Eli is a "dreamer." He has flitted from job to job, for the most part, not working. They live in a run-down trailer and

> he <u>doesn't paint</u> the place. He once said to me, when they had an apartment in Jerusalem which we had given them <u>money to buy</u> and we were <u>glad</u> they bought it [I: Uh huh] and then they went and <u>sold it</u> and made <u>practically nothing</u> on it and moved to (???). He has <u>no sense</u> of business at all [I: Uh huh] and yet <u>he's</u> in charge of a family. [I: Hmm] So, she does, anything he says goes. I don't <u>understand it</u>, but that's what the rabbi must have said, I don't know.

In this passage Sylvia voices her husband and herself as giving and helpful parents. She voices Eli as an impractical and irresponsible man and Betty as a woman who submits to the dictates of unreasonable men on the basis of their gender role and religious authority. While evaluating Eli and Betty thus and stating that she does not understand their behavior, Sylvia ventriloquates herself as a person who thinks for herself and is independent. Sylvia contrasts her son-in-law, Eli, with Bill, her 81-year-old husband. Speaking of Bill's highly regarded work as a volunteer for a service for older adults, Sylvia states that Bill "doesn't understand people who sit around and expect others to do things." The term *people who sit around* evokes the image of a *ne'er do well*, which is consistent with the way Sylvia has been voicing Eli. Elsewhere, Sylvia suggests that he is either too lazy or fearful to follow up on a job lead ("I can't go there, I can't ride, I can't do that"). Sylvia also voices Eli as deceitful. Eli made it known that he would like Betty's parents to help him purchase a bus he would use to start a business. When Sylvia and Bill visited them in Israel, they discovered that Eli's plans were vague and there were no signs of a bus. After Bill questioned Eli about his plans, Eli and Betty became insulted and walked away. For 3 months after that encounter, there was no communication between Betty and her parents. This was so painful to Sylvia that "after that time, I have—we have never criticized them because it was worse [voice shaking] for me to lose contact." Sylvia's coping by means of conflict avoidance offers a means for her to preserve a semblance of family solidarity (Schiffrin, 1996). Nevertheless, Sylvia is distressed over her daughter's working hard taking care of her three children and selling religious articles while Eli is not working. She said:

> I mean, why can't he be, go and work in a store? Why can't he? I don't understand it, because <u>I</u> had a <u>hard-working father</u>, <u>Bill</u> had a <u>hard-working father</u>, and <u>Bill</u> was a <u>hard worker</u>. <u>Daniel</u> [Janet's husband] was a <u>hard worker</u>. <u>My son's</u> a <u>hard worker</u>. What is this man? [laughing? crying?]

Considering that Sylvia only lists men here and asks, "What is this man?," she is double voicing Eli as deviant and something less than a man. In differentiating Eli from the other men in the family, she is positioning Eli outside the family and its gender norms (Schiffrin, 1996). In evaluating Eli in this way, she ventriloquates herself as a person who believes that men should work hard. Sylvia also positions Betty at a distance from the family. The case in point is Sylvia's report that Betty has cut herself off from her brother and his family. Even though Betty attended Lennie's wedding and sent gifts following the birth of her brother's children, currently

> she acts like she has no brother because he married a Gentile. And he has two kids that are the most <u>loving</u> children [crying], and they don't understand [voice shaking] why their aunt doesn't want to meet them.

Following this statement, Sylvia attributed Betty's behavior to the rabbis with whom she consults, who object to Jews marrying outside their religion and would not consider children from this marriage Jewish. But as far as Sylvia and others in the family are concerned, "we're *all* broken, *all broken up* [voice shaking]." Sylvia's distress over Betty's cut-off relationship with her brother and his family can be understood by revisiting the abstract of Episode 3, where Sylvia says that she wanted to have a family. When she describes the nonrelationship between Betty and Lennie's children, Sylvia indexes her confusion and despair over having loving grandchildren but not a loving family, which parallels the situations in her parents' and grandparents' homes. The word *broken* evokes an image of a divorced family in which relationships are fractured and reminds us that Sylvia's parents were estranged. Being "broken up" suggests emotional pain. In summary, Sylvia has been telling us who she is in the ways she has positioned herself in relation to those she has voiced. Table 2.1 describes the ways in which Sylvia voiced herself in the process of voicing Betty. It shows the discrepancies in the values of the mother and daughter, which may contribute to the emotional distance between them.

The analysis of voices in tandem with the structural analysis shows parallels between Sylvia's family of origin and her family of procreation (Table 2.2). Even though she wanted to and did have a family, the family she created replicated some of the conflict she experienced in her family of origin (Bowen, 1978). After her parents separated, Sylvia felt caught between two good parents, but subsequently was caught between her mother and mother-in-law and her children, among her three children, and among commitments to her children, parents, and work. Her sensitivity to Betty's position as a middle child seems to be a manifestation of her own conflict. Sylvia continues to be

Table 2.1 Sylvia's Voicing of Betty and Herself

Betty	Sylvia
Has a husband who does not work.	Expects men to work and to work hard.
Defers to authority of rabbis and impractical husband.	Thinks for herself; is practical and independent.
Not sensitive to parents' needs.	Cared for her parents.
Rejects family members who are not Jewish.	Accepts religious differences within the family.

Table 2.2 Parallels Between Sylvia's Families of Origin
and Procreation

Sylvia's Family of Origin	Sylvia's Family of Procreation
Loving grandparents but children are in conflict with each other.	Loving family but estrangement between daughter and son and son's children.
Caught between two good parents (after they separated).	Caught between in-laws and children; mother and children; among three children.
Parents were not happy (with each other).	
	Betty was not happy (within herself).
Upset over parents' conflicts (after they separated).	Upset over children's conflicts.

disturbed about the alienation between Betty and Lennie's family. Sylvia's story
and voicing show her disappointment in not having been able to have a
loving, conflict-free family.

The Interaction Between the Interviewer
and the Interviewee

The research interview, like other interviews, is negotiated by participants
whose interactional positions are different. I approached Sylvia as a researcher
trying to learn about the family context of the daughter's turn to Orthodoxy
and how she viewed, was affected by, and coped with this phenomenon; Sylvia
was a volunteer whom I had recruited through a parents' organization. I came
with a set of questions I wanted her to answer; she came with knowledge about
her life and questions about its meaning. During the course of the interview we
assumed a variety of interactional positions and enacted a number of roles. The
example presented earlier of the initial interaction in the interview (see page
52) shows how the role of Sylvia's husband in the interview process was negotiated. Sylvia seemed to want clarity about the participation of her husband, who
was present when I arrived. Her inquiry indicates that she perceived me as the
rule maker and she wanted to comply. I hesitated initially (this was one of my
first interviews for this project), stated that I would be focusing more on her
story than his, and concluded that I *did* want to hear about his side of the family
at some point. Bill then left the room, but he returned when Sylvia asked him
to help her describe his family. Subsequently, he went out to take care of some
errands. Early in the interview, I asked Sylvia to describe her maternal grandparents and her father's side of the family. Because she did not present much religious content in her depiction of her family, I inquired about their religiosity.
Then I asked her about the family in which she was raised. Her response was
the first occasion in which Sylvia cried during the interview. The following is
the full transcription of an excerpt that was abridged in Episode 1:

> **I:** Um, okay, how about the family in which you were raised?
>
> **Sylvia:** My mother and father and I was their only child [I: Uh huh] and
> uh, they both were <u>wonderful</u> parents, very <u>adoring</u>, but taking me
> everywhere [LP] This is the problem, I'm getting emotional [crying].

I: Oh, oh.

Sylvia: And it was hard for them [voice shaking]. 'Cause they were very good people, and everything was for me. They were not happy [LP].

Here we see Sylvia crying while recalling how good her parents were to her. She indexes her feelings by saying in line 110, "This is the problem, I'm getting emotional." This statement, followed by crying, suggests that she thought that she needed to account for her feelings to the interviewer. She continues with her narrative, but her voice shakes when she talks about her parents' having a hard time with each other while devoting themselves to her. In crying relatively early in the interview she seemed to be interactionally positioning herself as a client and the interviewer as a therapist (cf. Wortham, 2001). There were seven moments during this interview when Sylvia cried and at least ten when her voice shook or trembled. In all instances Sylvia was talking about pain that she had experienced in relation to family members. She told me how upset she was that Betty does not communicate with Lennie and his children three times and cried on each occasion. In addition, she made numerous references to times being "difficult," "hard," "bad," and "tough," and used the word *upset* five times. It appeared that by crying during the interview she was enacting her pain and helplessness, thus creating a parallelism between the self constructed in the narrative ("the narrated self") and the self that does the telling ("the narrating self") (Wortham, 2001). The most illuminating parallelism became apparent toward the end of the interview when I commented on how well she had coped with this situation. In the following exchange Sylvia resists the compliment while indexing her tears.

I: Well, I think you've coped with these situations very well.

Sylvia: Well, I don't know if I have or I haven't [laughing],

I: No, I think you

Sylvia: because <u>why can't I</u> talk about this without tears? [crying] I <u>knew</u> this was gonna happen. You know, you said, you wanted to interview me [laughing?], because <u>I don't</u> understand it. [I: Yah, yah] I don't know <u>why</u> things turned out the way they did.

Based on this segment, it appears that Sylvia accepted my invitation to be interviewed even though she anticipated that she would cry. Sylvia's consent despite her reservations is an enactment of her statement in Episode 3, line 572, that she accepted her mother's request to move in because Sylvia "didn't know how to say no." Her agreement to the interview is also in keeping with the social expectation that women be acquiescent. The transcript of this interview reveals how the two of us co-constructed the narrative. During the first half or so of the interview, I asked open-ended questions that invited lengthy responses. Within this space, Sylvia told stories. I frequently used back channel communications (e.g., hmm, uh huh), which allowed me to actively demonstrate involvement without interrupting her story (Tannen, 1989). Occasionally, we engaged in cooperative speech (Grice, 1975), where we would complete each other's sentences. Sylvia initiated discussions of episodes within her family life history without my prompting. At one point she asked, "Have I talked too much?" (I said no). As the interview moved along, I became more actively engaged in the construction of its meaning. For example, after hearing Sylvia's story, I asked how she explained her daughter's restricting her world to other religious people when the home in which Betty grew up was so open, to which she replied:

> **Sylvia:** I can't explain it. [I: Yes (both laughing)] I can't explain it, because the other two are still very open. [I: Uh huh.][noise] My son was really, harder on Betty while she was growing up, 'cause she wasn't able to enter the same activities as the little one. [I: Uh huh uhha] And I <u>know</u> that this was hard for her, and I <u>tried</u>, you know, my best. [I: Uh huh.] I had <u>so many things</u> going on in my life. [I:Yeah] [with in-laws]
>
> **I:** You were <u>really overburdened</u>
>
> **Sylvia:** I <u>was</u> overburdened, I was.
>
> **I:** with so many <u>responsibilities</u> for other people.
>
> **Sylvia:** I certainly was. That's what daughters did, you know!
>
> **I:** Yeah, right, right! [both laughing]
>
> **Sylvia:** I mean, it never occurred to me not to do it. That's what we did.

In this interaction, I introduced the idea that Sylvia was "overburdened," an interpretation that Sylvia readily accepted and acknowledged. Sylvia also agreed with my comment that she had "so many responsibilities for other people," which was an expansion of her statement on line 1267 about having "so many things going on." When Sylvia said, "That's what daughters did, you know!" she introduced a gender lens through which to interpret her caregiving. In this instance, she seemed to be positioning herself as an older woman who is telling the younger interviewer how things used to be, allowing Sylvia to move from the position of client that she assumed when crying to the more empowered position of knowledgeable older woman (cf. Wortham, 2001). The latter interpretation is supported elsewhere in the interview, where she explains that in the past families that did not have financial resources provided personal care.

DISCUSSION

The three levels of analysis have given us an idea about how Sylvia lived, how she viewed herself as a woman, and how she constructed her daughter. The structural analysis revealed that she grew up in a family in which love was intermingled with conflict and her goal was to have a harmonious family life. While pursuing this goal, she experienced struggles and reversals. Sylvia voiced herself within the preamble and four episodes as a dutiful daughter and daughter-in-law, a caring parent, and a responsible, independent adult, but she also spoke of feeling obligated to care for others and burdened by their demands. As shown in the analysis of her interaction with the interviewer, she complies with others' wishes despite her reservations, suggesting that she silences her own voice. Sylvia seems to have overtly acquiesced to traditional gender norms, but underneath was experiencing stress, anguish, and role conflict.

Sylvia voiced her daughter, Betty, as unhappy as a child and deferential to her husband and rabbis as an adult. Because Betty was not interviewed, we have a limited perspective on Betty's persona. From what Sylvia said, however, there appear to be commonalities between the mother and daughter. Both conformed to the expectation that women center their lives around their families. Both had three children and worked. Both appear to be acquiescent. Betty, however, adopted a religious ideology and lives in a community that supports traditional gender norms and confers with rabbis who sanction these norms. In contrast with her mother, who tried to be all things to all people despite the stress this engendered, Betty has reclaimed the traditional role of women (Kaufman, 1991) without, so it seems, conflict over competing wants and needs.

Except for the emotional distance between the mother and daughter and indications that Betty may have had emotional problems, this "negative case" example turned out to have much in common with the others in the study. Those mothers whose sons-in-law did not have steady or adequate employment were critical of their Israeli families for being insufficiently independent. A few of the families of origin were financially supporting their children in Israel; most, like Sylvia and Bill, provided help occasionally. Within the sample, most of the mothers and daughters assumed traditional gender roles, but mothers who were considerably younger than Sylvia and more influenced by feminist ideas were disappointed that their daughters were not more career minded than they turned out to be. Like those mothers in the sample who had other children who had married non-Jewish partners, Sylvia accepted interreligious marriage in her family and was distressed that this created a problem between her daughter and another child. Although the relationship between Sylvia and Betty was more fragile than that of other mothers and daughters, many mother–daughter relationships appeared to be complex.

B. Personal Reflections:
Revisiting and Reliving
an Interview

BACKGROUND

I came to qualitative research out of an interest in sociolinguistics, the study of language in use. My dissertation research used a mixture of methods to investigate the language styles of factory workers. Acquaintance with researchers at The Ohio State University who used sociolinguistic, ethnographic, and narrative methods of qualitative research, as well as membership in a postmodern feminist reading group at the same university, enhanced my interest in qualitative research. My articles about the relevance of sociolinguistics (Sands, 1988) and postmodern feminism (Sands, 1996; Sands & Nuccio, 1992) to social work evolved from these experiences. I used a combination of ethnographic and sociolinguistic methods in my research on interprofessional team interactions (McClelland & Sands, 2002; Sands, 1990, 1993) and, since moving to the University of Pennsylvania in 1990, have used a variety of other qualitative methods in my research.

The study of women who became Orthodox and their mothers derived from my personal life experience. I am the mother of a daughter who became Orthodox in her late teenage years, moved to Israel after graduating from college, and has been living there ever since, now married and a mother. When I first became aware of her religious change, I was alarmed because I found Orthodox Judaism sexist and repressive. I was concerned that she would be bound by religious laws and customs that would require that she become submissive and defer to male-dominated religious authorities that would impede her ability to fulfill herself intellectually. During the past 10 years, I have modified some of my initial impressions and have grown to accept the situation. Engagement in this study has increased my own understanding and appreciation of my daughter's religious orientation.

GETTING STARTED

In anticipation of spending my sabbatical in Israel, I began to collaborate with a colleague, Dorit Roer-Strier, who is on the faculty at the Hebrew University of Jerusalem. I told her of my interest in the impact of a child's becoming Orthodox on family relations; she told me of her interest in cross-cultural differences in the socialization of children and the processes of coping with change. We began to design the study long distance, during which time she formed a research team of students interested in our topic who explored the topic in the literature and conducted pilot interviews. I communicated with the team via e-mail and received minutes of the team's meetings. During my sabbatical in the winter and spring of 1997, an expanded research team continued to work on this study. The team consisted of women from Israel, Holland, South Africa, Italy, and the United States (some binational) who were diverse in their orientation to Judaism. Some women were raised in religious homes and remained Orthodox, some had become Orthodox, and others were less traditional or defined themselves as secular. The age span was from mid-20s to the 50s; some were mothers. The team fleshed out the parameters of the design, refined the interview questions, identified participants, and implemented some interviews and a focus group.

Most valuable to me was hearing the attitudes and feelings of team members who were or had become Orthodox. Listening to the opinions of and collaborating with women who could explain the thinking behind customs and behavior that at the time appeared illogical and excessive to me provided me with a balanced perspective that, I believe, reduced my bias and thus enhanced the trustworthiness of this research (Lincoln & Guba, 1985). The team served functions that are similar to those provided by peer debriefing and support groups (Padgett, 1998)—the generation of ideas, giving and receiving of support and feedback, and protection against bias.

INTERVIEWING AMERICAN MOTHERS

After I returned from my sabbatical, I began the process of recruiting American mothers and tracking down mothers of daughters who had been interviewed in Israel. I made some personal contacts through an organization called Parents of North American Israelis (PNAI) and had a "call" for participants published in the organization's newsletter. This resulted in my receiving inquiries from potential participants and a list of names of individuals whom I could contact. I conducted screening interviews by telephone during which I described the study and determined whether the individual met the study's criteria for participation (daughter must be age 30 or older, married, have at least one child, identify with an Ultra-Orthodox religious group, and live in Israel; mother must have raised her non-Orthodox). Recruitment through PNAI as well as the inclusion of mothers whose daughters had been interviewed in Israel resulted in a national sample that was diverse with respect to social class, the daughters' stream of Orthodox Judaism, and the families' religious affiliations while the daughters were growing up (Reform, Conservative, unaffiliated).

Sylvia was one of the first mothers whom I interviewed for this study. I recall being impressed with her intelligence and emotionally moved and saddened by her story. I admired her strength in raising a family, caring for parents, returning to the university, and working, and felt that she was a woman ahead of her time. I identified with her openness to the secular world and her desire to understand her daughter. Because I am more career centered than she, I had issues about my daughter's not fulfilling herself that were different from Sylvia's. I shared with her that I, too, was the mother of a religious daughter who had immigrated to Israel and, after our interview was over, answered her questions about my daughter and me. I felt that being a mother of a daughter who became Orthodox sensitized me to Sylvia's situation and contributed to our rapport. Apart from the questions on my interview guide, I instinctively knew what to ask and directions in which to probe, and Sylvia seemed to respond with openness. On the other hand, I did not explore deeply or question some issues, such as her portrayal of her daughter as a "perfect" child and Sylvia's ambivalence about helping her daughter and son-in-law, which are close to my own experiences.

When interviewing someone whose situation is close to one's own, one needs to be aware of personal reactions and determine whether they fit the research situation or are extraneous. Even though a participant faces a similar situation, she may not perceive or manage it the same way the interviewer does. I handled my personal reactions through introspection and writing interview summaries that included my personal reactions. The team members who identified, screened, and interviewed the religious daughters in Israel were also "insiders." Having interviewers who were raised or had become Orthodox gave us access to a population that is ordinarily closed to and suspicious of outsiders. In reviewing the transcripts of interviews conducted by these interviewers, it appeared that the participants were open and honest. One interviewer added questions to the interviews (e.g., "How have you changed over time in getting close to God?"), which probably were her own concerns but nevertheless enriched the data.

With respect to the interview with Sylvia, I expected her to focus more on religion than she did, but she made it clear to me early in the interview that religion was not the central axis around which this family rotated. In the following excerpt, which followed Sylvia's description of her grandparents (see Prologue), I inquired about her grandparents' religiosity:

> **I:** How were they in regard to religion?
>
> **Sylvia:** I never heard much about religion with them, I never
>
> **I:** You said you went to them on holidays.
>
> **Sylvia:** I used to <u>stay</u> with them. Well, we went for dinners, we went for—I was so little, I don't remember. But I know I used to go there if my parents were still away for a weekend I would stay with them. I was their <u>only grandchild</u> and so they really <u>loved me</u> and I <u>loved them</u>, But as far as <u>religion</u> is concerned I really don't know too much about it and I don't think, if they went to synagogue I never knew it.

Sylvia seemed to be telling me here (and elsewhere) that the critical factor in her family was love, not religion. When I realized that her construction did not match my expectations, I abandoned my set of questions and went with the flow. When Sylvia asked, "Have I talked too much?" I was already moving with her rather than against her. As I have evolved with this study, I have become increasingly flexible in my use of my interview guide. I continue to ask for a multigenerational family history focusing on religion, but allow the participant to lead. In the course of hearing Sylvia's story, I became cognizant of the pain that has been part of her life. I did not anticipate Sylvia's tears, but when they came I tried to respond empathetically. As noted, when she first cried she seemed to be positioning herself as a client and me as therapist. Toward the end of the interview, when I told her that she coped well, I positioned myself as and enacted the role of a supportive therapist. Although she was not sure how well she coped, she did accept my interpretation that she was "overburdened." It seemed to me that Sylvia felt validated in my recognition of the multiple demands on her life and her management of these demands. Furthermore, Sylvia appeared to have gained insight in the course of constructing her story.

INTERPRETIVE ISSUES

As I reflect on the analysis presented in Sylvia's Family Story, I acknowledge my own role in selecting lines and constructing episodes. My constructions emerged from repeated listening to the tape and reading the transcript and my recollections from being there and reviewing a summary statement I wrote following this interview. I attempted to make my analysis transparent by presenting examples from the transcript; space prohibits printing the transcript in its entirety. Nevertheless, it is possible that my decisions about what to include and exclude were influenced by my own subjectivity. I may have been overly sensitive to Sylvia's pain because of my own. On the other hand, I included her caregiving experiences even though my own such experiences were limited. I accept responsibility for the choices I made and recognize that another researcher may have made different selections. In support of my interpretation of Sylvia's narrative, I presented many examples of parallels that I found across episodes, between the narrating self and the narrated self (Wortham, 2001), and between Sylvia's characterizations of her family of origin and her family of procreation. I noted what I saw as repeated instances of the same kind of event occurring over and over in Sylvia's life and her recurrent use of the same word (e.g., loving parents, personality problems, and so on). These instances of intratextual parallels or consistencies contribute to the coherence of the narrative (Rissman, 1993) and the credibility of my interpretations (Lincoln & Guba, 1985).

To further corroborate the validity of my interpretations, I sent Sylvia a previous draft of this chapter and the transcript and subsequently met with her. During our "member checking" session, she identified some factual errors in the transcription and draft that I have since corrected and asked me to change some additional items to further protect the family's confidentiality. She told me that the story told in the chapter was "true," but I should not get the idea that everything was negative. She said that she has had a wonderful marriage and that, for the most part, relationships within the nuclear unit were good while the children were growing up. The difficulties with her mother and mother-in-law had to do with their strong personalities. On the other hand, they helped her—especially her mother, who encouraged her to complete college and credits toward a teaching certificate, enabling her to do so by caring for the children. During this meeting, I asked Sylvia to clarify what she meant by certain phrases she used during the interview. She said that she felt "caught between two good parents" after they separated to mean that she was not aware of their conflicts while she was growing up. She said that her mother would complain about Sylvia's father, which was upsetting to Sylvia because she loved and felt committed to both parents. Her father did not complain about her mother. I also asked Sylvia what she meant when she said "I wanted to make a family." I made this request because my repeated reading of the transcript and listening to the tape led me to believe that she had wanted to emphasize this point but she went off in another direction and I subsequently cut her off. Here is the selection we discussed:

> **Sylvia:** But I always had the intention, every Mother's Day, I had those mothers there, and I never knew what the hell was going to happen. [I: Uh huh] And, the kids would become involved because my mother, they didn't like what my mother said or, It was <u>very</u> unpleasant! And <u>I took it very hard</u> [softer] but, uh, we were still a family [voice shaking] [I: Uh huh] and I <u>never had had</u> [louder, voice shaking] you know
>
> **I:** You increased the number of people.
>
> **Sylvia:** [Louder] <u>I wanted to make a family</u>, you know. Inside I was being torn up.

Sylvia told me that she did want to have family around her, but there was so much tension in the family, "I never really had the family I really wanted." When asked to explain this further, she said, "I never really had a peaceful family." She was always worried about her mother or mother-in-law, who would tell her what she should do and how she should raise her children. Sylvia would have liked to have had a family in which people could talk to each other without arguing. This discussion with Sylvia was consistent with my interpretation that Sylvia both desired yet suffered over her desire to have a conflict-free family.

The transcript excerpt cited was one of a number of instances in the interview where I became acutely aware of errors I made in conducting the interview. In trying to show appreciation for Sylvia's growing up in a household of three persons here, I interrupted her train of thought. I identified other moments in the interview where I might have probed more deeply. The analysis of the interaction between the interviewer and interviewee was particularly challenging because I was both the interviewer and researcher. To conduct this analysis, I had to treat the text as if I were not a part of it. My interpretation is limited by my not having interviewed Betty. Had this occurred, I would have been able to compare the stories, voices, and interactional positioning of both mother and daughter and would have been able to see for myself whether Betty had some sort of personality problem. I would have been able to inquire into her perception of growing up in a family in which Judaism was viewed as a culture rather than a religion. I wonder how Betty felt about her maternal grandmother's presence in her parental home, and how she saw her relationships with her siblings in the past, and how she sees them now. I would want to know how she perceived her mother's simultaneous parenting, caregiving, and working. In addition, I would like to hear about her religious journey, her relationship with her husband, and her expectations of her husband, her children, and herself. Nevertheless, I do have an e-mail birthday message that Betty sent her mother last year that offers some glimpse into Betty's perception of her mother. It also confirms my interpretation of Sylvia. The following are excerpts:

Dear Mother,

It is your birthday

You have given me so much. . . .

You gave up your own pleasures

So I could have pleasure. . . .

In our house our father had the final word.

The mutual respect was tangible.

It was a perfect model

On how to conduct my own marriage. . .

Each child was a precious gem to you.

Each one you loved equally. . . .

You taught me the value of good relationships

With in-laws, your own mother, with friends.

You were always the one to forgive and make peace.

You were the beloved daughter, daughter-in-law, and friend. . . .

In short, you took me

And made me into a decent human being.

For your birthday, I am giving you an appreciation

It is truly a blessing to be your daughter.

The member checking interview also afforded me the opportunity to learn about the family's current situation. Sylvia and Bill did make the trip to Israel that they had planned but have not been back since. Nevertheless, Sylvia and Betty are now communicating regularly via e-mail. Sylvia was pleased to report that Betty and her family have moved to a large metropolitan area, where they have a nice apartment. Betty is currently holding two jobs. Eli borrowed money from Sylvia and Bill so that he could take a computer course. Reportedly he is now selling religious items over the Internet, but Sylvia does not know how successful he is at this. Today Sylvia is distressed over her daughter's and grandchildren's living far away in Israel and is worried about their safety. Because of her own and her husband's current health status, she doubts that they will be able to visit again.

CONCLUSIONS

Rehearing and reviewing an interview $3\frac{1}{2}$ years after it was completed afforded me distance from the interview situation and the benefit of having completed data collection for the study of American mothers and their daughters in Israel. Now that I have completed writing this chapter, I appreciate having had the opportunity to revisit the interview, perform this analysis, and be reflexive. I believe that this was a good interview insofar as it produced data that illuminated my research problem. I was able to obtain an in-depth understanding of a negative case and determine the extent to which it diverged from the others. From a personal perspective, participation in this interview and its analysis was humanly satisfying. In reliving this interview, I have lived more. Data analysis for this case and the others is never complete. With each reading one gains new insights.

Currently we are completing papers on the study of American mothers and their daughters in Israel and are collecting data for two studies of mothers and daughters where both live in the United States or Israel. One of our team members is conducting similar research in Holland. When the various components of this study are completed, we plan to consolidate them in a book that takes a cross-cultural perspective on families coping with religious change.

ACKNOWLEDGMENTS

I gratefully acknowledge the willingness of "Sylvia" to share her narrative and discuss its meaning. I also appreciate the valuable suggestions on a previous draft by Samuel Klausner, Deborah Padgett, Cynthia Salzman, and Stanton Wortham. The project of which this is a part would not have been possible without Dorit Roer-Strier and research team members Nicole Goldstone, Gail Gundle, Minny Mock, Pessla Stern, Evey Volk, and Jenny Weisberg.

REFERENCES

Anderson, K., & Jack, D. C. (1991). Learning to listen: Interview techniques and analyses. In S. B. Gluck & D. Patai (Eds.), *Women's words: The feminist practice of oral history* (pp. 11–26). New York: Routledge.

Bakhtin, M. M. (1981). In M. Holquist (Ed.), C. Emerson & M. Holquist (Trans.). *The dialogic imagination: Four essays*, Austin: University of Texas Press. (Originally published in 1935).

Bakhtin, M. M. (1984). *Problems of Dostoevsky's poetics* (C. Emerson, Trans.). Minneapolis: University of Minnesota Press. (Originally published in 1963).

Bell, S. E. (1988). Becoming a political woman: The reconstruction and interpretation of experience through stories. In A. D. Todd & S. Fisher (Eds.), *Gender and discourse: The power of talk* (pp. 97–123). Norwood, NJ: Ablex.

Bell, S. E. (1999). Narratives and lives: Women's health politics and the diagnosis of cancer for DES daughters. *Narrative Inquiry, 9,* 347–89.

Bloom, L. R. (1998). *Under the sign of hope: Feminist methodology and narrative interpretation.* Albany: State University of New York Press.

Bowen, M. (1978). *Family therapy in clinical practice.* New York: Jason Aronson.

Brown, L. M., & Gilligan, C. (1992). *Meeting at the crossroads: Women's psychology and girls' development.* Cambridge, MA: Harvard University Press.

Cameron, D. (2001). *Working with spoken discourse*. Thousand Oaks, CA: Sage.

Cohler, B. J. (1991). The life story and the study of resilience and response to adversity. *Journal of Narrative and Life History, 1*, 169–200.

Cortazzi, M. (1993). *Narrative analysis*. London: The Falmer Press.

Danzger, M. H. (1989). *Returning to tradition: The contemporary revival of Orthodox Judaism*. New Haven, CT: Yale University Press.

Davidman, L. (1991). *Tradition in rootless world: Women turn to Orthodox Judaism*. Berkeley: University of California Press.

DeVault, M. L. (1999). *Liberating method: Feminism and social research*. Philadelphia: Temple University Press.

Fonow, M. M., & Cook, J. A. (1991). Back to the future: A look at the second wave of feminist epistemology and methodology. In M. M. Fonow & J. A. Cook (Eds.), *Beyond methodology: Feminist scholarship as lived research* (pp. 1–15). Bloomington: Indiana University Press.

Freedman, J., & Combs, G. (1996). *Narrative therapy: The social construction of preferred realities*. New York: Norton.

Geertz, C. (1983). Blurred genres: the refiguration of social thought. In C. Geertz (Ed.), *Local knowledge: Further essays in interpretive anthropology* (pp. 19–35). New York: Basic Books.

Grice, H. P. (1975). Logic and conversation. In P. Cole & J. L. Morgan (Eds.), *Syntax and semantics*, vol. 3 (pp. 41–58). New York: Academic Press.

Gumperz, J. J. (1982). *Discourse strategies*. Cambridge, UK: Cambridge University Press.

Jack, D. C. (1991). *Silencing the self: Women and depression*. Cambridge, MA: Harvard University Press.

Kaufman, D. R. (1985). Women who return to Orthodox Judaism: A feminist analysis. *Journal of Marriage and Family, 47*, 543–51.

Kaufman, D. R. (1991). *Rachel's daughters: Newly Orthodox Jewish woman*. New Brunswick, NJ: Rutgers University Press.

Kelley, P. (1996). Narrative theory and social work treatment. In F. Turner (Ed.), *Social work treatment: Interlocking theoretical approaches* (4th ed., pp. 461–79). New York: The Free Press.

Labov, W. (1972). The transformation of experience in narrative syntax. In W. Labov (Ed.), *Language in the inner city* (pp. 354–96). Philadelphia: University of Pennsylvania Press.

Labov, W. (1982). Speech actions and reactions in personal narrative. In D. Tannen (Ed.), *Analyzing discourse: Text and talk* (pp. 219–47). Washington, DC: Georgetown University.

Labov, W., & Waletzky, J. (1967). Narrative analysis: Oral versions of personal experience. In J. Helm (Ed.), *Essays on the verbal and visual arts* (pp. 12–44). Seattle: University of Washington.

Laird, J. (1989). Women and stories: Restorying women's self-constructions. In M. McGoldrick, C. Anderson, & F. Walsh (Eds.), *Women in families* (pp. 428–49). New York: Norton.

Lincoln, Y. S., & Guba, E. G. (1985). *Naturalistic inquiry*. Beverly Hills, CA: Sage.

Linde, C. (1993). *Life stories*. New York: Oxford University Press.

McClelland, M., & Sands, R. G. (2002). *Interprofessional and family discourses: Voices, knowledge, and practice*. Cresskill, NJ: Hampton Press.

Mishler, E. G. (1986). The analysis of interview narratives. In T. R. Sarbin (Ed.), *Narrative psychology: The storied nature of human conduct* (pp. 233–55). New York: Praeger.

Mishler, E. G. (1995). Models of narrative analysis: A typology. *Journal of Narrative and Life History, 5*, 87–123.

Ochs, E. (1979). Transcription as theory. In E. Ochs & B. Schieffelin (Eds.), *Developmental pragmatics* (pp. 43–72). New York: Academic Press.

Olesen, V. L. (2000). Feminisms and qualitative research at and into the millennium. In N. K. Denzin & Y. S. Lincoln (Eds.), *Handbook of qualitative research* (2nd ed.). Thousand Oaks, CA: Sage.

Padgett, D. K. (1998). *Qualitative methods in social work research: Challenges and rewards.* Thousand Oaks, CA: Sage.

Reinharz, S. (1992). *Feminist methods in social research.* New York: Oxford University Press.

Rissman, C. K. (1992). Making sense of marital violence: One woman's narrative. In G. C. Rosenwald & R. L. Ochberg (Eds.), *Storied lives* (pp. 231–49). New Haven, CT: Yale University Press.

Rissman, C. K. (1993). *Narrative analysis.* Newbury Park, CA: Sage.

Roer-Strier, D., & Sands, R. G. (2001). The impact of religious intensification on family relations: A South African example. *Journal of Marriage and Family, 63,* 868–80.

Rosenwald, G. C., & Ochberg, R. L (1992). *Storied lives: the cultural politics of self understanding.* New Haven, CT: Yale University Press.

Sands, R. G. (1988). Sociolinguistic analysis of a mental health interview. *Social Work, 33,* 149–54.

Sands, R. G. (1990). Ethnographic research: A qualitative research approach to study of the interdisciplinary team. *Social Work in Health Care, 15,* 115–29.

Sands, R. G. (1993). "Can you overlap here?" A question for an interdisciplinary team. *Discourse Processes, 16,* 545–64.

Sands, R. G. (1996). The elusiveness of identity in social work practice with women: A postmodern feminist perspective. *Clinical Social Work Journal, 24,* 167–86.

Sands, R. G., & Nuccio, K. (1992). Postmodern feminism and social work. *Social Work, 37,* 489–94.

Sands, R. G., & Roer-Strier, D. (2001). *Divided families: The impact of geographic distance and religious difference on family relations.* Paper presented at the World Congress of Jewish Studies, Jerusalem, Israel.

Schafer, R. (1992). *Retelling a life.* New York: Basic Books.

Schiffrin, D. (1996). Narrative as self-portrait. *Language in Society, 25,* 167–203.

Smith, D. E. (1987). *The everyday world as problematic: A feminist sociology.* Boston: Northeastern University Press.

Stein, N. L., & Policastro, M. (1984). The concept of story: A comparison between children's and teachers' viewpoints. In H. Mandl, N. Stein, & T. Trabasso (Eds.), *Learning and comprehension of text* (pp. 113–55). Mahwah, NJ: Lawrence Erlbaum.

Tannen, D. (1989). *Talking voices: Repetition, dialogue, and imagery in conversational discourse.* Cambridge, UK: Cambridge University Press.

White, M., & Epston, D. (1990). *Narrative means to therapeutic ends.* New York: Norton.

Wortham, S. (2001). *Narratives in action: A strategy for research and analysis.* New York: Teachers College Press.

TRANSCRIPTION SYMBOLS

<u>Underlined word or part of word</u>	Emphasis
=	The words spoken by two speakers are continuous, i.e., latched
[LP]	Long pause
,	Short pause
.	Full pause

?	Upward inflection of the voice
italicized words	The words that are italicized were spoken with the feelings in brackets, e.g. [crying]
(???)	Uncertain about the word; it was difficult to hear this in the tape
[words]	Words spoken simultaneously by two speakers

Note: Where the interviewer did not take a full turn (e.g., where she said, "Uh huh"), I enclosed her words in brackets immediately following the participant's statement such as [I: Uh huh].

SYLVIA'S FAMILY STORY

Preamble: Loving Grandparents But Not a Loving Family

Abstract: Well, my memory is of <u>very loving</u> grandparents.

Orientation: My grandfather, was a <u>very fashionable</u> tailor and, uh, my grandmother was a homemaker and they had four daughters and a son. And uh I was <u>there a lot</u>, I was their <u>only grandchild</u> and so they really <u>loved me</u> and I <u>loved them</u>, and <u>my mother</u> came here at 9 months and she was the oldest. They had <u>lost two children</u> in Russia in pogroms, and then <u>the others</u> were born here.

Complications: But they were loving, as was the whole family, but the <u>family</u> was not a loving <u>family</u> The girls, the relationship between the sisters was not good. There was one sister, the youngest, they all, <u>adored</u>, but the rest of them, whenever they got together they used to fight. I never saw a <u>really good</u>, family relationship with my mother's family. They all went to college, every one of them, and, uh, <u>for that time</u> that was very good, but <u>personality-wise</u> it wasn't. One of my aunts once told me that the relationship between my grandparents wasn't so good, that my grandmother was more of a home woman and my grandfather evidently was more modern, although she dressed beautifully and all that.

Coda: My memory of it is so, slight and totally what people told me.

Episode 1: Caught Between Two Good Parents

Abstract: . . . I was their only child and uh they both were <u>wonderful</u> parents, very <u>adoring</u>. And it was hard for them [voice shaking] 'cause they were very good people, and everything was for me. They were not happy.

Orientation: He, he was quite-a-bit <u>older</u> than my mother, and he had been <u>married</u> <u>previously</u> and his first wife died and left three grown children. We lived in two apartments in the city, in-next door to each other. My father had a business downstairs on the first floor in purses and they all worked in the store.

Complications: And it was <u>very successful</u>, he was, but when the Depression came things got <u>really bad</u>. I know there was a lot of tension between my mother who was not too different in age from them. My father was hit very hard, he lost <u>all his business</u> and <u>a lot of money</u>. And my mother, was not a very, solid person. She could easily could argue, and she felt like uh that my dad hadn't pro<u>vid</u>ed for us, and she had a degree and she went back to work.

Resolution: After I got married, they separated. [crying] *"Never happy,"* Dad said, *"all these years"* because I-I felt so badly for them. It was <u>very hard</u> on me *caught between the two of them* [crying].

Coda: You have *two good parents* [crying] What do you do?

Episode 2: Living With My In-Laws

Abstract: And we lived with Bill's parents.

Orientation: Bill and I met during college and were married after I completed 3 years. We lived out of town so Bill could work in the war industry.

Complications: After the war, we, Bill went into business, and we didn't have any money. And Bill's parents were not wealthy people, but they <u>managed well</u>, and they always had a beautiful home. and I had been <u>alone</u> with Bill for 4 years. We came home with a 6-week-old baby, and we had no money. And I lived with Bill's mother for 6 years and she was <u>very helpful to me</u>, but she just interfered with <u>everything</u> we did.

Resolution: And finally, we got together enough money, and my mother helped me a little bit, and uh, Bill was earning money, and we got our own place. We built a house, a small place in Glenwood Hills

Coda: and we lived there for 40 years.

Episode 3: My Mother Moves In

Abstract: <u>I wanted to make a family</u>, you know. Inside I was being torn up.

Complications: And then my mother called me up one day [voice shaking], she was in Florida, she says, "I'm coming back, and I want to stay with you." Oh, my God, I just got out of my mother-in-law's place! Now, well [sighs], as I said, I didn't know how to say no, [softly and deliberately] and that caused so much tension with my children. And, uh, my mother was <u>very helpful</u>. She, in the kitchen, she helped me a lot, but [louder] you can't control other peo-ple's personalities, and my mother was <u>very hard</u> to get along with. And, uh, every holiday became a nightmare because if Janet didn't or Betty didn't want to sit next to my mother my mother would feel hurt. And it—then I, was upset [voice shaking] because my mother was hurt. And she didn't get along with Betty, my middle daughter, and she didn't get along with my son. She adored the little one, because she kind of helped raise her.

Resolution: And that lasted about 6 years. Oh, we had a big fight or something so she <u>did</u> get an apartment in town. She didn't have a lot of money but we tried, we uh helped her, and she got enough that she could maintain herself.

Coda: <u>I never</u>, from the time the children were born, I <u>never</u> was alone with them. I always had a mother or a mother-in-law in my (way???)

Episode 4: Caregiving With Other Things Going On

Abstract: And then our parents became ill.

Complications: And every Sunday . . . I'd go and spend the morning with [my mother], and very often she'd come back stay with us, and then we would take her home. And, that was, that was okay, and then [softly] she became ill, and then eventually she died. She was there for about 4 years. So, I, and then Bill's family started getting sick and I'll tell you, between the two of us we were running with them to doctors. And I still had kids at home, and I was running and it was very difficult because I tried to give everybody attention and I couldn't. Well, I went back to school around the late '60s, and it took me 3 years. And then I worked, I found a job, and uh, at a school until I got the certificate and then I got the job at a different school and on my lunch hour I'd go to my mother-in-law's apartment, and I would, uh, get her medicines set up for her, and then I would come back. And I knew I was under pressure, but it <u>had</u> to be done.

Resolution: But <u>we did</u>, I mean, <u>we just did it</u>. And Bill was <u>always</u> ready to help, you know. I didn't do it on my own, <u>he helped</u> when I couldn't do it, so.

3

Ethnography

JERRY FLOERSCH

A. Practice Ethnography:
A Case Study
of Invented Clinical Knowledge

The use of ethnography to understand practice in action offers rich inter-disciplinary opportunities for occupational therapists, anthropologists, sociologists, nurses, and social workers. Wherever there is a practice relationship, there are opportunities to study helping in every day contexts. Within and among the various disciplines there are manifold understandings of the principles and practices of ethnographic techniques, but there is general agreement on the central features: ethnography is holistic, inductive, and naturalistic (Creswell, 1994; Lincoln & Guba, 1985).

Tanya Luhrmann (2000), Deborah Connolly (2000), Norma Ware and colleagues (1999), Michael Rowe (1999), Elizabeth Townsend (1998), David Wagner (1993), Geoffrey Skoll (1992), and Lorna Rhodes (1991) have used ethnography to examine occupational therapists, social workers, drug abuse counselors, psychiatric nurses, and psychiatrists. Gerald A.J. de Montigny (1995) studied child welfare workers and used both oral and written narratives. Dorothy Smith (1987) offers specific methods for institutional ethnography in the study of every day life that, if adapted, could be called *practice ethnography*. Townsend (1998) and de Montigny (1995), for example, made significant contributions using Smith's method.

In contrast to institutional ethnography, I propose *practice ethnography*.[1] It does not focus on the institutional or organizational determinants of practice, although these matter. Instead, practice ethnography examines the process of practice and investigates how practitioners use theory in practice. See, for example, Gubrium's (1992) comparative ethnographic study of family therapy.

The setting for this study is a suburban community mental health center in the Midwest. The center serves 400 clients and is fortunate to have abundant state and local funds to provide the myriad case management, medication, housing, vocational, and social support services that severe mental illness often requires. For nearly a year, I followed and observed case managers who worked in five teams. The data for this chapter are from a case study of a client and associated team. In *Meds, Money, and Manners* (Floersch, 2002), I provide an in-depth historical-sociological and ethnographic analysis of the practice called *strengths case management.*

At the site of my field study, the state had administratively mandated the use of the strengths model. This simplified my research because practitioners were required to use a single model. Thus, managers were carefully instructed and supervised to think and write according to a strengths philosophy (Rapp, 1998)—nearly 90% of the managers studied had completed the strengths training. Familiarity with the strengths lexicon, an important first step in identifying the work of case management theory, was accomplished by my immersion into the training process and language of the model. This I did by attending a training seminar.

At the training, participants were told that strengths was significantly different from other models of management. In this model, case managers "assist people, who we call consumers, to identify, secure, and sustain the range of resources, both internal and external, needed to live in a normally interdependent way in the community" (Strengths Training Workshop, March 19, 1997). Thus, "in case management we're assisting people to get what they want" (Strengths Training Workshop, March 19, 1997). The workshop leader forcefully argued that strengths does not focus on defining consumer needs; it asks, instead, "what do you want?" The textbook theory and language behind strengths (Rapp, 1998) is, for me, an example of Michel Foucault's disciplinary knowledge/power.

Disciplinary knowledge/power points to how case management theory construes severe mental illness and the practices set against it. And it is in this way that social work techniques (e.g., strengths assessment and diagnostic schemes) are seen as "dividing practices" that work to place clients either inside a normal circle of behavior, or outside, among the abnormal (Chambon, Irvin, & Epstein, 1999). Thus, strengths theory defines what normal or appropriate management work is. Situated knowledge/power, on the other hand, refers to the strategic, contextual, or practical theories of manager work that are alongside but in the shadow of the more privileged disciplinary knowledge. I purposefully sought to investigate if these practice power realities existed and if so, what their unique or overlapping contributions were (I say more about my use of these terms in Part B).

In Section A, I will show how the strengths model, or disciplinary knowledge/power, suppresses a biomedical language of needs and illnesses and shuns a clinical language that focuses on "internal resources," focusing instead on "external resources." Case managers were trained to use assessment and goal plans to ask the client "what do you want?"; "what have you tried in the past?"; and "how can we get there from here?" In contrast, manager-situated knowledge/power referred to clinical concerns. For example, managers used the phrase "gets it" to refer to a consumer's ability to understand goals, steps, and action. No matter how much planning occurred, when clients failed to take the right steps to meet goals, a "natural consequence" was invoked. The expressions "low and high functioning" and "low and high need" were situated diagnostic languages used by managers for placing consumers along a continuum. The expression "doing for" signified that a consumer's illness required direct assistance, and a corollary phrase, "doing with," suggested they were capable of self-sufficiency but managers were needed "to walk alongside."

Strengths management creates a narrative of a textual, self-directed, apartment-dwelling consumer, but invented (situated) clinical knowledge performs unique work: it recovers illness, dependency, and irrational action. By comparing the two narratives, I will establish that in some instances the written and spoken do similar work; in other instances, the spoken accomplishes what the written cannot begin to do. By placing the written and spoken narratives side by side within natural settings of practice, practice ethnography permits the retrieval of social work's oral narrative from the shadow of the privileged written case record (Floersch, 2002; Silverstein & Urban, 1996).

My ethnographic technique involves five related steps: (1) identification of the disciplinary knowledge/power, or strengths language, (2) recording the oral narratives of management events, (3) reading the written text (i.e., case record) corresponding to the event, (4) comparing the oral and written strengths narratives with the invented or situated language, and (5) interviewing managers to confirm whether or not the language I identified as situated was a language acknowledged by the practitioner.

INTENSIVE CASE STUDY

I began following Robert closely in February 1997. By age 37, he had been a client for nearly 10 years; his diagnosis was schizo-affective disorder with a secondary substance abuse problem. In Figure 3.1, I have reproduced Robert's February monthly goal plan written in the strengths format. I found no situated language in Robert's case notes; they were concise, repetitive, and largely reported on activities (i.e., goals) that the case manager and consumer completed. To contrast the disciplinary and situated languages of managers, I first analyzed the written narrative. Manager case notes produced a "textual," self-directed Robert.

The Written Narrative

In Robert's case notes, managers identified his monthly goals or wants: "I want to handle my money," "I want to feel better emotionally," "keep my apartment clean," "I need more money," "I want to stay out of the hospital," and "I need to let the cleaning crew in my apartment." (In examining the July monthly goals of 400 consumers, I discovered that the goal "to stay out of the

---

Goal(s)

1. "I want to handle my money."
2. "I want to feel better emotionally."
3. "Keep my apartment clean."

Steps Toward Goals

1. Robert will meet with case manager for monthly money mgt. session by 2-28-97. Not accomplished 2-28.
2. 2-3-97 Our case management team will provide daily med drops by 2-28-97. Accomplished 2-28.
3. 2-3-97 Robert will take meds as prescribed by CSS psychiatrist by 2-28-97. Not accomplished 2-28.
4. 2-3-97 Robert will come into the center every Monday to have blood drawn for Clozaril level by 2-28-97. Not accomplished 2-28.

5. 2-3-97 The cleaning crew will clean Robert's apartment weekly (Tues.) and the team will assist in the clean up by 2-28-97. Not accomplished 2-28.

Progress Toward Goals

February 5, 1997 TCM 060 1400
I met with Robert today at his apartment to bring him his medication he [this typographical error is left to show it was copied from one month to the next] took it without any problems and was somewhat upset about his financial situation. Apartment very unhealthy, refusing to let cleaning crew assist him. [case manager signature and credential]

FIGURE 3.1 February Monthly Goal Plan

hospital" was typical.)[2] Progress notes were written to affirm or negate collaborative resource acquisition and goal attainment.

Written Progress Note: February 5th

After calling Robert numerous times, I went by his apartment for a med [medication] drop. Got no answer at the apartment. Left note on his door that his medication would be at the office and it's his responsibility to take his medications as prescribed.

Written Progress Note: February 10th

Provided Robert with daily med drop, watching him take. Discussed his attempt to take the van yesterday for lab [laboratory] work and the option of getting it done by Thursday.

Written Progress Note: February 14th

Case manager watched Robert take medication for the day. He reports that his sister took him to get lab work today. Apartment covered with magazine pictures. Robert was wearing an eye mask when he opened the door. Discussed ongoing struggle with obtaining weekly lab work— explored possibility of medication change; however, Robert states he is not interested at this time.

Written Progress Note (Event 1): February 24th

Provided Robert with daily med drop watching him take. He started off in pleasant mood, showing artwork. When conversation switched to his budget and apartment condition his attitude changed. He became argumentative and loud, seeming not to believe what I was saying. By the time the cleaning crew arrived, he'd had his fill of Jerry and myself, so he asked us to leave.

Written Progress Note (Event 2): February 24th

Assisted Robert in getting to the office for lab work. Spent time discussing his past involvement with a church. Resource Development staff offered support if Robert chooses to explore going back to work in the future.

Written Progress Note: February 26th

I met Robert at his apartment. He took medications without any problems. We ran to the pharmacy to pick up his medication. I dropped him back by his apartment. I encouraged Robert to clean his apartment. He stated that the apartment didn't need cleaning.

Written Progress Note: March 25th

Provided Robert with daily med drop, watching him take. He was very angry, regarding team no longer subsidizing his rent. He would not discuss any other topics, bringing everything back to that [rent].

Similarly, other records reported where and what occurred: "Robert and I went to the grocery store for a pack of smokes"; "Apartment very unhealthy, refusing to have cleaning crew assist him"; and "I met with Robert today at his apartment. We talked about some vocational options." Not only does this last note address Robert's desire to earn money, the manager also wants the record to show that the conversation and activity took place "at his apartment." Why? Medicaid specifically reimburses home visits. And, of course, strengths emphasizes "in vivo" intervention.

It is no coincidence that managers' textual narratives placed their work in apartments, grocery stores, and discount cigarette stores. Case managers produced, in Robert's case record, a "textual" community dweller. Thus, the manager's written text substantiated the theory—principle of normalization—and the policy of deinstitutionalization: the return of "patients" to the "normal" suburban community.

The Oral Narrative

In team meetings, hallway conversations, clinical meetings with the psychiatrist, or routine office chat, managers repeatedly used several phrases to describe their work with Robert: "doing for," "doing with," "gets it," "low functioning," "do him," and "natural consequences." However, these expressions never made their way into his case record. Most importantly, they were not part of the strengths lexicon. By juxtaposing the unwritten narrative with the written, one could easily see that the situated language was excluded from the case record.

Below, the oral narratives describe the same events that were referenced in Robert's written progress notes. I recorded the oral narratives while shadowing managers in their every day work (the situated language is underlined).[3]

Oral Narrative: February 5th Team Meeting

I saw Robert yesterday. He was in a good mood, maybe because the cleaning crew did not show. His apartment is a mess. Plates with food on it. I said to him, "You know, the cleaning crew is coming tomorrow. You better get the papers off the floor or tomorrow it goes into the trash…" He replied that this was his stuff and he wanted to help clean. I think we should be there <u>for him</u> when the cleaning crew comes over. He seems to be less anxious when we're there with the cleaning crew.

Oral Narrative: February 10th Team Meeting

CM13: Did the cleaning crew get over there?

CM2: No.

CM1: They're supposed to go today.

CM3: Who has got his daily med drop?

CM4: I do him today at 1 PM.

CM3: Okay, he's covered.

CM1: What are we going to do about the damage to the bathroom ceiling?

CM2: He's pretty good at repair work. Get him to do the research about the cost of the repairs.

CM1: What happens if he doesn't do it?

CM2: We can do it.

CM1: No, we shouldn't.

CM1: What about using the apartment maintenance workers?

CM2: What if tomorrow I do a goal plan and fix the holes with him? I don't mind helping him. I like the idea that he would fix it himself. If he knows he has to pay for it, then maybe he will do it.

Oral Narrative: February 14th Office Talk

He amazes me how he doesn't catch that apartment on fire. I would like to see the cleaning crew go through it. I think we should give him the <u>natural consequences</u> about that because we co-subsidize the apartment.

Oral Narrative (Event 1): February 24th Team Meeting

CM1: Who can do Robert Monday and Tuesday?

CM2: I can do him.

CM3: Are we still picking up medications on Friday? Did he have labs done last week?

CM2: I'm not sure. I doubt it. I'll call him today and see if he had labs.

Oral Narrative (Event 2): February 24th Office Talk

I'm finishing graduate school, but I've never had a class on house cleaning. Sometimes you get things done now, but later you find out it wasn't helpful. Sometimes if you do it <u>for them</u> now, it saves them later. But there isn't any way of knowing how the client will respond. For example, take Robert, we don't know if he really can "<u>get it</u>." But we must decide what we are doing.

Oral Narrative: February 26th Team Meeting

[The February 24th (Event 1) progress note was her written account of a home visit; below is her oral narrative of the home visit.]

CM1: Well, it started out okay. He talked about his art. But his cleaning crew arrived late. It didn't go well then. The cleaning crew student reported that Robert accused her of saying things. I think house cleaning will drop him. I think the need is there, but I think housekeeping wants to close him. He gets more worked up with the cleaning crew, then he reaches a point and he won't listen. We may have to—I hate to say this—but we may have to let the natural consequences step in.

CM2: I think it is okay for us to acknowledge that we have limitations. He has medication through today. If he misses lab again, he will not have enough medication. If we look at his outpatient treatment order, he is missing medication?

CM3: At what point do we make it a clinical issue?

CM1: I think we should pull more of our strings and tell Robert we are pulling out. His mother is giving him the message that we have said not to rescue him. We are going to subsidize only $100 instead of $200.

CM2: Should we get this in writing that we will pull our subsidy if he doesn't keep his apartment clean?

CM1: We can offer to help him but he must show us that he is willing to do it. He really struggles with our standard of cleanliness.

CM3: Yes, but with his piles of paper, it is a fire hazard.

CM4: Well, yes, my standards go down every time I go near the place. I think we should get the landlord to do an inspection. Maybe we don't have to set him up. Maybe we could go <u>with him</u> to the landlord's office.

Oral Narrative: March 25th Team Meeting

CM1: Robert's rent is going up to $435 a month. If we don't let it go to a month-to-month lease, it stays at $410. I think we should reevaluate his housing. How do we present this to Robert and give him choices?

CM2: We gave him a shot at an independent apartment. Now I think we should go to structured housing. Until this guy can get his emotions and substance abuse together he can't live alone. I bailed him out several times that I never reported.

CM3: We have the wrap-around services to keep him in his apartment.

CM2: Well, I'll play the devil's advocate. I don't think he can make it. At times, he is too <u>low functioning</u>.

CM3: Robert prefers and wants to live in his own apartment. On Friday, he was willing to cooperate. I agreed to give him another try, but this time we can't let it go for so long. I think it should be structured every day. He needs to get the clear message that if we are going to subsidize his apartment, then we should have some input. And, we must help control his diet, all he buys and eats is sugar.

CM2: Yes, okay. But we need this plan laid out. And we are looking at some kind of behavior-mod plan. We can tell him that this is our treatment plan, so if he wants to work with us, then I think we should put these things into the Outpatient Treatment Order.

CM3: This is a toughie. [Meeting ends without clear resolution]

The invented situated language of "doing for" and "doing with" functioned to guide manager action. "Doing for" justified daily med drops. "Doing for" was getting the job done; that is, "I can do him." In another oral narrative (March 13th, Breakfast Team Meeting), Robert's manager reported to the team that "sometimes I think Robert is like a small child and pushes us until we will make decisions <u>for him</u>."

Situated comments like these do not appear in the case record. In the situated expression "we will make decisions for him," we learn that Robert was not always rational. Sometimes he is "like a small child." In other instances— only in the oral narrative—they wonder if Robert "gets it." "Gets it" and "doing for" are situated terms that recognize illness and acknowledge that, given our current knowledge of medication, individuals like Robert have limited self-monitoring ability. "Doing for" expresses the managers' willingness to help regardless of the presence or absence of "initiative."

In sum, situated knowledge privileges illness over Robert's willpower and goal-oriented action. In the textual narrative, the disciplinary knowledge of community support service and strengths does not acknowledge the possibility of an irrational subject; instead, consumers like Robert are represented as subjects of goal-achievement treatment plans and notes. From a strengths disciplinary perspective, there are no illnesses, only individuals who lack goals or cannot achieve them.

Robert did not follow medication instructions and did not keep his apartment clean. These practical realities befuddled everyone and created conditions for situated understandings—"he doesn't get it." While strengths language lacks the concepts necessary to think clinically about irrational thought or action, the oral narratives recover a language of needs. Strengths does not make sense when individuals do not want medications or when they repeatedly overspend monthly budgets. From a case manager's standpoint, you may not want medication, but your illness makes you need it. I think this is why Robert and his managers do not list (see Figure 3.1) medications among wants. It is a need. And why does he need it? Strengths could not say. "Needs" are suppressed by its language of "wants."

After repeated attempts at "doing for" and "doing with," it seemed that Robert would never "get it." In tracing the unfolding drama in the written and oral narratives, one could see how the invented expression—"he doesn't get it"—became linked to another common expression—"natural consequences." Case managers did not use *natural consequences* in written narratives. It was instead part of the oral narrative's production of Robert: "We may have to—I hate to say this—but we may have to let the natural consequences step in." The condition of the apartment led managers to conclude that he "doesn't get it" and that natural consequences would be the next step. Regardless of his desire to live in the apartment, the team considered pulling the monthly subsidy, because "he is living in the community and he has to live by the rules."

Through this case study, I have shown that managers invented a common sense clinical language elided by strengths. Manager disciplinary and situated practices were aimed at the same effect—independent apartment living—but they operated on different objects of practice: goals and "rational" behavior and illness and "irrational" behavior. The situated expressions were aimed at the difficulties evident in helping relationships. Yet without clinical training, managers were left to invent what strengths avoided and, moreover, what strengths could not see because of its mandate to examine only *observable* goals and wants.

It is here that the theorist and practitioner of strengths management confronts a puzzling question: if the goal of deinstitutionalization and community support service is to produce consumer autonomy, what is the site for this change? For strengths management, the site is the external community and the rational, goal-setting subject who utilizes a wants debit and credit accounting of accomplishments. Strengths offers no theory or language of the self that could account for self-observation, self-monitoring, and self-regulation.

This was the most troubling problem—the full or partial recovery of the self from debilitating psychiatric symptoms had to be theorized and developed outside of the strengths model. Although I believe that managers' situated language (e.g., "doing for" and "doing with") represented an attempt to invent a clinical language of the self and the helping relationship, it was inadequate. A manager, for example, would "do for" a client who was "low functioning and high need" but say no to someone who was "high functioning and low need." This practical reasoning helped managers set clinical boundaries and ration resources, but it lacked a theory of the self and of the helper–recipient relationship.

Why can't clients "get it" and what is the site for "getting" something? Strengths management philosophy provides only one answer: external resource acquisition and goal attainment. Although the invented language approximated a more clinical understanding, it limited the manager to practice wisdom, which assisted but fell short of the needed clinical work.

B. Doing Practice Ethnography Among Mental Health Case Managers

In this section I retrace my experiences and techniques for conducting practice ethnography among case managers. First I discuss how specific methodologic assumptions guided my research. Second, I describe my research design strategy, including sampling and the significance of studying a single case of crisis. Third, because successful ethnography depends on gaining access to different types of lived experience, I discuss the recursive and continuous nature of negotiating access. And finally, I review my recording, documenting, and organizing techniques while also addressing writing concerns.

METHODOLOGY

Ethnography is not commonly used in social work research; thus, in preparation, I first thought about the philosophical underpinnings of the method and its usefulness for studying practice (Hammersley & Atkinson, 1995). I believe that we index our data-gathering techniques and methodologic assumptions to the specific object of study or practice research question. I needed managers' oral narratives of work and I wanted these to be untainted by surveys or questionnaires. I did not want to assume, a priori, how managers used strengths. Thus, I sought raw data in the lived experience of "actual" case management; practice ethnography was my preferred method for gathering oral narratives.

I had assumed that managers' situated knowledge would not be written and knew from years of experience that most practice is conversational. Thus, I needed to be in the open system of management, observing and recording oral narratives. I intentionally sought to serve the oral and written narratives up to ontological (the question of what exists) and epistemological (the question of what constitutes adequate criteria for making a knowledge claim) practice questions. All qualitative research makes some kind of ontological and epistemological assumption (Bryman, 1984; Smith, 1983). I posited that both disciplinary (textbook theory) and situated practice existed and that each had real practice effects (for an elaboration, see Floersch, 2002, pp. 215–20).

A central feature of ethnography is the emphasis given to the individual as agent in constructing the social world (see Hammersley & Atkinson, 1995). However, ethnographers must be careful in how they construe their research subjects, both through interpretations and actions based on those interpretations (Edelman, 1996). I wondered how my concepts, disciplinary and situated knowledge, might misconstrue the actual experience of case managers. Was I inventing situated knowledge myself? Still, I believed that research without concepts is impossible (Floersch, 2002). I posited that disciplinary and situated practices were constituent parts of a practice power totality, and that totality (ontologically) existed independent of rival thoughts about it.

Moreover, practice power is an object or structure that can produce effects in helping relationships. In other words, researchers and practitioners can have different theories of practice, but these theories point to one reality (i.e., practice power) that alternate theories compete to explain (Collier, 1994; Sayer, 2000). I was fully aware that my theory of practice power was concept dependent. Indeed, this enabled me to identify strengths as a specific form of disciplinary knowledge/power. In short, I used practice ethnography to gather lived case management experience to see (i.e., methodologically speaking) the hidden structures of practice power: the work of disciplinary and situated knowledge.

How did I select the theoretical concepts for my study? I started with Michel Foucault's concepts of bio-power and disciplinary schemes, and examined how scholars applied them to the study of social work.[4] I then used the concept of disciplinary knowledge/power to reference *strengths case management*. I did this to show that strengths theory had an inherent quality to produce helping effects; its property to produce effects was denoted by placing a (/) between knowledge and power (i.e., strengths disciplinary knowledge/power).

Most Foucauldian-inspired studies of social workers see disciplinary knowledge/power as regulating, controlling, and shaping the behavior and thoughts of clients (i.e., the making of a "case" of mental illness). To avoid reducing all practice effects to disciplinary knowledge/power, I needed a companion concept to capture the manager's specific, contextual, or strategic efforts. In this search, I found Foucault's discussion of the "specific" intellectual especially useful (Rabinow, 1984, 67–75).

In addition to Foucault's idea of the specific intellectual, I traced my adoption of situated knowledge/power to several related bodies of literature. First, there is the cognitive and learning literature on situated learning. Here, learning is seen as contextual, intersubjective, relational, and specific, rather than a direct extension of intrinsic capacity or teaching (Lave, 1988; Lave & Chaiklin, 1993; Rogoff, 1990). Second, there is the professional literature that denotes a practice reality separate from theory. This is known by a number of labels or concepts, including practice wisdom (Klein & Bloom, 1995), tacit knowledge (Imre, 1985; Sternberg & Horvath, 1999; Zeira & Rosen, 2000), personal practice models (Mullen, 1983), reflective practitioner (Berlin & Marsh, 1993; Schön, 1983), deliberative practitioner (Forester, 1999), and practitioner-researcher (Hess & Mullen, 1995).

A third body of literature I consulted was anthropological and philosophical. Anthropologists use the terms *local knowledge* (Geertz, 1983) and *situated lives* (Lamphere, Helene, & Zavella, 1997) to refer to particular cultural knowledge; the feminist philosopher Donna Haraway (1988) calls for an understanding of women's situated knowledge. Examining how these conceptualizations variously name personal knowledge, I saw agreement that "situated" knowledge/ power pointed to realities "disciplinary" knowledge/power could not capture or represent.

In contradistinction to the a priori disciplinary knowledge, these various conceptualizations see situated knowledge as dependent on activities or as knowledge in action. In short, I posited that together disciplinary and situated powers form a totality of practice and, at least theoretically, each referenced different kinds of practice work. Consequently, my research aim was to gather case management data to support a general knowledge claim about the work of situated knowledge and its relationship to strengths theory.

Obviously, managers did not use the term *situated,* just as no one used the category *disciplinary knowledge/power.* So, had I merely invented their situated knowledge? Again, I relied on methodology to clarify my construal of manager experience. Toward the end of the ethnography, I validated my understanding of situated practice by devising a structured interview schedule to compare self-reported expressions with practitioner perceptions.

For example, in the case of Robert, I queried managers concerning their perceptions I had coded as situated. Managers, although unaware of the common usage, recognized the expressions. And most important, they described to me the meaning and work each expression performed. This methodologic step allowed me to check out the case managers' understanding of the phenomena under study (Hammersley & Atkinson, 1995) and provided a measure of validity and reliability (Rissman, 1993). The oral narratives on Robert (summarized in Part A) contained the situated expressions (underlined for emphasis) that managers recognized and used.

Still, my study was not driven by a single theory that predisposed me to see from one perspective. In the spirit of grounded methodology, I remained open to leting the "data speak to me." For example, I did not approach the study with a preconceived notion that managers would spend their time inside three consumer life domains: medication (meds), money, and social manners. Indeed, I was surprised to find disciplinary and situated knowledge at work in three bounded domains. I will refer again to this discovery in the section on research design.

RESEARCH DESIGN AND SAMPLING

Constructing a research design for practice ethnography presents unique challenges. In part, it means deciding on the kind of research one needs ethnography to accomplish (see Hammersley & Atkinson's [1995] chapter on research design). Because I did not concern myself with a predetermined number of manager cases, for example, my investigations were not dependent on a sampling strategy. I chose an intensive case study of one team and branched out to study other managers as I gained familiarity and trust.

The practice ethnographer will inevitably occupy personal spaces requiring voluntary participation. Thus, I did not ask the director of the mental health center and its board of governors to mandate manager participation; I sought volunteers and was fortunate to have one case management team offer unqualified support. My sampling technique, then, could be characterized as convenient and self-selecting.

Practice ethnography will usually have self-selecting participants (informed consent requires this) and a small sample size. In general, ethnographic work must correspond to topics that are compatible with an inductive analysis. Such research projects are not tied to large samples and are more dependent on in-depth examination of specific cases.

I started with an ambitious plan to observe everything possible in the daily lives of managers. My goal was immersion. Soon, however, I realized that their daily work was highly regularized and bounded; thus, I adjusted my global strategy downward to specific observations of manager experiences in medication, money, and social manner life domains. I learned a most important lesson in the early months of ethnographic work: to remain flexible. This adjustment, again in the spirit of letting the data speak to me, resulted in the exploration and use of supplementary methods.

It was in this way that I learned that manager experience of medication management was integrally related to prescription assessment, delivery, compliance monitoring, and reporting. I examined 329 medical charts and generated frequency distributions of the type and number of medications prescribed for each consumer. By mixing quantitative with observational methods, I could place the experience of medication management in the wider context: the number of medications, the psychotropic categories, and the percentage of consumers on multiple medications. These data allowed me to think about the complexity (i.e., context) of situated medication management. In short, I studied how psychopharmacologic and situated knowledge were deployed in managing a consumer's medication experience.[5]

I made a second adjustment in data collection after observing suburban case managers. Because I often rode in cars with managers and consumers—from the main office to pharmacies, banks, grocery stores, donut shops, welfare offices, and back to the office—I could appreciate the extraordinary and tiresome effort of suburban driving (12,000 miles annually per manager). This led to yet another important finding. I collected data from mileage reimbursement forms so that I could tally the number of miles the entire project accumulated in carrying out management functions for 400 consumers (750,000 miles in one suburban county). With these data, I came to understand the centrality of the car in successful suburban case management. I was then able to turn to a literature on social geography to understand how the community reintegration of the suburban mentally ill unfolds within the cultural constructions of our automobile-centered culture and exurban life.

The urban political economy produces the *homeless* mentally ill, but in suburbia we also have the *car-less* mentally ill. I discovered in the data that "the landscape of a case manager" matters in how work is experienced. I offer these illustrations from data collected on medication and money to demonstrate how practice ethnography does more work than can be done solely with observation of oral narratives. By experiencing management in vivo, I learned how manager narratives were pieces of much larger contexts; thus, I used other data gathering techniques, both quantitative and qualitative.

THE SIGNIFICANCE OF STUDYING CRISIS

In addition to the intensive case study of a team, I also observed numerous managers from four other management teams, but ultimately I found it useful to follow one case study of crisis. Victor Turner (1974), an anthropologist, has shown how in the study of crisis, social structure is often made transparent. Likewise, I knew from years of practice experience in emergency rooms that mental health crises were windows into consumer lives. In the emergency room, for example, I could see and assess the quality and quantity of social supports. Ordinary life, in contrast, often masks the meaningfulness of relationships.

As a research shortcut into the structural relationship between disciplinary and situated knowledge, I studied a case where strengths had failed and practitioners were uncertain about how best to proceed. By studying cases where the preferred outcome—an independent, apartment-dwelling client—was not evident, one could see the relationship between disciplinary and situated practices and gain insight into the nature of strengths case management. I did not need numerous cases to see the disciplinary or situated language at work. I used instead the inductive method, starting with a particular case of crisis and working upward, toward confirming my understanding that practice power had two constituent parts.

ACCESS TO THE FIELD SETTING
AND ONGOING RELATIONS

How does one get permission to conduct practice ethnography? Once given access, how does the researcher become an insider? Here, I compare my experience at two different ethnographic sites. The first is with my strengths study. I chose this familiar field setting, where I had worked for nearly 15 years, so that I could draw upon already established trust with administrators, supervisors, case managers, staff, and consumers.

Ethnographers new to practice contexts must spend considerable time becoming familiar with routines and winning trust. Although my research participants were managers, consumers were necessarily included. Because mine was a practice question, I had to secure bottom-up (i.e., consumer and manager) and top-down (i.e., the board of governors, executive director, and supervisors) permission and access.

The first priority in practice ethnography is to build trust. There is no blueprint for this stage of work, but I think that social work skills at engagement offer advantages to the ethnographer in clinical practice settings. I initially secured access through the executive director, who channeled my proposal through the agency-based institutional review board (IRB). Upon receiving administrative approval, I attended an agency-wide staff meeting where I described the project. I avoided overuse of research language and said that "I wanted to study how case managers use a textbook model and when it did not work, what did they face?" I was later contacted and told that one team had agreed to participate. I had an entry point.

In practice ethnography, access to "what" is an important first but ongoing question. Because there are myriad levels of practice reality, it was necessary to identify which one would serve up the data appropriate to my research question. For example, it was not essential that I attend administrative or board meetings to collect data on how strengths management was practiced.

To maximize field observations, it is essential to identify a unit of analysis that represents a microcosm of the practice research question. For my study, the case management team was one such microcosm. Consequently, daily (5 days a week), starting at 8:30 AM, I attended their meetings and after each meeting selected a manager to follow for that day.

I shadowed managers wherever they did their work. Informal conversations with colleagues over lunch, in hallways, in the medication room, in the medical chart room, with consumers in the community, and during their daily transactions in and around the money management file cabinet. When I discovered that the file cabinet and the medication room were frequent sites of practice, I studied them by staying in one place and tracking the movements and aims of managers moving through that spatially circumscribed activity. In this way, I learned that access to what is never completely predetermined. As an instance of renegotiating access, I asked and was granted permission to observe in the medication room.

In human service organizations, a practice ethnographer does not negotiate absolute access. Doors open slowly to personal and private space. Always I asked consumers (even ones I had observed many times) if I could work with their manager. Before the first management event with a consumer, I asked the manager to prepare the consumer. And managers were reminded that consumers came first; if my presence compromised treatment, I expected the manager to request my absence. On only two occasions did this happen.

I negotiated access to sites as the study progressed, always indexing the sites where managers talked about or with consumers. For instance, when I learned that managers had received training through workshops sponsored by a university office, I inquired and received permission to be trained along with new managers. I used my field notes and audio transcriptions of the training as a window into the lexicon of strengths, rather than relying on the many texts and publications written by advocates and researchers.

RECORDING, ORGANIZING, AND WRITING

Ethnographic work is most idiosyncratic when recording and organizing field data. Documenting and translating practice narratives had two components: audiotaping and field notes. I found that managers and consumers were often uncomfortable with audio recorders, so I gathered approximately half the data with field notes. During a field event, I sought locations in the background of the action where I attempted to notate conversations verbatim. I audiotaped team discussions, but hallway, office, lunch, and automobile-based conversations were not taped. In numerous instances, I wrote field notes soon after the action occurred, relying on my memory of events.

I kept a daily journal of oral narratives, and when I discovered how medication, money, and social manners dominated work, I began to note in which domain the particular observation should be referenced. By developing this in vivo coding system, I hastened the analysis. For example, in the writing phase, I focused on how both components of practice power were at work in the three management domains.

Sometimes I simply kept a list of events. In the medication room, for instance, instead of observing an interaction and recording an oral narrative, I would query managers about the purpose of the trip. In one day, I might log 40 manager visits. Logging these recurring manager activities proved helpful in quantifying their experience (e.g., the entire project made 14,000 home deliveries in 1 year). How many times in 1 day, in other words, would a manager deliver medication to a consumer's home? Also, how did the manager qualitatively experience the delivery of medication? These were different questions, requiring different recording techniques.

Because I had budgeted for the transcription of audio recordings, I found it useful to read my field notes into an audio recorder and have them transcribed. In the strengths study, I coded and managed the data using standard word processing software; during analysis I worked almost entirely from the transcribed documents.

In the case study of Robert, recall my juxtaposition of the oral and written narrative of the same management event. This recording and organizing technique was my most original and productive; it required strict dating of the oral narrative and copious sifting through the case record. In the room devoted to some 400 case records, I worked from my field journal and first identified a particular consumer and the corresponding date of the oral narrative. Then, I looked for a written note in the case record matching this oral narrative. I either read the case note into a recorder or copied it into my field journal, always disguising actual names. With the written documentation and oral narrative of the same event in hand, I cut, pasted, and then merged the two into a single narrative, exemplified in the study of Robert.

I began analysis midway through the strengths project with numerous readings of the oral narratives. I discovered the language of "doing for," "doing with," and "gets it," for example. These expressions were so ordinary that I had paid little attention to them until I compared them with the written case notes.

It was also helpful to think about the paired usage of the oral expressions. For example, after I heard managers say that a client "doesn't get it," I learned more about "get it" and its meaning when I analyzed how they combined situated terms. "Get it" was often associated with a second phrase: "natural consequences." Natural consequences would not be deployed if workers reasoned that consumer illness produced a particular demand on the manager. For instance, a compromised cognitive ability might prevent consumers from balancing a monthly checkbook, resulting in a manager doing it for them. In the case of Robert, after many attempts at cleaning his apartment, they thought, "he doesn't get it." By doubting Robert's ability to "get it," or understand the situation, they used their situated language to reference his cognitive and emotional abilities. I coded the meaning of these situated terms, then, as mentioned, I queried managers about their perceptions (i.e., a form of triangulating the field note data). Here is one example of a manager's understanding of the term "gets it."

> I have one consumer that is like, she just doesn't understand. She thinks people just call the police on her and take her off to the hospital. She can't remember and she gets really manic—in people's faces and really scary out in the community—when she stops taking her meds. We can tell her and tell her, but she just doesn't get it that we don't just call the police on her. So, I mean, I think truly some people just don't get it. I think that is part of their illness.

(Re)presenting data in a concatenated story format that ties ideas, concepts, and data together requires more than research skills; writing occurs after the research fact. For example, writing practice, much like writing culture (e.g., Clifford & Marcus, 1986; Geertz, 1988), serves up postmodern challenges—authenticity and the reflexive research process.

Earlier, I discussed how I addressed the possibility of my inventing the findings regarding manager's situated practices. But I did not discuss the related and more difficult issue of the postmodern criticism of a single standpoint with which one sees and then writes about the other untainted by the ethnographer's perception and voice (e.g., Behar, 1993). Because I was a social worker and had written hundreds of case notes, I had insider information about the limits of written narratives. Indeed, my strengths study was motivated by a need to respond to historians, sociologists, and political scientists (see in Note 4 a list of such works) that have imagined that the written text alone reaches deep like a taproot into a social worker's subjectivity.

Did an insider view give me the privileged position with which to see case managers? As a practitioner, I do not think that my research is the *authentic* social work view as opposed to the *inauthentic* gaze of the nonpractitioner, or social scientist. Nor do I believe that a scholarly preoccupation with social workers' subjectivity is an unfounded research aim. And neither of these conclusions, drawn exclusively from written texts, is wrong. Instead, knowledge claims about practice are incomplete without the oral narrative.

In short, I saw the importance of the oral narrative because of my unique standpoint as both ethnographer and social worker. This means, more importantly, that I cannot claim to have written *the* strengths manager narrative. As a researcher/practitioner I brought my bias into the study and because I was foremost a researcher, managers certainly occupied a standpoint that I could not absolutely see or gain access to. Thus, practice ethnographers must be reflexive (e.g., Bourdieu & Wacquaint, 1992, pp. 36–9; Padgett, 1998, p. 110) about the research process and never foreclose on the social worker's stand-point. This is not to say that I invented the findings about managers' situated practice. Although I appreciated and incorporated the postmodern challenge, I also embraced a modernist perspective and sought to discover a practice real-ity that was independent of any particular standpoint—manager or mine (e.g., Edelman, 1996).

My research aims influenced how I organized, wrote, and disseminated the findings. I began the project with a specific ontological understanding of case management and practice power. Thus, I intentionally placed the policy and historical-sociological analysis in chapters before the ethnographic data because I wanted the reader to see how community support services (re)pro-duced specific power relations. In effect, I sought to have the reader under-stand the context first.

In writing, I also wanted to demonstrate that my data "spoke to me." For example, I found the tedious hours of driving represented a significant part of suburban case management. As I thought about the car, suburbia, and the physical stress of driving, I decided to (re)present my driving data in a specific chapter on the suburban landscape. I wanted the reader to feel the landscape before reading about the disciplinary and situated practices of money and med-ication management.

My writing was made immeasurably easier because I had organized my data and findings into medication and money domains; it felt natural to write a chapter-length discussion on each. By writing an intensive case study, I pre-sented each domain as integrally related to the others. Thus, Robert's case study became a chapter that demonstrated how disciplinary and situated lan-guage was used to represent an independent consumer and how my method of comparing oral and written narratives revealed situated knowledge/power.

From the beginning to its final publication (Floersch, 2002), my study spanned 5 years. If one is looking for quick turnaround, I advise against the use of ethnographic methods. Nevertheless, to (re)present strengths manage-ment as a close approximation to the reality of suburban case management, I felt an in-depth ethnographic approach was necessary.

My research aim was to challenge the view that textbook theory alone drives practice. Moreover, studies of practice, sometimes called intervention and outcome studies, typically focus on the treatment model—the disciplinary knowledge—and ignore the situated contribution of the professional. Indeed, situated work is often perceived by researchers as a deficiency, a sign of un-faithfulness (i.e., infidelity) to a model's prescriptions (in strengths, for exam-ple, see Marty, Rapp, & Carlson, 2001). Thus, a 5-year investment was worth the opportunity cost to dispel the myth that practitioner inventions are due to misapplied theory (e.g., strengths) and to challenge the methodologic reliance on written text.

I decided to publish a book-length manuscript because I felt my arguments were more robust when placed in their historical and contemporary context. Publishing in the form of a book, however, may not be optimal for achieving tenure. Unlike faculty in departments of anthropology and sociology, social work faculties are usually not as enthusiastic about book-length manuscripts. This is especially true in larger universities where hard science or medical model approaches hold sway. Before deciding upon the mode of presentation, a nontenured faculty member should weigh the values of peer-reviewed articles against books.

CONCLUSION

I believe practice ethnography is a much needed research method for two reasons. First, outcome and evaluation researchers tend to ignore the situated contribution of the practitioner—the practitioner must be empirically studied along with the outcomes. Studying practice requires analysis of written and oral texts because each registers different forms of practice power. Thus, to make a knowledge claim about a practice model's effectiveness, we can no longer turn a blind eye to the situated knowledge/power of the practitioner. Without ways of studying what some have called *noise* and others have called *infidelity,* practitioners' strategic knowledge in action will be reduced to a mere shadow of the more privileged textbook theory, model, or intervention. Studying situated practice and disaggregating its effect from disciplinary-driven practice is not easy, but easy should not be the criteria for undertaking research. Practice ethnography has the potential to put the practice back into research on therapeutic, clinical, and social service *relationships.* No matter how much we wish to reduce or control situated effects, it will remain a mad wish. Practice reality is necessarily made up of both disciplinary and situated knowledge/power.

This portrayal of practice reality requires a balanced view. Just as scholars adhere to a textbook approach, practitioners often believe that practice wisdom is superior. Although I found situated practice to be helpful in case management, it was also limited. Thus, a practice outcome may be produced by the situated alone, the disciplinary alone, or some combination. This will always remain an empirical question. Policymakers, researchers, and practitioners must work together to avoid over- or underestimating the power of knowledge in action.

NOTES

1. Because he specifically breaks down the subject/object dualism inherent in nonpractitioners studying professionals (see *What's Wrong With Ethnography*), Martyn Hammersley (1992) has called for *practitioner ethnography.* My use of the *practice ethnography* is aimed at a different purpose, complements Hammersley's definition, and does not require that a practitioner do the research.

2. Among 50 of approximately 400 clients, I found this same monthly goal,

written in similar fashion: "I want to stay out of the hospital."

3. I have used the abbreviation CM to mean case manager; CM1, CM2, and so on, refer to specific case managers.

4. Using case records to describe and explain social workers' disciplinary work has been a 1990s social science preoccupation. The following authors are exemplary in their use of case records: Karen Tice (1998) *Tales of wayward girls and immoral women: Case records and the professionalization*

of social work; Leslie Margolin (1997) *Under the cover of kindness: The invention of social work;* Mary Odem (1995) *Delinquent daughters: Protecting and policing adolescent female sexuality in the United States;* Elizabeth Lunbeck (1994) *The psychiatric persuasion: Knowledge, gender, and power in modern America;* Linda Gordon (1994) *Pitied but not entitled: Single mothers and the history of welfare, 1890–1935;* Regina Kunzel (1993) *Fallen women, problem girls: Unmarried mothers and the professionalization of social work, 1890–1945;* Theresa Funiciello (1993) *The tyranny of kindness: Dismantling the welfare system to end poverty in America;* Beverly Stadum (1992) *Poor women and their families: Hard-working charity cases;* Lori Ginzberg (1991) *Women and the work of benevolence: Morality, politics, and class in the nineteenth-century U.S.;* Andrew Polsky (1991) *The rise of the therapeutic state;* and Peggy Pascoe (1990) *Relations of rescue: The search for female moral authority in the American West, 1874–1939.*

5. For more on the analysis of medication management, see Longhofer, Floersch, & Jenkins (2003), "The social grid of community medication management."

REFERENCES

Behar, R. (1993). *Translated woman: Crossing the border with Esperanza's story.* Boston: Beacon Press.

Berlin, S., & Marsh, J. (1993). *Informing practice decisions.* New York: Macmillan.

Bourdieu, P., & Wacquant, L. (1992). *An invitation to a reflexive sociology.* Chicago: University of Chicago Press.

Bryman, A. (1984). The debate about quantitative and qualitative research: A question of method or epistemology. *The British Journal of Sociology, 35,* 75–92.

Chambon, A. S., Irvin, A., & Epstein, L. (1999). *Reading Foucault for social work.* New York: Columbia University Press.

Clifford, J., & Marcus, G. (1986). *Writing culture: The poetics and politics of ethnography.* Berkeley: University of California Press.

Collier, A. (1994). *Critical realism: An introduction to Roy Bhaskar's philosophy.* London: Verso.

Connolly, D. R. (2000). *Homeless mothers: Face to face with women and poverty.* Minneapolis: University of Minnesota Press.

Creswell, J. (1994). *Research design: Qualitative & quantitative approaches.* Thousand Oaks, CA: Sage.

de Montigny, G. (1995). *Social working. An ethnography of front-line practice.* Toronto: University of Toronto Press.

Edelman, M. (1996). Devil, not-quite-white, rootless cosmopolitan: Tsuris in Latin America, the Bronx, and the USSR. In C. Ellis & A. P. Bochner (Eds.), *Composing ethnography: Alternative forms of qualitative writing* (pp. 267–300). Bochner. Walnut Creek, CA: Altamira Press.

Floersch, J. (2002). *Meds, money, and manners: The case management of severe mental illness.* New York: Columbia University Press.

Forester, J. (1999). *The deliberative practitioner: Encouraging participatory planning process.* Cambridge, MA: The MIT Press.

Geertz, C. (1988). *Works and lives: The anthropologist as author.* Stanford: Stanford University Press.

Geertz, C. (1983). *Local knowledge.* New York: Basic Books.

Gubrium, J. F. (1992). *Out of control: Family therapy and domestic order.* Newbury Park, CA: Sage.

Haraway, D. (1988). Situated knowledges: The science question in feminism and the privilege of partial perspective. *Feminist Studies, 14,* 575–99.

Hammersley, M. (1992). *What's wrong with ethnography.* London: Routledge.

Hammersley, M., & Atkinson, P. (1995). *Ethnography: Principles in practice* (2nd ed.). London: Routledge.

Hess, P., & Mullen, P. (1995). *Practitioner-Research partnerships: Building knowledge from, in, and for practice.* Washington, DC: NASW Press.

Imre, R. (1985). Tacit knowledge in social work research and practice. *Smith-College Studies in Social Work, 55*, 137–49.

Klein, W., & Bloom, M. (1995). Practice wisdom. *Social Work, 40*, 799–807.

Lamphere, L., Helene, R., & Zavella, P. (1997). *Situated lives: Gender and culture in everyday life*. New York: Routledge.

Lave, J. (1988). *Cognition in practice*. New York: Cambridge University Press.

Lave, J., & Chaiklin, S. (1993). *Understanding practice: Perspectives on activity and context*. New York: Cambridge University Press.

Lincoln, Y., & Guba, E. (1985). *Naturalistic inquiry*. Beverly Hills, CA: Sage.

Longhofer, J., Floersch, J., & Jenkins, J. H. (2003) The social grid of community medication management. *American Journal of Orthopsychiatry, 73, 24–34.*

Luhrmann, T. M. (2000). *Of two minds: The growing disorder in American psychiatry*. New York: Knopf.

Marty, D., Rapp, C., & Carlson, L. (2001). The experts speak: The critical ingredients of strengths model case management. *Psychiatric Rehabilitation Journal, 24*, 214–21.

Mullen, E. (1983). Personal practice models. In A. Rosenblatt & D. Waldfogel (Eds.), *Handbook of clinical social work* (pp. 623–49). San Francisco: Jossey-Bass.

Padgett, D. K. (1998). *Qualitative methods in social work: Challenges and rewards*. Thousand Oaks, CA: Sage.

Rabinow, P. (1984). *The Foucault reader*. New York: Pantheon Books.

Rapp, C. (1998). *The strengths model: Case management with people suffering from severe and persistent mental illness*. New York: Oxford University Press.

Rhodes, L. (1991). *Emptying beds: The work of an emergency psychiatric unit*. Berkeley: University of California Press.

Rissman, C. K. (1993). *Narrative analysis*. Newbury Park, CA: Sage.

Rogoff, B. (1990). *Apprenticeship in thinking: Cognitive development in social context*. New York: Oxford University Press.

Rowe, M. (1999). *Crossing the border: Encounters between homeless people and outreach workers*. Berkeley: University of California Press.

Sayer, A. (2000). *Realism and social science*. Thousand Oaks, CA: Sage.

Schön, D. (1983). *The reflective practitioner: How professionals think in action*. New York: Basic Books.

Silverstein, M., & Urban, G. (1996). *The natural histories of discourse*. Chicago: The University of Chicago Press.

Skoll, G. (1992). *Walk the walk and talk the talk: Ethnography of a drug abuse treatment facility*. Philadelphia: Temple University Press.

Smith, D. (1987). *The everyday world as problematic: A feminist sociology*. Boston: Northeastern University Press.

Smith, J. K. (1983). Quantitative versus interpretive: The problem of conducting social inquiry. In E. R. House (Ed.), *Philosophy of evaluation: New directions for program evaluation*, no. 19 (pp. 27–51). San Francisco: Jossey-Bass.

Sternberg, R., & Horvath, J. (1999). *Tacit knowledge in professional practice: Researcher and practitioner perspectives*. Mahwah, NJ: Lawrence Erlbaum Associates.

Townsend, E. (1998). *Good intentions overruled: A critique of empowerment in the routine organization of mental health services*. Toronto: University of Toronto Press.

Turner, V. (1974). *Dramas, fields, and metaphors: Symbol, myth, and ritual*. Ithaca: Cornell University Press.

Wagner, D. (1993). *Checkerboard square: Culture and resistance in a homeless community*. Boulder: Westview Press.

Ware, N., Tugenberg, T., Dickey, B., & McHorney, C. (1999). An ethnographic study of the meaning of continuity of care in mental health services. *Psychiatric Services, 50*, 395–400.

Zeira, A., & Rosen, A. (2000). Unraveling "tacit knowledge": What social workers do and why they do it. *Social Service Review, 74*, 103–23.

4

Case Study Research

JAMES W. DRISKO

A. The Voice of the Consumer in Intensive Family Preservation Programs

Intensive family preservation programs came on the child welfare scene very suddenly in the 1980s. They claimed significant cost savings, an emphasis on family, and efforts to prevent out-of-home placements. The model joined program administrators' and funders' needs to reduce child welfare costs with a focus on families that had been prominent in professional circles since the late 1970s and was also being emphasized in politics (for somewhat different purposes). The early literature claimed impressive success rates. However, by the mid-1990s, several studies yielded conflicting findings regarding the general effectiveness of intensive family preservation programs (Bath & Haapala, 1994; Littell, 1995; Schuerman, Rzepnicki, & Littell, 1994).

In the early 1990s, the administration of The Brightside, a large human service agency in Western Massachusetts, sought to evaluate the effectiveness of its Intensive Family Intervention program. The Brightside was not required to undertake such a study, but administration wanted to examine their program's implementation and effectiveness. Having done some prior evaluation work for The Brightside, I was asked to develop a proposal for such a study. Because a parallel program, the Family Life Center, was run by the Massachusetts Department of Social Services (DSS) and shared the same referral pool, a comparative case study was proposed. The Brightside provided funding for the study ($12,500 for 1 year). Massachusetts DSS provided human subjects review and approved the study plan, data collection procedures, and protections for participants.

The two programs under study served families in the Greater Springfield/Holyoke region of Western Massachusetts. This region includes two moderately sized cities with very diverse populations and many smaller outlying communities with less diversity. Begun in 1989 under a Massachusetts DSS contract supplemented by foundation and private funding, the Brightside Intensive Family Intervention Program (IFI) serves 30 to 35 families per year. A team approach is used to provide intensive, family-centered, home-based services. Goals and objectives for IFI services are determined jointly with the family and, in practice, overlap considerably with the goals and objectives previously defined in the family's DSS service plan. Placement prevention through family strengthening is the objective for about three-quarters of IFI clients; the remaining one-quarter have the objective of aiding family reunification after placement. The IFI program is committed to the family as the most important child-serving institution, with emphasis on family empowerment, the dignity of individual family members, and the desire and capacity of families to change (The Brightside, 1990, 1991). Services employ a broad family systems theoretical orientation. Cultural differences are incorporated into understanding families and interventions are reviewed for cultural relevance and utility (The Brightside, 1990, 1991).

The Massachusetts DSS Family Life Center (FLC) offers programs across the state, although only the Greater Springfield office was examined. DSS initiated the FLCs to expand its capacity to serve families with multiple problems. Area-based DSS "social workers can request consultation, coordination, comprehensive assessments and/or short-term intensive home based intervention for their most needy families" (Massachusetts DSS, undated, p. 1). FLC staff, experienced child welfare workers with bachelor's degrees and considerable training, are assigned to FLC for a 1-year period. Short-term intensive family intervention services are offered by FLC "with the goal of supporting Area Offices in their efforts to help families live together" (Massachusetts DSS, undated, p. 6). During FLC short-term intervention services, the "Area Social Worker maintains primary case responsibility for the family. The FLC worker offers a service to the family as part of the overall service planning between Area worker and the family. The interventions will be shaped by the needs of the family as addressed through the Service Plan" (Massachusetts DSS, undated, p. 8). The FLC worker is part of a three-way team consisting of the family, the Area Office social worker, and FLC. Goals and objectives are defined and oriented by the DSS Service Plan developed by the Area worker.

Both programs viewed imminent risk of out-of-home placement and imminent family reunification as crises during which families were potentially the most motivated and open to change. "The goal of intensive intervention is to engage a family during the time of crisis while motivation and the potential for learning and change are high" (Massachusetts DSS, undated, p. 6). This view is consistent with many models of family therapy and Homebuilder's-style intensive family intervention programs (Kinney, et al., 1990; Whittaker & Tracy, 1990).

LITERATURE REVIEW

The two programs offered an opportunity to examine a number of factors identified as needing further research in the literature. First, the agency and institutional contexts in which intensive family prevention services were located had not been well identified or examined adequately (Warsh, Pine, & Maluccio, 1995; Wells & Freer, 1994). Studies comparing similar programs offered under private versus public auspices were noted as lacking and needed (Bath & Haapala, 1994; Pecora, 1993; Pecora, Kinney, & Mitchell, 1990; Wells & Freer, 1994). The Western Massachusetts programs offered such an opportunity. Second, studies of similar client populations in the same geographic region but served by distinct program types were lacking and needed (Frankel, 1988; Nelson, 1987/1988; Tracy & McDonell, 1991, Warsh et al., 1995; Wells & Biegel, 1990). The Western Massachusetts programs allowed the direct comparison of two different program types serving the same referral pool. Third, the literature did not clearly distinguish programs by their intended target populations (Dore, 1993). Many program models targeted families who were referred for child welfare services for the first time or as primary preventive services. Other programs targeted families who had previously been formally substantiated for child abuse or neglect as secondary or tertiary prevention services (Bath & Haapala, 1994; Frankel, 1988). Few studies of substantiated families were evident in the literature. The Western Massachusetts programs served a population already formally involved with the child welfare system (tertiary prevention services) which had rarely been studied.

Fourth, the literature noted that how a given theoretical orientation was actually enacted by program staff was not well examined (Wells & Biegel, 1990; Littell, 1994, 1995). Further, the fidelity of interventions (how closely they matched intended plans) was not well established (Raschick & Critchley, 1998). Because the two Western Massachusetts programs differed in service delivery philosophy and model, they offered an opportunity to explore these issues in detail. Staff training, caseloads, number of workers per family, duration of service, planned contact hours per week, and philosophy varied between the two programs while the referral pool was the same. Characteristics that distinguish the two programs are summarized in Table 4.1.

The study also intended to allow service consumers (client parents) to give their views about the programs in their own voices. The voices of the program consumers—state-substantiated child abusers often heading multi-problem families and often living in poverty and difficult environments—are rarely sought or reported in the professional literature (Corby, 1991). This contrasts markedly with efforts to understand consumer experiences in many other services directed to more affluent populations. Indeed, the prior literature used simple "Yes," "No," and "Not Sure" categories and 1 to 5 Likert scales to obtain quantitative client feedback in set formats. No prior qualitative research exploring the views of parents in family preservation programs was found. This qualitative case study research targets parents' (and other

Table 4.1 Summary of Program Differences

FLC	IFI
State Agency Auspices, Located in DSS Regional Office	Private Agency Auspices, Located on Private Agency Campus
Single Worker Team: BA level senior child welfare worker	Two Worker Team: MSW with mental health experience and BA level support worker
Program duration of 8 weeks with 3 to 5 contact hours per week	Program duration of 10–12 weeks with 6 to 10 contact hours per week

Both Programs served families with substantiated child abuse or neglect histories living in the same geographic region and referred by the same source.

participants') views given in their own voices instead of imposing prior categories (Patton, 1996; Pecora et al. 1995).

METHOD

The study was designed as a comparative case study (Feagin, Orun, & Sjoberg, 1991; Stake, 1995; Yin, 1984, 1994). The two programs were not viewed as "critical" or "pivotal" cases in the sense often used in selecting cases for studies of single, unusual, or novel cases. Each program was instead viewed as unique, but able to offer information that might be more telling for the purpose of effecting program changes (Patton, 1987, 1996).

The case study sought to examine the implementation, processes, and impact of the two programs using in-depth interviews with parents and other family members (as available). The study also used regular, in-depth discussions with staff, supervisors, select consultants, and administrators. Additional information was sought from some state child protective workers who had overall responsibility for each family case. The information gathered on each program (case) was cross-compared or triangulated to offer perspective and identify areas of ambiguity or disagreement.

Study Epistemology

The study employed a realist epistemological stance (House, 1991; Kazi, 2002). Empirical data were treated as central to description and interpretation, but building and refining theory was viewed as equally important. At the same time, the researchers' and participants' values and personal theories were viewed as sources of bias or misunderstanding that could not be fully eliminated. Strategies were included in the study design to identify bias and misunderstanding and to maximize credibility and verisimilitude (Drisko, 1997; Padgett, 1998).

Study Purposes, Audiences, and Interview Questions

The case study was part of a mixed-method research project reported elsewhere (Drisko, 1998). The quantitative component sought to document outcomes in a conventional fashion, which agency administrators knew was crucial to establishing the merit of the programs for funding purposes. The qualitative case study component was intended to provide more detail and suggestions useful to supervisor and program planners. The Brightside provided funding for the study ($12,500 for 1 year). The Massachusetts DSS provided human subjects review and approved the study plan, data collection procedures, and protections for participants. All participants (staff and families) were offered a summary of the study results.

The study had several orienting questions. Responses to these questions were sought from both staff members and parents. These questions included the following: How well did the implemented programs correspond to the programs described on paper? Did the public agency or private agency auspices of each program matter to parents? Did the implemented programs lead to, or toward, the outcomes sought by each program's designers? What components of the programs did the parents find most valuable? What program components did the parents believe lead to or toward the desired outcomes? What components were least helpful or unhelpful? Responses to these questions were intended to address the information needs of line staff, supervisors, program administrators, and funding sources. The questions were simultaneously intended to address the information needs of the academics with interest in intensive family preservation and child welfare service.

Sampling Among Participating Families

Given limited funding, single interviews were planned with families. Families were initially identified as potential participants by program staff. Approximately 30 families were sought, with an even split between the two programs. Midway into the study staff intimated (indirectly) that they were referring "more successful" cases to be interviewed. A change in sampling strategy was therefore initiated to ensure inclusion of less successful cases from both agencies. This change in sampling strategy ensured better theoretical representatives of the final study sample.

All staff agreed to participate in the study. Information from program staff was collected in a number of interviews with staff and administration as well as a series of monthly meetings with the program staff and supervisors. The group meetings reduced the time demands on the staff and served as a source of individual views and an informal focus group in which other staff reflected on and reacted to the comments of their peers.

DATA COLLECTION PROCEDURES

Data from families were collected using a semi-structured interview protocol. The interviews took place in parents' homes. They were done by the researcher and two master's-level students and were tape recorded. Each interview began with a review of informed consent and the signing of a consent form. No parent refused consent. Parent and staff interviews covered some similar content oriented by the questions described above. Additional questions to staff addressed what services each program offered, who provided them, how often, what worked well or poorly, what progress was evident, and future concerns for the families. Later on in the data collection process, staff were asked their views about the parents and the ability of some parents to make use of certain program components.

Data Analysis

Transcriptions of the interviews were carefully reviewed for accuracy before data analysis was begun. The collected data was then analyzed using Glaser and Strauss's (1967) constant comparative method. Open coding yielded more than 100 core categories. A high level of agreement on the assignment of codes was achieved and differences were discussed to identify potential areas of omission or bias and to achieve clarity on the codes. Axial coding followed in which text segments were combined into working categories or concepts. Differences across cases were also examined. Roughly 30 concepts (axial codes) proved applicable to the study. The third step, selective coding, involved joining theoretical or narrative categories into a working understanding of target phenomena (Strauss & Corbin, 1990). Selective coding was partially oriented by the initial study questions (e.g., Do agency auspices matter? What program features were helpful?) together with new concepts which were grounded in the parents' and staffs' unanticipated comments.

FINDINGS: THE FAMILY LIFE
CENTER PROGRAM

Both programs had proved highly successful in terms of a quantitative summary of outcomes as reported elsewhere (Drisko, 1998). Rates for placement prevention cases were 100% success for both programs at program termination and 91% for IFI and 100% for FLC at 6-month follow up. These rates were better than statistics for similar programs found in the published literature (Frankel, 1988; Littell, 1995). Rates for rapid family reunification were more variable: 75% for IFI and 0% for FLC at termination and 100% for IFI and 33% for FLC at 6-month follow up. Several family reunification cases proved to take longer than the planned 3 months owing to factors outside the control of families or program staff. Court delays and postponements, the lack of required housing (usually more bedrooms to separate children by gender or age), and the lack of substance abuse treatment were the sticking points. Both programs appeared highly successful in summary terms. This information was vital to some readers because it established that the programs were effective; thus, their components warranted further examination.

An unexpected pattern of differential referrals between the two programs was found. The FLC program, with its roots in child protective services, received most of the rapid family reunification referrals. The IFI program, with its family therapy philosophy, received most of the placement prevention referrals. Administrators and staff from both programs thought that this pattern accurately reflected the strengths of each programs, but that the pattern was unintended. Local DSS supervisors, who were familiar with both programs, apparently acted on their sense of the programs' different emphases and made referrals accordingly.

The Family Life Center

The Massachusetts DSS FLC serving Greater Springfield/Holyoke is a small program. There were just two line staff and a part-time supervisor. The program was housed in the DSS regional office, which was located in downtown Springfield, newly modernized and nicely furnished. The FLC staff, an African-American man and a White woman, were both veteran protective service workers.

As noted, FLC was referred more rapid family reunification cases than was IFI. FLC had a roughly 60% : 40% mix of rapid family reunification and placement prevention cases, respectively. The families tended to be located in urban areas, in housing ranging from large housing projects to older apartment buildings in various states of repair. Most parents did not identify "their" FLC worker as a DSS employee, perhaps because the parents and the FLC staff met jointly with the local DSS worker early on to clarify service goals. However, a few families who had had "very bad experiences" with local protective workers were quite aware the FLC worker was connected to this state agency. The program was mainly identified by the name of the worker: "What do I call the program . . . I call her Diane!" Parents reported FLC workers came from 2 to 6 hours per week, for 8 to 10 weeks. Most visits took place on weekdays. Sixteen FLC cases were included in the study.

Reasons for Referral

Most parents took some personal responsibility for the family's difficulties: "I couldn't handle them too much," or "They took him to this foster home because I hit him because I couldn't control him" were typical responses. Others located blame for the problems leading to referral in the children: "My boy was having problems in school so they took him," or "My daughter was having trouble after [sexual] abuse by [relatives]." A few said they did not want to be part of FLC: "For nothing I wanted, DSS made me do it" or "I just needed a larger apartment, not nothing else." Most FLC parents clearly stated they did not initially want or need to be in the program. "No! I was forced! They didn't tell me that it's your choice, you know? They just told me this is what you're going to do." When families were referred as part of a long-term reunification plan or for reassessment, parents' views regarding the goals of the program were less specific. This may reflect the more global nature of the program's involvement but, for some, appeared to be a source of confusion about FLC.

No parents viewed their family as being "in crisis" at the time of referral to FLC or at the start of FLC services. Instead they overwhelmingly viewed their situations as the norm: "Things weren't good, but they weren't much different than usual either." The crisis appeared to be more of a casework crisis, where changes in worker's views or actions evoked a crisis within the services, than a disequilibrium within the family system per se. FLC parents expressed many doubts about the program at its start. Many of these related to unresolved bitter feelings about prior child protective investigations and failures in follow through by prior services. "I didn't want people coming into my house, getting involved in my business." Another said "I was afraid of what they would think of me as a parent . . . I am embarrassed by much of my daughter's behavior." Nonetheless the concern, reliability, and persistence of the FLC workers impressed parents. Several parents noted they made the worker "jump through some hoops" to demonstrate reliability—and that the workers passed the tests.

What Has Changed and What Helped

About half the parents saw positive results due to FLC services. These included "my daughter's back in school," "I'm seeing my child more [in foster placement]," and "I'm in good drug treatment." A few located the change in their child exclusively: "My daughter's much improved . . . she's shaped up." The other half offered no detailed comment in response to this question.

A key positive aspect of FLC staff was that they "did not tell [us] what to do," unlike many other service providers. Parents made clear they felt like FLC staff were supports, facilitators, and collaborators, not "bosses and bullies." FLC staff were seen as "really trying to see it from my viewpoint," and "much, much easier to talk to [than the DSS worker]." The practice wisdom and skill of these veteran workers was immediately evident to the families. But building trust took more. Descriptions of the availability and follow through of the FLC workers often took the form of comparisons to protective workers. "She'd return my calls quick, and show up when she said she would come, not like those other people." Caring proved to require a combination of treating parents with respect, backed with follow through on the details. "He don't keep me waiting. I know I count with him."

The FLC was often described by parents as helping them work better with the local Area DSS worker. "She helped me find a way to work with the DSS, to see they had something to offer." "He helped me see how [the DSS worker] was trying to help me out, not just jerk me around like I thought at first!" In addition, FLC staff offered information, resources, and referrals. This was often stated as unlike the local DSS worker (many of whom said they *did* provide information and referral to FLC parents). In many respects, it appeared that the developing positive relationships with the FLC workers made their suggestions and ideas more palatable and more likely to be considered and tried out.

Hands-on assistance was another valuable aspect of the FLC program in the view of *all* the parents. Actually getting to appointments was initially aided by the presence of FLC staff: "She got me going. I couldn't plan out how to get there on my own." "His bringing the kids for visits really helped out . . . no transportation was a big problem in getting us to visit before." In addition, FLC staff helped organize access to many forms of continuing community services. This included help in organizing baby-sitting or similar services to facilitate the parent's attendance at such meetings. Most parents noted FLC did this to a much greater extent than their DSS Area Office Worker, despite the 5-hour per week direct contact limit. "He's much more available and does more things with us" than did the DSS workers. Still, several FLC families wished for more concrete help. FLC had a small budget for purchases on behalf of families, but none of the parents mentioned it. This surprised staff, because they frequently bought parents and children meals and ice cream from these funds.

What Did Not Help

About half of the FLC parents wished for extended services and worried about what would happen when the program ended. Such comments simultaneously spoke to the parents' sense of the value of the program and their concerns about their own abilities. Parents mentioned the importance of (1) careful work with the family to ensure they could maintain or continue changes on their own—often around obtaining services and keeping appointments; (2) emphasis on termination; and (3) the need for attentive follow up by the local DSS Area Worker. These aspects of the FLC program were not covered in detail; interviews were intentionally timed to precede any potentially negative impact of termination.

A few FLC parents wished for more concrete answers about the timing and prerequisites for family reunification. Although such answers generally involved court hearings and multiple procedural delays that were beyond the knowledge or control of the FLC worker, parents often viewed this uncertainty as a personal failing of their worker. This added both to the parents' sense of powerlessness and to the staff member's burden. Two parents asked for more specific guidance and direction: "There were, you know, these things I had to do to get the kids back . . . " One couple felt pressured by FLC staff: "They didn't much respect me and seemed to have a list of things for us to do."

One parent was enraged by a violation of confidentiality. "They told my business to people in this drug program without my OK. It really made a mess of things. I felt betrayed." This parent was court mandated to enter drug treatment prior to return of the children from placement and had had great difficulty in finding a slot in a program. The worker tried to use some connections to get the parent into the program and noted confidentiality was indeed broken. The worker also noted "that an important lesson was learned here, the hard way."

Program Length and Model

Half the FLC families felt 3 to 5 hours per week over 8 weeks was "too short" to achieve their goals. "It seems like we are just getting started and going, then it's wrapping up." One quarter felt this amount of contact was about right and another quarter felt it was too long. Families who felt the FLC program was of an adequate length often noted improvement in their relationship with the ongoing Area Office Worker as a result of the program. Two parents felt FLC was "too available" or "always around." No parent reported seeking FLC staff via the DSS Hotline for after-hours backup.

Most FLC families felt the single-worker model was fine, given the qualities demonstrated by "their" worker. "He's great. I couldn't ask for better." Yet some families noted the single worker model offered no room for choice if "personal chemistry" was not optimal, or for input from workers of different sexes: "I would have liked to talk to a woman about some of this." FLC families reported no issues regarding racial differences with workers. Client families felt the unavailability of the single worker, such as when the worker was ill, very deeply. Families felt respected by workers who were reliable and came consistently, so any form of interruption was a problem: "I wondered if he was really sick, or if it was like [protective services] all over again." These families had only 8 weeks of FLC in which to make changes.

Summary

The FLC program, as described by parents and staff, was implemented very much as intended by its planners. The program was extremely successful with placement prevention cases, but less so with rapid family reunification cases. The single-worker model was effective, but was viewed by families as lacking flexibility to meet some needs.

Families did not experience a crisis at time of referral, and many were initially very mistrustful of the FLC workers. FLC workers overcame such mistrust in most cases by demonstrating respect, concern, reliability, and avoiding telling parents what to do. Although not mentioned in the FLC program philosophy, relationship skills proved crucial to helping these families open up to problem solving help. The majority of FLC parents wished the service could be longer. Although considerable progress had been made, most parents expressed anxiety about the future and their ability to maintain progress on their own.

FINDINGS: THE INTENSIVE FAMILY INTERVENTION PROGRAM

The Brightside's IFI Program is also small. IFI employed five line staff, a supervisor, and a part-time administrator. The program was housed in The Brightside's campus, consisting of housing and a mix of various residential and day programs, was located in a commercial area of West Springfield. The offices were modern and well furnished. The IFI staff were White and consisted of two master's-level clinical social workers and three social workers with bachelor's degrees with some child welfare experience. IFI served about 40% more families per year than did FLC.

As noted, IFI was referred more placement prevention cases than rapid family reunification cases. Nearly 80% of IFI families had placement prevention goals. IFI families were widely spread, from urban areas to very rural areas, living in housing projects to older apartment buildings and isolated houses in various states of repair. Parents described the program using the name of the workers. Only one quarter of the IFI parents knew the program's agency auspices. All of these parents reported that they learned about The Brightside during trips with IFI workers to the agency to "shop for" or "check out" clothing and small household items available for them to keep. Parents reported IFI workers came from 6 to 8 hours per week for 10 to 12 weeks. Visits took place on weekdays and weekends, and often included evening visits. Twenty IFI cases were included in the study.

Reasons for Referral

Almost all the IFI parents were clear about the reasons for their referral to the program and who had initiated their referral. Most were quite specific and detailed: "There was a 51A due to neglect," or "the kids weren't up on their doctors appointments." However, a few responses were more global: "My DSS worker insisted on it." "DSS wasn't helping." Roughly three quarters of the parents were able to clearly specify the problems which led to their referral and the target goals for services. Almost all families reported that they were referred by DSS. In several cases the DSS worker's first name was given as the initial response.

Several parents noted that in their initial contacts with IFI staff they got a good explanation of the program, were asked to participate, and IFI staff had a "relaxed style." All of this was well received. One parent noted: "I wasn't forced, they asked instead of told. There were no surprises; they called before they came." Another said: "They weren't pushy, [they] explained things, [they] told me why I was here [in IFI]."

Parents did not report that their families were in crisis at the time IFI services began. "No, it was things as usual when we began." No disequilibrium within the family system was evident to parents or to IFI workers. Many IFI parents had doubts and reservations about the program. Some initially chose to hide out:

> They knocked on my door every day—even weekends—for 3 weeks. They left little sticky yellow notes and called . . . saying just when they were coming. When they did just what they said . . . I said, "What the heck," and let them in. They treated me with respect.

What Has Changed and What Helped

About one half of the IFI families noted specific positive progress. One parent said, "I feel mellower now, you know, calmer, slower. I don't explode with the kids." Another said, "I'm all caught up with the medical stuff, appointments. I guess I'm more organized. I know I'm more motivated." Still another mother stated, "I'm set with detox so now I can stop swinging at the kids when they upset me. I'm not so touchy . . . my fuse is longer. I can understand them better."

Some noted they had gained new skills and confidence in working with systems. "I've been able to get to doctor's appointments, to go to welfare. I couldn't do it before." One parent stated, "I learned how to talk to DSS. I got to know them better. I trust her [DSS worker] more." Another said, "I'm more motivated to get help, to keep the help coming." Still another said, "I've had a great deal of support . . . my depression's lifted." Some other parents did not directly respond to this question but later reported their parenting skills had improved. "They helped me get a handle on my temper . . . to maintain a good relationship with my daughter and keep it together when she bugs me." Some parents combined this with building skills to plan and organize. "She helped me figure out how to get to the appointments . . . to get it together."

A few IFI parents pointed to specific goals but felt little had changed. One parent said, "It's like the same stuff all over again. More trying to help her behave better, but no changes." Another said, "Not much [has changed] . . . we tried the same things over again to solve the same problems." Notably, both these parents viewed the problem as located within a child who had not changed. Viewed from a family systems perspective, this minimized their influence over the problem and likely reflected little motivation for the parent to be part of a solution.

Many IFI families reported a key source of change was feeling "cared for," even "treated like family." IFI staff listened empathetically and offered counseling, planning, and problem solving. Interestingly, some of the most effusive comments came from members of the three families in which severe, chronic mental illness was a prominent issue. "They don't always agree with me, but they tell it straight and try to build me up." The IFI staff member's strong clinical skills and their attention to relationship were reflected in the parents' descriptions, with very few exceptions. Three quarters of IFI parents highlighted these attributes *above* the importance of concrete help or information and referral.

Several others felt the combination of emotional and concrete services was the best part of IFI. Support for the parents' own personal needs, not only issues related to parenting, was reported by some as crucial to IFI's success. This was also described as quite unlike prior child protective services contacts, which (in the parents' descriptions) tended to blame parents and focus solely on the needs of the children. However, one parent with mixed feelings noted, "They did a lot for us . . . sometimes it bugged me but I never would have done it myself . . . getting the children to all their appointments."

What Did Not Help

About one fifth of parents identified some negative aspects of IFI. Three themes emerge: a wish for more concrete advice, concern over intrusion into family matters, and concern over losing the children. Some parents wished for more clear advice or more specific directions from IFI staff, who "didn't tell me what to do" (which was seen by other parents as a positive attribute). Another parent stated, "I resent the intrusion into my home." Another parent stated, "They took us to appointments . . . you knew what to expect . . . but sometimes it felt like a bit too much."

Another mother had concerns over intrusion and information sharing she felt was not the program's business. She had had a fight with her boyfriend that the IFI worker suggested should be reported to the police to protect the mother. The IFI worker also reported the fight to the DSS worker. The mother became concerned this would be used as "an excuse" to take her daughter away. Although this was not called a violation of confidentiality, it seemed to be one. The workers had struggled over their obligations as mandated reporters of abuse in this matter and felt obligated to report the incident to the DDS worker because it related to goals in the service plan and, in their view, could impact on the safety of the family's children.

Length and Model

Families were divided in their views of the program's length. Over half felt it was about right and several felt it was too short. Only one parent said IFI was too long. Those who felt it was too short often gave specific circumstances that led to this appraisal. "Ten weeks is too short if you're Court involved. Courts don't do anything in 10 weeks. They [IFI] are gone before anything can happen." "Our problems have been years in the making and are serious [involving significant mental illness]. They could assess the problem but it's too short to do much about it." "There was an interruption at the holidays." The parent who felt IFI was too long often also reported feeling intruded upon and minimally helped by the program. Yet even this parent noted that staff cared about her and were readily available if she needed them.

There were some additional comments addressing the intensity of the program and frequency of contact. One drug-involved parent noted "It's only 10 weeks long? It already feels like they've been here 3 months! . . . [pauses] I got a little too attached." Yet this parent wished for more help and appeared to be fearful about maintaining progress. Another parent said, "They come so often it feels like the week is gone and here they are again!" Despite these diverse comments, both felt the intensity of contact was "just right."

Parents strongly endorsed the two-person team model. Most thought that the team model was very useful and ensured consistent staff availability. The two staff team also allowed family members to make most use of the IFI staff person they felt most comfortable with, despite racial differences in many cases. The two-person model also allowed one staff member to baby-sit while freeing up the other staff member to accompany parents to appointments or interviews. There was no indication of problems in communication or consensus between team members in the parents' descriptions.

Summary

The IFI program, as described by parents and staff, was implemented very much as intended by its planners. The program was extremely successful in placement prevention and quite successful in rapid family reunification. The IFI workers were viewed as skilled counselors, very empathic and caring, although this was sometimes a mixed blessing. Some parents found this approach too intense and the high frequency of contact too intrusive. The two-person team model was strongly endorsed as beneficial.

Families did not experience a crisis when IFI services began and most were initially doubtful of the program. Quite quickly, IFI staff proved to most parents' satisfaction that they were available, reliable, concerned, and helpful. IFI staff were quite effective in enhancing parent's skills and improving interactions between parents and their children. Families did not indicate any sense of the family theory foundations of the IFI program. IFI staff were described as great counselors who were also concerned about the parents as individuals and could help improve communication between parents and their children. This was the only way in which a specifically family-based approach was evident.

STAFF COMMENTARY

Staff from both programs found the descriptions of parents to be helpful and very positive. They were surprised that there were not more negative comments. Staff could sometimes infer which parents had been critical (based on their concerns) and often understood the parent's responses as justified.

Program staff raised two additional comments. IFI staff were surprised that none of the parents had commented on IFI's emergency budget, which in one case had funded a septic system for a family, allowing reunification otherwise hampered by failed plumbing. The only mention of the provision of funds or clothing was made in terms of explaining how some parents knew about the agency auspices of the program: their visits to pick up clothing. IFI staff believed direct provision of funds could often "get a family moving" and generate progress from within the family and from other external systems. Parents did not report on this.

Staff from both programs noted some families appeared to be very concrete in their thinking and had difficulty in planning and organizing appointments in the community. FLC has access to a psychologist who tested several families in which this appeared to be a concern. Many of those tested (about 20% of FLC's cases) tested at borderline intellectual function (WAIS 70 to 85) and some as possibly mildly retarded (WAIS 55 to 70). The testing appeared valid. There is very little mention of intellectual limitation in parents in the child welfare literature generally and virtually none in the family preservation literature (Ray, Rubenstein, & Russo, 1995). This warrants further examination.

CONCLUSION

This qualitative case study compared two intensive family preservation programs serving the same referral pool but using different service models. Parents found both program models helpful but voiced many specific preferences. Agency auspices did not appear to interfere with acceptance or use of either service. However, the parents in these programs had all been previously substantiated for child abuse or neglect. Thus the parents had many misgivings about *any* family support/child protective program and its providers. Services designed for this population, unlike primary prevention programs, need to include measures designed to build trust and ensure parent autonomy. Extra time may be needed to gain the parent's trust and participation in such tertiary prevention programs.

Differences in theoretical orientation between the two programs were not conspicuous to the parents. However, efforts to support the dignity of the parents, show respect, and listen were valued. The small things that any middle-class consumer would expect routinely were very important to these parents: quick and reliable return of telephone calls, showing up for appointments on time, and calling to let them know of delays. All of these demonstrated concern and respect.

Feedback indicated that parents who fear intrusion or intimacy may find home-based family preservation services overwhelming. Efforts to devise less intrusive and frightening models may need to be developed for such parents. Staff feedback indicated flexible funding could be very helpful in empowering parents and making progress to family reunification where material roadblocks thwarted progress. Staff feedback also indicated that services for parents of borderline intellectual capacity need to be developed and wider awareness of cognitive planning needs to be included in family assessment and service planning. Both parents and staff indicated that court postponements often made them feel out of control and helpless and that lack of needed housing resources and substance abuse treatment slots often limited progress parents were motivated to make.

Feedback from these client/parents has addressed several aspects of family preservation program design and delivery rarely examined in the prior literature (Rodwell, 1995). More important, involving consumers directly in the evaluation and fine tuning of family preservation programs enacts a form of client empowerment (Rapp et al., 1994).

B. Doing Qualitative
Case Study Research

Working on this comparative case study helped identify several key dimensions of the "doing" of qualitative research. These relate to useful characteristics in the researchers, dealing with funders and proposals, working as a team, maintaining context, the process of collecting data, and the process of data analysis. Each will be discussed briefly.

CURIOSITY AND PERSEVERANCE

Anyone undertaking qualitative research needs to possess curiosity and to have perseverance. Curiosity drives you to ask others for their stories and to listen respectfully to what others have to say, however odd, offbeat, or irrelevant it may seem at first. Curiosity keeps you open and listening so you hear and understand the story a bit more their way. Curiosity also helps you make connections upon listening to tape recordings or reading transcripts, when you finally "get" parts of the story you did not understand at first. Perseverance keeps you listening, pushes you to ask for more, to dig a little deeper, to really "get it," to understand. Perseverance keeps you moving forward amid the mountains of tapes, transcripts, field notes, and data. Perseverance helps as you write the 14th draft. Qualitative research is hard work; curiosity and perseverance keep you going.

SOME ISSUES IN GETTING
FUNDED AND STARTED

Case studies and qualitative research are often misunderstood. To potential funders and administrators, qualitative research proposals with open-ended questions may seem too loose, too vague. On many occasions I've been asked,

"But what about specific answers and recommendations?" or "How will this approach get specific information?" True, qualitative researchers need to ask appropriate and generative questions, but experience indicates participants will provide detailed answers not only to the expectable questions, but will direct you to new, unexpected, and useful questions, too. However, the openness of the method may be unsettling to funders, sometimes requiring reassurance and examples of successful work to be persuasive. Yet once the report is written, I have never been asked about a failure to answer the orienting questions or about failure to offer useful recommendations.

Funders of qualitative research typically want a lot for their money (well, don't we all!). The costs of hiring and training, transportation, good tape recorders and tapes, doing interviews, training and paying transcribers, and doing data analysis are considerable. Doing this study for $12,500 meant no stipend for the principal investigator, an agreement to pay two master's students $2,500 each and another $1,250 in institutional overhead (one student also used study data for her master's thesis). The remaining funds barely paid the remaining bills. The budget did not allow, unfortunately, for a stipend for the parent's participation. Qualitative research is usually more labor intensive than quantitative research and often requires a very large proportion of the budget for core research tasks.

Good equipment is essential; too much effort goes into each interview to have a worthless tape at the end. Close work on transcription is also imperative (Drisko, 2001). Transcriptionists need to be trained on the coding conventions you wish to use and about the formatting of transcripts. (Do you want page numbers or not? How will the speakers be identified? How are emotional outbursts noted?) Original tapes should be compared to transcripts before coding, a process that takes at least as long as the original interview but maximizes the fidelity of the transcript.

ENTERING AND WORKING
WITH THE TWO PROGRAMS

Once the administrators had agreed to this study, the first step was to meet the staff at each program. All such meetings are crises: full of danger and opportunity. We introduced our roles, told a bit about our home lives and interests, and gave our clearest explanations of the project. Staff members asked some questions, joked a bit, found the people we knew in common. One joke centered on, "Sure, they're not evaluating us." We admitted we were studying staff, but to see how the programs were implemented, not to evaluate their personal performance. Both staffs proved to be professional, friendly, and helpful. Cooperation was terrific. Still, about midway into the project the issue of evaluating staff performance reemerged at an IFI team meeting, again as a joking aside. Curiosity kicked in and I noticed (had the insight) that none of the "really difficult" cases discussed in staff meetings had been referred for interviews. I asked if we might interview some of these difficult cases. There was a brief silence, followed by a worthy discouraging rationale: "These parents are really mistrustful and bringing in new people would only make our job harder." We researchers did not wish to interfere or potentially cause harm. Nonetheless I ventured, "I wonder if parents might feel you are trustworthy if you gave them the opportunity to talk about the program even given their difficulty." Conversation ensued and the ice broke. One staff person admitted concern that she would "look bad." Clarification, reassurance, and some joking followed, leading to the chance to interview two difficult families. Both of these difficult families reported that the program was helpful and that they felt staff were trying hard. They did have reservations and complaints, but not about the staff or the program per se (I expect their comments may have been "cleaned up" a bit, but I also think these parents were honest, given their openness and level of detail regarding their concerns).

The staff, in turn, was surprised and very much affirmed by the parents' feedback, which they received after the families had terminated from the program. After this, the staff was receptive to my request that we needed to interview a number of these difficult families to learn what made them difficult and how they thought the programs could be improved. The study sampling improved. Notably, this story centered on only one program, but I later learned it had been shared between the programs, although not by any of the research team. The other program referred difficult cases, too.

ENTERING, INTERVIEWING, AND LEAVING THE FAMILIES

Entering the lives of parents and families, even for a single interview, was still more challenging. We knew that these parents likely had reasons to be mistrustful of strangers. As noted, parents' responses to the initial "ice breaker" question (Have you been in any similar program?) routinely brought forth comparisons to child abuse investigations. In these investigations, parents felt they were threatened with the removal of their children—which indeed had happened to some—intruded upon, and treated disrespectfully. We researchers all felt there was an implicit message conveyed in these stories regarding the threat we posed, despite our good intentions. It was saddening and somewhat scary. Still, in no more than 90 minutes, these same parents opened up as we talked and (usually) became more direct and revealing. Despite their mistrust, these parents gave us their time and insights and told us about their family life, doubts, and small triumphs. For some, their sense of helplessness in the face of the legal system was defeating to hear. For almost all, their doubts about their ability to make it on their own, after the programs ended, was sobering. All these parents gave us a gift.

LEAVING THE PROGRAMS

Once the interviews were completed, we had little contact with the program staff until the report was completed. One unknown result was the quantitative summary of program effectiveness (Drisko, 1998). Staff were very pleased that their work was generally so effective and were not surprised that family reunification often was *not* rapid due to external delays and problems in finding resources. Staff and administration alike were very pleased their programs had some of the best outcomes found in the published literature—despite the fact that they worked with families who were already substantiated for child abuse or neglect and not as preventive programs. Administration and staff were both pleased that the research had broken some new ground in specifying the impact of intellectual limitations on family preservation work. All thought this was an area worthy of further study in the child welfare world generally.

Staff from both programs were finally assured that they were not being personally evaluated, which had now become a kind of running joke with the researchers. This was despite the fact that two violations of confidentiality were noted in the report.

WHERE'S THE CONTEXT?

Many more connections to local political trends, trends within the child welfare profession, and with community resources could have been made in reporting this study. Different disciplines, sociology and anthropology most prominently, would likely emphasize such contextual linkages in reporting a case study. In this comparative case study, emphasis was instead placed on the programs and families. This was a choice, made to emphasize the views of the families and to generate information optimally useful to the study funders. For social workers, this utilization-focused case study approach often fits well with our values and research purposes.

The first report of this study was a monograph over 100 pages in length. Researchers have to make many decisions that reduce the detail of a report to meet publisher's page-length expectations. In this case, a local emphasis was adopted, pointing to the contexts framed by participants' statements rather than by issues evident on a larger scale. Cross comparison between the programs was undertaken by offering more detail on each program in the parent's own words, rather than via linkage to external influences they did not specifically identify.

DATA ANALYSIS

The data collected for this study filled two 36-inch deep file cabinets, including notes and transcriptions. The average interview transcript ran 48 pages, single spaced, with a 3-inch right margin for coding. It was a daunting amount of paper and difficult to manage.

Data analysis was done manually for this project. Each researcher wrote open codes in the margins, drawing a bracket to indicate the content to which the code was attached. Coded segments often overlapped. In the initial coding work, the student qualitative analysts tended to be concrete in their interpretations of text and to assign relatively few codes per page. After discussion among the researchers, codes were assigned not only to literal statements but also to passages that conveyed a compelling meaning. Reviews of such codes were undertaken by at least two analysts, both of whom had to clearly comprehend the content warranting the assigned code. High inter-coder agreement was common. Differences in coding led to clarification of the study purposes and some good fun.

Selecting quotes to represent codes in the final report brings additional choices. Space limitations require the use of selective illustrations, which runs the risk of losing complexity and credibility (Drisko, 1997). Some codes and concepts were purposefully demonstrated using multiple illustrations and some lengthy quotes to better convey the voices of the participants. It was also hoped that these lengthy quotes would provide a better sense of the parents' voices to readers of the report.

SELF-REFLECTION

Both qualitative interviewing and qualitative data analysis require considerable self-reflection from the researcher. It is not difficult to line up a series of quotations that convey just about any idea from many lengthy interviews. One challenge is to observe biases and determine how they distort data collection and analysis. In this project, researchers held different views about change, emphasizing the individual or the family. In some instances, the data analyst's personal views led certain quotations to be interpreted as either consistent inconsistent with the program's written philosophy. The data just "read" differently. Self-awareness led to the identification of these differences. Group discussion led to a consensus view that IFI's family theory-based treatment philosophy was not clear in the parent's comments. We agreed families were strengthened but that conspicuous, family theory-based interventions were not clearly evident. We also came to believe that there would be few obvious indicators of such a family theory philosophy in the views of individual family members. The theory appears to work at a level of abstraction (patterns of interpersonal interaction) that were not discussed by parents.

EMPATHY: ANOTHER VITAL
RESEARCHER CHARACTERISTIC

Qualitative researchers must "walk in the shoes" of others. Moving from an external understanding to (a better approximation of) an internal one is difficult work. Qualitative researchers take on the authority and responsibility to report the views of people with very different lives and views of the world. Time in setting builds awareness and relationships become more open over time, but empathy is still required. Perhaps we can never fully know the internal views of others, but the effort to learn is worthy and important, and a key task of qualitative researchers. It is always done better with empathy.

ACKNOWLEDGMENTS

The author wishes to acknowledge The Brightside of Western Massachusetts for funding this project and The Massachusetts Department of Social Services for providing the human subjects review and authorizing access to the client families. The author also wishes to thank the parents who participated for giving of their time and knowledge with warmth and grace, despite difficult circumstances.

REFERENCES

Bath, H., & Haapala, D. (1994). Family preservation services: What does the outcome research really tell us? *Social Service Review, 68*, 386–404.

The Brightside. (1990). The Brightside's Intensive Family Intervention Project Description. (Available from The Brightside, 2112 Riverdale Street, West Springfield, MA 01089).

The Brightside (1991). Brightside Intensive Family Intervention–Summary of second project year FY'91. (Available from The Brightside, 2112 Riverdale Street, West Springfield, MA 01089).

Corby, B. (1991). Sociology, social work, and child protection. In M. Davies (Ed.), *The sociology of social work* (pp. 87–105). New York: Routledge.

Dore, M. (1993). Family preservation and poor families: When Homebuilders is not enough. *Families in Society, 74*, 545–56.

Drisko, J. (1997). Strengthening qualitative studies and reports: Standards to enhance academic integrity. *Journal of Social Work Education, 33*, 187–197.

Drisko, J. (1998). Utilization-focused evaluation of two intensive family preservation programs. *Families in Society, 79*, 62–74.

Drisko, J. (2001). Transcription. Retrieved January 12, 2001 from URL:

http://sophia.smith.edu/~jdrisko/transcription.htm.

Feagin, J., Orum, A., & Sjoberg, G. (Eds.). (1991). *A case for the case study*. Chapel Hill: University of North Carolina Press.

Frankel, H. (1988). Family-centered, home-based services in child protection: A review of the research. *Social Service Review, 62*, 137–57.

Glaser, B., & Strauss, A. (1967). *The discovery of grounded theory*. Chicago: Aldine.

House, E. (1991). Realism in research. *Educational Researcher, 20*, 2–9, 25.

Kazi, M. (2002). Realist evaluation for practice. Paper presented at the 6th Annual Conference of the Society for Social Work and Research, San Diego, CA.

Kinney, J., Haapala, D., Booth, C., & Leavitt, S. (1990). The Homebuilders program. In J. Whittaker, J. Kinney, E. Tracy, & C. Booth (Eds.), *Reaching high-risk families: Intensive family preservation programs* (pp. 31–64). New York: Aldine de Gruyter.

Littell, J. (1994, December). What works best for whom in family preservation? Paper presented at the 8th Annual National Association for Family Based Services Conference, Boston, MA.

Littell, J. (1995). Debates with authors: Evidence or assertions? The outcomes of family preservation services. *Social Service Review, 69*, 344–51.

Massachusetts Department of Social Services. (Undated). DSS Family Life Center program description. (Available from Massachusetts DSS, 24 Farnsworth Street, Boston, MA 02210).

Nelson, K. (1987/1988). Research on family-based services. *Prevention Report*. National Resource Center of Family Based-Services, Winter 1987/88 Report.

Padgett, D. (1998). *Qualitative methods in social work research*. Thousand Oaks, CA: Sage.

Patton, M. Q. (1987). *How to use qualitative methods in evaluation*. Newbury Park, CA: Sage.

Patton, M. Q. (1996). *Utilization-focused evaluation*. (3rd ed.). Thousand Oaks, CA: Sage.

Pecora, P. (1993). Intensive family preservation programs. *Violence Update, 3*, 1–2.

Pecora, P., Fraser, M., Nelson, K., McCroskey, J., & Meezan, W. (Eds.). (1995). *Evaluating family based services*. Hawthorne, NY: Aldine de Grutyer.

Pecora, P., Kinney, J., & Mitchell, L. (1990). Selecting an agency auspice for family preservation services. *Social Services review, 64*, 288–307.

Rapp, C., Kisthardt, W., Gowdy, E., & Hanson, J. (1994). Amplifying the consumer voice: Qualitative methods, empowerment and mental health research. In E. Sherman & W. Reid (Eds.), *Qualitative research in social work* (pp. 381–95). New York: Columbia.

Raschick, M., & Critchley, R. (1998). Guiltiness for conducting site-based evaluations of intensive family preservation programs. *Child Welfare, 77*, 643–62.

Ray, N., Rubenstein, H., & Russo, N. (1994). Understanding the parents who are mentally retarded: Guidelines for family preservation programs. *Child Welfare, 73*, 725–43.

Rodwell, M. (1995). Constructivist research: A qualitative approach. In P. Pecora, M. Fraser, K. Nelson, J. McCroskey, & W. Meezan (Eds.), *Evaluating family based services* (pp. 191–214). Hawthorne, NY: Aldine de Grutyer.

Schuerman, J., Rzepnicki, T., & Littell, J. (1994). *Putting families first: An experiment in family preservation*. Hawthorne, NY: Aldine de Grutyer.

Stake, R. E. (1995). *The art of case study research*. Thousand Oaks, CA: Sage.

Strauss, A., & Corbin, J. (1990). *Basics of qualitative research: Grounded theory procedures and techniques*. Newbury Park, CA: Sage.

Tracy, E., & McDonell, J. (1991). Home based work with families: The environmental context of family intervention. In Lewis, K. (Ed.), *Family systems application to social work: Training and practice*, (pp. 93–108). New York: Haworth.

Warsh, R., Pine, B., & Maluccio, A. (1995). The meaning of family preservation: Shared mission, diverse methods. *Families in Society, 76*, 625–6.

Wells, K., & Biegel, D. (1990). *Intensive family intervention services: A research agenda for the 1990s*. Final report of the Intensive Family Intervention Services Research Conference, Cleveland, OH, September 25–26, 1989.

Wells, K., & Freer, R. (1994). Reading between the lines: The case for qualitative research in intensive family preservation services. *Children and Youth Services Review, 16*, 339–415.

Whittaker, J., & Tracy E. (1990). Family preservation services and education for social work practice: Stimulus and response. In J. Whittaker, J. Kinney, E. Tracy, & C. Booth (Eds.), *Reaching high-risk families: Intensive family preservation programs* (pp.1–12). New York: Aldine de Grutyer.

Yin, R. (1984). *Case study research*. Beverly Hills, CA: Sage.

Yin, R. (1994). *Case study research* (2nd ed.). Thousand Oaks, CA: Sage.

5

Mixed Methods
in a Dissertation Study

DEBORAH GIOIA

A. The Meaning of Work for Young
Adults With Schizophrenia

Mental health professionals and family members often debate about whether individuals with severe mental illness (SMI) "should" work competitively. It is not always an easy or obvious decision, and the ensuing discussions are linked to personal experience with mental illness as well as to the prevailing science at any given time. The issues in the debate may revolve around protecting individuals from extra stress, minimizing stigma or shame in the workplace, and/or encouraging people to get back to their prior routines. Mental health researchers currently make the point that competitive employment is a developmentally and therapeutically valuable goal for persons recovering from severe mental illness (Anthony & Blanch, 1987; Becker & Drake, 1993; Akabas & Gates, 1993; Strauss & Davidson, 1997; Mueser, Salyers, & Mueser, 2001). If asked, mental health consumers themselves view work as part of recovery, but family and friends may not agree with these assertions and opt to protect their relative from workplace stress.

What appears to be a striking omission in prior studies is the failure to ask consumers directly about the value and meaning that work holds for them. We assume work is valuable in general, but we often fail to ask those with disabilities to articulate this important aspect of their lives.

This study provides the "inside perspective" on the meaning of work from those whose expert opinion holds the most relevance for vocational rehabilitation. Several notions ultimately guided the formulation of the research questions for this study:

1. Vocational rehabilitation and supported employment for adults with schizophrenia have not produced encouraging rates of employment. Actual rates of full- or part-time competitive employment have rarely risen above 50%

(Harding et al., 1987; Harding & Keller, 1998; Breir et al., 1991; Fabian, 1992; DeSisto et al., 1995; Rogers et al., 1997).

2. Prior studies have indicated that medication compliance, symptom stability, psychosocial services, flexible employment policies, social support, and pre-illness employment history contribute to work reentry, but pre-illness employment history is in fact, the only known predictor of future vocational functioning (Anthony & Jansen, 1984: Anthony et al., 1995).

3. Widespread use of novel neuroleptic medications (e.g., risperidone) has led to a quicker return to baseline functioning for many individuals (Marder & Meibach, 1994). There are indications that better work recovery may be associated with newer medications (Nuechterlein et al., 2000; Rollins, 2000).

4. The choice to work in competitive settings for pay benefits overall function-ing (Mowbray et al., 1995; Bell & Lysaker, 1995, 1997; Bell, Lysaker, & Milstein, 1996; Priebe et al., 1998).

5. Most studies have missed the unique point of view of individuals regarding work in their lives and the meaning it holds for them (Fabian, 1989, 1992; Estroff, 1995; Harris, Bebout, & Freeman, 1997; Strauss & Davidson, 1998).

6. Civil rights legislation has attended to vocational recovery issues of the mentally ill with the passage of the Americans with Disabilities Act (ADA) of 1990 and the Ticket to Work and Work Incentives Improvement Act (TWWIIA) in 1999.

7. Work is an important developmental task, especially for young adults (Super, 1957, 1963). For those with schizophrenia, there is significance attached to these valued social roles (Stein et al, 1999; Stein & Wemmerus, 2001).

PURPOSE OF THE STUDY

The main purpose of this mixed method study was to develop a grounded theory about the meaning of work for young adults with schizophrenia. Grounded theory provides a method for building new theory from the bottom up through a process of careful and constant comparison of the data (Glaser, 1978; Strauss & Corbin, 1990). According to Glaser and Strauss (1967), grounded theory is deduced from prolonged engagement with each individual informant, comparing his or her responses to the data al-ready collected. Although the notion of the value of rehabilitative work in schizophrenia is not new, what is new is developing a theory on the meaning and role of competitive employment in the life of persons with schizophrenia.

Nested within the main intent of developing new theory in this area was a desire to pay attention to subjective processes. First, it was essential to provide a depth of understanding about work and its meaning in the lives of 20 young adults with schizophrenia from their point of view. Second, it was equally important to understand why some individuals, despite difficult psychotic episodes and persisting symptoms, recover sufficiently to obtain competitive employment and how they go about obtaining work. Next, there was a need to provide a deeper understanding of the range of factors (both internal and external) that contribute to a working life over three distinct phases of the illness: (1) premorbid, (2) illness prodrome including initial episode, and (3) postdiagnosis/recovery. A fourth goal was to contribute a qualitative analysis to emerging themes of work reestablishment at the individual level. Last, it was of value to use selected quantitative data to support or challenge the emerging qualitative theory.

We understand little about employment or vocational recovery in young adults with SMI, because symptom recovery has been the predominant outcome studied. Symptom stability has taken the place of full symptom recovery in the minds of most rehabilitation specialists, because we now know that individuals can have favorable vocational outcomes while experiencing symptoms (Jacobs et al., 1992; Marrone et al., 1998). It was an important research priority that the full lived experience of employment (symptoms and non-symptoms) was explored through interviews. Other methods (e.g., observations) may have also achieved the research purpose. Methods are a means and not an end in research, because the world of the subject and our renderings of that world take precedence over methods and measures (Charmaz & Mitchell, 2001).

Analyzed qualitative and quantitative data from one male pilot subject were utilized to develop a guiding focus for this study. The themes from the pilot data provided a framework for future questions and for comparisons with data from later interviews. I began the theory building with several of these a priori notions derived from the pilot study. These notions, combined with the current vocational rehabilitation literature, suggest that competitive work had important restorative value in illness recovery.

The pilot subject provided multiple examples in his interview of how work as a carpenter assisted him in developing coping strategies to combat his symptoms (e.g., pounding nails to distract him from his voices). In his narrative, he provided a succinct and elegant metaphor about building a staircase for the first time in his life and working to build an internal "staircase" to assist him with his symptoms. This metaphor gave him a rubric for handling new and unsettling challenges of his illness, one step at a time, with the simplest of tools at his disposal.

As new subjects were interviewed and their narratives transcribed and coded, I was able to challenge my initial theory about work as a restorative process, and thus link the concept of work restoration with the new data. A concern was whether work was going to be beneficial and restorative for all

20 subjects in this study, or would factors other than work account for overall positive outcomes and recovery?

The pilot research and the a priori guiding research questions (listed below) helped to refine the development of the semistructured interview guide (pp. 143–146). Developmental career theories from the field of career counseling (Super, 1963; Lent & Brown, 1996) were also extremely informative in the grounded theory process as a means of understanding normative vocational development. This parallel to normative theory has generally been absent from vocational research on schizophrenia.

This research was not undertaken to provide a definitive answer to this complex problem; the nature of this heterogeneous disorder precludes a simple solution (Bellack & Meuser, 1993). Instead, this study was undertaken to derive themes from subjective accounts about the interaction of schizophrenia and work. It became evident that people with this disorder have the capacity to work and also possess great clarity in articulating the choices they make in their lives. Each individual made important contributions to increased understanding about work-related strategies, resources, and potential barriers encountered from their first jobs in adolescence to their current job functioning.

RESEARCH QUESTIONS

This research was guided by the following questions:

1. What makes it possible for some persons with schizophrenia to return to competitive employment postdiagnosis?

2. What are the external supports that assisted the individual in his or her return to work?

3. What are the internal resources and strengths that assisted the person in the return to work?

4. What are the normal contributions of adolescent and young adult vocational development that endure postillness and provide the potential for a positive outcome of work reentry?

5. How does the person feel that his or her vocational life has changed as a result of their schizophrenia?

METHODS

This study was supported by a predoctoral National Institutes of Mental Health (NIMH) grant (R03 MH60481). It received institutional support from my dissertation chair at the University of Southern California (John Brekke, PhD) and from the parent study at the University of California, Los Angeles (Keith Nuechterlein, PhD).

The study was designed as multimethod, utilizing both qualitative and quantitative data. Although a case could be made for being solely qualitative, a design decision was made to employ both in-depth interviews and standardized measures to integrate different perspectives or multiple ways of knowing. Mixed methods were also used to strengthen grounded theory development and provide an additional source of validation or data trustworthiness (Creswell, 1994; Tashakkori & Teddlie, 1998; Padgett, 1998; Kelle, 2001). This combined approach was integrated throughout all phases of the study.

Creswell (1994) described designs that capture the various ways in which qualitative and quantitative data can be "mixed." Reviewing options offered by Creswell, I viewed this study as dominantly qualitative, or "QUAL-quant." This appeared to be the best fit because the main questions of the study were explored with in-depth interviews. The themes from the qualitative analyses were enhanced by analysis of the quantitative data (scale scores from measures used in the UCLA parent study). Thinking about the study in grounded theory terms generated the following sequence of activities:

1. Recognition that the vocational rehabilitation has generated only one validated theory (work prior to illness best predicts work postillness).
2. Initial review or "read" of all the transcribed interview data and memos.
3. Code or label sections of data.
4. Create a quantitative data set in SPSS from scaled measure responses.
5. Group or collapse initial codes to form themes/categories using a software program known as NVIVO (Richards, 1999).
6. Link categories and derive higher order constructs for the data relationships.
7. Visually map the data as a further descriptor of the arrangement of categories/themes.
8. Triangulate the qualitative and quantitative data for theory building.
9. Display and describe mixed method data in the dissertation results.

PARTICIPANTS

The 20 participants in this meaning of work study were recruited from a longitudinal NIMH-sponsored study ($N = 87$) at UCLA. Each person was selected purposively to ensure that the sample was rich with experiential participants, that is, those who had been in a competitive work environment. This selection procedure is also known as *intensity sampling* (Morse, 1997).

All 20 subjects were known to me prior to their consenting to participate in this project. Some were clients I case managed and others I knew through casual encounters in my position as clinical coordinator for the parent study. This potential limitation will be discussed later in this chapter.

The young adults (10 men and 10 women) initially met research diagnostic criteria (RDC) for schizophrenia or schizoaffective disorder as assessed by the Structured Clinical Interview for DSM IV (SCID; Spitzer, Endicott, & Robins,

1978) and the psychosis sections of the Present State Exam (PSE). They were all medication adherent at the time of the study interviews, most taking risperidone, at doses tailored to their symptom needs. Participants were living in a variety of independent and semi-independent settings in the community.

The primary selection criteria for the study were that the participants had worked competitively at any point prior to diagnosis and for any length of time. The criteria specified that the person be in some stage of work recovery (currently working, between jobs, or actively job seeking). Amount of time worked after diagnosis was not specified. There was no lower limit placed on hours worked because the study was about the process of work restoration and its meaning rather than obtaining an actual job. As a result, participants worked anywhere from 8 to 60 hours per week. The work needed to be for a competitive wage (usually minimum hourly wage or above).

I initially approached potential participants and informed them about the study. If they agreed to participate, a mutually agreed upon interview time and site in the community was arranged.

DATA COLLECTION PROCEDURES

In-Depth Interviews

Interviews took place in one or two sessions that lasted 1 to 2 hours each. Interviews were audiotaped and later transcribed with permission of the participants. The interview guide was developed to address key topics of work function in a sequence that made sense to the informant (Padgett, 1998; Lofland & Lofland, 1995; Kvale, 1996). It also followed a conceptual model of the illness trajectory.

The open-ended questions were developed from a variety of sources, including (1) my 15 years of professional and personal contact with this population; (2) the literature on vocational theory and work reformulation; and (3) a developing conceptual framework about work as a beneficial part of the recovery process. Questions concerned three identified phases: (1) premorbid work history, (2) work history during illness onset, and (3) postdiagnosis work history.

Questions about the pre-illness or prodrome period, usually confined to the first interview, were intended to capture healthy work functioning. Illness onset through illness recovery constituted the second interview. This dual path of illness and work, which evolved as part of the interview process, became an important feature of the model because these two important life trajectories overlapped for each individual.

Scaled Measures

The quantitative data were collected at the end of the second interview. The six scales were chosen because they adequately assessed vocational and nonvocational outcomes or they assessed positive and negative symptoms that have been hypothesized as having effects on work outcome (Bond, 1992;

Tsang et al., 2000). These scales, which were administered biweekly in the parent protocol, reflected domains of importance in studies of individuals with schizophrenia: (1) symptom variables, (2) social and vocational outcomes, and (3) perception-of-self ratings.

The symptom measures were the Brief Psychiatric Rating Scale (BPRS) (Ventura et al., 1993), and the Scale for the Assessment of Negative Symptoms (SANS) (Andreasen, 1982). The BPRS is a 24-item scale used to assess positive psychiatric symptoms on a 7-point scale (from *not present* to *extremely severe*). It has excellent interrater reliability with median Pearson and intraclass coefficients ranging from 0.67 to 0.88. SANS is composed of four global subscales (affect, poverty of speech, apathy, and anhedonia) rated along a 6-point severity scale. The intraclass coefficients range from 0.81 to 0.91 for individual items.

The social and vocational outcome measures were the Strauss/Carpenter Outcome Scale (SCOS) (Strauss & Carpenter, 1972, 1974), and the UCLA Social Attainment Survey (Goldstein, 1978). The SCOS is a three-item global measure of hospital time, social functioning, and time spent as a student or worker. The items are rated from 4 to 0, with 0 being the lowest outcome level. The UCLA Social Attainment Survey compliments the SCOS and adds seven 5-point ratings on particular aspects of social functioning (e.g., heterosexual relationships, friendships, leadership).

Measures that assessed perception-of-self were The Rosenberg Self-Esteem Scale (RSES) (Rosenberg, 1965) and Lehman's Quality of Life Interview (QOLI) (Lehman, 1988). The RSES is a 10-item self-report measure used with a variety of populations, including those with mental illness. Cronbach's alpha of the RSES for this study was .92. Lehman's QOLI assesses daily circumstances across eight life domains on a 7-point Likert scale. Cronbach's alphas range from 0.77 to 0.87 for the eight domain scales, although only the global quality of life item was utilized in this study.

RESULTS

In a mixed method study, displaying findings is a complex task. Therefore, a framework for the results needs to be introduced. First, description of the study sample will be summarized quantitatively (demographic, vocational, and clinical characteristics). Second, the emergent narrative themes will be stated and samples of dialogue that capture each theme displayed. Finally, qualitative and quantitative themes will be represented in a conceptual map (visual display).

As noted, a guiding premise of the grounded theory analysis was discerning whether work would be viewed as restorative for any, some, or all of the young adults in this sample. If so, how was work a restorative process? Additionally, it was important to understand what factors (internal and external) contributed to work as a positive outcome.

Demographic Characteristics

The sample, evenly divided by gender, had the following racial/ethnic makeup: 10 Caucasians, 5 Latinos/Latinas, 4 African Americans, and 1 Asian American. The mean age of the sample was 29.3 years, with a range of 21 to 37 years. Twelve participants had never married, 2 were currently married, and 4 had dependent children. With regard to housing, 10 lived with family members, 6 lived in their own apartments, and 4 resided in board and care homes. Average level of education was 13.8 years.

Vocational Characteristics

Twelve individuals had postsecondary education and of those, 4 had college degrees. Although all participants had worked since becoming ill, only 13 were employed at the time of their interview. Of the total sample, 14 were still receiving either full or partial government support in the form of Supplemental Security Insurance (SSI) or Social Security Disability Insurance (SSDI). In terms of a livable wage, 7 individuals were earning above the minimum wage at the time of the interview. Of those earning less ($n = 12$), 9 still described their jobs as part of their long-term career path.

There was a striking difference between the average number of jobs held prior to illness (7.7) and the average number of jobs held after (1.5). This finding is consistent with other studies and with anecdotal evidence of reduced vocational functioning. The overall lower number of jobs postdiagnosis was also related to the longer duration of time to first job postdiagnosis (mean = 25.00 months, [SD] $\pm$ 21.57). The average job tenure of combined full-time and part-time jobs pre-illness was 32 months; the average job tenure postillness was only 7.4 months. Because illness onset ranged from age 18 to 35, the pre-illness period during which work careers were initiated varied considerably.

Clinical Characteristics

The average length of time since diagnosis was close to 4 years (44.7 months). Participants were medication adherent at the point of the interviews due to their involvement in the parent study where adherence was monitored with pill counts and blood monitoring. Thus, this sample is atypical when compared to other community samples of persons with SMI.

Both positive and negative symptom scores portray a fairly remitted group. Two of the individuals had persistent auditory hallucinations at the time of the interview but these did not appear to interfere with their work functioning or their participation in the study.

Psychosocial Characteristics/Outcomes

Paired t-test analyses indicated RSES and QOLI (Life in General) as measured at baseline in the parent protocol and again during this study did not show any significant changes over time. Interestingly, the mean scores for both measures were well within general population norms.

Stages in Vocational Development

Super's model (1957) was applied to assess if there was a decline in developmental stages and tasks after the onset of schizophrenia. From the description of work given in the interview, vocational stage pre-illness and postdiagnosis was assessed for each individual. Only 1 of 20 participants rose to a new vocational stage postdiagnosis; the others stayed the same or decreased.

QUALITATIVE THEMES

Ten qualitative themes emerged from the interview data; some were anticipated from the pilot study but others were serendipitous (Padgett, 2002). The themes were clustered within the three phases of illness and work history (premorbid, symptom onset, and postdiagnosis/recovery). It is possible that these themes could have been recoded and further collapsed. However, because this study was exploratory in nature, the decision was made to display all 10 across the three categories for a rich description of the grounded theory.

Premorbid Phase: Early Work History

Theme 1: Reaching Back Participants spoke with ease, excitement, and pride about their earliest work experiences. There were no parameters placed on choosing one's earliest work experience and some individuals "reached back" to as early as age 6 to respond to this question. One woman recalled picking and selling fruit from her father's tree to raise money for a youth organization:

> "When I was a little girl, the first thing I remember about working is selling peaches, on a side street, from my parents' peach tree. And I made about $7.00 and was very proud of that."

Theme 2: Familial Messages Participants spoke about the influence of positive and negative remarks made by important adults in their lives. This theme emphasized family attitudes about work expressed both verbally and nonverbally. One woman, who spent most of her childhood doing her school homework in her Dad's barbershop, stated, "Well, I had ideas about being a beautician because I watched my Dad everyday and wanted to be like my Dad (pause) and own my own business."

Theme 3: Growing Up With a Mentally Ill Parent Seven of 20 participants had a parent who was mentally ill. One man spoke about how his mother's mental illness affected her own career and his life. "(Mom) tried different jobs, but had real problems staying with jobs . . . she never really got a certain career going in a certain area. I knew there was a problem but I never knew exactly what it was. My sister and I lived with my Dad."

Theme 4: First "Paid" Job Most members of the sample had a first job between ages 15 and 16. The responses to this question provided a framework for understanding what factors contributed to early work success. Families or concerned adults in the community often served as a resource in obtaining these first jobs. One woman recalled, "I worked in the summer program tutoring trumpet players. It is a special program for low-income students . . . um, my music teacher, Mr. Presley, was the one that recommended me to apply for it."

Theme 5: Educational Support for Career Choice This theme addressed the role of the high school guidance counselor in facilitating career goals. In this sample, two individuals never received their diploma or GED. One Latina woman's story reflected a lack of direction or good information regarding career choices: "Um I forgot his name but um yeah. I met with him 'cause see I wanted to go on to college, but I wasn't doing so well in high school . . . he didn't really encourage me, kind of discouraged me, uh money wise. Because . . . I didn't know you could go to junior college and transfer the credits and it wouldn't be so expensive."

SUMMARY OF PHASE ONE

The relative normalcy of the individuals' premorbid development revealed in the first interviews was striking. Thus, normal vocational development was occurring on schedule for most of the sample. Aspirations for adult work roles were evident in participants' responses.

Illness Prodrome and Initial Episode—Effect on Work

Theme 6: Symptom Recovery and Messages About Work Participants reported that psychiatrists gave two somewhat contradictory messages after diagnosis. The first was, "If you rest, recuperate, and take your medication work or school may be possible after some undefined amount of time." At other times, they would offer a second, less-encouraging, message: "Work may no longer be a viable option for you." The choice of which message was delivered seemed to hinge on whether the individual was responding well to medications and psychosocial interventions. Why they gave particular advice to some patients and not others was not clear. One young man recalled this phenomenon:

"Well, it was weird, in the beginning I heard, uh, you know, he's never gonna recover. And then I heard there's a chance he's gonna recover. And then I heard, he probably will recover but I've always got to take my medication."

Theme 7: SSI and SSDI Benefits Decisions Concerns about vocational recovery lead many individuals and families to apply for SSI (or SSDI) benefits immediately. Sometimes family members make the decision for the individual. One woman with a very young daughter stated, " . . . my mother applied for welfare for my daughter first, as soon as I became ill."

SUMMARY OF PHASE TWO

These narratives portray the powerful impact that schizophrenia has on one's thinking and functioning as a worker. Instead, one becomes a *patient*, a dependent life role where it is assumed that professionals and family members will step in and begin planning *for* and not *with* the person. In no instance had anyone asked participants about their work abilities, echoing other studies of this type (Baron & Salzer, 2000). This represents a serious omission in the psychiatric rehabilitation of young adults.

Postdiagnosis, Illness Recovery, Work Attempts, and Ongoing Work

Theme 8: View of Self as Worker A sense of empowerment and a rise in self-esteem can be welcome byproducts of competitive work, extending to nonvocational areas of life. One woman said, " . . . I guess feeling normal again [having a job] made me want to start dating other people."

Theme 9: Struggles, Supports, and Strategies Competitive work is not without its unpredictability and stress. Interpersonal problems on the job and medication side effects can add extra burdens to the workday and impinge on the ability to work successfully. One woman who had a lengthy career pre-illness stated, "I was working in the pharmacy, cashiering and dispensing medications to customers. And I never told them about my illness and they fired me for being too slow. I just—I can't move as fast as I used to . . . I get more nervous than I used to."

Theme 10: Experiential Knowledge and Sharing of Work Advice With Newly Diagnosed Individuals This theme was related to the final question posed to most of the participants: "What advice would you give to others about returning to work?" The question was provided as a summation and integration experience. Four subthemes emerged: (1) take a gradual approach, (2) utilize your determination and perseverance, (3) follow medical advice, and (4) work is good for you. One woman said, "I would definitely encourage them to go to work right away because I think it definitely helps you. You need to have structure . . . it helps you to have less symptoms or whatever. It gives you structure and it forces you to be normal and like everybody else and also you can make money so you can do other things."

SUMMARY OF PHASE THREE

These narratives were instrumental in supporting the finding that work was challenging, but ultimately gave more than it took away. In fact, work was seen as restorative by all of the individuals in the study whether they were working at the time of the interview or not. This further contributed to the

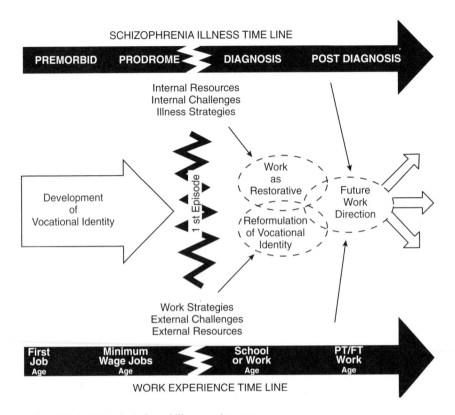

FIGURE 5.1 Individual work and illness trajectory

grounded theory finding that work was a restorative process for persons with schizophrenia. As a result of the study complexity, a graphic representation (Figure 5.1) proved to be important to the analysis of the data and to the development of the grounded theory.

First, 20 individual maps were created to graphically understand themes common to all participants. The global Individual Work and Illness Trajectory (shown in Figure 5.1) was created to display the intersection between internal and external forces in work and illness that enable the individual to navigate his or her vocational career path despite the onset of schizophrenia. In all 20 cases, the restoration of self and work reformulation occurred as a result of internal and external resources and strengths. The headings of internal and external resources on the individual map refer to specific items tailored to that individual (e.g. family assistance with job finding).

Mapping provided additional dimensions of rigor and trustworthiness to the formation of the grounded theory. The results were credible in that the portrayal of the work histories seemed plausible. They also fulfilled the elements of both dependability and transferability of the data (Lincoln & Guba, 1985). When mapping is used to elucidate those conditions closely tied to a phenomenon, very little data are lost for analysis (Strauss & Corbin, 1998).

THREE MAJOR FINDINGS OF THE STUDY

1. Work for this population was a healthy, normative, and therapeutic goal. The following four points about work address the broader issue of why it was seen as restorative:
   a. Work represented a beneficial change in the lives of young adults.
   b. Work was a structured life activity that enabled individuals to make sense of their world.
   c. Work was a normalizing activity that facilitated adult development, especially after it had been disrupted by schizophrenia.
   d. Work provided important monetary and social rewards that were helpful boosts to self-esteem and motivation.

2. Working prior to the first episode of schizophrenia emerged as extremely helpful for individuals who began to work competitively after their diagnosis. The reasons included more than just having prior work skills. Access to internal resources and external supports provided linkages that facilitated the individual's work trajectory.

3. Families and other social network supports provided a strong link to work reestablishment. This link enabled families to be part of a team effort to enhance functional community outcomes.

In addition, Super's vocational theory (1957) was supported; that is, vocational development achieved prior to illness can be identified and revived, despite the severity of the illness. All of the young adults in my study were able to reignite work skills or recapture a vocational stage even though they had experienced a profound disruption due to their illness.

DISCUSSION

The findings of this study have importance for the following stakeholders: (1) individuals with schizophrenia, (2) family members and network friends, (3) mental health providers, (4) mental health policy planners, and (5) state Departments of Vocational Rehabilitation (DVR). If the grounded theory is strengthened in future studies, dissemination of the findings to these groups will be even more critical.

Young adults with schizophrenia still possess the normal hopes and dreams that others their age express. They value making a societal contribution, earning a living, and advancing into a career of their choosing. The young men and women in my study stated that work provided them with the structure, the social rituals, and the status to feel normal. For those with persistent symptoms, it provided a distraction from the endless preoccupation of following their own thought patterns.

This study did more than confirm previous findings that those who worked prior to their illness were more likely to work successfully postdiagnosis (Anthony & Blanch, 1987; Tsang et al., 2000). It also began to explain the why and the how of work recovery. However, studies of individuals who did not work prior to becoming ill will need to be undertaken to refute or support the finding that work is restorative.

B. A Process Essay: The Path of a Doctoral Student

Reflexivity is an important component of any qualitative study, because the researcher is the primary tool of the research. Schwandt (1997) notes that reflexivity allows researchers to be critical of their own biases and opens the door to examining ways in which they are a part of the setting, context, and social phenomenon of the study. Studies begin well before the start date on an official form and it is very likely that sparks of interest in the topic have existed for years in the researcher's mind, long before the first participant enters the study. The need for advance time when applying for funding assists in this process of reflexivity by clearing out a reflective space for the researcher.

As Denzin and Lincoln (1998) point out, qualitative researchers abstract from the world as the study design emerges. In my case, this was very true. This essay will be structured along three reflexive themes that were directly related to my study: context, co-construction, and consumer-driven research.

PERSONAL AND PROFESSIONAL CONTEXT

In 1993, I began my doctoral education at the University of Southern California (USC) School of Social Work in Los Angeles. I arrived at the university door filled with unease about my ability to succeed in academia and carve out a place for myself as a new researcher. I also arrived with 15 years of direct clinical experience working with young adults with schizophrenia and their families. This experience was a major impetus for seeking an advanced degree. I had heard many stories of illness and recovery over the years, and I listened intently to the concerns of those involved in this life-altering disorder.

Schizophrenia is typified by an onset in young adulthood with roughly 95% of diagnoses made between the ages of 17 and 27; the average age of onset is slightly later for women than men (Brekke & Slade, 1998). The illness has a population risk rate of 1% and equally effects men and women.

I was concerned with whether young individuals who experienced this significant life event would be able to have satisfying adult lives, including the ability to work competitively if desired. Their vocational concerns, voiced to me over the years, connected strongly with my own views and triggered my research questions. I knew that to effectively answer these questions, I would need to seek a doctorate, and there was never any doubt that the doctorate would be in social work. These questions about work and its meaning remained steadfast throughout my early years of coursework, my qualifying exams, and right up to the final keystroke of my dissertation.

My interest in learning about satisfactory work outcomes for young adults with schizophrenia was also fueled by personal experiences. I had seen my own relatives struggle to maintain a work life despite major depression and bipolar disorders. As a single parent, I needed work that was personally meaningful to me yet still met basic survival needs.

The research method(s) that I would use to formulate and answer questions about work and its meaning were not at all clear in the early days of just keeping up with the demands of the doctoral program. I did not know all that much about qualitative research, but I knew that I would need a method that would incorporate more than just responses to items on a standardized form. In many respects, I was similar to doctoral students in other disciplines who do not begin as blank slates but rather have a strong hunch or hypothesis to guide their research (Cotner et al., 2000). It was here that reflexivity, or self-reflection, interacted with my research methods courses and jumpstarted the dissertation process.

Crabtree and Miller (1999) state that knowing yourself, and how you affect and may be affected by the research enterprise, are central to the success of a qualitative study. One of the things I knew about myself was that after spending 15 years working as a clinician in a longitudinal study of schizophrenia, I was frequently dissatisfied with quantitative modes of data collection. I watched individuals make their answers fit the structure of the response scales and I struggled along with them, frustrated because their stories could not be told. I had also learned many things about individuals and their families over the years as a case manager, and this information was a source of inspiration (as well as potential bias).

CLINICAL CONTEXT

There were some pivotal events in my clinical work that influenced this study's development. The father of one patient asked me repeatedly whether anything had been written documenting personal accounts of individual work recovery postdiagnosis. He felt that this type of information would at least give him and his son some hope for rejoining the competitive work world. This father was appropriate in his request, but there was little to give.

On another occasion, one of the patients sitting in the waiting room at the UCLA clinic provided further impetus for the study. He was a bit older than the others, had been ill for several years, and had tried a variety of competitive jobs. After I presented some rudimentary ideas about the study, he said, "Debbie, you *have* to do this study!" "Why?" I asked. "Because, you don't understand, for me, it's *where the rubber meets the road*, it's *that* important."

I never forgot the passion of his remark. It was the jingle from a Michelin tire ad in the 1960s, which emphasized the importance of the traction on any kind of wet, snowy, or dry road surface. This was a powerful nod of approval and one that kept me going during times of fatigue and discouragement.

Through interactions with individuals and their families, I acquired confidence about the emerging research ideas and questions. I developed a concept paper describing a mixed method design and gave it to a senior researcher at UCLA. This quantitative researcher did not feel that the project had merit, nor did he feel that I would find anything noteworthy by analyzing in-depth interviews. If I had been swayed by these discouraging comments, the study might never have been launched. Fortunately, I listened to the right voice and did not abandon the project.

NEW RESEARCHER CONTEXT

How do we know whether we have what it takes to frame a study and whether we have the energy and resources to complete it? The chair of my dissertation committee, Dr. John Brekke, and I had many discussions about my ideas and what methodology would be most suitable. Doctor Brekke has been a leading NIMH-funded researcher who had utilized mainly quantitative approaches to data, but he also had a deep interest in the subjective experiences of individuals with SMI and had published a journal article in this area (Brekke & Bradshaw, 1999). He encouraged me to draft a proposal of my research idea and submit it for a workshop sponsored by NIMH.

In June 1998, I was invited to attend the grant-writing workshop with other doctoral students in social work from across the country. I was pleasantly surprised when the first speaker, a senior NIMH staff member (the late Dr. Ken Lutterman) spoke with great enthusiasm about the merits of qualitative research. He directed us to a book entitled *Tell Them Who I Am: The Lives of Homeless Women* (Liebow, 1993), a work I had read and admired. Hearing that there was at least some appreciation for qualitative methods at NIMH, I journeyed forward and submitted my application for a predissertation grant to the NIMH in December 1998.

While waiting for the decision on my proposal, I continued my qualitative education in any way that my budget allowed. I attended the First International Qualitative Methods Conference in Edmonton, Canada, a high-energy forum for researchers to present the findings of their studies. There were many disciplines represented there (e.g., nursing, anthropology, and education) but very few, if any, social workers. There was also very little on mixed method designs. Nevertheless, my enthusiasm was increased by rubbing shoulders with other attendees and my investment in the methodology flourished.

Although I could not afford to attend other conferences on a student's budget, I could begin to slowly build my qualitative library. This was a great investment and one I would recommend to the new researcher. Each academic term, I would peruse the qualitative methods course offerings in other disciplines at USC and buy one or two texts. I also discovered qualitative listservs and web pages (pp. 209–210), leading publishers, and interdisciplinary journals that featured qualitative studies.

As this part of the journey developed, the annual meetings of my professional organizations (Society for Social Work and Research, Council on Social Work Education) were accepting qualitative proposals for presentations and forming qualitative interest groups. Attendance at these professional forums allowed me to discover like-minded social workers and form new collegial friendships.

It was while attending the International Schizophrenia Congress in Santa Fe in the spring of 1999 that I received word that NIMH had positively reviewed my research proposal. My score was excellent and I did not have to resubmit! With this dissertation grant, I was able to craft the study as I had hoped and complete it in within the 1-year time frame. After many months of consideration, hesitancy, extraordinary personal effort, and more than a few tears, I felt I had arrived as a new mental health researcher.

INTERSECTING CLINICAL AND RESEARCH CONTEXTS

Few templates exist for doctoral students as they consider whether to pursue a qualitative (or mainly qualitative) dissertation. In the academic world, we understand that there are factors, other than the research question(s), that shape the use of methodologies (i.e., committee members, funding, time). It still pains me when doctoral students post questions on qualitative listservs about committee members' struggles with understanding the methodology.

In my case, my methodological mentor was an outside committee member from the USC School of Education. Arriving at some methods consensus with my entire committee early in the research was a crucial component of the iterative process of the study and an important step toward a successful dissertation experience. As stated, the research begins before it begins. Seeking and procuring mentorship in qualitative research is a frustrating but necessary struggle.

Students may discover, as I did, that the research journey has to be managed in creative and persistent ways. My own led me to attend national and international conferences, seek out exemplar articles, and reach out to professors in other disciplines on the USC campus and elsewhere. It was a little tricky at times, but ultimately very enriching.

The title of a paper I found on the Internet captures the process: *Lonely days and lonely nights: Completing the doctoral dissertation* (Germeroth, 1990). Although the journey has a lonely quality to it, we usually come to realize that we are not alone—many others have succeeded before us. But it is not always evident how these successful others were able to complete this daunting task.

A dissertation is usually our first independent piece of research, a time when we can contribute knowledge to our field of practice. In conducting the study, we pose our questions and examine a context where, if we are fortunate, new discoveries abound daily. It can be an exciting journey. The dissertation as a journey metaphor was helpful to me as I tried to capture the process.

Each of us who completes a dissertation and successfully defends it has the opportunity to add our voice to the discussions of the personal meaning of doctoral research. These process stories about dissertation experiences, especially qualitative dissertations, are far too few and too brief to enrich our learning and they often omit the emotional impact on the researcher (Gilbert, 2001). We can learn from our mistakes and relish the personal successes of others, hoping to replicate the best features of their research experiences in our own work. We tend to learn about the practical aspects of research from fellow students who are just a bit ahead of us in the pipeline, but that can be hit or miss on both the practical and emotional level.

Universities are beginning to offer workshops and support sessions featuring advanced doctoral candidates and new PhDs who share their experiences and passion about their work. The Universities of Michigan and Pennsylvania have dissertation workshops available to their candidates. Further information is available from their Web sites:

http://www.umich.edu/~qualnet/call.htm

http://www.upenn.edu/gsc/programs/phd_support/diss_wkshp/workshops.html

These sessions fill up quickly, pointing to the desire for a supportive social context. Sharing the finished dissertation with peers can be a celebratory forum and reinforce the process for all involved.

CO-CONSTRUCTION OF THE DATA

Qualitative or mixed method research designs have not been widely used in understanding complex outcomes (such as work) in a complex disorder (such as schizophrenia). One way to capture the complexity of a phenomenon is to engage in co-construction. As described, the researcher brings a personal context to the study and provides the forum for the data to be collected; the participant brings a personal story and possible answers to the research questions.

Co-construction of the data is context dependent. The physical, cultural, and social community surrounding the individual is integral to understanding the data. I learned so much from being in my respondents' homes and neighborhoods as they told me about their work history. If one is beckoned to tell his or her story with an attentive audience at hand, there is a relaxation into the narrative and an evocation of the feelings that accompany the remembered time. On one occasion, it meant grabbing a certificate of work achievement off of the wall and sharing it with the same sense of pride as the day it was received. Environment can assist in the reenactment of retrospective accounts.

The humbling part of co-construction is acknowledging that this study and its findings never belong solely to the researcher. They are literally constructed and co-created over long periods of involvement. In my case, the main research question came out of the persistent inquiries of parents asking about when their son or daughter might be able to return to work. There was never an easy answer to this question and thus over time, a research topic was born.

My connection to the interviewee was deepened in many ways in this co-construction of the data. Due to the fact that the research was work focused rather than symptom focused, I was able to journey with individuals on a healthier path. Of course, we spoke about symptoms and their interference in one's life and work ability, but we also spoke about times when they worked and were not ill, and the successes and joys they had as workers living in society.

If you have ever worked with or known someone with schizophrenia, you know that it is quite common to see diminished or dampened affect. The times when joy is registered on their faces are a great gift, and to know that somehow you shared in the co-creation of that uplifting experience is very special. Almost across the board, the individuals in my study said that no one else had made such in-depth inquiries into their work history, especially since becoming ill. As a researcher, it was very clear that these were not individuals with a blank slate of work involvement. Tapping that prior involvement can provide a window into vocational development that could be helpful in work restoration efforts.

CONSUMER-DRIVEN RESEARCH

Consumer-driven research is similar to participatory action research (PAR). Reason (1998) defines PAR as "establishing liberating dialogue with impoverished or oppressed peoples." On reflection, many of my respondents fit this description of poverty and oppression. They lived on low government-subsidized incomes (SSI or SSDI) that rarely is enough to cover living expenses. Many of the board and care homes I visited were not well kept, but options for better housing were limited without earning extra income.

However, if persons with SMI seek employment they risk losing this income as well as eligibility for Medicaid and MediCal benefits. Thus, decisions about adding work to their lives are complex.

Because I did not attempt to undertake a change process or set any agenda with the participants, my study was not PAR. But it was consumer driven in the sense that it originated with consumer (and family) concerns. Persons with SMI are a much-studied group, but they are rarely asked to help set the research agenda. A future study of work and its meaning should be designed with PAR methods in mind.

The findings from this study did generate a booklet of guidelines for families designed to demystify the process of seeking employment and urge family members to let their relative pursue competitive work as part of the recovery.

One future aim would be to develop this document as co-created, consumer driven, and personally meaningful for a wider audience, thereby having a potential impact on workplace policies for persons with SMI.

CHALLENGES IN MIXED
METHOD RESEARCH

Although it is not my intention to discourage would-be mixed methodologists, I will review three key issues that might be helpful in thinking through potential problems. I think this is particularly important because, as stated, there is so little sharing of this kind of information.

First, there is nothing easy, fast, or simple about this type of research and ensuring its rigor becomes even more demanding. Not only will you be handling qualitative data, but you will need to construct an SPSS data set as well. You may not analyze all of the data for your dissertation, but you will be happy to have it for future analyses.

There is no precise template to follow in mixed methods, and your mixing may not proceed quite as intended; it really depends on your study questions. There are several books (listed in the References for this chapter) that I found helpful in my study. I would recommend carefully reading the sections on rigor and trustworthiness in Padgett (1998) and Creswell (1994) prior to starting your study. I utilized Padgett's *Threats to Trustworthiness* diagram (1998, p. 95) within my dissertation to demonstrate that even though traditional (quantitative) standards for reliability and validity do not apply to qualitative studies, other strategies are available. You can use these to inform your dissertation committee and subsequent audiences that you have thought about these confounding issues.

Second, the process of transcribing interviews, formatting the text for computer software, and creating a quantitative data set are all very labor intensive (or very costly if you choose to pay someone for these services). Transcribing qualitative data is especially risky if the transcriber is unfamiliar with qualitative analyses. Be certain that you have duplicates (or triplicates) of all your interview tapes. Things happen and tapes can easily be lost. Tape duplication can also be expensive. My recommendation would be to cost out your budget (whether you have a grant or not) so that you can anticipate and budget for these expenses. Analysis of the data may be stalled otherwise.

Third, build in some immersion time with your data early in the analysis phase. You may have to take a vacation to do this, but it will be worth it. I sent my children to their grandparents for a month, closed the blinds, pretended that I was not missing the California sun, and embarked on this solitary journey, this vision quest with my data. This was a time when I recognized that I would only use part of the quantitative data. This was not quite what I had anticipated, because I had hoped to have a truly integrated qualitative and quantitative study. But I came to terms with this by realizing that these data would be there for me in the future. For example, I was able to use some of the narratives about the Americans with Disabilities Act (ADA) along with analyses of key clinical, outcome, and psychosocial variables to produce two articles for publication in leading journals of psychiatric rehabilitation, one of which was recently published (Gioia-Hasick & Brekke, 2003).

My hiatus also helped me to reflect on how much work meant for me. To complete the study, I had to stop working as a psychiatric social worker at UCLA. I saw my monetary resources dwindle rapidly and recognized that the work I was doing on my dissertation was not seen as valued by people who worked in the professional world. This was more difficult emotionally than I had anticipated.

In summary, the value and vitality of this study rested on four important points: (1) it was one of the few studies to ask participants directly about what work means to them; (2) it was the only known study to examine the intersection of illness and vocational development through use of mixed methods; (3) it was the only study to attempt to answer the question of restoration of work functioning by highlighting pre-illness contributions to vocational development; and (4) it enabled the development of a grounded theory and model of work history that was interrupted but still held restorative capacities for the young adults in this study. I was deeply grateful for the opportunity to participate and learn from these 20 individuals and their families.

ACKNOWLEDGMENTS

This study was funded by the National Institute of Mental Health (RO3 MH60481). This study was conceived from questions asked by relatives of young adults with schizophrenia. I am grateful to them for planting this seed for the study within me. I am also grateful to the 20 participants who shared their stories of working competitively with a mental illness. My understanding was increased because of them. Finally, gratitude is extended to my dissertation chair, mentor, and friend, Dr. John Brekke, for his encouragement of my pursuit of this knowledge even though qualitative work was not his area of expertise.

REFERENCES

Akabas, S. H., & Gates, L. B. (1993). Managing disability in the workplace: A role for social workers. In P. A. Kurzman & S. H. Akabas (Eds.), *Work and well-being*. Washington, DC: NASW Press.

Andreasen, N. C. (1982). Negative symptoms in schizophrenia: Definition and reliability. *Archives of General Psychiatry, 39*, 784–8

Anthony, W. A., & Jansen, M. A. (1984). Predicting the vocational capacity of the chronically mentally ill. *American Psychologist, 39*, 537–44.

Anthony, W. A., & Blanch, A. (1987). Supported employment for persons who are psychiatrically disabled: An historical and conceptual perspective. *Psychosocial Rehabilitation Journal, 11,* 5–23.

Anthony, W. A., Rogers, S. E., Cohen, M., & Davies, R. R. (1995). Relationship between psychiatric symptomatology, work skills, and future vocational performance. *Psychiatric Services, 46,* 353–8.

Baron, R. C., & Salzer, M. S. (2000). The career patterns of persons with serious mental illness: Generating a new vision of lifetime careers for those in recovery. *Psychiatric Rehabilitation Skills, 4,* 136–56.

Becker, D. R., & Drake, R. E. (1993). *A working life: The individual placement and support (IPS) Program.* Concord: New Hampshire-Dartmouth Psychiatric Research Center.

Bell, M. D., & Lysaker, P. H. (1995). Paid work activity in schizophrenia. *Psychosocial Rehabilitation Journal, 18,* 25–34.

Bell, M. D., & Lysaker, P. H. (1997). Clinical benefits of paid work activity in schizophrenia: 1-year followup. *Schizophrenia Bulletin, 23,* 317–28.

Bell, M. D., Lysaker, P. H., & Milstein, R. M. (1996). Clinical benefits of paid work activity in schizophrenia. *Schizophrenia Bulletin, 22,* 51–67.

Bellack, A. S., & Meuser, K. T. (1993). Psychosocial treatment for schizophrenia. *Schizophrenia Bulletin, 19,* 317–36.

Bond, G. R. (1992). Vocational rehabilitation. In R. P. Liberman, (Ed.), *Handbook of psychiatric rehabilitation.* Vol. 166. Boston: Allyn and Bacon.

Breier, I., Schreiber, J. L., Dyer, J., & Pickar, D. (1991). National Institute of Mental Health longitudinal study of schizophrenia: Prognosis and predictors of outcome. *Archives of General Psychiatry, 48,* 239–46.

Brekke, J. S., & Slade, E. S. (1998). Schizophrenia. In J. B. W. Williams and K. Ell (Eds.), *Advances in mental health research: Implications for practice.* Washington, DC: NASW Press.

Brekke, J. S., & Bradshaw W. (1999). Subjective experience in schizophrenia:

Factors influencing self-esteem, satisfaction with life and subjective distress. *American Journal of Orthopsychiatry, 69,* 254–60.

Charmaz, K., & Mitchell, R. G. (2001). Grounded theory in ethnography. In P. Atkinson, A. Coffey, S. Delamont, J. Lofland, & L. Lofland (Eds.), *Handbook of Ethnography.* Thousand Oaks, CA: Sage.

Cotner, T., Intrator, S. Kelemen, M., & Sato, M. (April 2000). What graduate students say about their preparation for doing qualitative dissertations: A pilot study. Paper presented at the Getting Good at Qualitative Research Symposium, annual meeting of AERA, New Orleans, LA.

Crabtree, B. F., & Miller, W. L. (1999). *Doing qualitative research* (2nd Ed.). Thousand Oaks, CA: Sage.

Creswell, J. W. (1994). *Research design: Qualitative and quantitative approaches.* Thousand Oaks, CA: Sage.

Denzin, N. K., & Lincoln, Y. S. (1998). Introduction; Entering the field of qualitative research. In N. K. Denzin, & Y. S. Lincoln (Eds.), *Collecting and interpreting qualitative materials.* Thousand Oaks, CA: Sage.

DeSisto, M. J., Harding, C., McCormick, R. V., Ashikaga, T., & Brooks, G. W. (1995). The Maine and Vermont three-decade studies of serious mental illness: I. Matched comparison of cross-sectional outcome. *British Journal of Psychiatry, 167,* 331–8.

Estroff, S. E. (1995). Brokenhearted lifetimes: Ethnography, subjectivity and psychosocial rehabilitation. *International Journal of Mental Health, 24,* 82–92.

Fabian, E. S. (1989). Work and the quality of life. *Psychosocial Rehabilitation Journal, 12,* 39–49.

Fabian, E. S. (1992). Longitudinal outcomes in supported employment: A survival analysis. *Rehabilitation Psychology, 37,* 23–33.

Germeroth, D. (1990). *Lonely days and lonely nights: Completing the doctoral dissertation.* Paper presented at the annual meeting of the Speech Communication Association, Chicago. Retrieved May 5, 2002 from URL: www.dept.usm.edu/~idv/html/bibliography/dissertation_process.htm

Gilbert, K. R. (2001). *The emotional nature of qualitative research.* Boca Raton, FL: CRC Press.

Gioia-Hasick, D., & Brekke, J. S. (2003). Use of the Americans with Disabilities Act (ADA) by young adults with schizophrenia: *Psychiatric Services, 54,* 302–04.

Glaser, B. G. (1978). *Theoretical sensitivity.* Mill Valley, CA: The Sociology Press.

Glaser, B. G., & Strauss, A. L. (1967). *The discovery of grounded theory: Strategies for qualitative research.* Chicago: Aldine.

Goldstein, M. J. (1978). Further data concerning the relation between premorbid adjustment and paranoid symptomatology. *Schizophrenia Bulletin, 4,* 236–43.

Harding, C. M., Brooks, G. W., Ashikaga, T., Strauss, J. S., & Breier, A. (1987). The Vermont longitudinal study of persons with severe mental illness: II. Long-term outcome of subjects who retrospectively met DSM-III criteria for schizophrenia. *American Journal of Psychiatry, 144,* 727–35.

Harding, C. M., & Keller, A. B. (1998). Long-term outcome of social functioning. *Handbook of social functioning in schizophrenia.* Needham Heights, MA: Allyn & Bacon.

Harris, M., Bebout, R. R., & Freeman, D. W. (1997). Work stories: Psychological responses to work in a population of dually diagnosed adults. *Psychiatric Quarterly, 68,* 131–53

Jacobs, H., Wissusik, D., Collier, R., & Stackman, D. (1992). Correlations between psychiatric disabilities and vocational outcome. *Hospital and Community Psychiatry, 43,* 365–69.

Kelle, U. (2001). Sociological explanations between micro and macro and the integration of qualitative and quantitative methods. *Forum: Qualitative Social Research, 2.* Retrieved October 26,

2001 qualitative-research.net/fqs-texte/1-01/1-01kelle-e.htm

Kvale, S. (1996). *Interviews: An introduction to qualitative research interviewing.* Thousand Oaks, CA: Sage.

Lehman, A. F. (1988). A quality of life interview for the chronically mentally ill. *Evaluation and Program Planning, 11,* 51–62.

Lent, R. W., & Brown, S. D. (1996). Social cognitive approach to career development: An overview. *The Career Development Quarterly, 44,* 310–21.

Liebow, E. (1993). *Tell them who I am: The lives of homeless women.* New York: The Free Press.

Lincoln, Y. S., & Guba, E. G. (1985). *Naturalistic inquiry.* Thousand Oaks, CA: Sage.

Lofland, J., & Lofland, L. H. (1995). *Analyzing social settings: A guide to qualitative observation and analysis.* Boston: Wadsworth.

Marder, S. R., & Meibach, R. C. (1994). Risperidone in the treatment of schizophrenia. *American Journal of Psychiatry, 151,* 825–35.

Marrone, J., Gandolfo, C., Gold, M., & Hoff, D. (1998). Just doing it: Helping people with mental illness get good jobs. *Journal of Applied Rehabilitation Counseling, 29,* 37–48.

Morse, J. M. (Ed.). (1997). *Completing a qualitative project: Details and dialogue.* Thousand Oaks, CA: Sage.

Mowbray, C. T., Bybee, D., Harris, S. N., & McCrohan, N. (1995). Predictors of work status and future work orientation in people with a psychiatric disability. *Psychiatric Rehabilitation Journal, 19,* 17–28.

Mueser, K. T., Salyers, M. P., & Mueser, P. R. (2001) A prospective analysis of work in schizophrenia *Schizophrenia Bulletin: Special Issue, 27,* 281–96.

Nuechterlein, K. H., Gitlin, M. J., Subotnik, K. L., Bartzokis, G., Fogelson, D. L., Siegel, B. V., & Ventura, J. (May, 2000). Risperidone is associated with better work recovery after onset of schizophrenia. Presented at the 55th Annual Scientific Convention and program of the Society for Biological Psychiatry, Chicago, IL.

Padgett, D. K. (1998). *Qualitative methods in social work research: Challenges and rewards.* Thousand Oaks, CA: Sage.

Padgett, D. K. (January, 2002). Paper presented at Society for Social Work and Research Symposium, San Diego, CA.

Priebe, S., Warner, R., Hubschmid, T., & Eckle, I. (1998). Employment, attitudes toward work, and quality of life among people with schizophrenia in three countries. *Schizophrenia Bulletin, 24,* 469–77.

Reason, P. (1998). Three approaches to participative inquiry. In N. K. Denzin & Y. S. Lincoln (Eds.), *Strategies of qualitative inquiry.* Thousand Oaks, CA: Sage.

Richards, L. (1999). *Using N Vivo in qualitative research.* London: Sage.

Rogers, E. S., Anthony, W. A., Cohen, M., & Davies, R. R. (1997). Prediction of vocational outcome based on clinical and demographic indicators among vocationally ready clients. *Community Mental Health Journal, 33,* 99–112.

Rollins, A. (2000, October). Presentation at 4th Biennial Research Conference on Work: Informing and enhancing employment practices for persons with serious psychiatric disability through research. Philadelphia, PA.

Rosenberg, M. (1965). *Society and the adolescent self image.* Princeton, NJ: Princeton University Press.

Schwandt, T. A. (1997). *Qualitative inquiry: A dictionary of terms.* Thousand Oaks, CA: Sage.

Spitzer, R. L., Endicott, J., & Robins, E. (1978). Research diagnostic criteria: Rationale and reliability. *Archives of General Psychiatry, 35,* 773–82.

Stein, C. H., & Wemmerus, V. A. (2001). Searching for a normal life: Personal accounts of adults with schizophrenia, their parents and well-siblings.

American Journal of Community Psychology, 29, 725–46.

Stein, L. I., Barry, K. L., Van Dien, G., Hollingsworth, E., & Sweeney, J. K. (1999). Work and social support: A comparison of consumers who have achieved stability in ACT and clubhouse programs. *Community Mental Health Journal, 35,* 193–204.

Strauss, A., & Corbin, J. (1990). *Basics of qualitative research: Grounded theory procedures and techniques.* Thousand Oaks, CA: Sage.

Strauss, A., & Corbin, J. (1998). Grounded theory methodology: An overview. In N. K. Denzin & Y. S. Lincoln (Eds.), *Strategies of qualitative inquiry.* Thousand Oaks, CA: Sage.

Strauss, J. S., & Carpenter, W. T. (1972). The prediction of outcome in schizophrenia: I. Characteristics of outcome. *Archives of General Psychiatry, 27,* 739–46.

Strauss, J. S., & Carpenter, W. T. (1974). The prediction of outcome in schizophrenia: II. Relationships between predictor and outcome variables: A report from the WHO International Pilot Study of Schizophrenia. *Archives of General Psychiatry, 31,* 37–42.

Strauss, J. S., & Davidson, L. (1997). Mental disorders, work, and choice. In R. J. Bonnie & J. Monahan (Eds.), *Mental disorder, work disability, and the law.* Chicago: University of Chicago Press.

Super, D. E. (1957). *The psychology of careers: An introduction to vocational development.* New York: Harper & Bros.

Super, D. E. (1963). Vocational development in adolescence and early adulthood: Tasks and behaviors. *Career development: Self-concept theory.* New York: College Entrance Examination Board.

Tashakkori, A., & Teddlie, C. (1998). *Mixed methodology: Combining qualitative and quantitative approaches.* Thousand Oaks, CA: Sage.

Tsang, H., Lam, P., Ng, B., & Leung, O. (2000). Predictors of employment outcome for people with psychiatric disabilities: A review of the literature since the mid '80s. *Journal of Rehabilitation, 66*, 19–31.

Ventura, J., Lukoff, D., Nuechterlein, K. H., Liberman, R. P., Green, M. F., & Shaner, A. (1993). Manual for the expanded brief psychiatric rating scale. *International Journal of Methods in Psychiatric Research, 3*, 221–4.

INTERVIEW GUIDE

I. Questions about work experience (premorbid)
  A. Early occupational goals (establishing one's early identity as a worker)
    1. *Global:* I would like to begin by asking when you first thought about yourself as a person who would work one day? How old were you?
    2. What did you think about doing as a job or career?
    3. *Probes*
      a. How did you come up with the idea?
      b. Did you share it with anyone? (Who?)
      c. Was the response to your idea generally encouraging or discouraging?
      d. Did you experience any guidance or support for this career decision?
        (1) From whom?
        (2) Explore the responses of each person mentioned in the narrative.
  B. Family work ethic and values
    1. *Global:* Did your parents work during your childhood? Tell me briefly about their jobs? What kind of message(s) verbal or nonverbal did they give you about work?
    2. *Probes*
      a. Were there other relatives whose jobs you admired? Tell me about that.
      b. Were there stories about these relatives and their work struggles that became family lore? Who told these work stories and how often were they told?
  C. First job and/or discussion of any jobs held before the illness
    1. *Global:* What was your first job? (Obtain lots of description.)
    2. *Probes*
      a. How did it feel to work for pay? To get your first paycheck?
      b. How long did you keep that job? Did you have any other jobs?
      c. Was the work interesting to you?

II. Questions about work experience (at initial episode and prodrome)
  A. Work status at illness onset
    1. *Global:* Were you working at the time you became ill?

2. *Probes*
   a. How did you handle your symptoms and work?
   b. Did you understand what was happening to you?
   c. Did you leave your job due to your symptoms or to the length of your recovery?
   d. Did anyone help you handle work-related dilemmas (boss, co-worker, family member)?

  B. Expectations about work after illness episode
    1. *Global:* Did you expect that you would be able to work again? (Describe.)
    2. *Probes*
      a. What were you told by your doctor about your work future?
      b. How did that information affect you?
      c. What were you told by your family about work?
      d. Did you apply for benefits right away?

III. Questions about work experience (on-going, recovery stage)
  A. Early phase of recovery
    1. *Global:* At what point in recovery do you remember thinking about work again?
    2. *Probes*
      a. Did you visualize yourself working again or not? How did that feel?
      b. Did your symptoms respond quickly to medication or did it take awhile?
      c. Did you have a job to return to or were you looking for a new job? (Describe.)
      d. What convinced you that you would be ready to work again?
      e. What level of support did you receive from family and professionals about returning to work?

  B. Job seeking
    1. *Global:* What was it like to look for work after dealing with schizophrenia?
    2. *Probes*
      a. How did you motivate yourself to undertake the task of job hunting?
      b. What kinds of difficulties or obstacles did you discover during job hunting?
      c. Did you decide to select a different type of work after your illness?
      d. How did you find the jobs to apply for?
      e. Did you have any help from anyone during your job search? (Explain.)
      f. What was the most useful resource in your job search?

  C. Work Restoration
    1. *Global:* Tell me about the first job you were offered.

2. *Probes*
   a. Did you consider the amount of stress in the job before you agreed to take it?
   b. Did you use any vocational support to obtain the job? (Why or why not?)
   c. Did you disclose your diagnosis to anyone after the job offer? (Tell me about that.)
   d. How were the first few days on the job?

D. On-going work
  1. *Global:* Have you had one or multiple jobs since your diagnosis? (Explain.)
  2. *Probes*
   a. How have you handled the work-versus-benefits issue? Did you lose any benefits?
   b. Have you had periods of unemployment since you began working?
   c. If yes, how did you cope with those periods?
   d. What has been your greatest struggle in your attempts to work?
   e. What or who has been your greatest source of support?
   f. Have negative symptoms (loss of motivation, feelings) been a difficulty at work?
   g. Have positive symptoms such as ongoing auditory hallucinations or delusions made it difficult for you on the job? (Explain.)
   h. How have your relationships been with your co-workers? Your supervisor?
   i. Has it been difficult to fit into the social culture of the workplace? (Explain.)

IV. Personal Attributes
  1. *Global:* What do know about *yourself* that has made it possible for you to work?
  2. *Probes*
   a. Has your view of yourself as a worker changed since becoming ill? (How?)
   b. What does work add to your life?
   c. What would your life be like without work?
   d. Have you developed new coping mechanisms since your return to work?
   e. Is there anything you plan to do differently as you continue to work?
   f. Did you seek out any training to help with your current or future positions?
   g. What have you learned about yourself in the process?

V. Policy Considerations
  1. *Global:* What do you know about policies that protect persons with disabilities in the workplace? Do these laws cover mental disabilities?

2. *Probes*
   a. Have you ever heard of the Americans with Disabilities Act?
   b. Did the employer bring to your attention any information about workplace protections or the ADA (e.g., orientation, pamphlets, handbook)?
   c. Is it important to you that there are workplace policies in place?
   d. Would you know how to ask for an accommodation? How would you do this?
   e. Who would you go to in the company?
   f. What workplace accommodations could you imagine requesting?

LISTSERVS AND WEB ADDRESSES

Web Sites I Have Found Helpful With Mixed Method Discussions and Resources

http://www.qsrinternational.com/resources/publications.asp

http://www.ualberta.ca/~jrnorris/qual.html

http://www.qualitative-research.net/fqs/fqs-eng.htm

http://www.nova.edu/ssss/QR/web.html

http://www.sagepub.co.uk/frame.html?

http://www.sagepub.co.uk/journals/details/j0331.html

I Subscribe to This Listserv from the University of Georgia

QUALRS-L@LISTSERV.UGA.EDU

6

Evaluation Research

AMY BARR

A. A Qualitative Evaluation of a Supported Housing Program for Homeless Persons With Severe Mental Illness

Although homelessness among those with serious psychiatric disorders remains a significant problem in New York City, considerable progress has been made during the past decade in developing a range of supportive housing alternatives that combine principles of community mainstreaming and service integration. The New York/New York Housing Program, enacted in 1990, created over 9000 units of supervised housing for homeless persons with mental illness and an additional 1500 units will be finished by 2004. The addition of these units has played a significant role in bringing the overall shelter census of single adults from a high of 9300 in 1990 to 6778 per night in 1999 (New York State Office of Mental Health, 2000), but an upsurge in the numbers of homeless individuals due to a post-September 11 economic downturn has brought new demands for shelter and affordable housing.

The provision of additional housing units has not met the needs of some homeless persons with mental illness who account for disproportionate amounts of all health care, shelter, and social service spending on the population. Numerous studies show that this relatively small group of homeless persons with mental illness accounts for a large proportion of total public spending for mental health and homeless services in New York City (Brauth, 1995; Salit & Mosso, 1997; Kuhn & Culhane, 1998; Culhane, Metraux, & Hadley, 2001).

The figures are staggering: 7% of mental health service users account for over half of all Medicaid spending for mental health services. The average annual per capita cost for this group is $50,000, three quarters of which is spent on hospitalization (Brauth, 1995). A study of high-cost Medicaid-eligible psychiatric patients treated at New York City's public hospitals (which provide over half of Medicaid-funded inpatient psychiatric treatment in the city) found that the majority were homeless, diagnosed with schizophrenia, and abusing drugs and/or alcohol (Salit & Mosso, 1997). Homeless people with mental illness stay longer in the hospital than their housed peers, largely because of the limited placement options for them. One study showed that the lack of placement options for some homeless patients resulted in a minimum of $17,500 in unnecessary hospitalization costs per admission. It is estimated that homelessness costs New York City's hospitals $100 million per year in preventable medical expenses, more than half of which are incurred by homeless people with mental illness (Salit et al., 1998).

When homeless people with mental illness and/or substance abuse disorders are not in the hospital they face living on the street, in jails, or in shelters. On any day, there are close to 8000 people with mental illness in New York's prisons and jails. Annually, 15,000 persons are treated for mental illness in the city jail on Riker's Island (Barr, 1999).

Homeless people with severe psychiatric problems and histories of drug abuse stay in shelters longer and incur more costs than the non-mentally ill homeless. An analysis indicates that there are three classes of shelter users: transitional, episodic, and chronic. Contrasted with people who have a one-time stay or frequent short stays, chronic shelter users have extremely long stays. Eighty-five percent of these chronic users are diagnosed with mental illness or serious medical problems. Only 10% of users of shelters for single adults account for a majority of all shelter days (Kuhn and Culhane, 1998).

The addition of new supportive housing units and creation of services such as intensive case management and Assertive Community Treatment (ACT) teams have helped many homeless individuals. However, numerous studies suggest that a small group has not been effectively engaged in services and consequently cycles repeatedly through the health care and social service systems. This puzzles clinicians and policy makers alike: Do these people want to stay on the street? Are they "too sick" to accept help unless they are forced to? Is drug use or sociopathy to blame? If they are not willing or able to accept help through the de facto service system, then what do they want?

This report has four sections. This first describes the two different models of housing placement encountered by members of the control and treatment groups to establish a context for the experiences that they discuss. The second section describes our research methods. The third section presents information gathered from our 40 in-depth interviews, and the fourth summarizes the work and presents some conclusions.

MODELS OF CARE FOR HOMELESS
PEOPLE WITH MENTAL ILLNESS

The *linear continuum of care* (the traditional model of services received by the control group) and the *housing-first approach* (received by the treatment group) share the goal of helping people develop the practical, interpersonal, and self-management skills to sustain permanent independent housing within the community. But the two programs differ markedly in how they pursue this goal (Tsemberis, 1999).

Briefly, the continuum of care approach requires consumers to demonstrate *housing readiness* before they are placed into the community. This may include a period of sobriety, compliance with mandatory mental health treatment, and living successfully in supervised congregate housing or single-room occupancy (SRO) situations. In contrast, the housing-first model places homeless individuals with mental illness directly into their own scatter-site apartments within the community and *then* offers them a range of supportive and treatment services based on their own perceived needs and preferences (Carling, 1993).

Most professionals in the field adhere to the continuum of care approach, and this is the model that dominates New York City's service system for homeless mentally ill people. An alternative housing-first approach is taken by Pathways to Housing (PTH), a nonprofit agency based in Harlem. In this program, homeless persons with mental illness and/or substance abuse issues move directly from the street or institutions into scatter-site apartments. Clients are then offered a range of treatment and vocational and supportive services based on self-identified needs and choices. The program is tailored to the so-called hard-core homeless mentally ill, many of whom have already been rejected or have refused services through the traditional model (Tsemberis, 1999).

The New York Housing Study

As noted, the two approaches were part of a randomized trial known as The New York Housing Study (NYHS), which was supported by the New York State Office of Mental Health (OMH), with funding from the Substance Abuse and Mental Health Services Administration (SAMHSA). The target population for the NYHS was the hard-to-reach, dually diagnosed homeless. Specifically, persons were eligible for inclusion if (1) in the prior 30 days, they spent at least 15 days living on the streets or in other public places (shelters did not fulfill this criterion); (2) they showed a period of housing instability over the prior 6 months; and (3) they had a DSM-IV-TR axis I diagnosis. No other clinical or social characteristics such as substance use or criminal history were considered relevant to participation in the study.

Participants were recruited by outreach teams and through referrals from two state psychiatric hospitals. Ninety-nine (44%) were randomly assigned to the Pathways to Housing/Housing First condition (treatment) and 126 (56%)

were assigned to the Treatment as Usual/Linear Continuum of Care condition (control).

The purpose of the NYHS was to compare the two groups with respect to housing stability, substance abuse/treatment utilization, mental health symptomatology/treatment utilization, and ratings of quality of life. Although the study is ongoing, at 24 months the treatment group had spent a greater proportion of time in stable housing (74% versus 34% of their time) (Tsemberis & Eisenberg, 2000). The treatment group also showed a lower rate of heavy alcohol use at 24 months, despite a lower utilization of substance abuse treatment. No significant differences were found between the groups in regard to heavy drug use. There were also no differences between groups for psychiatric treatment utilization or symptoms or in ratings of their quality of life (Tsemberis & Eisenberg, 2000). In summary, the NYHS demonstrated that the Pathways to Housing model increased the proportion of time individuals spent in stable housing without increasing drug or alcohol use or psychiatric symptoms.

METHODS

In selecting participants, we might have drawn 20 individuals at random from each of the two groups. However, we elected to sample from the treatment group at random, but draw a stratified quota sample from the control group. This choice emanated from our goal of eliciting perspectives from control group members who were at various points in the service system as they were experiencing them. Within the control group, five participants were recruited from each of these strata: (1) literally homeless, (2) depending on shelters, drop-in centers, and other forms of crisis-based housing, (3) transitional living (group homes) arrangements, and (4) in permanent residences (their own apartments).

As participants in the NYHS, participants talked with staff by phone on a monthly basis. Between June and December 2001, staff inquired whether participants might be interested in participating in our study of homelessness. Those who agreed were given a telephone number to call to schedule an informational meeting. As the quota in each of the strata was filled, that group was closed to referrals.

Initial meetings were held at either the Pathways to Housing Program offices in Harlem or in mutually agreed upon locations in the field. Participants had the opportunity to review the proposed study verbally and in writing and were given the opportunity to discuss any questions or concerns they had. They were given a copy of the consent form for review and discussion prior to signing. They were also given a copy before participation began and offered the option of being interviewed at that time or setting up an appointment at a later time. During the course of the consent process participants were informed, "This is a study to learn more about the experiences you have had as a homeless person in New York City and about your opinions regarding the mental health, substance abuse and social services programs you have had contact with." Participants also agreed to allow us to have access to quantitative data from the NYHS study.

Participants were paid an honorarium of $28 for their time and transportation costs. Data collection, which was carried out from June to December 2001, involved in-depth open-ended interviews. Interviews were audio taped with permission of the participants. All participants were assured confidentiality, that their participation would not affect the services they were receiving, and that the tapes would be available to the study team only. Interviews lasted approximately 1½ hours.

The interview guide consisted of five sections (pp. 143–146). Participants were asked to give basic demographic information, such as where they were born, age, marital status, educational history, and work history. Next, they were asked to describe in detail their current residential status, including the circumstances that led up to the particular placement or condition and their opinions about housing status. They were then asked to describe the residential status that they felt best suited their needs and what obstacles they felt prevented them from securing such a placement, including both internal and external factors. At the conclusion of the interview, participants were asked to describe their goals in life in whatever manner they chose. The interviews were conducted using an unstructured format giving respondents the opportunity to talk about what they chose without being led to respond in a specific direction.

Interviews were taped and transcribed verbatim. The researchers coded the transcripts to identify themes related to factors contributing to success or failure in achieving residential stability. Examples of phenomena were collected and analyzed in an effort to find commonalities and differences within and between the two groups.

To reduce bias, negative cases from both groups (people who disliked or had been asked to leave the Pathways program and people who found permanent housing through the traditional system) were examined.

FINDINGS

Access to Services

Participants in both groups reported that to achieve housing stability in the community they needed financial and practical assistance to obtain necessary resources, including assistance with rent vouchers and money management. They wanted these services without the mandate of treatment or required periods of residence in transitional housing programs. But they also knew that these services were extremely difficult to access through a public mental health system characterized by bureaucratic inefficiency, scarce resources, and long waiting periods. A 50-year-old man in the control group with a history of severe depression and alcoholism put it this way:

> "I just wish things could move. There is so much paperwork. It makes
> people give up. It takes too long. I hope they find a way around that.
> Housing . . . mental health, in everything. That's why people give up.
> You gotta go here, you gotta go there. These people are sick. They don't
> have that energy. Sometimes there's a lack of understanding. These people
> don't have energy to go through all this."

Extended stays in shelters and other crisis-based housing while participating in prescribed treatment protocols is usually necessary before resources can be mobilized and placement is offered. Case management loads are high and attention to individual needs and preferences inadequate. Many participants in the control group reported these environments compromised their need for independence and safety. Consequently, they continually cycled in and out of shelters and other crisis-based housing or they resisted engagement in the system entirely. As one man stated: "They have an open door policy. Really a revolving door policy. You just keep going round and round and it's on you. It's really a spirit of you have to help yourself. And if you fail for any reason, it's you that failed."

The Pathways to Housing program offered immediate placement and coordination of benefits and ongoing support with practical needs and money management. Once financial access to housing is secured, participants are more receptive to other services such as mental health or substance abuse treatment. Members of the control group felt that they were offered services they did not need or services they were unwilling or unable to take advantage of while homeless.

Housing Preferences

Participants reported they wanted the option of living alone, without intensive supervision, and in mainstream housing. Autonomy, privacy, and choice were central to their decisions to accept or remain in housing. The majority of transitional housing placements participants were offered while they were homeless did not conform to these preferences. As one control group participant stated:

> "I just really need a place to stay. I really need to be left alone. Just require
> being more independent. It wasn't a problem being with the mentally ill.
> I felt like I was being guarded, being watched. I was always being
> rehearsed. It was very uncomfortable to me. It wasn't a favorable living
> situation at all."

Participants also reported a preference for separation of treatment and housing. Placement in transitional residences required compliance with medication as well as mandated mental health and substance abuse treatment. As one man explained:

> "It was hard for me to get accepted by certain places cause I wouldn't take
> medication. I got kicked out of places 'cause I wouldn't take it. A lot of

places, even program, day programs, it's hard to get accepted. They want to slap me on medication they don't know me from a hole in the wall. I feel like I am a rabbit or a guinea pig in a science experiment."

Participants resisted "mental health housing" because they felt it increased stress and stigma and put them at greater risk of discrimination in the larger community. As one woman who lived in a supervised home reported:

"In the neighborhood I've been spit at, and everything else. It's coming from the fact that I'm a mental patient. People look down on mental patients for some reason. We don't have our rights or something. People at the grocery store take advantage of you. They give you the incorrect change. They feel like they can get away with it."

In contrast, participants in Pathways appreciated the anonymity and freedom they experienced in the program. As one participant stated:

"I feel I'm just part of everything that's okay. Or what seems to be okay. I don't think I would want to live around other people in the program. Or in the same apartment as people in the program."

Another participant discussed the benefits of living stably in the community:

"I have roots. I have a community that's mine, or I feel that's mine, where I belong. I feel comfortable there. It's a great feeling. But you don't know about it till you lived it. In other words, you probably grew up in a well-established area. You feel at home there. If I took you out of the area you would feel the difference. But if you never had an area, you don't know you're homeless. Now I know what the benefits are."

Feelings About Mental Health
and Substance Abuse Treatment

Participants indicated housing and practical assistance should come prior to, or at least in conjunction with, treatment. They also wanted to have a greater voice in decisions about their mental health and substance abuse treatment, saying that they felt more capable of taking advantage of treatment if not in "survival mode."

Having a choice about participating in treatment did not mean that they would reject it. As one man said:

"That's why I like Pathways. House people first. How can you help people if they are out there? When you house a person you put him together then you can deal with him piece by piece. When he's out there, he's not together. He is in pieces. And you don't know which you can deal with. When you house him you get to know him. Then you deal with him. If he has a drinking problem deal with that. If he has a mental health problem deal with that. That's why people like it here."

Pathways participants also reported that the stability and sense of responsibility they gained through living independently had a positive effect on their mental health. One man reported:

> "I can kind of know now when I'm headed towards a depression and I have a choice . . . It's gotten a lot better. For a long time I would go through periods when depression would just descend on me and I just became immobilized and kind of dead feeling. I didn't want to deal with anything. It's still kind of a mystery to me but it's better. It's a lot better than it was. Now I feel like there's a choice about giving into it or not."

Quality of Life

While homeless, participants reported their all-encompassing concern was with daily survival and shelter needs. The hopelessness and shame they experienced prevented them from setting goals, investing in their own futures, and refraining from self-destructive behaviors. One man explained:

> "It's a syndrome. I know one guy who says he isn't good enough to be with other people. The real street people, I mean there were people at (the shelter) we had to toilet train they had been on the street so long. People who were living there would help them delouse. When I was at (the shelter) I thought if I get out of here I'm never coming back. I think some people had been there, left and came back. For some people that was the pattern. Something they were used to. They were too tired to go any further. They had given up hope."

Once removed from the shelter environment, participants reported they could begin to hope for a future. As one Pathways participant reported:

> "It's a lot easier to make friends, have a job, whatever. You get a little bit of the criteria of what people expect from normal people: a fairly decent place to live, your own money, a job. From there, people can do just about anything they want."

Once housed, the participants assigned to Pathways were able to look beyond daily needs for food, shelter, sleep, and safety. They reported engaging in a variety of new activities such as self-reflection, education, work, and creative pursuits. As one man summarized:

> "I want to go back to school. Maybe get off social services. I don't know. I've just started thinking about it. It took a couple of years after getting out of (the shelter) just to get out of survival mode. There was still that fatality about things."

Another participant discussed how his life changed for the better after he moved into an apartment:

> "Being by yourself, having your apartment, you settle down and it's yours. You could sit back and be like, this is mine. I went through a lot to get

this. How was my life back then? It was bad. How can I make it better? How I thought I could make it better was going to school. That's the first thing. Going to college."

SUMMARY AND CONCLUSIONS

These study findings suggest that individuals engaged in the Pathways program because they were offered the necessary resources and supports without a long wait or complicated bureaucratic procedures and without having to yield control over their own lives. They stayed in the program because it offered them what they felt they needed on their own terms.

All participants reported that they wanted independent housing in the community, and that given the proper supports they could retain their housing despite their mental health or substance abuse problems. They were not homeless because they wanted to be; they simply had no place to live safely and comfortably.

The process of meeting housing readiness criteria through the traditional model took too long and conflicted with fundamental values held by many. While they waited, individuals gave up, dropped out, or otherwise remained at the mercy of a system that they felt diminished them and kept them from becoming active participants in their own lives. They reported feeling hopeless and like they were "in the military," "being punished," or seen as "animals."

In the quantitative portion of the NYHS study, responses to a measure of quality of life showed no differences between the groups. This was in sharp contrast to what was revealed in the interviews. Out of 20 people in the control group, 19 reported their only goal was to "get an apartment of their own."

Participants in the treatment group had an apartment and their goals encompassed work, education, and realization of creative pursuits like painting and writing poetry. This difference was manifested in the tone and nuances of their speech, their eye contact, and even in their dress. It was also manifested in their ability to look back and reflect on their lives. As one Pathways to Housing tenant stated:

> "One year of college. Then this homeless thing happened. Like I said I was homeless for 18 years. That basically was my career. It always stands a grim reminder that some people had a career in the last 10, 20 years. I had a career of being homeless. I had that as a career instead of a career. I spent 18 years doing that. Now I spent the last 3 years, I like to think of it as a resurrection. But I had a 20-year career of being homeless. I can't do anything about that except look to the future."

As the participants in our study made clear, mental illness and substance abuse present harrowing challenges. But their stories suggest that clinicians and policy makers need to reexamine assumptions about what severely mentally ill people with substance abuse problems can and cannot accomplish given these challenges. As this study shows, these clients wanted to be moved directly into their own apartments in the community with minimal requirements. The quantitative evaluation of the Pathways to Housing program demonstrated that this can be done, and that it can work. Our findings shed light on how and why supported housing can make a difference.

Yet, for many service providers and policy makers, allowing homeless people with mental illness and substance abuse problems to live in the community without restrictions is nearly unthinkable. This creates a cycle in which the lack of support for such programs limits awareness of their potential (Pathways accounts for just 400 of the 10,500 supportive housing units in New York State).

Providers as well as politicians express concern about threats to public safety posed by housing these clients on their own with minimal supervision. However, as one Bellevue Hospital clinician observed, "The Pathways approach can't be less safe than letting these people continue to deteriorate in the streets. Right now there are virtually no good options available for them." The clinician further noted that an expansion of the Pathways program could enable Bellevue to discharge over half of its homeless mentally ill patients with substance abuse problems immediately; they have been medically stabilized and are awaiting placement.

In recent years, there has been increased awareness of the presence of this core group of clients that the public mental health service system has left behind. The lack of housing options for this group has taken its toll in human costs and in the costs incurred by excessive hospitalizations, public shelters, and incarceration. As one member of the control group noted, "[the system] has been afraid to take a chance on people like me." The findings from this qualitative evaluation build on the quantitative findings in demonstrating that policy makers and clinicians need to reconsider taking those chances.

B. The Angels Are Breaking
Their Wings

THE BACKGROUND OF MY STUDY

I interviewed 40 people for this study. For 10 years before that, I shuttled homeless people with mental illness in and out of psychiatric units and drug treatment centers with their belongings in trash bags. I did this study because I thought I could help make things better for them. On some days I was so full of these people, so occupied with the sadness or triumphs they shared with me that I thought of nothing else; I felt that their stories lived in me.

I saw myself as a researcher, getting the truth out or bearing witness, and it was an exhausting and exciting mission. I can still see every one of their faces, recall the way they sat or made a joke as if they were sitting in front of me now. They haunt me in a way, perhaps because nothing has turned out quite the way I imagined it would. During the 10 years I worked in an emergency room and through 2 years of setting up this study and gathering data, I swore many times that I would do them justice. I was going to do something to make their lives better. Research is a painfully slow process.

Years ago, when I was a social worker in the psychiatric emergency service of a large urban hospital, I met a man named Warren. They called Warren a *frequent flyer* because he seemed to spend more time in the hospital, or at least in the emergency room, than anywhere else. I got to know Warren. He came to the hospital to get his medicine, to get out of the rain, or for a sandwich and some conversation. I was the one he came to for help. Most of the time he was not admitted. His usual complaint, that he saw angels falling to earth, did not meet criteria for an admission to the psych unit. So he came to visit for while and then I sent him back out. Warren did not have a home. I do not know where he slept.

Warren was a big man, but he was shy and awkward and spoke in a whispery voice. He was full of secrets. You had to lean over to hear him and sometimes he giggled at his own private jokes with his hands over his mouth like a little boy. One day I asked him, "Why does seeing angels bother you? Aren't they beautiful?" Warren edged closer to me and whispered, "They're breaking their wings."

Warren had schizophrenia; he had it since he was a teenager. Sometimes he tested positive for cocaine, sometimes he did not. He smoked cigarettes until they burned his fingertips and you had to take them out of his hand and put them out. He sang songs he made up that were so sweet and filled with sorrow you wanted to cry. I never really learned much about his history or how he lived when he was not with me in the emergency room. His story changed every time I saw him.

I liked to think that there were people throughout the social service system of the city looking out for Warren. Sometimes he would show up with a new pair of sneakers or a jacket. He seemed to have no contact with family anywhere and no friends. We were his friends.

If Warren had any place where he felt at home it was probably the hospital waiting room. He had spent his life in and out of institutions of various sorts, and he had been to prison for something or other, so they said. I liked Warren. He was gentle to me, and so lost and alone. I worked in the ER screening patients until I was 8 months pregnant and Warren followed me around to make sure nobody hit me. "Just watching your back Mama," he would say. I tried to look out for him too, getting him a bed when he really looked bad; sneaking sandwiches and juice packs into his pockets when he was hungry. That was the best I could do for him. It was not nearly enough.

Managed care had taken over by then and hospital stays were short, 3 days at the most. Sometimes care managers made patients sleep in what they called 24-hour chairs (four men and women in one room divided by a curtain) to save money. Nothing was accomplished in 24 hours. It was just 24 hours out of hell before you got sent back. After he was discharged, Warren was placed in a number of "adult homes" and he would run away or get kicked out within a week. He did not like sharing a room; the place was filthy and had mice; they would not let him smoke cigarettes; the food was bad; he had a fight with the day nurse because he said she treated him like a child. "I'm a man," Warren explained, "I need to live like a man."

People like Warren made everybody mad. "He couldn't be helped," they all said, and he was not. They gave him more medication, more groups, another placement. Nobody asked what he wanted. I had no perfect answers. The mental health system has so many tangled arms I could not begin to think I could sort it all out. But Warren and I were stuck in the middle of it, and it was slowly killing him. After awhile it started to tear out something in me.

We had a really bad winter one year. It seemed to snow all the time. The emergency room stayed crowded and at some point the administration decided that Warren should not come by anymore. I was "only encouraging him" they said. Those sandwiches were for "real patients." Warren was a "resource drain."

I did not see him for months and when I finally did he limped down the corridor leaning on a cane. His feet had frozen and thawed so many times that his feet were riddled with gangrene and he could not walk right. He was dirty and smelled like urine and he muttered to himself. He would not look at me at all. He was admitted to the unit and he broke another patient's arm in a fight and he spent 72 hours in restraints. He was put on a "do not admit" list.

The last time he came in he did not seem to know who I was. Hospital security chased him out of the waiting room and into the street. I never saw him again.

I knew a lot of people like Warren through my work at the hospital. They drifted around and then they just disappeared. Some got lucky; most did not. We treat them at best like errant children or patients and at worst like criminals. We shuffle them in and out of sad places and then throw up our arms in surprise and blame them when they do not get better. I thought that many of the people who were making crucial decisions about "what Warren needed" never knew him as anything more than a diagnosis code and a long unpaid bill. I have seen the places he was sent to live, and I have wandered through the shelters he slept in and visited him in jail. They were not places I would want to call home. I saw the medication bottles rattle out of his pockets and hit the table so I could carry them to security (again). There was nothing I could give Warren in the hospital that could make him better because when he got out, he had nowhere to go. Warren did not want or need another prescription; he wanted a place he could feel at home in. It seemed to me to be a terrible and wasteful way to do business and I did not want to be part of it anymore. So I left.

In the fall of 2000, I went back to school to study health policy and management at New York University's Robert F. Wagner School of Public Service. I studied statistics, finance, and political theory so I could make sense of some of the information that was available about homeless people with mental illness and the different types of housing programs that were available to them. I took a course in the philosophy of qualitative research, but never had coursework or experience in the methods. Meanwhile, I went to conferences, read the newspaper, did literature searches, and read death reports from the New York State Commission on Quality of Care (the government watchdog group that investigates allegations of abuse and neglect in adult homes for the mentally ill.)

In the winter of 1999, I followed the murder trial of Andrew Goldstein after he had pushed Kendra Webdale in front of a New York City subway train during a psychotic episode. He too had been in and out of many programs—he could not get the help he needed from them. As a response to the death of Ms. Webdale, The New York State Legislature passed Kendra's Law, which essentially added nothing to available programs except a court mandate that clients had to accept them or get locked up. It seemed a very misguided response to a tragic occurrence. Did we really want to criminalize mental illness? Wasn't there a better way? The New York State budget for mental health services alone surpassed $4 billion, more than the gross national product of some countries.

I read two great articles at that time, one a feature story that appeared in *The New York Times Sunday Magazine* entitled "Bedlam on the Streets" (Winerip, 1999) and the other was a report on homelessness and the institutional circuit (Hopper et al., 1997). Both poignantly described the inadequacy of the current public mental health system and inspired me to study it further. I came back to my memories of the frequent flyers of the emergency room again and again from different angles and tried to understand the different pressures that created and sustained the different systems designed to serve them. I tried to find a focus and a means to study it as part of my pursuit of a master's degree in public health policy.

THE METHOD OF INQUIRY:
GENERAL AND APPLIED

I thought qualitative methods would be well suited to my goals. I had been telling stories about the men and women I met in the emergency room for years. My only plan when the study started was to give homeless people with mental illness the opportunity to tell their own stories and formally document them. I chose qualitative methods because they seemed a way to keep people whole in documenting their experiences about why programs did or did not work for them and what they thought would help.

I wanted to give outsiders an opportunity to see the mental health system from an insider's perspective. This perspective had to be presented in a way that was credible and grounded in facts that were readily digestible so people would listen. The statistics were well documented—the growing numbers of people with mental illnesses in jails, in and out of hospitals, on the street, in the shelters—the budgets for homeless and mental health services that went up and up. I was not interested in generating more numbers. I wanted to portray real people in trouble.

My graduate advisor at NYU, Dr. Jan Blustein, introduced me to Sharon Salit, a senior grant analyst at the United Hospital Fund. Sharon was very passionate about moving a qualitative study like mine forward. Her own research on high-cost users of mental health services in the New York City public hospital system and her previous work in that system had convinced her of the timeliness and the necessity of understanding more about this population from a new perspective. Jan had recently completed a qualitative study on another topic sponsored by United Hospital Fund and her reputation as a research scientist was well known and respected by senior staff at the foundation. After discussing the project at length with me, she agreed to supervise a study and ensure that the project was carried out in accordance with high standards of ethical, fiscal, and scientific responsibility. The fulfillment of this supervisory role by Dr. Blustein was a critical factor in the project eventually receiving funding. The three of us—Sharon, Jan, and I—worked together to get the project off the ground.

We originally attempted to have a large public hospital in New York City agree to sponsor the study, but after a long process of trying to get Institutional Review Board (IRB) approval from that institution, the deal fell through. At around the same time, Sharon introduced me to Dr. Sam Tsemberis, founder and Executive Director of Pathways to Housing, Inc. As it turned out, there was an immediate opportunity to piggyback a qualitative study onto a randomized trial of the Pathways program that was nearing the end of a four-year, federally funded grant studying over 200 Pathways and control group participants.

Doctor Tsemberis was interested in enriching the evaluation of his program by adding qualitative data to provide greater depth and explanatory power. He had seen many homeless, mentally ill individuals enter his program since its founding in 1993 and had found the changes remarkable. However, although it appeared from preliminary analyses of the data that differences in housing stability were significant and positively related to participation in the Pathways program (the experimental condition), efforts to distinguish the quality of life of program participants in the experimental and control groups had not been fruitful.

Pathways operated according to a completely different paradigm from the majority of programs in the public mental health system. Although numerical measures demonstrated success in keeping residents housed without associated increases in substance abuse or psychiatric symptoms, Pathways was still met with considerable resistance from mental health care providers. Outsiders to the program had real fears about what went on in tenant's apartments when they were not being supervised closely or made to comply with recommendations for mental health or substance abuse treatment. The idea that homeless people with severe mental illness and substance abuse disorders could be placed in independent apartments in the community without restrictions and not self-destruct was simply foreign to providers. By adding qualitative data to the evaluation, Dr. Tsemberis hoped to answer questions about how the program worked.

Piggybacking on a study already underway had considerable benefits. Our study team had access not only to a large, randomized sample of participants, but also 3 years' worth of quantitative data about program outcomes, including how many days participants slept in a shelter or were hospitalized for psychiatric reasons or for substance abuse treatment.

Because the facts of their lives had been documented, I had the freedom to design a qualitative addendum that could capture the lived experience of participants. Clearly, two people in two different programs can each drink three beers in a month, have four therapy appointments, and one overnight stay in a hospital, yet have a completely different experience or quality to their lives. I wanted to look at this kind of difference.

From the initiation through completion of the study, I consulted with experienced researchers in several disciplines who helped me frame the project, develop a sampling strategy, gather and understand the data, and write and edit the final report. I used successful grant proposals as models for my own, had experienced researchers walk me through the IRB reviews, asked for recommendations for relevant literature, and sent out drafts of everything I wrote asking for comments and suggestions. The opportunity to utilize the skills, experience, and expertise of others was tremendously helpful to me.

DEVELOPING THE INTERVIEW PROTOCOL

The interview questions were developed with consideration for (1) what had already been asked in the quantitative study, (2) how it had been asked, and (3) what had already been found. The quantitative interview was an exhaustive structured questionnaire that took several hours to be administered. We developed the qualitative protocol by addressing the same question (does the program work?) from a different perspective: that of the consumer.

I did not ask specifically about the program at all or about participation in treatment for drug abuse. Participants were told on the consent form, "This is a study to learn more about the experiences you have had as a homeless person in New York City and about your opinions regarding the mental health, substance abuse and social service programs you have had contact with." After that I asked, "Why don't you start by telling me how old you are and where you were born."

With some participants I did not have to ask another question over the course of a two-hour interview. People talked about what was important to them and they often talked about housing. They also talked about how their lives were shaped by having a home or not, or being in a particular program or not.

During the pilot study, the interview format went through several changes as we discussed how structured or unstructured it should be. My own style of interviewing is to offer very little structure. I do not like asking predetermined questions because I think it leads people to talk about what I think is relevant, but not necessarily what they think is important. The goal of this study was to offer a consumer perspective of why a program did or did not help them stay housed, and the effect that housing stability or instability had on them. Although the pilot interview was much more structured, I found that it had too many questions and I spent a lot of time looking at my list of questions and less time really listening to the natural unfolding of the participant's contributions. In other words, my questions got in the way.

However, I did find that without some kind of outline, I forgot to address certain topics altogether. I worked well with a list of domains that I thought of as points I wanted to cover in the interview. It was not necessary in this case to have a lot of questions. In the end my cheat sheet had five domains I wanted to address, including demographics and four questions: Where are you living now? Where would you like to be living? What are your obstacles? What are your goals? Because most specific questions about use of services and treatment had already been asked in the quantitative interviews, this interview offered participants the space and time to talk about what had not been asked.

I found that participants wanted to talk and were forthcoming about their experiences; interviewing was a joy to me. The idea that people with mental illness could not or would not offer valuable information about their own experiences was completely unfounded.

I also found that when my colleagues on the study read the transcripts they were surprised by the content: the interviews offered something new, something unexpected. Many people commented on how "articulate" the participants were, and it was true.

ENTERING THE FIELD AND INTERVIEWING

People in an agency (or a hospital or a school) are working. I remember scores of bright-eyed and bushy-tailed medical students with pen and paper in hand taking up space in the emergency room and how irritated I was with them. When I went into the field to begin the study, I considered myself an unwanted distraction and in the way. I tried to be not only as unobtrusive as possible, but capable of adding something positive to the environment.

I brought treats and was respectful of the space, additional energy, and time I was requiring from agency staff. It helped that the participants seemed to enjoy being interviewed, and left the room smiling and shaking my hand. When I returned, participants who were at the agency for other matters called out to me to say hello. If not a happy addition, I was at least an innocuous presence.

It was also assumed that because I had experience with the homeless I would be able to handle myself appropriately. The agency personnel ultimately could not have been more helpful, friendly, or enthusiastic about helping me out and I could not be more grateful to them.

In regard to interviewing, I had had some practice. My job as a clinician in the psychiatric emergency room was to get the story. People who arrive in the emergency room are usually in some sort of crisis. They are scared, frazzled, and often in pain. As a social worker, I needed to gather a great deal of information quickly, toss out parts of the story that seemed irrelevant, and pass on the rest of the information in a way that someone else could understand and use. I was not the person patients came to for fixing, forgiveness, or salvation. I just listened and documented information. I must have spoken to thousands of people over the years; I was very comfortable in that role.

Perhaps the most important skill I learned in the emergency room (relevant to my work as a qualitative researcher) was how to make people feel safe enough to open up: You take the time to look people in the eye, listen carefully to what they are saying, and demonstrate you are listening with an attentive stance and gentle probes when appropriate. Interviewing is different from regular social interaction in that the conversation has a specific goal: to gather information. For this reason, I occasionally had to interrupt or move the conversation in a different direction. However, this had to be done without allowing the participant to feel cut off or pushed around. My guidance had to be unobtrusive, and this takes practice.

In the past I had experienced occasional difficulty in drawing someone out. I was not flustered by individuals who had unusual ways of expressing themselves or interacting socially. I was also, sadly, very familiar with the level of pain many of them had endured in their lives. There is a way you listen to horrible stories when they are all new to you, but then you reach a point where you have heard so many of them that they run together like paint.

I used to cry in the car on the way home when I first started working in the emergency room. After a while I did not cry anymore, although I would like to feel that I still heard people, and that their pain still resonated with me. I developed professional boundaries. I also became aware that there are certain kinds of stories I cannot listen to over and over again. My own level of professional detachment was something I considered when I decided to start qualitative interviewing. This is research, not therapy and not friendship (although it feels a little like both sometimes). I was not fixing anybody. I was not there to save the day; I could not. But it is hard not to become immersed in the lives you are learning about. You have to be careful not to drown.

It was good for me to have been an interview subject before I started listening to the stories of others. I had experienced being interviewed in a manner that was unpleasant and diminishing and I was not going to do that to my participants. I was aware of being seen as the researcher and therefore as a person with power. I drew upon my own previous experiences and recalled feelings of wanting to please, fear of reprisal, wanting to be understood, and perhaps most importantly, wanting to have the intimate details of my life respected and handled gently. I thought having people tell me their stories was as a gift, which takes courage and trust to give. Accepting this gift demanded both gratitude and sensitivity. I always ended my interviews by saying thank you (and meaning it).

I know that sometimes when my respondents talked about their lives they relived them in the telling. They felt sad, they got angry. They may have gone home and been unable to sleep, because it all came back—because I asked them to bring it back. I had to sit with that. One woman spoke at length about her history of abuse, although I tried to move her on to other topics. She was crying and it was hard for her to talk about her memories, but she used them as a way to help me understand how much better her life had become in the Pathways program. Whenever I opened doors, I tried to gently close them. I tried to have people walk away from me with their defenses back in place. I never knew what was waiting for them after they left the interview.

Respondents asked for sandwiches, packs of cigarettes, and help getting a new case manager. Most had so little and I always walked away with so much. It made me feel guilty, unjust somehow. Still, it was important to set firm guidelines about what my role was in their lives, which was someone who would document their words. I think because I was very clear about this, my participants accepted it and felt that the opportunity to reveal themselves was enough to make it worthwhile. The money offered as compensation was certainly welcome, but I do not believe that participants spoke to me just for the money.

ISSUES OF RACE, GENDER, AND SOCIAL CLASS

There were great interviews and difficult ones, but I do not see the outcome as dependent on the outward similarities between the participant and me. It seems, in fact, a false assumption that, because I share a certain race, age, gender, or socioeconomic background with someone, I will understand them. I interviewed people with severe mental illness who had lived on the street, the majority of whom were men of color in their 30s and 40s. Our pasts and our current circumstances were very different. However, I do not think these differences impeded our exchange.

Qualitative research is a sense-making process no matter who you are interviewing. We all get hurt and feel lonely at times. And we have all felt the pure delight of connecting with another person or doing something well. These are the commonalities that I drew upon, but I was only trying to come close enough. You cannot crawl inside.

Some differences inspired anger and distrust, even momentary hatred. This study overlapped with the September 11 terrorist attacks on the World Trade Center. Remarking on my race, one African American man said to me,

> "I hope you don't get upset, but people die everyday. I have been inside the WTC and seen how humongously big that place was. And I can

imagine the day that it crumbled with all those people in there that died. The majority of them White. Cause see, all the wrong that White people have done to Blacks, it's coming back on ya'll. You all get killed in multitudes."

This was said to me 1 week after my husband ran toward the Brooklyn Bridge covered in ashes. What did I say? Nothing. I just listened.

When respondents talked about alcohol and drug abuse or mental health treatment they often said, "You don't know anything about this." They made assumptions based on my appearance and my affiliation with a large university. Sometimes they were not very nice about it. Once when I asked a question a man responded, "You must be stupid." Perhaps the most negative reactions I received were for being a social worker, a profession some saw as populated by miserable, judgmental, inept people who made a living exploiting the miseries of others. But I reminded myself that these reactions were not about me; I was just the wall on which these images were projected. I used these reactions as a way to understand what it is like to be in their world. If I felt bullied, small, or embraced, I used that information to understand what they might have felt.

ANALYSIS AND FINDINGS

Recruitment went smoothly; so did the interviews. The study hummed along with great promise. Although I originally planned to conduct 50 interviews, I ended up doing 40. *Saturation* aptly describes what happened after 6 months in the field. Interviews seemed to give more of the same information. I was also tired. As themes and patterns became clear, the interviews started to feel redundant.

Making sense of the data was where I had the most difficulty. It was like I was in a car speeding down the highway toward an eagerly anticipated destination when I ran off the road. I had 40 great interviews and not the foggiest idea of how to make sense of them.

I did the interviews and transcribing myself, enabling me to know the material I had gathered extremely well. Listening to the tapes, I saw every interviewee as a whole person sitting in front of me. I knew where every great quote was and who said it. I had met with participants in the two groups and saw how starkly different they were. I read the transcripts and reread them and marked them up and then started over again with clean copies. I coded with 10 different themes in mind, and when the pages were full of multicolored sticky tabs I tore them all out. Once I concretized my ideas in specific codes they seemed wrong. It was an amazing amount of paper to sort through. I felt I did not know how to make sense of it. Or, perhaps I did not know how to put my observations into words that would make sense to anyone else.

The interviews were transcribed verbatim, although it was ultimately what was not said that most impressed me. I interviewed one man in a basement shelter in lower Manhattan. The floor was crowded with people sitting in old chairs with all their belongings falling out of bags at their feet. It was dark and the place smelled sour and mildewy. Most residents seemed to be staring out into space and I could not find a staff member anywhere. The din of the small space was miserable. When I finally found a social worker, she had no record of my appointment or even of the resident I was supposed to meet. "Who? There's nobody here by that name" (he had been there almost a year).

It turned out he was there after all, a smiling gentleman with a briefcase sitting at an empty table. It was so dirty I did not want to sit down. It was a place I did not want to spend an hour in, let alone a year. Yet when I asked the man what he thought of it he said, "The accommodations are very nice, very pleasant." This is what was picked up on the tape.

Yet it was the face of this man and all the others crowded into and forgotten in this sad, dirty place that stayed with me. He seemed so confused, so helpless to alter his circumstances, so resigned to this fate that had left him in such a dark place. He had been sleeping sitting up in a chair for over a year, using his sneakers as a pillow so nobody would steal them. He kept telling me he was there because he was "a schizophrenic" as if that was the way schizophrenics must live. Yet he just waited patiently. He talked about waiting for permission to live in society again, for the day that someone would tell him he was okay and he could resume life along with the rest of us. He said, "one day they award you." He had no fight in him—he was thankful for being given anything at all. It was deeply troubling, but it was not said aloud. I wanted to pluck him right out of there and take him somewhere (anywhere) else.

Later on in the study, I could tell as soon as I saw a participant whether he was a Pathways person or a control group member, even though I knew the participants had been randomly assigned and had started off in the same place.

Those in the Pathways program had developed a sense of themselves as having a place in the world that mattered. For a long time I thought it was the apartment itself, but participants kept telling me, "It's just an apartment." The change in the participants seemed to come about not just because they had been given an apartment, but because they had assumed a role in relation to their own lives based on personal choice. They were treated like adults, not like patients or children or animals, as some of the control participants compared themselves to. They were in control of the decisions being made about their lives and restored to a place where they could have some dignity.

I thought of how many times a Pathways person said *I* rather than *they* during an interview, made a joke, or talked about personal goals. I thought about the friendships they had been able to make or artistic pursuits they had begun. One man talked about cleaning the apartment of another Pathways tenant who was less capable, and how proud he was that he finally was useful to someone. I remembered how a respondent walked into the room, challenged something I said, or looked me in the eye during an interview. The people who had been in the Pathways program got something by being in that program that changed the quality of their lives. One man called it a "resurrection."

Something happened inside the Pathways program, but it did not happen in a way that could be captured easily in words and certainly not in numbers. A special community had been created, a community tied together by wellness, not sickness. Not everyone benefited; some were too ill to take charge of their lives. But even they looked back on the Pathways program as a grand and missed opportunity. I felt sorry for the people who were not given the chance to be there at all.

Respondents in the control group seemed to live in an environment where their individuality was routinely ignored, or at least was seen as secondary to their sicknesses. Theirs was a world in which they were asked to play no meaningful part, just to accept blindly what was given (or taken away). Once they became "sick," the life they had known was gone. They entered a new world, a shadow world, where the days ran into each other. Nothing expected, nothing gained.

As a qualitative researcher I felt I had the capacity to take all this in but I did not know how to bring it back out. I felt as if policy makers would have to meet all 40 participants and spend the day with them to even begin to understand. I hated the idea of flattening any of these wonderfully full human beings into paper.

CONCLUSION AND RECOMMENDATIONS

The man I spoke to in the shelter is probably still there, waiting patiently, the despair palpable around him in that airless space. All over the city, people sleep in chairs, on subway platforms, and in hospital beds. Some wake up every day to lives of misery, and there is nothing I am going to do about it today. Research is a slow, methodical process and it takes time for our work, no matter how laborious, to circle back and make a difference. It is hard to know this and keep plugging away.

There are programs like Pathways that demonstrate that something better is possible. Part of doing this project was recognizing that just because you know something is wrong and have an opinion about a solution, it does not mean that you have the power to make it happen. But some of the homeless mentally ill do not have that kind of time. As one participant asked, "How long can you hold your self-esteem? How long? Life moves. Everything moves."

During the study, I interviewed a man who was still living on the street. Feeling helpless to make a difference in his life, I said, "I wish I could offer you more. The best thing I can tell you is that now you'll have 25 bucks to get lunch." He replied, "That's better than nothing. I'm hungry. I just hope that the next person doesn't have to go through this. Since I got a little older I think its maybe worth doing something for the next guy." It's too late for Warren. His wings are broken.

ACKNOWLEDGMENTS

I am indebted to Dr. Jan Blustein for making this project possible, and for her continuing support and guidance. I am thankful to The United Hospital Fund (UHF) for their financial sponsorship. At UHF, Sharon Salit gave her enthusiasm, considerable skills, and generosity of spirit to all phases of the work, from development through completion.

I feel privileged to have been allowed inside the Pathways to Housing program by Dr. Sam Tsemberis, and to see the fruits of the tireless efforts he makes on behalf of his clients. Doctor Leyla Gulcur and her team of NYHS staff could not have been more accommodating or welcoming, and I owe the smoothness of recruitment to their efforts. Special thanks are due to Dr. Kim Hopper, whose expertise in homelessness research, which he shares so readily, is an inspiration to me. At NYU, Dr. Beth Shinn worked with us to develop sampling strategies, the interview protocol, and analyze the findings of the NYHS. Doctor Deborah Padgett worked with us in preparing the research for human subjects review. Most of all, I am thankful to the men and women who have shared the stories of their lives with me with such grace and honesty. They deserve so much more than they have been given.

REFERENCES

Barr, H. (1999). *The Need for Discharge Planning for Incarcerated People with Mental Illness in New York.* New York: Executive Summary of Joint Project commissioned by The Correctional Association of New York and the Urban Justice Center.

Brauth, B. (1995, October). *Cycles of Relapse and Remission Among Medicaid Eligible Users of Mental Health Services in New York City.* Presentation by the NYS Office of Mental Health to the Institute for International Research on Mental Health and Substance Abuse Services, Orlando, FL.

Carling, P. J. (1993). Housing and supports for persons with mental illness: Emerging approaches to research and practice. *Hospital and Community Psychiatry, 44,* 439–44.

Culhane, D., Metraux, S., & Hadley, T. (2001, May). *The Impact of Supportive Housing for Homeless People with Severe Mental Illness on the Utilization of the Public Health, Corrections and Emergency Shelter Systems: The New York-New York Initiative.* PhiladelphiaCity?: Center for Mental Health Policy and Services Research, University of Pennsylvania.

Hopper, K., Jost, J., Hay, T., Welber, S., & Haughland, G. (1997). Homelessness, severe mental illness, and the institutional circuit. *Psychiatric Services, 48,* 659–65.

Kuhn, R., & Culhane, D. (1998, April). Applying cluster analysis to test a typology of homelessness by pattern of public shelter utilization: Results from the analysis of administrative data. *American Journal of Community Psychology, 26,* 207–32.

New York State Office of Mental Health (OMH). (April 21, 2000). Housing: Governor Pataki, Mayor Guiliani announce New York/New York II. Press Release. www.omh.state.ny.us/ omhweb/omhq/ q0699/housing.htm

Salit, S., & Mosso, A. (1997, April). High cost users of mental health services in the New York City public hospital system. Internal memorandum of the

Office of Behavioral Health, New York City Health and Hospitals Corporation.

Salit, S, et al. (1998, June 11). Hospitalization Costs Associated with Homelessness in New York City. *New England Journal of Medicine, 338,* 1734–40.

Tsemberis, S. (1999). From streets to homes: An innovative approach to supported housing for homeless adults with psychiatric disabilities. *Journal of Community Psychology, 27,* 225–41.

Tsemberis, S., & Eisenberg, R. (2000). Pathways to housing: Supported housing for street-dwelling homeless individual with psychiatric disabilities. *Psychiatric Services, 51,* 487–93.

Winerip, M. (1999, May 23). Bedlam in the streets. *New York Times,* 42–65.

PART II

Methodological
Issues—New and Old

The chapters in this second half of the book represent another approach to our goal of improving the supportive infrastructure of qualitative research. Although several topics are familiar (e.g., using qualitative data analysis software, ethical issues, writing and dissemination), others are relatively new (or at least underdeveloped) in the literature on qualitative methods (e.g., methods for analyzing data in a cross-language context). All of the chapters in Part II offer a more advanced discussion of methodological issues that are central to the enterprise (and too important to omit from a comprehensive text on qualitative research).

Chapter 7, by Tazuko Shibusawa and Ellen Lukens, addresses one of the oldest yet least-explored frontiers in qualitative methods—how English-speaking researchers approach the transcription, translation, and analysis of non-English-language data. It is surprising that so little has been written about this subject given that (1) so many ethnographies have been conducted among non-English-speaking peoples; (2) the English-speaker's standpoint has dominated the literature in qualitative research; (3) interest in cross-cultural studies has skyrocketed in recent years in the practice-based professions where multi-ethnic (multilanguage) encounters are increasingly routine; and (4) the vast majority of qualitative reports are published in English (although sometimes translated from the first language of the author if he or she is not English speaking). Thus, Tazuko and Ellen's English-language standpoint is not only reflective of their work but broadly representative of the ways things are in the field. We look forward to future studies from other linguistic vantage points.

The complexities of dealing with cross-language qualitative studies are many—conducting interviews, transcribing them, and analyzing their content is challenging enough in a single language. Translating non-English texts into English sets the stage for a number of concerns, for example, what to do with words or idiomatic phrases that have no comparable terms in English? What if meaning comes not from word-for-word translation but from the arc of a narrative that collapses when translated? So many phrases in other languages defy translation (think, for example, of *zeitgeist* and *shadenfreude* in German, or *panache* and *savoir faire* in French). There are also "culture-bound syndromes" of physical or emotional ailments that have no equivalent forms in Western medicine. Although the conundrums of language and culture often stymie, we cannot shy away from them as long as we value cross-cultural understanding and interchange. If not made more transparent, the process of translation will leave the qualitative methods family—where language reigns supreme—vulnerable to the charge of cultural filtering and distortion. Tazuko and Ellen have done an admirable job of capturing these complexities and producing a workable collaborative model for others to follow.

Chapter 8, by James Drisko, is about a topic that has become de rigeur in qualitative research: computer software for qualitative data analysis (QDA). With each newly updated version, QDA programs have become more sophisticated and responsive to the researcher's needs. Yet the same caveats apply as before: QDA programs offer far greater efficiency for storing, managing, and retrieving data but they cannot replace the human brain. A qualitative study can only be as good as the researcher who conducted it—all decisions about abstracting meaning must come from the investigator. The same can be said about newer technologies such as speech recognition software. Although the laborious task of transcription continues to consume inordinate amounts of time, computer-generated speech recognition is at a primitive stage and lacks the capacity to detect the nuances of pitch and intonation that underlie the richness of human utterances (Eisenberg, 2002). Whatever their limitations, QDA software programs are here to stay and Jim's overview draws on his long-term expertise to keep the reader informed and up to date.

Chapters 9 and 10 focus on the nurturing, interpersonal aspects of pursuing rigor that are crucial for maintenance of the research instrument of qualitative studies. In Chapter 9, the importance of mentoring is reflected in the dialogue between Dennis Shelby and his former doctoral student, Ida Roldan, as they revisit her journey into the world of Puerto Ricans with HIV/AIDS. Dennis and Ida reflect on the influences of culture, ethnicity, social class, and gender as challenges and opportunities for deeper insight. Their mentoring relationship, viewed through the lens of clinical theory, facilitated Ida's growth both personally and professionally. Mentors with expertise in qualitative methods are still in short supply, but with each successful pairing we have a template for others to follow.

Even scarcer than mentors are peer debriefing and support (PDS) groups, the subject of Chapter 10. In this chapter, I have the privilege of joining with two doctoral student advisees to report on our experiences in forming and maintaining PDS groups within a social work doctoral program. Perhaps because they are so rare, PDS groups receive scant attention in the literature. Yet they can be invaluable in complementing the power differential inherent in mentoring and in harnessing the spirit of the collectivity to enhance rigor as well as provide instrumental and emotional support.

In Chapter 11, Deborah Waldrop discusses the ethical dilemmas peculiar to qualitative research. Although generally more beneficial and less risky for participants than quantitative studies, qualitative studies nevertheless present potential hazards related to vulnerability and loss of privacy. In addition, qualitative studies conducted in communities and practice settings pose unique challenges for researchers seeking Institutional Review Board (IRB) approval, especially when working at multiple sites (Wolf, Croughan, & Lo, 2002). For example, there is the tremendous burden of having to get approval from several IRBs representing community and practice institutions (and the added risk that they will give conflicting advice about the study protocol). Also, what happens if one's collaborators are at institutions or agencies that do not have an IRB, or they are not formally affiliated at all? (The latter would be true in community action studies where lay individuals are invited to become partners.) Recent federal requirements that all study investigators must undergo human subjects protections training and certification add yet another layer of complexity and burden to multisite community-based studies. Still, ethical concerns need constant vigilance given the flexible, ever-changing aspects of qualitative inquiry.

In Chapter 12, Margareta Hydén and Carolina Överlien take us to a residential treatment center in rural Sweden to illustrate how techniques of narrative analysis can be used to reveal the dangers of disclosing sexual abuse, especially when staff are ill-equipped to handle the Pandora's box that such revelations can open among the troubled young women in their care. Together with Chapter 2 by Roberta Sands, these chapters demonstrate the power of rigorous narrative analysis as a mode of inquiry that is neither arcane nor remote from real-world problems.

There are other forms of analysis related to talk such as conversation analysis (CA) and discourse analysis (DA), both of which focus more on the mechanics (structure and sequencing) of utterances in social exchanges rather than their story-telling qualities (Gubrium & Holstein, 2000). Beginning in the 1970s, Foucault infused DA with a strong sociopolitical frame of reference designed to expose how language reflects and reinforces power relations inherent in Western society (1972). Rooted in phenomenology and ethnomethodology, CA and DA have not been as popular as other qualitative approaches among practice-based researchers, but this could easily change as the palette of qualitative methods becomes more diversified and colorful.

Chapters 13 and 14 represent topics that are crucial points of departure for discussions of the place of qualitative methods in the larger quantitative world. Chapter 13 is devoted to a more expansive (and I hope thought-provoking) discussion of mixed methods and their advantages with respect to serendipitous findings—the latter a primary strength of qualitative methods. When used appropriately, mixed methods lend hybrid vigor to a study and offer the additional opportunities for concatenation—another theme developed in the chapter.

Chapter 14 addresses a common dilemma facing qualitative researchers—writing and publishing qualitative reports. The difficulties of finding suitable outlets for dissemination are a constant source of frustration for qualitative researchers and the recent boom in qualitative studies has tightened the bottleneck even further because peer-reviewing expertise lags behind. This chapter is devoted to practical suggestions for writing reports and producing manuscripts that will have an easier time during the review process (and hopefully be accepted). There are still factors we cannot control (e.g., selection of reviewers, lack of agreement on standards, etc.) but well-written, rigorous studies will go a long way toward widening that bottleneck.

Chapter 15 is devoted to a reprise of earlier themes (from the Introduction) revisited through the lens of three interrelated issues affecting qualitative research in the future: theoretical thinking, social responsibility, and globalization. Discussion of each of these reveals tensions within the qualitative family—pitting those for versus against theoretical thinking, those who argue that postmodernism has the closest links to socially responsible research (versus those who disagree) and the difficulties of balancing global versus local concerns amidst the paradox of two trends: economic globalization and ethnoreligious conflicts. Part II—and the book—close as they began: with an invitation to the reader to embark upon the journey of discovery that is qualitative research.

REFERENCES

Eisenberg, A. (2002, August 1). Teaching machines to hear your prose and your pain. *The New York Times*, p. 69.

Foucault, M. (1972). *The archaeology of knowledge*. New York: Pantheon.

Gubrium, J. F. & Holstein, J. A. (2000). Analyzing interpretive practice. In N. L. Denzin & Y. S. Lincoln (Eds.), *Handbook of qualitative research* (2nd ed.) (pp. 487–508). Thousand Oaks, CA: Sage.

Wolf, L., Croughan, M., & Lo, B. (2002). The challenges of IRB review and human subjects protections in practice-based research. *Medical Care, 40*, 521–9.

7

Analyzing Qualitative Data in a Cross-Language Context

A Collaborative Model

TAZUKO SHIBUSAWA AND ELLEN LUKENS

Although the majority of cross-cultural and cross-national qualitative research has been conducted by monolingual, English-speaking researchers (Esposito, 2001), the effects of their linguistic and cultural standpoint on the research process has received little attention. Furthermore, the influence of the translators and interpreters, who are usually native to the culture being investigated, is rarely discussed (Temple & Edwards, 2002). As noted by anthropologists and linguists, cultures have different verbal interpretations of reality and thought (Whorf, 1956). Different cultures ascribe different meanings to words and narratives according to their world view (Barnes, 1996). Thus, cross-language research involves meaning-based translations rather than word-for-word translations (Esposito, 2001). The way in which monolingual English-speaking researchers arrive at meaning-based translations, however, has remained largely invisible, which in turn has led to a lack of rigor in demonstrating cultural transferability of qualitative data. Thus, although considerable discussion surrounds the development of culturally sensitive research instruments in quantitative research (Dumka et al., 1996), little comparable attention has been paid to methods for analyzing qualitative data in cross-language research (Esposito, 2001; Twinn, 1997, 1998). There is a need to explicate the process of translating and analyzing non-English data.

The purpose of this chapter is to describe our approach to analyzing qualitative data in a cross-national and cross-language context in Japan and to present the model that emerged from this process. We will present a collaborative model for analyzing data collected in a non-English language (in this case, Japanese) in an English context. Discussion will focus on the decisions that were made at each juncture of the analysis involving (1) methods for translation and coding, (2) cultural filters that became evident in the process, and (3) the negotiation of differences to enhance the generation of themes without privileging either perspective.

Table 7.1 Contexts for Cross-Language Qualitative Research by Monolingual (English-Only) Researchers

Researchers*	Respondents	
	English-speaking	Non–English-speaking
Intranational (within the United States)	**A** 1. Native English-speaking respondents 2. Bilingual respondents (e.g., Native Americans, Latino(a)s, Asian Americans)	**B** 1. Non–English-speaking respondents (e.g., first-generation immigrants, temporary residents) 2. Bilingual respondents (e.g., Native Americans, Latino(a)s, Asian Americans)
International (cross-national)	**D** 1. Native English-speaking respondents (e.g., UK, Australia, Ireland, Canada) 2. Bilingual respondents (e.g., English-speaking Singaporeans)	**C** 1. Non–English-speaking respondents**

*American-born monocultural native English speaker.

**Location of current study.

There are at least four alternative ways to depict cross–national and cross-language studies, depending on the targeted study population and the standpoint (and location) of the researcher. Table 7-1 illustrates the case when the researcher is an American-born monocultural English speaker. Proceeding clockwise, studies conducted in the United States with English-speaking respondents (mono- or bilingual) are situated in Cell A and U.S.-based research conducted in a non-English language is situated in Cell B. Cross-national studies with non–English-speaking respondents are located in Cell C, and those conducted with English-speaking respondents are in Cell D. Although problems of translation and transcription affect studies portrayal in both Cells B and C, our study's site in Japan places it in Cell C.

Each of us brought expertise and cultural backgrounds to the study. Lukens (E.L.) has worked solely in the United States with families of persons with severe and persistent mental illness (SPMI) as both a clinician and researcher. Shibusawa (T.S.) is a bilingual researcher and a clinician trained in the United States and Japan with expertise in cross-cultural practice and research with families and older adults. In 2000, we collaborated on a cross-national study of the experiences of Japanese and Americans who have siblings with chronic mental illness. Together, we planned to use our combined skills and knowledge to identify the common and differing experiences of siblings in the United States and Japan. This report draws on the sibling focus group data collected in Japan.

PREVIOUS STUDIES

Although many qualitative studies have been conducted in languages other than English, almost no attention has been given to issues surrounding translation in qualitative research: how it influences analyses and results. Twinn conducted and analyzed data from in-depth interviews (1997) and focus groups (1998) conducted in Hong Kong in Cantonese and reported encountering several complexities as an English-speaking researcher. Most of these centered around difficulties finding English-equivalent words for words or constructs in Chinese and differences in grammatical structure between Cantonese and English.

Twinn also noted challenges posed by multiple translations that lead to differences in the generation of codes, which in turn become artifacts of the translation process that undermine the analysis. In one study, Twinn (1997) compared the codes from Cantonese transcripts with those from an English translation of the same transcripts. She found that there were slight differences between the codes, but the overall themes were the same. In another study, Twinn (1998) concluded that translation can confound the quality of the data and recommended that data be analyzed in the original language. She did not, however, present evidence to support this contention.

Esposito (2001) described her attempts to enhance rigor in collecting and analyzing cross-language focus group data. During Spanish-language focus groups, Esposito (a monolingual English speaker) observed the group behind a one-way mirror with a simultaneous interpreter translating the conversation into English. The simultaneous English interpretation was audiotaped and transcribed, then compared to the "direct" English translations of the focus group transcripts. Esposito demonstrated the complexity and financial costs involved when attempting to uphold methodological rigor in arriving at valid language translations.

CONTEXT OF THE STUDY

The analytic methods presented in this chapter were utilized as part of the Sibling Project, which was conducted under the auspices of the National Alliance for Research on Schizophrenia and Depression (NARSAD) and the National Alliance for the Mentally Ill (NAMI) of New York State. E.L. was the principal investigator. The purpose of the original study was to assess the impact on adult well siblings of having a brother or sister with SPMI using a multimethod design. Data were collected through focus groups, in-depth individual interviews, and a statewide survey. Through these combined qualitative and quantitative approaches, the investigators aimed to add depth and breadth of understanding to research on siblings and SPMI as a critical first step toward designing proactive interventions that attend to the differing needs of family members across system levels.

After completing the focus groups in New York, we had the opportunity to expand the research by conducting focus groups among Japanese well siblings residing in Tokyo. This provided a rich opportunity to explore and describe similarities and differences among sibling responses in two different cultures (Lukens et al., 2001).

METHODS

Focus group methodology (Krueger & Casey, 2000) was chosen for several reasons. First, we wanted to provide a forum for participants that would yield various perspectives and attitudes, trigger thoughts and response patterns, and uncover diversity of opinion that might not be revealed through individual interviews. Such groups have the potential to elicit unanticipated and in-depth information as well as group perspectives. Through this process, participants had the opportunity to develop their own thinking in the presence of others who faced similar experiences. This information is collected through the voices of the respondents rather than through predefined categories or hypothesis-driven frameworks (Krueger & Casey, 2000; Morgan, 1996).

Sample

In both New York and Tokyo, participants were recruited using convenience sampling techniques. Siblings in Tokyo were recruited through mental health professionals. In New York, we also promoted the research and solicited volunteers at open meetings of the local chapters of NAMI, an advocacy and self-help organization for family members and friends of persons with mental illness.

The New York sample included 19 adult siblings who participated in one of five focus groups. In Tokyo, 19 adult siblings participated in one of three focus groups. The groups were relatively similar in demographic characteristics, although there were some important differences. In the focus groups conducted in Tokyo, 13 participants were female and 6 were male, and the age range was 35 to 60 years. In the New York study, 16 females and 3 males participated in focus groups, with an age range of 25 to 73 years. The New York sample was more ethnically diverse (16 Caucasians, 2 African Americans, and 1 Asian American).

Data Collection

All of the focus groups were conducted in 2000. The format was identical except for minor adjustments made to be culturally sensitive in Japan or to uphold confidentiality in New York. For example, the facilitator in the Japanese group acted more formally and addressed the participants by their last names. In the New York group, only first names were used to protect identity. Groups in both countries lasted approximately 2 hours and were held in a private conference room at the sponsoring university or agency. Each respondent participated in only one focus group. Prior to beginning a group, participants provided informed consent regarding study purpose, confidentiality procedures both within and outside the groups, and the rights of study volunteers, following an approved Institutional Review Board protocol. They then completed a brief demographic questionnaire. The groups in New York were conducted in English by a native English speaker; the groups in Tokyo were conducted in Japanese by a native Japanese speaker. All sessions were audiotaped.

After the researchers introduced the project, participants were asked to introduce themselves by first name in the United States and by last name in Japan. They were then asked to write down their responses to a single open-ended question: *Please list at least five ways, both negative and positive, that having a brother or sister with mental illness has affected different aspects of your life.* Five minutes were allotted for this task, after which participants were invited to begin to discuss their responses. The paper-and-pencil procedure was used as a starting point to generate discussion.

In both New York and Tokyo, the researchers facilitated the discussion in collaboration with a colleague. In both sites, the response to the project was positive—discussion flowed easily and the participants appeared comfortable and eager to talk. In New York, each participant was paid $10 as a token of appreciation for their time. In Tokyo, each participant was given a prepaid telephone card equivalent to $10 (a common form of compensation used by other researchers in Japan). In this chapter, we will focus on our analyses of the Japanese data.

DATA ANALYSIS

Grounded theory was used to guide the analyses (Glaser, 1978, 1992; Glaser & Strauss, 1967). Through this inductive approach, codes and categories are derived from the text and then interpreted and compared (Glaser, 1978). We employed a thematic analysis approach by starting with open coding, then clustering codes into families of concepts or categories, and finally capturing emergent themes from the clusters of codes (Coffey & Atkinson, 1996). To proceed with the analysis, each audiotaped session was transcribed verbatim in the original language. In both settings, random segments were checked against the audiotapes and corrected to ensure accuracy. Our overall goal was to examine culturally specific similarities and differences in content in the American and Japanese focus groups.

Initial Data Analysis Plan

A key objective was to examine the content of the Japanese transcripts for culturally specific and/or sensitive material. We initially followed Twinn's approach (1997), in which she coded and generated themes from English translations of audiotaped interviews and compared them to codes and themes

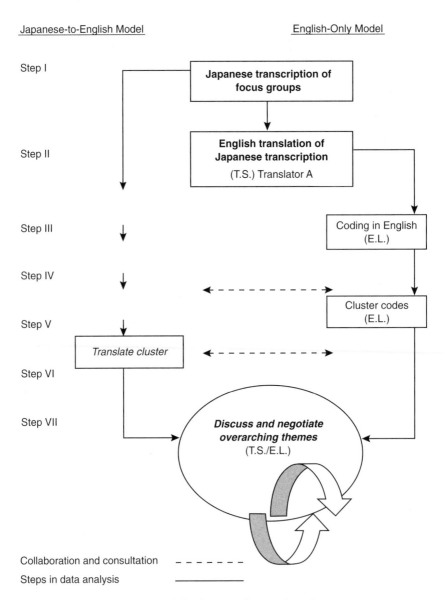

FIGURE 7.1 Original Analysis Model: Schematic diagram based upon methods used by Twinn (1998)

generated from the Chinese language transcripts. Thus, we devised a protocol to compare and contrast independent analyses of the Japanese transcripts by T.S. (in Japanese) and E.L. (in English) (Figure 7-1). This protocol involved seven steps: (1) transcription of focus groups in Japanese, (2) translation of the transcripts into English so that E.L. and T.S. could code them independently, (3) coding, (4) code clustering, (5) identify overarching themes, (6) translation of T.S.'s themes into English, and (7) comparison of themes. We planned to work independently so as not to contaminate the coding process and then come together at the end to examine and resolve differences.

English Translation of Japanese Transcripts. The way in which data are translated requires careful thought as translation can misrepresent the phenomenological perspectives of the participants (Twinn, 1997). There were two possible ways to translate our data: (1) directly from the audiotaped dialogue of the focus groups (simultaneous translation/transcription), and (2) transcribe first in Japanese and then translate into English (sequential transcription). We decided on the latter option because it allowed a more careful review of the translation process. To assess accuracy, we completed two different sets of translations for each focus group, one by T.S. who is bilingual and bicultural and the other by "A," who is not bicultural and thus represented a point of view "culturally" closer to the Japanese participants. Although we had two translated transcripts in hand, we decided to work only with one because, according to Twinn (1997), using two translated versions can lead to inconsistent codes that are an artifact of the difference in translation rather than the coding process. Because differences were relatively minor, we decided to use T.S.'s transcripts because she had compiled comments and notes on problems with the translation and difficulties capturing the meaning in English. We referred to the translation by "A" whenever differences in coding between E.L. and T.S. occurred to examine if the discrepancies were due to translation rather than content.

Establishing Coder Agreements. Before working independently to code the transcripts in the respective languages, we first coded a selected portion in English to establish preliminary agreement on the coding process. While doing so, we quickly found ourselves discussing the meanings of words and phrases. We also found that E.L. had omitted certain codes and themes that T.S. had coded and vice versa. Most of these differences reflected *emic* versus *etic* perspectives. E.L. represented the *etic* perspective because she stood "outside" the Japanese culture, and T.S. represented the *emic* perspective because she was Japanese born and fluent in the language.

Both viewpoints provided unique perspectives. E.L. noted cultural nuances that were overlooked by T.S. because of her familiarity with behaviors or verbal expressions. T.S. also brought depth of understanding and an appreciation of cultural trends and mores that were not recognizable to E.L. In this particular situation, T.S.'s perspective was further enriched by the fact that she had lived in both societies and had studied the differences in family traditions and relationships in the United States and Japan.

Table 7.2 offers an example of how we coded differently because of our respective cultural filters. T.S. coded "not telling family about their child's mental illness" as "shame," whereas E.L. did not code this segment at all. Rather, she connected the segment with the respondents self-observation several lines later. E.L. then coded the last sentence in the paragraph as the friend's

Table 7.2 Assessing Coder Agreement: Coding from English Translation*

English Translation of Japanese Transcript	Coding by E.L.
942 Some families won't take their children (to doctors) who've gotten sick, and some don't tell their	Family denial/secrecy
943 families. I told people over 10 years ago that I have two siblings who are ill, but I have a friend	
945 whose daughter became ill in her 20s. [I saw her the other day, but for 10 years, she says,	Secrecy/stigma
946 "oh, she just got a little sick." She won't even tell me, and I'm her friend.] so she's shocked by it	
947 (having her daughter ill). So, yes, professionals, too, but I'd like education for awareness. [If	
948 they said things, then I can say things to them, but I think its difficult to say something to	Ambivalence re: reaching out
949 people that don't say anything, who are traumatized by it.]	

English Translation of Japanese Transcript	Coding by T.S.
942 [Some families won't take their children (to doctors) who've gotten sick, and some don't tell their	Shame
943 families.] I told people over 10 years ago that I have two siblings who are ill, but I have a friend	
945 whose daughter became ill in her 20s. [I saw her the other day, but for 10 years, she says,	Disclosure of sibling's illness
946 "oh, she just got a little sick". She won't even tell me, and I'm her friend.] so she's shocked by it	
947 (having her daughter ill). So, yes, professionals, too, but I'd like education for awareness. If	
948 they said things, then I can say things to them, but I think its difficult to say something to	
949 people that don't say anything, who are traumatized by it.	

* Selective coding for illustrative purposes.

inability to reach out when people are secretive. T.S. did not code this because in Japanese culture people tend to refrain from talking about personal issues with others and she did not think that what the respondent said carried any particular meaning. In addition to cultural differences, E.L.'s wealth of expertise with siblings of persons with severe mental illness gave her a different perspective from T.S., who lacked this expertise. E.L. has worked for many years as both a clinician and researcher to assess and document the particular needs of individuals as they confront the mental illness a family member. In our analysis we worked together to minimize the gaps and maximize the richness of the perspectives.

Revised Data Analysis Plan: Addressing Issues of Cultural Transferability

As we proceeded, we decided that coding and clustering codes independently limited our ability to identify subtle differences that would only become apparent through constant comparison of our respective codes. We therefore decided to code independently in small segments (three pages of transcript) and then come together, with T.S. coding the Japanese transcripts in Japanese and E.L. coding the English translation. T.S. then translated her Japanese codes into English to engage in dialogue with E.L. In this way, we found that clarification of cultural differences emerged from the differences in codes and subsequent dialogue about the differences.

We agree with Barnes (1996): culture can become lost if qualitative researchers do not make it explicit throughout all stages of their research. Had we not worked together throughout the coding and code clustering process, we would have missed much of the nuanced material. Figure 7.2 presents our revised analytic model. Unlike our original plan (Figure 7.1), the revised model provides links between the two researchers for ongoing collaboration, leading to an iterative process of analyzing the data without privileging either perspective.

Negotiating and Resolving Different Interpretations: From Code Clusters to Themes

We also found that our differing perspectives influenced the ways codes were clustered to generate themes. Table 7.3 shows an excerpt where participants discuss their perceptions of their ill siblings when they have conflicts with them.

E.L. clustered these codes as "anger/frustration and burden" whereas T.S. clustered the codes as *amae*, a Japanese construct that translates as "interdependency" or "indulgence" in helping the sibling with illness. From E.L.'s perspective, the burden was intensified by the perception that "time stood still" for the person with mental illness, that is, that when the sibling became mentally ill, his or her emotional development stopped. Thus the well siblings were required to bear the brunt of the affected sibling's immature behavior.

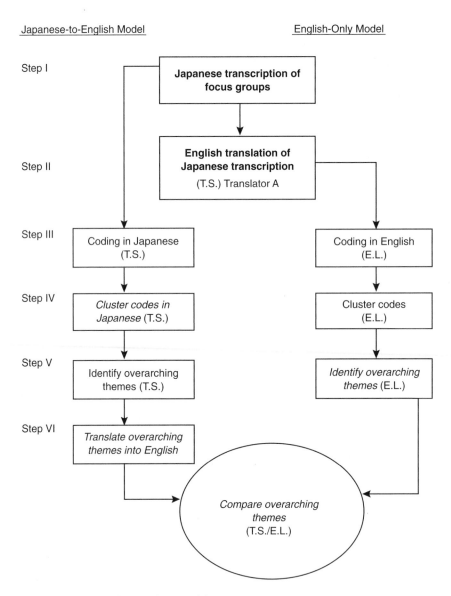

FIGURE 7.2 Revised data analysis model.

T.S. clustered the codes as *amae* (accepting and allowing the sibling to depend on them) because of her understanding of family relationships in Japanese culture. She reasoned that the well siblings felt that that they needed to indulge their sibling whose emotional development had been thwarted by the onset and chronicity of their illness. For well siblings, their own maturity and responsibility could be compared to Japanese parents, especially mothers, who accept and indulge their children's dependency (Lanham & Garrick, 1996).

Table 7.3 Negotiating Overarching Themes*

	E.L. codes English-only model	Overarching theme	T.S. codes** Japanese-English model
And so when the older (well) siblings get sick, because I'm her sister right above her (ill sibling), and she's my younger sister right after me, and I think I might end up getting involved with her.	Anticipated burden	Impact on self ———▶ Concern re: notion of self ↓ Sense of responsibility	*Family care-taker role* ◀———

* Selective coding for illustrative purposes.

** Coded in Japanese and translated into English.

The Japanese concept of *amae* was introduced to the West by Doi (1973) and was later comprehensively reviewed by Johnson (1993). By accepting the role of the "parental" caretaker, the well siblings accept *amae* with illness, and are more capable of tolerating the actions that disrupt their own lives. T.S.'s definition of *amae* as a code cluster was extended to include the need for Japanese well siblings to fit into the "mature" role in the family even when younger. This "reversed" the traditional hierarchy of Japanese family relationships where older children are expected to take care of their aging parents as well as their younger siblings (Johnson, 1993).

We discussed the different interpretations of burden and dependency *(amae)*. E.L., informed by her study of siblings in the United States, thought that the code clusters could be categorized under a theme of "Impact on Self." In the US sibling study, the code clusters under this theme had included *fear, anger, stigma, burden, hope, and loss* (Lukens, Thorning, & Lohrer, 2002).

T.S., however, noted that the "Impact on Self" theme would not be appropriate for the Japanese data because the notion of "self" is conceptualized differently in US and Japanese cultures. Many have noted that, although Western cultures emphasize personal autonomy and self-determination, individuals in Asian cultures view the self in relation to others (Markus & Kitayama, 1991; Triandis, 1988). For example, in Japanese families, it is the eldest son's duty to care for elderly parents as well as younger siblings. But if the eldest son has a severe mental illness, then younger siblings are expected to take on his role. The well sibling's maturity, which in such a case involves acceptance of the older sibling's immaturity, can be viewed as a reflection of this notion of taking on family roles. Thus, the well sibling is affected, but not necessarily in the same way as in the United States. The Japanese well sibling may not think that he or she has a "choice" so much as a "duty" in responding to an ill sibling. Thus, the theme of "Impact on Self" would distort the experiences of Japanese well siblings.

After considerable discussion about cultural differences in the concept of "self," we concluded that "sense of responsibility" was a more appropriate theme. This construct allowed space for differences in the way siblings in different cultures experience their relationship with a brother or sister affected by mental illness, but also fit Japanese notions of "family obligation."

Addressing Rigor

In pursuing this analysis, we followed several strategies to enhance the rigor of the work (Miles & Huberman, 1994; Padgett, 1998). These included (1) engagement, (2) triangulation, and (3) auditing and record keeping.

Engagement. Both T.S. and E.L. have had extensive experience working with caregivers and were well versed in the literature. This knowledge, and the decision to facilitate the groups ourselves, served to ground us in relating to the sibling participants. The participants responded well to the fact that we had knowledge of their concerns and that we were willing to listen. They appeared quite comfortable with the focus group format. In addition, the Japanese focus groups were co-led by our colleagues in Japan who were known to the families through their work with *Zenkaren*, the Japanese equivalent of NAMI.

Triangulation. Several types of triangulation have been identified (Denzin, 1978), but we were particularly focused on observer triangulation (i.e., ourselves as multiple observers) to complete this analysis. The combined perspectives represented in our on-going discussion enriched the analysis immeasurably.

Auditing and Record Keeping. As we have described throughout this chapter, a critical component of our analysis was through our record keeping. We used our notes to record our own reactions and outline points of agreement and disagreement to continually document our process.

SUMMARY AND CONCLUSION:
LESSONS LEARNED

In the course of this study, we became keenly aware of the dearth of research explicating methods for analyzing data in a non–English-language despite the large number of cross-cultural studies reporting findings based on non–English-language data. We were only able to find four studies that addressed methods for cross-language analysis (Esposito, 2001; Twinn, 1997, 1998; Temple & Edwards, 2002). The extent to which issues of cultural and linguistic transferability has been glossed over in qualitative research is a major concern given the central role of language in qualitative research. To address methodological rigor, researchers must first fully describe how they arrive at accurate and meaningful translations.

Monolingual researchers must rely on native translators and collaborators to represent the culture that is being investigated, yet few describe this collaboration and its impact on the study (Temple & Edwards, 2002). This can be attributed in part to the longstanding dominance of Western culture reflected in research by American-born researchers (e.g., anthropologists). Machida (1996) observed that U.S.–Japanese psychological research tends to be dominated by the Western context as opposed to the reverse. In most studies, the role of the native informants who guide the monolingual researcher is rendered invisible. Cultural transferability can only be established when neither Western nor non-Western privileges the other. A collaborative model that includes a systematic approach for cross-national researchers to discuss, negotiate, and resolve language and cultural differences provides an important step for addressing methodological and cultural rigor in qualitative research.

ACKNOWLEDGMENTS

We would like to express our appreciation to Dr. Junichiro Ito and Dr. Iwao Oshima in Tokyo, and Ms. Helle Thorning and Dr. Steven Lohrer in New York for their commitment and support for the mission of this project. We also are indebted to Dr. Deborah Padgett for her expertise in qualitative methods and for adding rigor to our work. This study was partially funded by the Center for the Study of Social Work Practice, a joint program of Columbia University School of Social Work and the Jewish Board of Family and Children's Services. Finally, we would like to express our sincere gratitude for the sibling participants in our study.

REFERENCES

Barnes, D. M. (1996). An analysis of the grounded theory method and the concept of culture. *Qualitative Health Research, 6* (3), 429–34.

Coffey, A., & Atkinson, P. (1996). *Making sense of qualitative data: Complementary research strategies.* Thousand Oaks, CA: Sage.

Denzin, N. K. (1978). *The research act: A theoretical introduction to sociological methods* (2nd ed.). New York: McGraw-Hill.

Doi, T. (1973). *The anatomy of dependence.* In J. Bester (Trans.). Tokyo: Kodansha.

Dumka, L., Stoerzinger, H., Jackson, K., & Roosa, M. (1996). Examination of the cross-cultural and cross-language equivalence of the parenting self-agency measure. *Family Relations, 45,* 216–22.

Esposito, N. (2001). From meaning to meaning: The influence of translation techniques on non-English focus group research. *Qualitative Health Research, 11* (4), 568–79.

Glaser, B. (1978). *Theoretical sensitivity.* Mill Valley, CA: Sociology Press.

Glaser, B. (1992). *Basics of grounded theory analysis.* Mill Valley, CA: Sociology Press.

Glaser, B., & Strauss, A. (1967). *Discovery of grounded theory.* Chicago: Aldine.

Johnson, F. A. (1993). *Dependency and Socialization: Psychoanalytic and anthropological investigations into Amae.* New York: New York University Press.

Krueger, R., & Casey, M. (2000). *Focus groups: A practical guide for applied research* (3rd ed.). Thousand Oaks, CA: Sage.

Lanham, B. B., & Garrick, R. J. (1996). Adult to child in Japan: Interaction and relations. In D. W. Shwalb & B. J. Shwalb (Eds.), *Japanese childrearing: Two generations of scholarship* (pp. 97–124). New York: Guilford Press.

Lukens, E., Shibusawa, T., Thorning, H., Lohr, S., Ito, J., & Oshima, I. (2001). A cross-national comparison of the needs of well siblings of persons with schizophrenia. [Abstract] *Proceedings from the International Congress on Schizophrenia Research,* pp. 14, 99.

Lukens, E., Thorning, H., & Lohrer, S. (2003). *Sibling perspectives on severe mental illness: Reflections on self and family.* Manuscript submitted for publication.

Machida, S. (1996). Maternal and cultural socialization for schooling: Lessons learned and prospects ahead. In Shwalb, D. W. & B. J. Shwalb (Eds.), *Japanese childrearing: Two generations of scholarship* (pp. 241–259). New York: Guilford Press.

Markus, H. R., & Kitayama, S. (1991). Culture and the self: Implications for cognition, emotion, and motivation. *Psychological Review, 2,* 224–53.

Miles, M., & Huberman, A. (1994). *Qualitative data analysis* (2nd ed.). Thousand Oaks, CA: Sage.

Morgan, D. (1996). Focus groups. *Annual Review of Sociology, 22,* 129–52.

Padgett, D. K. (1998). *Qualitative methods in social work research: Challenges and rewards.* Newbury Park, CA: Sage.

Temple, B., & Edwards, R. (2002). Interpreters/translators and cross-language research: Reflexivity and border crossings. *International Journal of Qualitative Methods, 1* (2), Article 1. Retrieved July 15, 2002. www.ualberta.ca/~ijqm

Triandis, H. C. (1988). Cross-cultural contributions to theory in social psychology. In M. H. Bond (Ed.), *The cross-cultural challenge to social psychology* (pp. 122–140). Newbury Park, CA: Sage.

Twinn, S. (1997). An exploratory study examining the influence of translation on the validity and reliability of qualitative data in nursing research. *Journal of Advanced Nursing, 26,* 418–23.

Twinn, S. (1998). An analysis of the effectiveness of focus groups as a method of qualitative data collection with Chinese populations in nursing research. *Journal of Advanced Nursing, 28* (3), 654–61.

Whorf, B. J. (1956). *Language, thought and reality.* Cambridge, MA: MIT Press.

8

Qualitative Data
Analysis Software

A User's Appraisal

JAMES W. DRISKO

Interest in qualitative research has increased markedly in the past decade across many disciplines. During this time, qualitative research has become more common in refereed journals and in a growing selection of texts and methods-oriented books (Denzin & Lincoln, 1994; Padgett, 1998). Several efforts to create standards for qualitative research and reports have been published (Altheide & Johnson, 1994; Drisko, 1997; Leininger, 1994) as have several books and articles addressing qualitative data analysis (QDA) (Dey, 1993; Tesch, 1990). Along with these books and articles, conferences and workshops on qualitative research and qualitative methods have increased. In the past few years, many of these workshops and papers have cited the use of QDA software tools.

During this same period technology has been a major factor in the economic growth of the United States and Europe and computer technologies have led the way. The use of QDA software shares in the cachet of technology and is sometimes used to enhance the apparent rigor of qualitative proposals and research papers. The status of QDA software is quite striking given that pencil and paper techniques of data analysis can generally be just as effective. Marketers of QDA software, from software creators and distributors to workshop promoters, publicize the special features of their products. Most of these features offer little to the typical user and generally go unused. None offer automatic enhancements to the rigor or meaningfulness of qualitative research.

Qualitative research may be done very effectively using pencil and paper methods (Drisko, 1998). In fact, enhancements in noncomputerized office technology make the old methods easier for today's researchers. Coding can be done with highlighters of multiple colors, xeroxing makes the sharing of printed results easier and can also make the results of cut and paste techniques much more durable, and Post It notes make locating sections of text a simple task.

The greatest challenge to excellence in qualitative research remains the lack of access to well-trained and experienced teachers and mentors. Although their numbers appear to be increasing in many social science disciplines and professions, most remain expert in one or two research approaches and one or two data analysis techniques. Few educators have training and experience in multiple approaches to qualitative research, yet the differences among advocates of different approaches are often significant. Qualitative scholars make excellent critics of each other's work, but often lack appreciation of other researchers' purposes and premises. They may also have limited training in the methods applied by other scholars. Thus, epistemological critiques and challenges to methodological adequacy are made without sufficient attention to the philosophical premises, research purposes, and methods a researcher has applied (Drisko, 1997). Wider training and exposure to qualitative research and methods is still needed (Padgett, 1998).

Space limitations in journals are another serious challenge to excellence in qualitative research (Drisko, 2000, 2001). Statements of methods are routinely very brief and often include multiple, conflicting, research approaches (e.g., grounded theory and phenomenology). Upon closer review, the named methods may require different forms of data collection, sampling strategies, and data analysis (Tesch, 1990).

Journal reviewers must require excellence in qualitative research, but editors and journal managers could assist by working to create formats that fit the greater page-length requirements of qualitative reports. At the same time, researchers must take greater care in describing their research methods and ensuring that multiple methods are consistent or mutually enhancing. Such improvements in qualitative research may be obtained with or without the use of computers and QDA software.

Qualitative research is defined by the use of nonnumeric data. This is most often, but not always, text-based data, that is, words. In this chapter, *text* will be used to designate all forms of data stored in electronic file formats. *Text* is used broadly in discussions of computer-assisted QDA software processes and products despite the increasingly narrow and misleading use of the term. Several QDA software products can be used to study images, audio files, and video files as well as word-processed text data. However, the predominance of textual data, coupled with the hermeneutic and/or constructivist turn of many qualitative researchers and software developers, has led to the use of *text* as the signifier for qualitative data. As video and audio technologies mature, a broader alternative may be needed.

This chapter will open with a description of what QDA software does and numerous reminders of what it does not do. Commentary on learning to use the software and user feedback follows. Contact information for learning more about specific QDA products concludes the chapter.

INTRODUCTION TO QDA SOFTWARE

Although some researchers used mainframe computers for linguistic content analysis many years ago, the growth of computerized QDA software blossomed in the late 1980s and throughout the 1990s with the widespread use of the personal computer (Richards & Richards, 1994; Kelle, 1995; Weitzman & Miles, 1995). Early works on the use of computers in social research made no mention of these products (Madron, Tate & Brookshire, 1985; Schrodt, 1984). Early versions of QDA software (i.e., The Ethnograph) were solely text-based and required numerous steps for core procedures such as coding a segment of text. They had very steep learning curves and required expensive hardware for the time, such as extensive RAM and high-capacity hard drives. The products were also severely limited by the capacities of the computer hardware, which limited the number of pages (or bytes) that could be managed at one time (Kelle, 1995; Weitzman & Miles, 1994, 1995).

In the past few years QDA software products have become more similar, more sophisticated, and more numerous (Alexa & Zuell, 1999). My own recent on-line review found about 25 different QDA products (listed at the end of the chapter) and Evans (2002) lists a distinct set of 33 content analysis products (using statistics). Some products Weitzman and Miles (1995) reviewed in the mid-1990s are no longer available.

The great majority of contemporary QDA products use graphical interfaces, making a wide range of tools readily available via icons or drop-down menus (at least for those without visual impairments). Some recent QDA tools focus on data in audio and video formats, expanding the nature of qualitative research and reports. Today, computer hardware poses no significant limitations to the use of most of these products, although the use of video files requires expensive equipment and specialized video editing software.

Although articles, books, and online resources offer considerable information about QDA software, hands-on experience with a human instructor seems to be the best way to begin. Comments from participants in my workshops on QDA software and numerous requests for help from new users on QDA listservs indicate that these products can initially be daunting to use. At the same time, a few hours of introduction and hands-on experience appears to free all but the most anxious user to play and explore independently. A beginner's workshop also helps users make better use of available CD and online tutorials for QDA software. The first step is to understand what QDA software does, and how it can be useful to high-quality qualitative research. Further information on QDA resources can be found in Software Resources and Qualitative Listservs (pp. 206–210).

THE BENEFITS OF COMPUTERIZED QDA

Managing Data

The movement toward using computers in qualitative research began at the level of managing data. Word-processing software allowed greater flexibility in the editing and revision of typed materials, most often interview transcripts and field notes (Weitzman & Miles, 1995). As personal computers and word-processing software made text revision, editing, and storage quicker and easier, computers entered the world of qualitative research. This introduction was little noticed at first.

Managing data is still the key attribute of QDA software (Drisko, 1998; Richards & Richards, 1994). The software allows compact storage of transcriptions and related electronic materials (images, sound files, and video files). It also allows the saving and storage of each successive iteration of the data analysis, allowing recovery of preliminary decisions and creating an electronic audit trail for internal and external use. Storage of paper and pencil iterations is also possible, but requires enormous storage space and is often challenging due to the sheer volume of cut-and-pasted copies generated.

The ability to quickly share data sets and associated analytic information with colleagues at a distance is one of two new contributions of QDA software. Electronic copies of data and iterations of analysis may also be e-mailed (or sent via diskette) to colleagues in remote locations. This communication is quick and compact, unlike its pencil and paper alternative: mailing many large boxes. Some QDA software can also merge the work of several researchers working on the same data, further easing collaborative efforts. Simultaneous collaborative qualitative research among researchers in remote locations was simply not feasible until QDA software and electronic communications came along.

The ability to create hyperlinks among data elements is the second innovation made possible by QDA software that has no paper and pencil parallel. Some writers and qualitative researchers want to organize their data in nonlinear fashion. Computer software makes nonlinear organization easy to produce using hyperlinks. *Hyperlinks* are connections among data. Most people know hyperlinks as the hot spots or underlined text on web pages that allow instant movement from one data source (or file location) to another. Because the user selects among these links, the resulting journey through the data is not fully defined by the original author. This process of data organization produces nonlinear connections among data.

Many current QDA products allow users to define hyperlinks among different parts of textual data and even among different types of data (text, images, sound, and video). These constructions may or may not reflect a consistent conceptual argument (Kelle, 1997; Ranwez & Crampes, 1999). Some hypertext documents aid hermeneutic text analyses, providing a means for multiple interpretations. Less conspicuously, many QDA products use hyperlink technology to link data with analytic content such as codes and memos. With hyperlink technology, QDA software allows users to create, save, and display nonlinear connections among data. Such displays are possible with relative ease on computers and can be made available at great distances and at any time using internet technology.

Some current QDA software allows the analysis of images, audio files, and video files. In these cases, images may be linked or hyperlinked to other text or images. They may also be coded by marking specific content. Audio and video files require additional software for editing, but QDA software can be used to mark beginning and ending points in sounds files and video images, noting content of specific interest. These coded sections of audio or video files may be linked or hyperlinked to text and still images. One technical challenge remains, however, in that editing video files may require software not (yet) widely available on personal computers (e.g., Adobe Premiere, Ulead Video Studio). Standards and conventions for reporting qualitative research using audio and video files are lacking, and will need attention in the future to make optimal use of these vivid technologies.

Preparing the Data

Before data are ready for use in QDA software, they must be carefully reviewed and edited. I think of this process as "preening" the data. This review ensures that the data to be analyzed are as complete and accurate as possible. It is a vital preliminary requirement in qualitative research. Preening the data set also obligates in-depth involvement with the data. Comparing the data in audio and print formats, or handwritten and word-processed formats, exposes the researcher to the data in small, often random, segments. In this way new meaning, nuances, or questions may emerge to enliven the data analysis.

Text Segmenting, Coding, and Retrieval

In all qualitative data analysis, the researcher must identify meaningful and relevant passages of text or other data (Miles & Huberman, 1994A; Tesch, 1990). This involves an ongoing, iterative set of assessments and judgments about the meaning of the content related to one's research purposes. Researchers may choose to "cast the net" broadly or narrowly. In pencil and paper methods, researchers mark text segments and then apply some tag or code to them for later retrieval. Almost all contemporary QDA software allows quick marking of text using the mouse to highlight the text of interest. Almost all QDA software also allows quick coding of the selected text with a user-created code name. All QDA software will generate a list of assigned codes and most will also generate a list of the frequency of use for each code.

The text segmenting and coding process is quick and easy in almost all contemporary QDA products. This represents a significant improvement in ease of use from the early versions of these products. Text is first segmented (highlighted) using the mouse. Second, a code name is applied to label and identify the text segment in a separate step. However, the set of steps used to code text and the variety of ways coding differ markedly among these programs. For example, NUD•IST 4 (QSR, 1995) only marks words, lines, or paragraphs of text. The results often include words and phrases that are unrelated to the author's desired text segment, which makes review and analysis of these segments confusing. In contrast, ATLAS.ti (Muhr, 1994) and Hyper-RESEARCH (Hesse-Beiber et al., 1994) allow the user to define text segments of any length and eliminates unrelated content. To some, such a difference might be unimportant; to others it is essential.

QDA software differs in the number of ways coding can be done. The more flexible QDA products allow alteration of the program interface, specifically the use of "floating" and resizable windows in which codes are listed. They also provide icon or drop-down menu options for assigning new codes, coding from a existing code list, and applying in vivo codes (using the text itself as the code label). To some users, these features will make the time-consuming process of coding easier; for others they will be unimportant.

Multiple codes may be applied to the same text passage in all QDA software. Coded text segments may overlap or be embedded. These relationships among codes and related text segments form the foundation of many search and filtering tools used in QDA software products.

Not all QDA software allows work with images, audio, or video files. In those programs that go beyond text, segmenting images typically involves dragging the mouse over the designated section of the image to produce a small rectangular box around the selected content. Code names are then typed in as text, and coded image content automatically appears in inverted or highlighted colors to make it conspicuous.

Audio and video files are coded using operating system utilities. That is, using a Windows or Apple OS utility, a window containing a timer, beginning and end markers, and start, stop, rewind, and fast forward buttons appears. Most users find these tools much like those on a cassette or CD player. The researcher finds the beginning of the designated section of "tape" and applies the beginning or start marker. The researcher then moves forward to find the end of the section and applies the end marker. The result is a subsection of the material, which may be labeled with a code. As with text, multiple, overlapping, and embedded segments of all data types (text, images, audio, and video) may be marked and coded. Search tools for images, audio, and video, however, are few and rudimentary in comparison to search tools for text.

Searching Text

Contemporary QDA software includes a wide range of text search features. All QDA programs allow simple searches for specific words or phrases and the use of wildcard searches. A simple search is analogous to those done with the "Find" command on a word processor. Wildcard searches allow identification of multiple word forms. In most wildcard searches, an asterisk is used to represent all possible prefixes and suffixes. For example, *cause would find *cause* and *because;* talk* would find *talk, talks, talked,* and *talking.* A few programs also allow searches using a string of different words and wildcards to locate all instances of a concept. That is, a search for *cause, "since, how come,* and *due to"* may be combined into a single search for equivalent word forms conveying similar content. Most QDA software also includes Boolean search functions in which multiple words, phrases, or codes are located. For example, a researcher might wish to search for segments of text in which the words *listened* and *heard* were both present. Many QDA programs include a variety of search tools that allow identification of text to which multiple, overlapping, or embedded codes have been assigned. For example, a researcher might wish to find all text to which both the codes *violence* and *drinking* were assigned. Some of these search functions have a considerable learning curve.

The key advantage of electronic text searches is that *all* instances of the text are located. The computer has no moments of inattention, distractions, or interruptions. Yet the researcher must still examine these text segments and determine if they are indeed meaningful for the identified research purposes. Not all instances of a word or phrase are necessarily germane given their context and manner of usage. "Autocoding" features in some QDA software sound like a qualitative researcher's panacea, yet they amount to little more than search functions. The software may indeed find and code all instances of a given word or phrase, but only the researcher can determine if these assignments are really warranted. Autocoding may serve as a rough form of content analysis by establishing word frequencies, but dedicated content analysis software is more appropriate to such statistical tasks (several content analysis software packages are listed in Appendix A).

Filtering Text

The filtering features found in almost all QDA software divide and collate the entire data set into more manageable subsets. Text segments, codes, and annotations are all subdivided and compiled. (Filtering features, however, are not yet applicable to images, audio files, or video files). At the most elementary level, a researcher can subdivide text content for review or analysis based on specific coded characteristics. For example, types of cases may be coded as *hospital care, nursing home care*, or *home care*. The content of the texts for each subgroup can be analyzed separately and the results compared across types of cases to establish similarities and variations in processes and responses.

Filtering features become still more helpful once text has been segmented into meaningful units and codes assigned to them. Again, all text and materials in the research project can be divided into subsets for review and analysis using one or more codes, words, or phrases. QDA software allows such filtering of data in several ways. A researcher can generate a filtered subset of text to print out and review (this subset will include only segments of text to which a given code has been assigned). Such results allow review of coding consistency and allow identification of text that establishes the boundaries to code assignment rules. Some QDA programs allow printing or file output of all text within a certain number of words or lines from a specified keyword.

Alternately, the researcher can locate and print out all instances of text to which several codes have been assigned in specified combination. For example, we may wish to see if the code "using" was assigned before or after content coded as "high risk behavior."

The ability to filter text and to save the results of filtering operations helps researchers delimit the boundaries of the systems under study. Such "systems closure features" distinguished some early QDA products from competitors (Weitzman & Miles, 1995). However, in contemporary QDA software the ability to filter subsets of data and save the analyses of these subsets is much more common. Many QDA software products include systems closure features, whether they are so labeled or not.

Memos and Annotation

Most QDA software allows users to create and store notes or memos about the research project and data analysis. Almost all QDA products allow the researcher to attach a note or definition to texts and codes. Others allow the researcher to annotate virtually all components of the data set. The differences among the programs are numerous, including variations in memo length, format, and the ease of use of the annotation features. The importance of specific annotation features remains a function of analysis type and user preference. Some users note specific omissions in annotation features. For example, Barry (1998) notes that ATLAS.ti does not allow annotation of the files that represent original data. On the other hand, ATLAS.ti allows editable annotation of the research project as a whole, of text segments, of codes, and even of other memos. User needs and preferences are central to determining which QDA product provides optimal memoing and annotation features.

Networking Features

Some QDA software products include features that organize the creation of visual network maps. Network maps display the relationships among selected components of the project. These components may, but do not necessarily, represent concepts or theory. Network mapping features help in the creation of data matrices or arrays as described by Miles and Huberman (1994a, 1994b), grounded theories as described by Glaser and Strauss (1967) and various forms of hermeneutic analysis.

The QDA software tools help the researcher define and delimit the concepts or components to be networked, organize them visually, and specify the relationships among the concepts. For example, NUD•IST generates a hierarchical tree network display in which researcher-defined higher-order concepts branch out to lower-order components. ATLAS.ti generates flexible network maps in which the user defines both the organization of the components (i.e., vertical, horizontal, reciprocal) and allows labeling of the nature of the relationships among components. ATLAS.ti will also automatically generate networks based on coding frequency and can generate "code forests" displaying user-coded data in a tree and branch format.

Researchers and academics have long drawn such network maps on napkins or plain paper, but alternations in the content and relationships are difficult and often require starting over for clarity. Computerized network maps may be easily revised and always remain legible and tidy. All computer QDA networking features are rudimentary in comparison to other software options, but nonetheless get the job done. NUD•IST networks are stick figure hierarchies; ATLAS.ti networks are small rectangles containing text labels connected by lines. The content is clear but the result is not sophisticated in comparison to network images created by dedicated concept mapping software such as Inspiration Software's Inspiration (a tool used by students of all ages) or MindJet's MindManager. Flow-charting software can also produce clear displays of components and their relationships. More importantly, QDA networking features may help researchers move from data and preliminary conceptualization to true theory building and testing.

THE LIMITATIONS OF QDA SOFTWARE

QDA software can be a very useful tool, but it does not replace the primary role of the researcher as analytic decision maker. Qualitative data analysis requires ongoing and reflective decision making by the researcher in conjunction with peer reviews and feedback from respondents (member checks). The actual judgments about the meaning, relevance, and importance of any given data must always be determined by the researcher and not by the software alone.

Miles and Huberman (1994a) note that pencil-and-paper QDA may be costly, time consuming, and fraught with errors. Computer-assisted QDA is also costly, time consuming, and may include errors of judgment due to researcher omission and commission. Computerized searches are surely complete, but coding assignments done by the researcher are only as good as is the care of the researcher in determining the meaning of the associated content. Computers may save complete versions of an ongoing analysis, but the final form of the data analysis is only as good as the researcher's knowledge, skill, budget, and perseverance can make it. Interpretations and assignments of meaning are not done by computer, but only organized and managed by computer.

Specific concerns about QDA software center on distancing researchers from the data (Seidel, 1991) and "decontextualizing" the data (Agar, 1991; Denzin, 1988). The computer may indeed be used to seek words or phrases out of context. QDA programs do differ in the prominence given to the raw data versus the researcher-assigned analytic content (Drisko, 1998). ATLAS.ti opens a large text window by default; NUD•IST opens to the project components. Whether such emphases alter user attention and analytic decision making is not at all clear. Barry (1998) notes that people who have not had much experience with the software often make such comments. Lee and Fielding (1995) note some researchers simply stop using QDA software if it distorts their approach to data analysis. Again, the researcher is always responsible for ensuring that the results of computerized QDA are meaningful and consistent with the research purposes.

Mason (1996) notes a concern that QDA software may promote a "variable-oriented" approach to data analysis. Several QDA products allow SPSS-formatted output of data that have been coded into nominal- or ordinal-level variable formats. However, using QDA software for quantitative coding purposes is an extremely cumbersome process.

On the other hand, the qualitative analytic strategies articulated by Miles and Huberman (1994a, 1994b) involve identifying and creating visual arrays of concepts in a format that appears similar to statistical path analysis modeling. It seems once again that qualitative researchers vary in research purposes and related analytic strategies. QDA software may lead some toward a more atomistic approach to data analysis, but others may adopt such a strategy purposefully to meet their intended research objectives. In any case, QDA software is not a strong tool for statistical analysis and may be applied to more, or less, contextualized analyses.

Yet another concern is that use of QDA software may promote a homogenization of methods. Coffey, Holbrook, and Atkinson (1996) argue that QDA software may narrow analytic options and push qualitative researchers who use it toward code and retrieve approaches to qualitative research, most likely grounded theory (see also Lonkila, 1995). Yet Lee and Fielding (1996) found that many other types of qualitative research also used QDA software and that these alternate approaches constitute 69% of all citations mentioning QDA software. Lee and Fielding (1995) also found that users of QDA software are more likely to stop using the software than to alter their analytic approaches due to its structure or limitations. Software use does not seem to be homogenizing QDA methods. On the other hand, it is quite possible that newer generations of qualitative researchers, unfamiliar with a range of analytic options, may be more prone to use only those options a given QDA product makes available.

Grounded theory is prominent in the orienting structures of many QDA products. Familiarity with grounded theory is widespread, leading to its frequent citation as an analytic method (Wells, 1995). It is also worth noting that grounded theory, like computer technology, has considerable cachet. Still, several studies claiming to apply grounded theory do not move from the descriptive identification of patterns within the data to a conceptual level of analysis (Drisko, 2001). That is, the theoretical linkages among the data elements are not specified in the final report. Here again, researchers must be responsible for understanding the methods they seek to employ and to report them fully. There remains a clear and compelling need for both breadth and depth in the training of qualitative researchers.

SPECIAL FEATURES IN QDA SOFTWARE: USEFUL TOOLS OR MARKETING FLUFF?

Some special features of QDA software can have limited practical utility. HyperRESEARCH's "hypothesis testing" features obviously assumes the qualitative researcher has a specific hypothesis to test (Hesse-Beiber et al., 1994). Many qualitative researchers do not view their work in this manner.

Indeed, this set of sequential filtering and searching operations can help structure a review of the data, but most other QDA software can achieve the same result.

Similarly, NVivo's (Richards, 1999) ability to display text in color may be useful for some forms of analyses, but seems a small step forward. Another recent innovation, the ability to edit text after data analysis has begun, allows for correction of errors missed in the data transcription and preening. NVivo and WinMax allow such editing. This is a useful improvement but hardly a transformative one. Another innovation, the use of file formats that can be opened directly by word processors, such as Rich Text Format, may be easier for the researcher than is use of ASCII text. Yet this change mainly improves convenience. Overall, these special features will appeal to few users. The growth in shared features, coupled with improvements in ease of use, seem much more important than are these unique features.

At this time, an analysis begun on one QDA product cannot be transferred to another. This is because the computer codes applied to the data set differ for each product. The ability to transfer a dataset and analysis from one program to another without loss of codes and memos already applied would make exploration across QDA software products much easier. Thomas Muhr, creator of ATLAS.ti, has proposed the use of XML data tags as a common approach that could be shared across QDA products. If the independent creators of several products adopt this XML standard, it could allow greater experimentation and comparison without lost effort. Such a standard would also allow more complete and fair product comparisons. Time will tell if standardization of file formats is possible in this small and competitive market niche.

OTHER RESOURCES

Weitzman and Miles (1995) offer an excellent, though now dated, sourcebook on a much wider range of software applicable to qualitative data analysis and display than is addressed here. The challenge of their book is that it requires a knowledgeable reader to follow the terminology in full, but it is nonetheless useful to novices for its portrait of the range and variety of qualitative research approaches and analytic methods. Kelle (1995) edited a volume on theoretical and methodological issues related to QDA software use. The book offers in-depth discussions of many issues briefly mentioned in this chapter. The journal *Qualitative Health Research* now offers regular articles on the influence of computers on qualitative research. These varied commentaries address practical issues, methodology, and user experiences.

A wide range of on-line resources about QDA software are also easily available. Few, however, detail its use. The listservs of ATLAS.ti and QSR provide useful feedback to users, and often spin off threads of conversation on analytic issues beyond computers. They should also be considered a resource for questions on analytic methods; well-known authors offer commentary from time to time. These listservs also provide an opportunity for researchers with common interests to find each other internationally. A number of disciplines have developed qualitative research listservs to expand joint research projects and to share teaching resources. URLs and addresses for products and listservs are provided in the section titled Qualitative Listservs (pp. 209–210).

USING QDA SOFTWARE:
THE USER'S EXPERIENCE

Most newcomers are drawn to QDA software as a way to make their work faster and easier. This hope will be only partially realized for those who stick with the process, but the yield is real and positive. QDA software can be a big help if it fits with one's needs and analytic purposes. Still, pencil and paper can do all that software can do, except for sharing and merging datasets with colleagues at a distance and creating hyperlinks among information.

QDA software is often expensive, with single-user editions costing from $225 to about $300. Some products offer reduced prices to students. All of these software products have a steep initial learning curve—newcomers often find it daunting. Most QDA products offer demo or trial versions as free internet downloads or on low-cost CDs. These demo versions will run for only a limited period of time (usually 30 days) or will manage and analyze only a small data set. Unfortunately, most demo software does not include the tutorial content included on the full versions.

Most users find that a workshop with hands-on exposure is the best way to begin using QDA software. Unfortunately, such workshops are not easy to find and can be quite expensive when run by consulting companies. Introductory workshops on QDA software are increasingly available at academic conferences. These workshops break the ice by helping new users gain confidence and by providing a forum for all kinds of questions. Workshops seem to make independent exploration more productive and fruitful.

Still, there is no substitute for doing a "real" QDA project, over some time, to understand and master the core program features. Software listservs host many calls for help from users who (appear) to have lost data or who (appear) to have lost program features. Typically, the responses are quick (although not instantaneous as desired!) and helpful. Most users inadvertently engage program features they do not understand, and simply need to move a few files or click an icon to find the lost data (really).

Some users become enamored of QDA software. Perhaps this is because the software requires some time to learn and because qualitative research can be difficult. The challenge of qualitative data analysis, or resistances to it, make the program seem much more controllable and compliant than is the large and unstructured data set. One doctoral student told me: "It's amazing. You click on a button and things happen *immediately*. It makes me feel slow." Such reactions are also common among workshop participants. That the software is only performing operations that the researcher has defined as useful and appropriate seems unnoticed. Another student gave a presentation on her research and spent about two thirds of her time discussing the software rather than her analytic contributions to an excellent study. It appeared that the technological cachet overshadowed the researcher's decisions and findings, although few of us would think of giving such credit to paper and pencil or a word processor. Ongoing support for qualitative researchers, and emphasis on their human analytic work, is always needed.

There are some differences in software choice due to the kinds of computer one owns. Mac users tend toward HyperREARCH and NUD•IST whereas IBM/Windows users tend toward ATLAS.ti and NVivo (developed by NUD•IST creators Lyn and Thomas Richards). HyperREARCH and NUD•IST were originally Apple/Mac programs (but are available in Windows versions); ATLAS.ti and NVivo are Windows programs (that can only be run on Macs using Windows emulator software). I first encountered ATLAS.ti as a DOS program, which happens to look identical to today's Windows versions, graphical interface and all. Most users stay with what they learn initially, for better or worse. Alexa and Zuell (1999) note some QDA products simply put a graphical face on older text-based program code, whereas others make much better use of recent graphical options.

"SO, WHAT SOFTWARE DO YOU USE?"
A PERSONAL NOTE

In 1996 I obtained a small grant from the Clinical Research Institute at Smith College School for Social Work to purchase and explore several QDA programs. I tried out six programs for some time. I also became familiar with the updates to these products and have experimented with three newer products. Analytic induction (Znaniecki, 1934) and grounded theory (Glaser & Strauss, 1967) coupled with Pattons' (1996) utilization-focused evaluation generally orient my work.

With some experience I found that ATLAS.ti suits me very well, but I know researchers with similar core QDA orientations who use HyperREARCH and NUD•IST effectively. WinMax is yet another similar program.

What made ATLAS.ti stand out? ATLAS.ti makes text prominent so I do not lose sight of the context in which specific text is embedded. Reading the text in context often helps me return to the moment of the interview. Sometimes I recall the scene vividly, almost eidetically. ATLAS.ti also has an icon-rich interface that makes it easy to accomplish many tasks. Icon buttons for all sorts of features are always instantly available and serve as little reminders, too. Placing the mouse on an icon generates a balloon display describing its functions, which was very helpful when I was learning to use the program.

The ATLAS.ti user interface can be easily altered to make coding more efficient. I routinely code with the "code extras list" expanded to fill the right side of the screen so I can see the codes I have already assigned. Finally, ATLAS.ti has a sense of humor. The program opens with a chord from the Beatles. The program also has an icon called the "Frustration Button" which has no analytic purpose. The icon activates program creator Thomas Muhr saying "I hate computers" in a very frustrated voice; he is British, and his accent makes it even more poignant. I use the button often because it helps me get beyond my moments of frustration. All computer programs should have such a button. Be warned: my needs and interests (and sense of humor) may not parallel those of other qualitative researchers.

I recently attended a fine introductory workshop on HyperRESEARCH. The latest version of this product seemed a lot like ATLAS.ti despite some clear differences in its look and organization. I was reminded of an early comment about NVivo from a veteran QDA software developer and trainer whose work I regard highly. This insider said NVivo seemed like "ATLAS.ti with colors." Indeed, my own later evaluation uncovered more similarities than differences between these two programs.

The QDA software market is maturing. Features and processes are becoming more similar across product brands. There may be some meaningful differences in program features and character, but similarity has increased dramatically in the past 6 years. Users should select the QDA software based on their analytic purposes and goals, ideally after exposure to two or more programs.

COLLABORATION AND QDA SOFTWARE USE

Collaborative qualitative research will always have challenging moments, but joint computerized QDA will surely add to the burden. Lee and Fielding (1995) report that differences in analytic approach, pacing of work, and views about merging joint work can all be sources of conflict among collaborative computerized QDA users. My own work suggests that differences in emphasis and understanding couple with ego and personal style whether the analysis is computerized or not. However, adding the frustrations and learning curve for using software jointly can only add to the challenge.

Collaborative researchers need structured analytic assignments and regular, structured opportunities to share their views and work toward a consensus when possible. When differences linger, a lead researcher must take responsibility for making final decisions and taking action. Still, reporting differences (when page length allows) increases the credibility of qualitative research in most cases. Differences and divergences often point toward content we do not yet fully understand.

Whether done individually or as part of a group, computerized or manually, qualitative data analysis can be an isolating experience. A good deal of data management and analytic work takes place alone. Researchers need to balance such analytic work with other tasks and activities. Good qualitative research requires peer review from time to time during data collection and data analysis to maximize reflexivity, self-awareness, and reflection on the project as a whole. It also requires that tentative findings (descriptive or conceptual) be member checked with participants to ensure their credibility. Balancing analytic work with external human reviews helps counter isolation.

SUMMARY AND CONCLUSION

Computerized tools for qualitative research are still new. QDA software offers researchers a fine way to manage, organize, analyze, and report their work. The products are increasingly sophisticated and relatively easy to use. Many supports for users of QDA software are now available internationally. New opportunities to examine and display audio and video data, and to generate hypertext, are emerging in the most recent QDA software. QDA software makes much more feasible long-distance collaboration among qualitative researchers. Perhaps the use of QDA software will become commonplace and less, as some now see it, an adventure in high technology. QDA software can enhance qualitative research, but does not automatically offer insight, self-awareness, or empathy. The human researcher, the software user, remains the real qualitative data analyst, as it should be.

ACKNOWLEDGMENTS

I acknowledge the Smith College School for Social Work Clinical Research Institute for funding the purchase of several qualitative software programs used in preparing this chapter.

REFERENCES

Alexa, M., & Zuell, C. (1999). *Commonalities, differences and limitations of text analysis software: The results of a review.* Retrieved May 24, 2002 from http://www.gesis.org/Publikationen/Berichte/ZUMA_Arbeitsberichte/documents/pdfs/99_06.pdf

Agar, M. (1991). The right brain strikes back. In N. Fielding & R. Lee (Eds.), *Using computers in qualitative research* (pp. 181–194). Newbury Park, CA: Sage.

Altheide, D., & Johnson, J. (1994). Criteria for assessing the interpretive validity in qualitative research. In N. Denzin & Y. Lincoln (Eds.), *Handbook of qualitative research* (pp. 485–499). Thousand Oaks, CA: Sage.

Barry (1998). Choosing qualitative data analysis software: Atlas.ti and Nudist compared. *Sociological Research Online,* 3 (3). Retrieved December 1, 2000 from the World Wide

Web: www.socresonline.org.uk/
socresonline/3/3/4.html

Coffey, A., Holbrook, B., & Atkinson, P.
(1996). Qualitative data analysis:
Technologies and representations.
Sociological Research Online, 1 (1).
Retrieved May 20, 2002, from
http://www.socresonline.org.uk/
socresonline/1/1/4.html

Denzin, N., & Lincoln, Y. (Eds.). (1994).
Handbook of qualitative research.
Thousand Oaks, CA: Sage.

Denzin, N. (1988). Qualitative analysis for
social scientists. Book review. *Contemporary Sociologist, 17* (3), 430–2.

Dey, I. (1993). *Qualitative data analysis: A
user-friendly guide for social scientists.*
New York: Routledge.

Drisko, J. (1997). Strengthening qualitative studies and reports: Standards to
enhance academic integrity. *Journal of
Social Work Education, 33,* 185–97.

Drisko, J. (1998). Using qualitative data
analysis software. *Computers in Human
Services, 15* (1), 1–19.

Drisko, J. (2000). *It's not just anything goes:
Qualitative data analysis methods.*
Juried workshop presented at the
4th Annual Society for Social Work
and Research Annual Meeting,
January, Charleston, SC.

Drisko, J. (2001). *What makes a publishable
qualitative report?* Juried symposium
paper presented at the Society for
Social Work and Research Annual
Meeting, January, Atlanta, GA.

Evans, W. (2002, March). *Content analysis
software.* Retrieved May 6, 2002, from
http://www.gsu.edu/~wwwcom/

Glaser, B., & Strauss, A. (1967). *The
discovery of grounded theory.* Chicago:
Aldine.

Hesse-Biber, S., Kinder, T., Dupuis, P.,
Dupuis, A., & Tornabene, E. (1994).
HyperRESEARCH [manual]: *A content analysis tool for the qualitative researcher.* Randolph, MA:
ResearchWare, Inc.

Kelle, U. (1995). An overview of computer-aided methods in qualitative
research. In U. Kelle (Ed.), *Computer-aided qualitative data analysis: Theory,
methods and practice* (pp. 1–17).
Thousand Oaks, CA: Sage.

Kelle, U. (1997). Theory building in
qualitative research and computer
programs for the management of
textual data. *Sociological Research Online, 2* (2). Retrieved May 20, 2002,
from http://www.socresonline.org.uk/
socresonline/2/2/1.html

Lee, R., & Fielding, N. (1995). User's
experiences of qualitative data analysis
software. In U. Kelle (Ed.), *Computer-aided qualitative data analysis: Theory,
methods and practice* (pp. 29–40).
Thousand Oaks, CA: Sage.

Lee, R., & Fielding, N. (1996). Qualitative data analysis: Representations of a
technology: A comment on Coffey,
Holbrook and Atkinson. *Sociological
Research Online, 1* (4). Retrieved
May 11, 2002, from http://www.
socresonline.org.uk/socresonline/
1/4/lf.html

Leininger, M. (1994). Evaluation criteria
and critique of qualitative studies.
In J. Morse (Ed.), *Critical issues
in qualitative research methods*
(pp. 95–115). Newbury Park,
CA: Sage.

Lonkila, M. (1995). Grounded theory as
an emerging paradigm for computer-assisted qualitative data analysis. In
U. Kelle (Ed.), *Computer-aided qualitative data analysis: Theory, methods and
practice* (pp. 41–51). Thousand Oaks,
CA: Sage.

Madron, T., Tate, C. N., & Brookshire,
R. (1985). *Using microcomputers in
research.* Beverly Hills, CA: Sage.

Mason, J. (1996). *Qualitative researching.*
Thousand Oaks, CA: Sage.

Miles, M. A., & Huberman, A. (1994a).
*Qualitative data analysis: An expanded
sourcebook* (2nd ed.). Thousand Oaks,
CA: Sage.

Miles, M. A., & Huberman, A. (1994b).
Data management and analysis methods. In N. Denzin & Y. Lincoln
(Eds.), *Handbook of qualitative research*
(pp. 428–44). Thousand Oaks, CA:
Sage.

Muhr, T. (1994). *ATLAS/ti* [manual]: *Computer aided text interpretation and theory building* (2nd ed.). Berlin: Author.

Padgett, D. (1998). *Qualitative methods in social work research*. Thousand Oaks, CA: Sage.

Patton, M. Q. (1996). *Utilization-focused evaluation* (3rd ed.). Thousand Oaks, CA: Sage.

Qualitative Solutions and Research [QSR]. (1995). *User's guide for QSR NUD•IST*. Distributed by Sage/Scolari.

Ranwez, S., & Crampes. M. (1999). *Conceptual documents and hypertext documents are two different forms of virtual document*. Retrieved May 10, 2002 from http://www.cs.unibo.it/ ~fabio/VD99/ranwez/ranwez.html

Richards, L. (1999). Data alive! The thinking behind NVivo. *Qualitative Health Research, 9* (3), 88–93.

Richards, T., & Richards, L. (1994). Using computers in qualitative research. In N. Denzin & Y. Lincoln (Eds.), *Handbook of qualitative research* (pp. 445–62). Thousand Oaks, CA: Sage.

Schrodt, P. (1984). *Microcomputer methods for social scientists*. Beverly Hills, CA: Sage.

Seidel, J. (1991). Method and madness in the application of computer technology to qualitative data analysis. In N. Fielding & R. Lee (Eds.), *Using computers in qualitative research*. Thousand Oaks, CA: Sage.

Tesch, R. (1990). *Qualitative analysis: Analysis types and software tools*. Philadelphia: Falmer Press.

Weitzman, E., & Miles, M. (1994). Choosing computer programs for qualitative data analysis. In M. Miles & A. M. Huberman (Eds.), *Qualitative data analysis: An expanded sourcebook* (2nd. ed.) (pp. 311–17). Thousand Oaks, CA: Sage.

Weitzman, E., & Miles, M. (1995). *Computer programs for qualitative data analysis: A software sourcebook*. Thousand Oaks, CA: Sage.

Wells, K. (1995). The strategy of grounded theory: possibilities and problems. *Social Work Research, 19* (1), 33–7.

Znaniecki, F. (1934). *The method of sociology*. New York: Farrar & Rinehart.

Software Resources

CORE QDA SOFTWARE PRODUCTS

- ATLAS.ti   www.atlasti.de
- The Ethnograph   www.qualisresearch.com/
- HyperRESEARCH   www.researchware.com/
- Kwalitan   www.socsci.kun.nl/maw/mt/software/kwalitan/
- MARTIN   www.son.wisc.edu/resources/simonds/
                        martin/martin.htm
- MAXqda   www.maxqda.com/ (Replaces WinMAX)
- NUDIST •   www.qsr.com.au/
- NVivo   www.qsr.com.au/
- Qualrus   www.ideaworks.com/Qualrus.shtml

Information, demo versions, and purchase of many of these products can be arranged through Scolari Publications at www.scolari.com *or* www.scolari.co.uk. Susanne Friese, QDA software developer and international trainer, from Qualitative Research & Consulting in Stuttgart, Germany, offers her comparison of four programs at http://www.quarc.de/overview.html (English language version).

AUDIO AND VIDEO PRODUCTS

- Annotape   www.annotape.com/
- C-I-SAID   www.code-a-text.co.uk/
                                [C-I-SAID is also called Code-A-Text; a
                                subset product is called CTANKS]
- Interclipper   www.interclipper.com
- Qualitative Media Analyser   www.cvs.dk/qma.htm

LARGE-SCALE DATABASE PRODUCTS

- AnSWR   www.cdc.gov/hiv/software/answr.htm
- EZ-text   www.cdc.gov/hiv/software/ez-text.htm

MAPPING SOFTWARE

- Decision Explorer   www.banxia.com/demain.html
- CmapTools   http://cmap.coginst.uwf.edu/
- Inspiration   www.inspiration.com/

HYPERTEXT TOOLS

- HyperSoft   www.hypersoft-net.it/Def-eng.htm
- Storyspace   www.eastgate.com/Storyspace.html

SPECIAL PURPOSE PRODUCTS

- Ethno2 (Event Structure Analysis software)   www.indiana.edu/%7Esocpsy/ESA/
- MacSHAPA (Observational Data Analysis)   www.aviation.uiuc.edu/institute/ acadprog/epjp/macshapa.html
- QMETHOD (for Q sort technique)   www.rz.unibw-uenchen.de/ ~p41bsmk/qmethod/
- The Observer (Observational Data Analysis)   www.noldus.com/products/index.html
- SPIRE (Visual Data Display)   www.pnl.gov/infoviz/

WORD PROCESSOR ADD-ONS

- TAMs   http://tux.educ.kent.edu/ %7Emweinste/tams/tams.html

PRODUCTS UNDER CONSTRUCTION

- CodeRead   www.unc.edu/~aperrin/CodeRead/

MAINLY CONTENT ANALYSIS PRODUCTS

Oriented to statistics and keywords in context.

- INTEXT   www.intext.de/intexte.htm
- Textquest   www.textquest.de/tqe.htm
- VisualText   www.textanalysis.com/

William Evans of the University of Georgia offers links to many content analysis software resources at www.gsu.edu/~wwwcom/

Alexa and Zuell (1999) take stock of a varied mix of 15 content analysis and QDA software at: www.gesis.org/Publikationen/Berichte/ZUMA_Arbeitsberichte/documents/pdfs/99_06.pdf (English language version)

Qualitative Listservs

QUALITATIVE RESEARCH FOR
THE HUMAN SCIENCES

Organized by Judith Preissle. QUALRS-L@uga.cc.uga.edu. To subscribe, send as message text: subscribe qualrs-l <your name> (example: subscribe qualrs-l Jane Doe) to listserv@uga.cc.uga.edu

QUALITATIVE SOFTWARE

Organized by Ann Lewins. To subscribe send as message text: join qual-software your name (example: join qual-software Joe Dokes) to mailbase@mailbase.ac.uk

ATLAS.TI

Organized by Thomas Muhr. To subscribe send as message text: SUB ATLAS-TI yourfirstname yourlastname yourinstitution (example: SUB ATLAS-TI Ray Lincoln, Some Fine College) to listserv@atlasti.de

Q.S.R. FORUM

Organized by T. and L. Richards, creators of NUDIST. To subscribe send as message text: subscribe QSR-Forum yourname (example: subscribe QSR-Forum Penny DuForge) to mailing-list-request@qsr.com.au

PROFESSIONAL GROUPS

The Council on Social Work Education
Qualitative Interest Group

Convened by James Drisko. To subscribe, send an e-mail with your e-mail address to jdrisko@smith.edu

The Society for Social Work
and Research Qualitative Interest Group

Convened by Deborah Padgett. To subscribe, send an e-mail with your e-mail address to deborah.padgett@nyu.edu

Qualitative Research in Management
and Organization Studies

To subscribe send as message text: subscribe qualnet yourname to major-domo@listserv.bc.edu or e-mail Gaiser@bcvms.bc.edu

Narrative Psychology

Organized by Andy Lock. To subscribe send as message text: subscribe psych-narrative your name to majordomo@massey.ac.nz

American Evaluation Association Discussion List

To subscribe, send as message text: subscribe evaltalk your name to listserv@ua1vm.ua.edu or e-mail EAL@ua1vm.ua.edu

9

The Role of the
Mentoring Relationship
in Qualitative Research

IDA ROLDAN
AND R. DENNIS SHELBY

This chapter explores and illustrates the role of the mentoring relationship and its use to facilitate rigor in qualitative research. Its builds upon ideas in Shelby (2001) and uses work between a mentor and a student to illustrate several concepts. The first step in discussing the role of mentoring in qualitative research is to explore definitions of the term. *Webster's Third New International Dictionary* defines *mentor* as (1) a close trusted experienced counselor or guide and (2) a teacher, tutor, or coach. These two definitions point to the qualities of the mentor and what the mentor does.

All professions—medical, legal, clinical—prescribe some period of supervised work applying the knowledge gained through books and lectures. Social work students have clients and are closely supervised in their early efforts to translate coursework into the dynamic (and often much more nuanced) world of real people and real problems. The physician is first a student, then an intern, and then a resident, with differing levels of supervision at each point in training. New police officers are sent out for a period with training officers, again to translate their learning from the relative safety of an academy to the complexities of life on the street. In a similar vein, why would we possibly turn doctoral students loose on a project as complicated as a dissertation, and not offer them close guidance?

The role of the mentor is central to this process when qualitative methods are involved. Researchers must interact with their participants while simultaneously gathering data and striving for balance between sensitivity and objectivity. We must articulate our findings in a coherent manner, hopefully with a new view on a phenomenon, and always grounded in the data derived from our interaction with the population and the phenomenon of interest (Glaser & Strauss, 1967).

The mentor's role is in this process of translating theoretical concepts into dynamic use in the real world. As Freud (1913) said, one cannot learn to play chess from a book. As educators, we need to address the important issue of how we convey and teach the complexities of actually doing qualitative research. Kennedy (1997) notes that mentoring is one of several vital areas of academic duty: ". . . [mentoring] is more like training than teaching; it resembles the journeyman–apprentice relationship that once characterized artisan guilds (p. 97)." In their study of successful academic programs, Haworth and Conrad (1997) describe mentoring as an aspect of the broader component of interactive teaching. Consistent with the themes of this chapter, Kennedy views mentoring as a transformation of classroom teaching. As students become more advanced, they must learn to function outside of the classroom.

This chapter describes common difficulties we encounter as qualitative researchers and how the mentoring relationship is useful in helping the student as well as enhancing rigor. The central idea of this chapter is that the mentoring relationship can and should be used to meet these standards. Dissertations in particular evoke tender feelings and a sense of vulnerability in students. This points to the importance of trust and confidence that the mentor knows what he or she is doing and has the student's best interests at heart. As methodologies continue to multiply, standards for rigor will be slightly different, depending upon the epistemological roots of the method (Drisko, 1990). As the mentor helps the student understand and meet these standards, the relationship becomes critical.

When working with a student, Erickson's statement: "true mentorship, far from being a showy form of emotional sympathy, is always part of a discipline of outlook and method" (1964, p. 124) should serve as a guide. The purpose of this relationship is to facilitate the student's knowledge and sophistication in general and his or her study in particular. Although there usually is a personal alliance, the ultimate task is to assist the student's learning, not merely cheer on his or her efforts. While acknowledging the myriad emotional issues evoked by a dissertation, the mentor and student tend to them only in terms of the task at hand: executing and completing a systematic inquiry about a phenomenon or group. This perspective acknowledges the intellect and skills that students bring to the task, but also pushes them ahead.

The alliance between student and mentor is crucial because the student is engaged in data collection and analysis using methodologies that require considerable use of self. Grounded theory (Glaser & Strauss, 1967; Strauss & Corbin, 1998), naturalistic inquiry (Lincoln & Guba, 1985), interactive interpretivism (Denzin, 1997), biographical (e.g., Atkinson, 1998), and phenomenological (e.g., Giorgi, 1985) approaches require immersion in the research participants' lives to produce results that are rich, thorough, trustworthy, balanced, coherent and, most importantly, useful to practitioners. Narrative methods (e.g., Riessman, 1993), while approaching the data in a very different manner, still involve the interface of the self with the selves of the participants.

Social work graduate students tend to be drawn toward live data derived from interviews. They want to interact with their participants and engage in the complexity of their lives. However, such intense engagement brings strong forces into play. Many students want to study vulnerable populations, which in turn raises human subjects concerns. Other students want to conduct research on a topic that has personal relevance to them and their lives. Although there usually is some personal experience that draws us to a topic, it is a matter of degree. The closer a phenomenon is to a student's life, the greater the chances for anxiety to emerge and affect the conduct and course of the study.

Central to the mentoring relationship is the student's interaction with the data as well as the mentor's interaction with the student and the data. These interactions allow for careful scrutiny and attention to bias. In this chapter, we address five topics that reflect our own experience in a mentoring relationship between a dissertation advisor (R.D.S.) and doctoral student (I.R.). These are resistance to immersion, the tension between objectivity and sensitivity, transferences and countertransferences, the role of clinical and social science theories, and a common pitfall of mentoring.

This chapter also demonstrates how clinical concepts from psychodynamic theory can be used to assist the student in producing research that is rigorous and offers an in-depth understanding of human experience. Thus, some of the same issues central to clinical practice (e.g., resistance, transference, countertransference, and content versus process) can be applied, albeit with some modifications in scope and purpose (Shelby, 2001). Examples are provided that highlight our experience in a mentor–student relationship.

RESISTANCE TO IMMERSION

Graduate students conducting qualitative research are usually surprised by the inadequacy of their coursework as preparation. Although methods courses are a good foundation, the demands of a full-scale dissertation can be daunting. One of the many tasks of the mentor is to help the student adhere to the procedures of the method she or he has chosen. Because the qualitative researcher is the instrument of data collection, he or she can easily become lost in the collection and analysis of the data as well as in the feelings evoked by the data (Shelby, 2001; Padgett, 1998; Strauss & Corbin, 1998). Anxiety has a way of interfering with adherence to these procedures especially when the require becoming immersed in the group and phenomenon under study.

> I.R.: When I was doing my study of AIDS in the Puerto Rican community, I collected my data at a community methadone clinic. My interviews with HIV-infected drug addicts evoked many painful feelings associated with my personal experience with a family member. Although I gradually developed positive relations with the research participants and enjoyed talking to them, I found myself dreading my visits to the methadone clinic. Interestingly, I found that my dread disappeared once I arrived at the clinic. Once I processed these feelings with my mentor,

I realized that my dread was based on my fear that I would discover that one of my participants had died or was hospitalized and that feelings of powerlessness and loss would emerge.

R.D.S.: The dread of death is part of living with AIDS. It is a high-stakes disease, and Ida's study indicated death and its consequences were very much a part of her participants' lives as well as other fears. In some populations, such as middle-class white gay men, the fear of death from AIDS has receded into the background with the advent of the newer antiviral medications. However culture and social class impart complex differences in how the disease is experienced and managed. In Ida's study, the men were worried about going to hell and the women were worried about the care of their children.

Ida encountered people who were not taking their antiviral medications to keep their T-cell counts low to retain their disability payments. She saw individuals whose problems with medication compliance resulted in their exclusion from the newer, more powerful medication regimens. Some of this data was horrifying to us, but it is the participants' lives and how they view the world that is central to qualitative research.

I.R.: Certain events during the pilot phase of my study led me to some of the major categories that later emerged in this study. When I interviewed staff at several Chicago community agencies providing services to the Puerto Rican HIV/AIDS infected population, it became apparent that their locations were well-kept secrets in the community. Most of these institutions either had no signage or their services were disguised. For example, my main recruitment site was part of a family health center. The other recruitment site was part of a methadone clinic. Nowhere at these sites was there any outward evidence that HIV/AIDS patients were being seen there. There seemed to be a conscious effort to disguise HIV/AIDS services by integrating them with the more "acceptable" services to the community. Also, most agencies I approached refused to give me permission to conduct the study at their agencies. They refused to support my study because they "wanted to protect their client's confidentiality."

As I approached the data collection phase, recruitment became extremely difficult. Access to participants was almost impossible. It became clear that participants were not going to talk to me unless the staff supported the idea of this study. Therefore, developing trust with the staff was crucial during this time. One of the ways to win the staff's trust and support was to be willing to "get down and dirty." At first I was referred the most difficult cases. I was expected to go out into the roughest areas of the neighborhood (sometimes at night) and visit clients who were ill yet had refused the staff's efforts to help. Once the staff saw that I was willing to do whatever it took to reach these clients, they adopted me as one of their own. Their support made this study possible.

R.D.S.: As a mentor I was impressed with Ida's tenacity in her efforts to work her way into the population at the clinic and gain their trust. An important aspect of this was her observation that even though she was Puerto Rican, she was not being welcomed and dealt with as a fellow Puerto Rican. As we discussed this more, she came to realize that she was being viewed and dealt with as a *gringa* (a white woman).

I have observed this phenomenon with other ethnic minority students who, when they first approach their own group, are viewed as White, and/or representative of a White institution. This can be hard for the students, who want to contribute to knowledge about their own group but find themselves distrusted and viewed as an outsider. Ida's difficulties in finding a cooperative agency had a familiar ring. There were no signs on the door; a veil of secrecy seemed to surround the provision of services to Puerto Rican people with HIV infection.

Ida made the decision on her own to reveal her family history that indicated she was all too familiar with the world of the Puerto Rican injection drug user with AIDS. The change this disclosure brought about was quite profound as the participants began to open up to her and share the complexity of their lives. Although the mentor ultimately needs to focus on the task at hand, feelings of admiration for the student and her efforts are not unusual. These feelings are part and parcel of the mutual dynamics of the mentoring relationship. I found myself admiring Ida's courage as she went into dangerous neighborhoods, but I also worried about her safety and wondered if her husband would blame me if something happened.

OBJECTIVITY VERSUS SENSITIVITY

Strauss and Corbin define *objectivity* as "the ability to achieve a certain degree of distance from the research materials and to represent them fairly. . . ." *Sensitivity* is "the ability to respond to the subtle nuances of, and cues to, meanings in the data" (1998, pp. 42–3). Because the researcher is the instrument of data collection in qualitative research, he or she will naturally become immersed in and influenced by the data. As this process occurs, sensitivity is enhanced. The challenge is how to become immersed yet maintain a balance between objectivity and sensitivity (Strauss & Corbin, 1998).

Padgett (1998) states that examining one's biases requires ongoing vigilance throughout the course of the study. She adds that we do not necessarily need to eliminate our personal beliefs and biases, but instead need to be aware of their impact on the study. Although the process of recognizing and working through a bias and its implications can be painful, it is also freeing in that it leads us to a deeper level of understanding of the issues and of ourselves.

I.R.: My interest in this study originated in 1992 when my brother died of AIDS. But the major question emerged long before my brother died. As my family began to face the possibility of my brother coming home and needing care, a crisis emerged. During this time, it became apparent that this family crisis was different from all the rest. It was then that I began to wonder what kept my "typical Puerto Rican family" from responding the way they would normally respond when a member is terminally ill. Instead, concerns about casual transmission and what to tell neighbors and family emerged. It became clear that this was not to be public knowledge, that there was fear and shame connected to having a son or brother with AIDS.

At my brother's funeral, I was again struck by how often people whispered the word *AIDS*. When family members talked about others who had died of AIDS, they would invariably say, "They said it was cancer, but we know." I became curious about my community's attempts to keep the AIDS epidemic a secret from the outside world. This was a first step toward objectivity in that I knew something felt wrong but was not sure what it was.

Although personal experience can increase sensitivity, it can also interfere with maintaining analytic distance. In my study, the word *bochinche* continued to emerge in the data. Having grown up hearing this word, I assumed I knew what it meant. To me, it simply meant *gossip*.

Perez-Foster (1998) warns us of the pitfalls of the clinician's cultural countertransference when working with clients from his or her own group. She reminds us that the clinician needs to be mindful and aware of predetermined ideas about how the cultural environment has contributed to the client's presenting problems (Perez-Foster, 1998). The same cautions apply for the bicultural qualitative researcher.

Strauss and Corbin (1998) note that what respondents tell us is not always apparent; we may have to look for hidden or obscure meanings that are not evident in the data. In our discussion about *bochinche*, Dennis worked with me to capture its meaning in English. We realized that the data were leading us into the Puerto Rican culture's strong beliefs about the spirit world, body humors, and redemption. HIV/AIDS transmission was viewed as almost a magical process, not viral. There seemed to be a supernatural quality to the participants' view of their family's understanding of their illness.

At this time, Dennis became aware of my tendency to translate the data through a *gringo* lens. My fear of presenting my culture as primitive led to less-than-accurate translations of meaning. Because I was encouraged to stay as close to the data as possible, I decided to include untranslated Spanish words in the dissertation when these words defied translation. For example, we decided to keep *bochinche* in Spanish because it captured a cultural idiom that could not be directly translated.

R.D.S.: As we worked with this aspect of the analysis, I was repeatedly reminded of what to me was a painful and eye-opening encounter with a friend who was from an old Spanish family in the Southwest. He had grown up in a Spanish-speaking household and English was his second language. As a college student, he had taken French to help erase his accent. When I asked why he went to such great lengths, he replied, "you have no idea how offended White people are by Spanish accents."

I later encountered similar experiences with other friends who, in the midst of a party, broke into *Spanglish*. To me, this sudden eruption of a hidden aspect of their lives was a joyous event. But later the same friends reported feeling mortified that they had "let it out" and were working at "packing it back in."

So here we were at this interesting point. The data pointed to a bilingual and bicultural approach. From a cross-cultural perspective, beliefs about diseases do not require strict adherence to germ theory. But for Ida it represented being "too" Puerto Rican and portraying her culture in a less positive light. I thought that Ida needed encouragement to make this study reflect the complexity of her culture, not a sanitized *gringo* version. I believed that, like my friends, Ida was working at "packing it back in." I was also aware of the considerable anxiety that can emerge when exposing rich yet hidden aspects of ourselves and its impact on data analysis.

> I.R.: As Dennis sensed my conflict and anxiety about those aspects of myself and my culture that I felt were misunderstood by mainstream society, he gently encouraged me to analyze my resistance. I believe this was one of the most challenging times for me as I came to face those aspects of my culture about which I felt shame.

Perez-Foster (1998) suggests that submerged within the clinician's deeply personal cultural beliefs and idealization are her attitudes about her own ethnicity. These attitudes are often kept silent or disavowed, yet they clearly emerge and operate in a countertransferential capacity in a qualitative study. With Dennis' help, I came to understand that part of my struggle had to do with what Winnicott (1971) refers to as a sense of my true self as acceptable. This struggle is common to many immigrant groups when the mainstream culture fails to provide a facilitating environment in which the true self is acceptable (Antokoletz, 1993).

As I struggled with this, Dennis enthusiastically immersed himself in the data and challenged me to contextualize the experience of the Puerto Rican HIV-infected person. His excitement, curiosity, and respect for the study, me, and my culture allowed me to trust him and the process. I was learning and being challenged in ways I could not have imagined. In many ways, Dennis provided the holding environment necessary for me to grow and learn. His calm manner, humor, and sharp intellect made this process not only less painful but integrative.

> R.D.S.: The tension between sensitivity and objectivity often involves going beyond the "master narratives" that have evolved for particular groups. As researchers, we often ascribe great explanatory power to these narratives and carry these ideas into our research efforts. The paradox comes when these narratives become confining and relegate members to a particular way of life.

For example, the master narrative of gay men is something like this "I was a sissy kid and was tormented for being that way, I was different from other boys." This narrative makes gay youths victims, often ignoring their strengths, talents, skills, and gutsiness. Similarly, the master narrative "women are subjugated by the patriarchy" and "women only value relationships and connections," threatens to ignore the talents and contributions of individual women and the fact that women can be quite competitive in their own right.

As researchers we must go beyond the master narrative if we are to discover something new and different. I have worked with students who struggle with this form of bias. One was studying adults who were diagnosed with learning disabilities at some point in their youth. The master narrative of this group tended to be, "Everything was fine until I went to school and then the trouble started." The student used a biographical approach to explore how individuals managed and adapted to their disability. In his biographical accounts, many participants indicated that their first feeling that something was wrong emanated from their parents and emerged long before going to school. Although these data were right before his eyes, he at first ignored it.

As a mentor I was excited because it was something new that had great implications for working with this population and understanding the developing sense of self, that is, a sense of "something being wrong" was in play long before they entered school. At first the student had trouble acknowledging this, wanting to begin the story with school. Gradually, though, he came to realize the extent to which he had subscribed to the master narrative and its biasing influence.

TRANSFERENCES AND COUNTERTRANSFERENCES

The student's transference (or countertransference) to the people under study, as well as participants' individual transference reactions to the student, can be significant factors. Listening for these phenomena as they are expressed in ongoing consultation or in early writing can help the student develop an objective, balanced, and deep perspective on the group under study.

What distinguishes transferential phenomena in qualitative research is the specificity and intensity of emotional reactions. This is why we use a clinical term rather than a term from the methodological literature such as *bias*. A very specific painful feeling can affect a great deal of the data analysis and collection. If identified, such feelings can be contained and their damage minimized.

When the student is from an ethnic minority group, he or she may feel pressured to convey that group in a positive light. This can be a complex quandary. Ida's initial interest was sparked by her relatives' less-than-heroic response, and she explored what she felt was a "problem" in how the Puerto Rican community dealt with AIDS. From the beginning, she was examining what could be considered a "less-than-admirable" response among her own people.

I.R.: In my study, the participants were initially resistant and suspicious of me. Their individual transference reactions were that I was a *gringa* (white) middle-class professional woman. This led to concerns about my ability to understand their experience. A certain amount of self-disclosure was necessary on my part to convey that our worlds were not so far apart. Yet, it was not enough that I was Puerto Rican. I also had to reveal my own personal experience with HIV/AIDS.

As I discussed this experience with Dennis, he helped me become aware of my countertransference reactions to the participants. I was insulted that my ethnic identity was being questioned—that I was seen as a *gringa*. This transference reaction had stirred up an old uncomfortable feeling within me about being judged as "less Puerto Rican" than others. This was a deep internalization from my family. Because I was the first child born in the United States, I was always called *la Americana*.

This fear probably explains my outrage at not being accepted by my own group. Only after a "prolonged period of engagement in the field" (Padgett, 1998) did the participants seem less guarded and suspicious. Ultimately, deciding to self-disclose about my personal experience allowed participants to feel safe enough to tell their stories.

As themes emerged in the data, being Puerto Rican allowed me to use my personal experience to understand how culturally specific understandings of disease influence the experience of illness. The data showed that participants' families and friends believed that the HIV/AIDS illness was caused by an infiltration of impurities and/or spirits (Roldán, 1999). Once again, I found myself getting stirred up by the data and began to reflect on this idea that disease was caused by impurities and an imbalance of body humors.

A central aspect of a mentor's role is to listen for these phenomena and to intervene with the student to promote a deeper exploration. When such experiences are used to facilitate the process of recursive questioning, a deeper, multifaceted, and dynamic understanding of the phenomenon under study can evolve. As Dennis urged me to further explore these phenomena, I began to appreciate how fearful and vulnerable my community felt when faced with HIV/AIDS.

I also became more sensitive to the notion of *bochinche* that continued to emerged as a central theme. Participants suggested that their primary reason for keeping their illness secret was to protect themselves and their families from the rejection, shame and humiliation that *bochinche* would inflict on them. My experience in the Puerto Rican community had been similar. Everyone feared it. No one wanted to be the target of *bochinche*.

R.D.S.: The mentoring alliance implies an ability to talk about and reflect on painful feelings and thoughts, but since this is research, not therapy, we use it to further the study (though enhanced self-knowledge usually occurs). This was an interesting time in our work. To me, the idea that fears of HIV infection were spread via *bochinche* made perfect sense. But Ida was reluctant. We would talk about it, but it would not make it onto the written page in a clear and succinct way.

Students are often hurt and incredulous when they find themselves rejected or marginalized by their own group in much the same way that they are marginalized by the larger society. Racism, sexism, and homophobia are all transmitted via enactments. This information comes to us in a myriad of ways, especially in how we are treated by others. At times we are dealt with in subtly demeaning ways, at other times in a more dramatically and obviously devaluing manner. It comes via interchanges in which we are viewed as "less than," and it may be completely out of the awareness of the person treating the other as "less than." This can impart an often-elusive quality to the analysis of the data. The student may know something is wrong, but may not be able to pin down what is actually happening.

STUDYING THE FAMILIAR
AND THE UNFAMILIAR

The previous discussion focused on work with a student who was exploring something more familiar than unfamiliar. Here, we must acknowledge a paradox: when a qualitative study is conducted properly, the familiar must begin to feel unfamiliar (Ely, 1991). The researcher will hopefully encounter data that tell a different story, or offer a different view than previously held.

Ida's ideas came from her interaction with the data and her participants, not solely from personal experience. Her understanding of the experience of her population changed considerably. Hence, it became "unfamiliar" despite her having lived through her family's experience with the death of her brother.

My own experience in studying partners of men with AIDS and men who were HIV-positive involved the same phenomenon (Shelby, 1992; Shelby, 1995). A population with whom I had done extensive clinical work became unfamiliar as the theory evolved and deepened. I began to feel quite naïve in my understanding of the experience. As a result, my clinical perspective changed. I began to use the findings of the studies as one theoretical framework with which to listen to the experiences of my clients.

When students approach a population or topic that is distant from their personal experience, the initial interviews are a very important time for the involvement of the mentor. When using grounded theory, data from early interviews are crucial to the analytic process of labeling and memoing, which are the first steps in establishing a new framework with which to understand current and future data. It is in the early stages that students tend to use familiar concepts, in part because the respondents and the data seem so unfamiliar. Active work with the mentor as this point will help ensure that a new framework is developed rather than simply relying on familiar concepts applied to the unfamiliar.

THE ROLE OF CLINICAL AND SOCIAL SCIENCE THEORIES IN QUALITATIVE RESEARCH

Many students want to explore some aspect of a broader theory or situate their study within a theoretical framework. If the research is for a dissertation, they will be required to review relevant literature and to place their study in the historical progression of knowledge in the area. At the risk of creating an artificial dichotomy (but for purposes of discussion), theories about the human experience can be classified as clinical theories and social science theories. Clinical theories are based on clinical practice and knowledge derived from encounters with clients. Whereas psychodynamic theories are rooted in Freud's idea of a dynamic unconscious, behavioral and cognitive theories focus on individual cognitions and behaviors at a more conscious level.

Social science theories inform our understanding of the human experience from a different perspective, one embedded in basic concepts such as social class, status, and social structure. Although such theories assume that various forces are at play in shaping behavior or meaning (e.g., racism and sexism), they do not locate causation in the unconscious mind. Instead, they focus on influences such as social roles and statuses, social interaction, and socioeconomic (or other) stratification systems.

Students in a professional school doctoral program will tend to choose a problem for study that has its roots in their practice experience (versus a problem rooted in social science theory). They usually come to the dissertation well versed in a clinical theory and want to use that theory in their own research. The challenge then becomes how to use a clinical theory in the conduct of qualitative research because it was designed to inform and guide clinical encounters. An additional complication occurs with psychodynamic clinical theories because their precepts are based on the unconscious mind.

We can think of any personal theory—whether clinical or social science—as part of the personal value system of the researcher and therefore as a source of useful information, but also a potential source of bias. If the student enters a qualitative study embracing a personal theory, she or he risks being attracted to nuances in the data (or, worse, creating such nuances) to cohere with this theory. It is in this way that a priori theories become a value system (Lincoln & Guba, 1985) similar to other sociocultural norms and beliefs.

Again, the relationship with the mentor can serve a valuable function. Research interviews are not clinical interviews. In the case of grounded theory, the researcher is developing a new interpretative framework (although a personal theory may influence the form and points of emphasis of the emergent theory). Researchers who seek to frame their findings within clinical or social science theories must strive to let their data speak for itself. The mentor's oversight and input will help ensure that data analysis focuses on the data as the ultimate authority.

A COMMON PITFALL OF MENTORING

R.D.S.: While we have advocated for the mentoring relationship in qualitative research, we must also address the potential problems of a close
alliance between the student and mentor. The biggest danger is a sense of
"you and I against the world" or, in the case of a dissertation, the rest of
the committee. The mentor must encourage the student to work with the
other committee members, as they are the first "outsiders" to read and
evaluate the qualitative report. Committee members represent the "community of scholars" and offer early critiques of the ideas and overall coherence of the document. As a mentor, I always assume that something
has been missed and hope that my colleagues will find it.

As mentors we must maintain a balance between our alliance with the student and with our colleagues. Ultimately, strangers will read and evaluate the
dissertation, and at some point the student will have to stand alone to defend
his or her ideas. A combination of mentoring and peer group support (described in Chapter 10) is ideal because students then have both peers and
senior faculty responding to their efforts.

In qualitative research, a central evaluative concept is coherence. The research questions, methodology, epistemological basis for the method, presentation of the findings, and discussion of the findings must all come together in a
coherent document. The close relationship between mentor and student that
evolves over a number of years, if too isolated, threatens to undermine coherence and clarity. The feedback of others is crucial to finishing the document
and identifying ideas that are not well elaborated or grounded in the data.

CONCLUSION

This chapter addressed how the mentoring relationship can and should be
used to enhance rigor in qualitative research. Although the standards for rigor
vary between (and within) qualitative methodologies, the mentoring relationship is central to virtually all epistemological approaches. In this context, we
discussed difficulties that can beset researchers conducting qualitative research
for the first time: resistance to immersion, objectivity versus sensitivity, transference and countertransference, the role of clinical and social science theories, and a common pitfall of mentoring. We also offered suggestions on how
the mentoring relationship can assist the researcher who encounters these
difficulties.

For students trained as practitioners, the mentor can help make the transition from clinical interviewing to research interviewing and assist in monitoring personal and professional beliefs so that they do not overwhelm the study.
Although the student–mentor relationship runs the risk of becoming too
isolated from the broader community of scholars, the dissertation committee and/or peer support group can provide helpful feedback to offset this

potential imbalance and enhance the overall coherence of the final report. When combined with other forms of intellectual and emotional support, mentorship can be a powerful means of ensuring the student's future success as a researcher.

ACKNOWLEDGMENTS

We learned a great deal as we worked on the project described in this chapter, not just about I.R.'s topic, but the complexity of minority status and what can be termed a "bicultural" identity. Qualitative conversations R.D.S. had had over the years with Tom Kenemore, Jim Drisko, Jeane Anastas, and Deborah Padgett influenced his work with I.R. There is something deeply satisfying about the multifaceted nature of qualitative research and conversations and the multifaceted deeper understanding rigorous efforts provide.

REFERENCES

Antokoletz, J. C. (1993). A psychoanalytic view of cross-cultural passages. *The American Journal of Psychoanalysis, 53* (1), 35–53.

Atkinson, R. (1998). The life story interview. *Qualitative Research Methods Series*, Vol. 44, Thousand Oaks, CA: Sage.

Denzin, N. (1997). *Interpretive Ethnography*. Thousand Oaks, CA: Sage.

Drisko, J. (1999, January). Rigor in qualitative studies and reports. Paper presented at the Society for Social Work and Research, 3rd annual conference, Austin, TX.

Ely. (1991). *Doing qualitative research: Circles within circles*. London: The Falmer Press.

Erickson, E. (1964). *Insight and responsibility*. New York: W.W. Norton

Freud, S. (1913). On beginning the treatment. *The standard edition of the complete works of Sigmund Freud* (p. 123), Vol 12. London: Hogarth.

Giorgi, A. (Ed.) (1985). *Phenomenology and psychological research*. Pittsburgh, PA: Duquesne University Press.

Glaser, B. G., & Strauss, A. L. (1967). *The discovery of grounded theory: Strategies for qualitative research*. Hawthorne, NY: Aldine de Gruyter.

Haworth, J.G., & Conrad, C.F. (1997) *Emblems of quality in higher education: Developing and sustaining high-quality programs*. Boston: Allyn & Bacon.

Kennedy, D. (1997). *Academic duty*. Cambridge, MA: Harvard University Press.

Lincoln Y. S., & Guba, E. G. (1985). *Naturalistic inquiry*. Newbury Park, CA: Sage.

Padgett, D. K. (1998). *Qualitative methods in social work research: challenges and rewards*. Thousand Oaks, CA: Sage.

Perez-Foster, R. M. (1998). *The power of language in the clinical process*. Northvale, NJ: Jason Aronson.

Riessman, C. K. (1993). Narrative analysis. *Qualitative research methods series*, Vol. 30. Thousand Oaks, CA: Sage.

Roldán, I. (1999). The Puerto Rican family's experience when a member has HIV/AIDS. Unpublished Doctoral Dissertation, the Institute for Clinical Social Work, Chicago.

Shelby, R. D. (1992). *If a partner has AIDS: Guide to clinical intervention for relationships in crisis*. New York: Haworth.

Shelby, R. D. (1995). *People with HIV and those who help them*. New York: Haworth.

Shelby, R. D. (2001). Using the mentoring relationship to facilitate rigor in qualitative research. *Smith College Studies in Social Work, 70* (2), 315–27.

Strauss, A., & Corbin, J. (1998) *Basics of qualitative research* (2nd ed.). Newbury Park, CA: Sage.

Winnicott, D. W. (1971). *Playing and reality*. New York: Tavistock/ Routledge.

10

Peer Debriefing and Support Groups

Formation, Care, and Maintenance

DEBORAH PADGETT,
REJI MATHEW,
AND SUSAN CONTE

The idea of a self-help group for qualitative researchers—and especially for students doing qualitative research for the first time—makes a lot of sense. Labeled a *lifeline* for qualitative researchers (Ely, 1991), peer debriefing and support (PDS) groups have received surprisingly little attention in the literature on qualitative methods. One of several "strategies for rigor" (Padgett, 1998), PDS can be a valuable tool to guard against bias in all phases of a qualitative study (Lincoln & Guba, 1985).

Although qualitative researchers have engaged in extensive (and occasionally contentious) debates about rigor, a general consensus has emerged that rigorous methods are an attainable and essential goal. Endorsement of this position has come from a variety of professional disciplines including education (Lincoln & Guba, 1985; Schwandt & Halpern, 1988), medicine (Silverman, Ricci, & Gunter, 1990; Mays & Pope, 1995; Frankel, 1999), and nursing (Sandelowski, 1986; Kahn, 1993; Morse, 1994) as well as social work (Beeman, 1995; Padgett, 1998; Reid, 1994; Ruben, 2000).

It is reasonable to ask why PDS is any more important for qualitative as opposed to quantitative studies—couldn't all researchers benefit from it? Generic doctoral student support groups have existed for some time as sources of intellectual and emotional support that complement the role of the dissertation sponsor or mentor (Meloy, 1994; Simmons, Gates, & Thompson, 2000). But we believe that a crucial need arises from the role of the researcher as instrument in qualitative research. Quantitative researchers have numerous safeguards available for enhancing the rigor of their work—starting with the choice of research design (for internal validity), going to probability sampling techniques (for external validity), and continuing with the choice of measures (for reliability and measurement validity). No such safeguards are available in qualitative methods where a sink-or-swim mentality often prevails. It is difficult to overstate the emergent and flexible nature of a qualitative study and the pitfalls that can hamper its successful completion.

This chapter has three objectives: to (1) describe the role of PDS as a meta-strategy for enhancing rigor in qualitative research; (2) present an example of how PDS groups were initiated and used by doctoral students in the social work doctoral program at New York University; and (3) propose a set of guidelines for implementing PDS in a variety of settings.

PDS AS A META-STRATEGY FOR RIGOR
IN QUALITATIVE RESEARCH

Qualitative researchers have created parallel standards of rigor reflecting procedures attuned to the flexible and iterative nature of their form of inquiry. Thus, *reliability* and *validity* have been replaced by terms such as *credibility* and *trustworthiness* (Lincoln & Guba, 1985).

Drawing on the cumulative works of pioneers in qualitative methods such as Anselm Strauss, Barney Glaser, Yvonna Lincoln, Egon Guba, and Norman Denzin, the first author (Padgett, 1998) identified six strategies for enhancing rigor in qualitative research. The earliest of these strategies, *triangulation* and *negative case analysis*, emerged from Glaser and Strauss' Grounded Theory approach in sociology (1967). Triangulation of data collection refers to the validating potential of using two or more types of data (e.g., interview data plus written documents) to capture the same phenomenon. Negative case analysis occurs during the lengthy process of data analysis and interpretation and refers to the deliberate search for disconfirming cases to test the accuracy and completeness of the researcher's interpretations.

Another early strategy, *prolonged engagement*, is the hallmark of ethnographic fieldwork in anthropology and has been embraced and expanded upon by subsequent generations of qualitative researchers (Guba & Lincoln, 1989). Qualitative researchers rely upon far greater depth of vision and familiarity with respondents than quantitative researchers.

Three more recently developed strategies—*member checks, auditing,* and *PDS*—were advanced by Lincoln and Guba (1985) as part of their groundbreaking efforts to establish separate criteria for rigor in qualitative research. Member checking (verifying one's data and interpretations with study respondents) helps guard against investigator bias. Auditing, or leaving an audit trail, is a process of oversight made possible by careful documentation of all aspects of the study and decisions made. Auditing by an outside researcher familiar with qualitative methods assists in reducing researcher bias. It also enhances the reproducibility of the study (Schwandt & Halpern, 1988), that is, sets the stage for verifying the findings all or in part by reproducing or retracing the steps in collecting and analyzing the data.

We would argue that PDS is a meta-strategy for enhancing rigor because it reinforces the importance of the other five strategies and provides a forum for integrating them into a qualitative study from its inception to its completion. Although PDS may be considered unsuitable for some types of qualitative approaches, the vast majority of qualitative researchers can benefit significantly from its use.

PDS DEFINED AND OPERATIONALIZED

PDS has been defined as "the process of exposing one's self to a disinterested peer in a manner paralleling an analytic session for the purpose of exploring aspects of the inquiry that may otherwise remain only implicit within the inquirer's mind" (Lincoln & Guba, 1985, p. 308). Lincoln and Guba discussed four valuable functions of PDS: (1) it helps expose researcher biases; (2) it gives the researcher a forum for testing ideas and emerging hypotheses and getting constructive feedback; (3) it provides concrete suggestions to the researcher for improving methodological rigor; and (4) it gives the qualitative researcher as instrument an outlet for exploring and clarifying feelings that emerge during the study and for distinguishing those that interfere with the study from those that do not.

Each of the words in the phrase *peer debriefing and support* has meaning and significance. *Peers* are important as group members because they do not have the power differential and potential pitfalls inherent in student–faculty (or mentee–mentor) relationships. *Debriefing* is critical for the qualitative researcher who is spending extraordinary amounts of time in the field as well as in analyzing and interpreting the data. *Support*—instrumental and emotional— is an essential part of the experience. PDS groups are not only guardians of "virtue" (i.e., rigor), but also offer assistance ranging from news about the latest computer software to advice on ethical issues to tips on handling a demanding dissertation advisor. Of course, the group's prime function is task oriented rather than socioemotional—members whose needs go beyond an agenda of improving their research are urged to seek counseling in an appropriate venue.

The actual implementation and operation of PDS tends to be open to a "whatever works" approach (Ely, 1991). Group composition can vary from multidisciplinary to monodisciplinary, from novices only to a mix of less and more experienced researchers. Groups may be as small as 2 or range up to 8 to 10 members with the obvious drawbacks to participation as size increases. Frequency of meetings, usually monthly, should be regular (infrequent and/or irregular meetings make it more difficult to maintain momentum and an ongoing agenda). Finally, groups may maintain an open-door policy for new members or vote to become closed for a period of time to enhance continuity.

As with any rigor-enhancing strategy, there are drawbacks and demands attendant with PDS groups. First, there are the risks associated with any group process—imbalance and domination by one or a few members, drifting away from the agenda, and overly harsh or overly indulgent feedback. Second are the challenges of logistics—how to organize the group initially and how to recruit, retain, and renew membership so that the group can evolve and serve its members' needs.

Even an egalitarian PDS group needs leadership or facilitation. The peer facilitator is pivotal in addressing potential problems and safeguarding the mission of the group. PDS also needs the involvement of an experienced qualitative researcher (usually a faculty member) who can (1) provide occasional infusions of expertise (e.g., conduct exercises in coding and analysis); (2) answer "factual" questions (e.g., availability of computer software and institutional review board (IRB) concerns about qualitative studies); and (3) assist in procuring resources (e.g., reserving meeting space or obtaining funds to bring in outside speakers).

A CASE EXAMPLE OF PDS
IN A UNIVERSITY SETTING

At our school, PDS had its origins in the rapidly growing numbers of doctoral students interested in carrying out qualitative research for their dissertations and the scarcity of faculty with appropriate expertise. The PDS groups were intended to complement a doctoral-level course on qualitative methods added to the curriculum in 1996.

Our first decision was whether to reach out to join existing PDS groups in other schools at the university (education and nursing). Although our colleagues were amenable, the students ultimately decided to stay home, partly because of the logistics of scheduling (our doctoral program is a part-time evening program and most students have day jobs) and partly due to a desire to—at least at the outset—focus on in-house concerns.

In January, 1999, PDS group formation began, initiated by the first author (D.K.P.) and facilitated by the co-authors (R.M. and S.C., who are doctoral students). Responding to a mailed invitation sent to all doctoral students who had finished their coursework, approximately 20 students expressed interest and two meeting times were selected to meet their busy schedules—a Thursday evening and Saturday afternoon. The faculty advisor (D.K.P.) assisted in reserving meeting space and in sending out monthly notices for subsequent meetings, but her primary role was to provide supervision for the peer facilitators and serve as a link to the doctoral program's leadership.

Each group had a peer facilitator working under the supervision of a faculty member with qualitative methods expertise—Susan worked with the Thursday evening group and Reji with the Saturday morning group. Groups agreed to meet monthly, to set agendas one month in advance, and to remain in contact via e-mail and telephone.

THE ROLE OF THE PEER FACILITATOR
AND FACULTY ADVISOR IN PDS GROUPS

The peer facilitator's role in PDS has been crucial for a number of reasons. She or he is the group's archivist, keeping track of meeting agendas and introducing and orienting new members. During meetings, the facilitator keeps the group on task and reminds members of the need to stay focused on the agenda they have jointly agreed upon. She also tries to optimize participation by all members and to keep the tone of meetings supportive and constructive.

During the first year, the two facilitators met regularly with the faculty supervisor to discuss issues that arose and to give feedback on group concerns. As would happen in almost any program, the groups provided a forum for members to voice pent-up concerns and misunderstandings that often arise during thesis advisement for qualitative dissertations. Faculty advisors accustomed to seeing only quantitative studies, for example, might unwittingly put students in a bind by requiring hypotheses when research questions are a far better fit. Sometimes, the faculty supervisor needed to remind group members that these concerns are virtually universal and not easily remedied.

To address misunderstandings about methods, a seminar on qualitative methods was offered to all dissertation advisors to discuss how proposals for qualitative studies are likely to differ from those for quantitative studies. Rigorous qualitative methods were described and their distinctiveness highlighted.

It is helpful to build in rotation of peer facilitators every few months to prevent burnout and share the work (the same can be said for faculty consultants). Rotation also gives new facilitators a chance to exercise their leadership skills. One of our groups is on its third facilitator and the transition has been smooth thus far.

PDS AS A META-STRATEGY FOR RIGOR:
CASE EXAMPLES

As mentioned, PDS provides a framework for addressing strategies for rigor in qualitative research. In our experience, some of the difficulties encountered by group members stemmed from making the transition from advanced practitioner (with all of the associated expectations regarding status and authority) to the more humbling status of seeking to learn from the expert, that is, the respondent. Underlying this change in status and role was a deeper cognitive shift—the transition from using clinical theories as the primary framework for understanding human behaviors and emotions to a more flexible and emergent approach that would be open to serendipitous findings.

Complications arose for the students who had chosen to study "the familiar" (Ely, 1991) rather than venture into new terrain. Examples included a student in a mixed race marriage who chose to study mixed race couples or a student who chose to study adolescent problems in her own ethnic community.

One strategy for rigor, *prolonged engagement*, was resisted by some group members who were initially uncomfortable in reaching out to informants to seek a more extended relationship involving multiple meetings and lengthy interviews. These members were concerned about the time needed to engage in these relationships and by the challenges inherent in meeting the schedules of busy respondents.

Led by the facilitator, the group reviewed the importance of prolonged engagement and urged reluctant members to redefine the research relationship as ongoing and to incorporate this new attitude into their recruitment of respondents.

Another strategy for rigor, *member checking*, was made easier by this shift toward prolonged engagement because consulting with one's informants about interpretations of the data requires return visits and rapport. Although the PDS group could not be directly involved in member checking, it provided a forum for each researcher to discuss dilemmas, for example, a respondent who asks that portions of audiotapes be erased because of their sensitive nature. If a respondent took issue with the researcher's interpretations and posed a countering viewpoint, the PDS group was there to urge the researcher to honor her ethical commitments or, in the latter situation, offer suggestions to help the researcher negotiate a compromise with the respondent.

Triangulation, another strategy for rigor, can take a number of forms during PDS. Group members periodically reminded one another to seek out additional forms of data whenever possible (e.g., observation or useful documents) to compare to interview data for corroboration. *Triangulation by theory*, that is, offering additional theoretical perspectives or interpretations to the analyses, can also occur in PDS. For example, a group member studying young immigrant women who had attempted suicide was asked to reconsider her data from an alternative standpoint to the cultural interpretation she had adopted. She did not discard her hunch that suicidal behavior was a response to rigid cultural traditions that provided few outlets for redemption if a young woman has brought shame to her family. But she did put it to the test.

By playing devil's advocate, the group challenged this interpretation and urged the student to perform *negative case analysis*, a strategy for rigor that involves deliberately seeking out disconfirming cases. When her new data analyses revealed risk factors that were common to suicidality among young women in general, a more nuanced interpretation was developed (following several spirited group discussions), which emphasized the additive (rather than root cause) effects of cultural factors.

The final strategy for rigor, *leaving an audit trail*, was initially viewed as quantitative, that is, an intrusive process of logging the many decisions made during data collection and analysis. To counter this, the facilitator urged members to consider positive aspects of enhancing a study's auditability. For example, leaving an audit trail enhances rigor by establishing for outside scrutiny what decisions were made and how biases were addressed. The message was simple: creativity does not preclude accountability and rigor. In this light, the time required for auditing seemed worthwhile rather than a distraction.

During the group meetings, a new reason for auditability surfaced—documentation for ethical purposes. Because several members were studying highly sensitive topics, their ability to navigate IRB Committee oversight and to carefully balance the concerns about emotional distress arising during the study was much smoother when they assured the IRB of their meticulous attention to documenting all aspects of the work.

We would be misleading the reader if we implied that rigor was the only agenda of the PDS groups—routine concerns invariably arose ranging from how much to pay informants to how to dress for the initial interview. But the groups never lost sight of their raison d'être, either.

PDS ACROSS THE SPAN OF A RESEARCH PROJECT: SUGGESTIONS FOR IMPLEMENTATION IN A VARIETY OF SETTINGS

PDS groups can be used in a variety of settings—university, institute, medical center, or social service agency—by as few as two individuals working together. Obviously, the surrounding environment plays a role in PDS—a university-based doctoral program versus the evaluation department of a struggling agency will likely have different capacities to support PDS. Nevertheless, extensive resources are not necessary for its successful deployment beyond space and time for regular meetings. Like qualitative research in general, PDS is a low-tech, labor-intensive enterprise. Its greatest demand is commitment from members.

PDS can assist in all stages of a qualitative study: formulating the research problem(s), deciding on how (if at all) to triangulate types of data collection, co-coding data to check for investigator bias, co-auditing notes and documentation of the data analyses, and reading and responding to drafts of the report. What is most important is that members of the group have training and/or education in qualitative research to anchor the process in knowledge of the methodology. Without a common ground and shared vocabulary, group members will find themselves unable to fully contribute and to stay on task.

In addition to background knowledge of qualitative methods, members in PDS groups need to enter the process with a commitment to be active and cooperative participants. This raises the thorny issue of dealing with a bad apple—a group member who is not participating or is disrupting the process by pulling the group away from its agreed-upon agenda. The facilitator may want to gently guide the group back on task or, in extreme cases, ask the member to leave.

PDS groups depend on flexible but persistent attention to updating agendas and adhering to them. They are especially helpful in urging members to set (and keep) deadlines and to stay the course despite life's many distractions.

SUGGESTED EXERCISES FOR
PDS GROUPS GETTING STARTED

Below are a few suggestions for tasks a new PDS group could pursue to get things moving:

1. Agree on outside readings in advance and discuss them in the group meeting. These readings could include exemplary published qualitative studies or new books or articles describing the methodology in more detail.

2. Select one or more transcripts of interviews and co-code the manuscripts, debriefing on decisions made about the coding. Another option is to have the faculty advisor participate, leading the discussion as a co-coder.

3. Stage a mock defense of the research proposal or of the completed dissertation. In either case, a group member has a chance to present the methods, defend them to a knowledgeable audience, and make refinements to improve the study. This could be done for a grant proposal to a foundation or government agency as well.

4. Devote one or more sessions to discussing ethical issues: how to ensure protection of respondents and at the same time minimize bias. The various strategies for rigor can be addressed from this standpoint. Prolonged engagement and member checking, for example, require repeated contacts with respondents and should be addressed at the time consent is given so that respondents know beforehand what lies ahead.

   Triangulation of data collection, which involves gaining access to personal documents or agency records, requires specific consent. Leaving an audit trail and carrying out negative case analysis, along with any other activities involving disclosure of research data during PDS, require absolute guarantees that the identity of respondents will be kept confidential—use of pseudonyms (and preferably case numbers) is mandatory.

5. Feature the work of one or two members at each session and ask them to provide copies of reading materials in advance, for example, drafts of the proposal or final report, transcripts and coding memos, and excerpts from personal logs or journals highlighting special dilemmas or concerns.

GROWING PAINS, RENEWAL,
AND OTHER CHALLENGES

As our PDS groups gained acceptance and appreciation from dissertation advisors and the doctoral program in general, they also encountered growing pains. Like any self-help group, the PDS groups developed norms that helped regulate and rationalize their operation. For example, prospective members are asked to speak to the facilitator and get oriented before joining the group.

If a group member is not actively involved in dissertation work and in the group itself, he or she might be urged to take a break and return when ready to benefit from PDS and make a contribution. Every member is expected to be available to pair off at some point with another member to assist in co-coding, auditing, and so on outside of group meeting times.

Sometimes group norms have to be revisited to accommodate inevitable change over time. A natural outgrowth of group formation has been a sense of belonging and cohesion and this can bump up against realities of growth. As one of the groups grew large and unwieldy (up to 12 members), members have been reluctant to break their bonds and split in two.

Another of the groups disbanded due to the loss of members to graduation or withdrawal. At this writing, it is in the process of regrouping and recruiting new members; a third group is being formed by a cohort of students who took the qualitative methods course together and finished their comprehensive examinations. This process of group formation by cohort is an ideal scenario because members already know one another and all begin at the same stage of dissertation development. As trajectories begin to diverge (some students move quickly, others fall behind), the groups may end up splitting and/or merging with others.

PDS groups are bound to give rise to the gamut of human emotions, both negative and positive. For example, members might feel a sense of loss (and envy) when a member graduates or they might perceive inequity in discussions about the inevitable (but seemingly unfair) unevenness of dissertation advisement.

But there is also the warmth and camaraderie that compels members to show up on the coldest of wintry Saturday mornings, shivering and warming themselves over steaming cups of coffee. There are celebrations of major rites of passage, for example, graduation or getting the proposal accepted, as well as of smaller victories, for example, an interview that left respondent and researcher exhilarated. There were words of encouragement to a member having medical problems and, sadly, a sharing of grief when another member was tragically killed in an auto accident.

This sense of bonding can bring potential hazards by inculcating an us–them mentality. For this reason, it is important for PDS groups to maintain a healthy relationship with a faculty member as well as the parent program and not stray too far away. Program standards can change or new resources become available (e.g., the latest QDA software). Room space may be needed for meeting. If too isolated, PDS groups also run the risk of losing touch with (or alienating) doctoral faculty who worry that misinformation is being shared or propagated by the groups.

When well maintained, PDS groups perform the vital function of helping to socialize members as developing scholars. The group process emulates a future in which collaboration and cooperation are essential to carrying out research and assuming roles of professional leadership. Would-be qualitative researchers come to recognize that they are the research instruments and the study depends on them to succeed. Alone, we might veer off course. In groups, we have a common purpose and a forum for increasing the trustwor-thiness of our work.

ACKNOWLEDGMENTS

We would like to thank the NYU School of Social Work Doctoral program for making the PDS groups possible. We are especially grateful to the doctoral students who participated in the groups and shared their thoughts and experiences with us. They were Deborah Langosch, Judith Slane, Jane Politi, Greg Klot, and Josephine Wong in the Saturday group, and Karen Marschke-Tobier, Nahid Westwood, Roy Laird, David Rappaport, and Dede Greenstein (who died in a tragic auto accident and is greatly missed) in the Thursday group. Their intellectual involvement and emotional support have been invaluable.

REFERENCES

Beeman, S. (1995). Maximizing credibility and accountability in qualitative data collection and data analysis: A social work research case example. *Journal of Sociology and Social Welfare, 22*, 99–114.

Ely, M. (with Anzul. M., Friedman, T., Garner, D., & Steinmetz, A. M.). (1991). *Doing qualitative research: Circles within circles.* London: Falmer.

Frankel, R. M. (1999). Standards of qualitative research. In B. F. Crabtree & W. L. Miller (Eds.), *Doing qualitative research* (2nd ed., pp. 333–46). Thousand Oaks, CA: Sage.

Glaser, B. G., & Strauss, A. L. (1967). *The discovery of grounded theory: Strategies for qualitative research.* Hawthorne, NY: Aldine de Gruyter.

Guba, E. G., & Lincoln, Y. S. (1989). *Fourth generation evaluation.* Newbury Park, CA: Sage.

Kahn, D. L. (1993). Ways of discussing validity in qualitative nursing research. *Western Journal of Nursing Research, 15*, 122–6.

Lincoln, Y. S., & Guba, E. G. (1985). *Naturalistic inquiry.* Beverly Hills, CA: Sage.

Mays, N., & Pope, C. (1995). Rigour and qualitative research. *British Medical Journal, 311*, 109–12.

Meloy, J. M. (1994). *Writing the qualitative dissertation: Understanding by doing.* Hillsdale, NJ: Erlbaum.

Morse I. (1994). (Ed.) *Critical issues in qualitative research methods.* Thousand Oaks, CA: Sage.

Padgett, D. K. (1998). *Qualitative methods in social work research: Challenges and rewards.* Thousand Oaks, CA: Sage.

Reid, W. J. (1994). Reframing the epistemological debate. In E. Sherman & W. J. Reid (Eds.), *Qualitative research in social work* (pp. 464–81). New York: Columbia University Press.

Ruben, A. (2000). Standards for rigor in qualitative inquiry. *Research on Social Work Practice, 10*, 173–7.

Sandelowski, M. (1986). The problem of rigor in qualitative research. *Advances in Nursing Science, 8*, 27–37.

Schwandt, T. A., & Halpern, E. S. (1988). *Linking auditing and metaevaluation:*

Enhancing quality in applied research. Newbury Park, CA: Sage.

Silverman, M., Ricci, E. M., & Gunter M. J. (1990). Strategies for increasing the rigor of qualitative methods in evaluation of health care programs. *Evaluation Review, 14,* 57–74.

Simmons, L. E., Gates, M. F., & Thompson, T. L. (2000). Processing issues related to culture, gender orientation, and mentoring. In S. D. Moch & M. F. Gates (Eds.), *The researcher experience in qualitative research* (pp. 83–93). Thousand Oaks, CA: Sage.

11

Ethical Issues in Qualitative Research With High-Risk Populations

Handle With Care

DEBORAH WALDROP

Qualitative research is a "journey of discovery" that can be simultane-ously challenging and inspiring in amazing and unforeseen ways (Padgett, 1998a). The privilege of learning from informants by listening to and observing them in their environment can produce insights that may surprise and intrigue, but sometimes distress the investi-gator. Because qualitative methods are used to examine situations in great de-tail, ethical concerns that might otherwise go unnoticed are more clearly in focus.

Extending well past the process of meeting institutional guidelines, ethical issues and dilemmas are present throughout the course of a qualitative study (Ely, et al., 1991; Strauss & Corbin, 1998; Tutty, Rothery, & Grinnell, 1996; Weiss, 1994). Some of the discoveries made in the field can gen-erate moral ambiguity (Weiss, 1994) and uncertainty, but I would argue that this discomfort is an important and even desirable component of the qualitative research experience. Being uncomfortable makes us more aware and alert, stretches our thinking, and enriches our insight about the very struggles and experiences of the marginalized or oppressed popula-tions we study.

This chapter explores some of the complex ethical issues that emerge while conducting qualitative research. It will not serve as a comprehensive how-to guide for ethics because most qualitative methods textbooks cover the basics (see, for example, Berg, 2001; Miles & Huberman, 1994; Padgett, 1998b; Tutty, et al., 1996). I will offer selected examples from the trenches and discuss how existing guidelines do and do not provide guidance. These examples are my own and those shared by colleagues. Twenty years of clinical social work experience inform the perspective from which I write, but I have also attempted to integrate ethical guidelines and examples from other disciplines.

WHO IS VULNERABLE?

The Code of Federal Regulations (CFR) (2001) defines minors, pregnant women, prisoners, mentally retarded, and mentally disabled persons as vulnerable populations. Families can also be vulnerable to harm because of their socioeconomic, minority, or other stigmatizing status (such as having a member who uses illicit drugs or has HIV) (Demi & Warren, 1995) or if they are homeless (Choi & Snyder, 1999). Other at-risk groups include the terminally ill and their caregivers, frail elders, and grandparents who are raising grandchildren. Understanding the experiences of those at risk provides an important perspective for practice (Appelbaum, 1989; Gilgun, 1994) as well as policy or program development (Choi & Snyder, 1999; MacPherson, 1988; Minkler & Roe, 1993). The importance of exploring the stories and experiences of vulnerable groups is expressed eloquently in the words of Meredith Minkler and Kathleen Roe:

> We chose to focus on black grandmothers raising the children of crack involved parents because of the often profound ways in which the drug epidemic has changed the experience of grandparent caregiving. By examining the lives of one group of African American grandmothers as they cope with the consequences of the epidemic, we hope to illuminate their unique experiences and concerns. At the same time, however, we will endeavor to direct attention to the broader implications and issues raised as these effect a variety of diverse population groups. (Minkler & Roe, 1993, p. 12)

REVIEW BY INSTITUTIONAL REVIEW BOARDS

Charged with the daunting task of upholding the principles of (1) Respect for Persons, (2) Beneficence, and (3) Justice (National Commission for the Protection of Human Subjects of Biomedical and Behavioral Research, 1979), Institutional Review Boards (IRBs) are often assumed to protect the organization (university, hospital, or federal agency) from liability, but their raison d'être is solely to protect human subjects. Originally developed to monitor biomedical research, IRBs can cause delays for behavioral and qualitative researchers. When individual members have limited understanding of qualitative methods, IRBs may require additional layers of protection to address perceptions of potential psychological harm or intrusion.

Research with vulnerable groups is not prohibited by the CFR, but the qualitative researcher may need to educate hesitant or unknowing IRB members about qualitative methods and reassure them regarding the principles of voluntary participation, protection of confidentiality, and the unequivocal right to withdraw from the study. The experiences of a colleague who was studying young people who had engaged in "cutting" (nonsuicidal self-mutilation) illustrate this extra vigilance:

> My study had already been approved by my university IRB, but before being allowed to recruit research participants at another institution by posting flyers, I was asked to meet with their IRB. Their concerns were about risk factors related to the sensitive nature of the topic, screening techniques for participants (was the person a risk to him- or herself?), as well as safeguards for participants who might decompensate during an interview and for my physical safety (when and where I would interview the participants). Although frustrated with the delay at the time, I appreciate the rigor and seriousness with which my study was handled, primarily because of the IRB's interest in protecting vulnerable people.

INFORMED CONSENT: ONGOING
AND NEGOTIATED

Standard requirements include a brief description of the study protocol, full identification of the researcher and sponsoring organization (with contact information), assurance that participation is voluntary and can be terminated at any point, and information about any risks or benefits associated with the study (CFR, 2001). However, true informed consent can be jeopardized by many factors, including social isolation and a desire for human contact (even with a researcher) (Kayser-Jones & Koenig, 1994), multiple ongoing stressors that make concentration and understanding difficult, or an absence of sobriety.

The participant's capacity to consent has been defined as the ability to comprehend information relevant to the decision, consider the choices as they relate to personal values and goals, and communicate with others verbally or nonverbally (Appelbaum, et al., 1987). Assessing decisional capacity is crucial among high-risk participants, particularly those whose cognitive function may be impaired (Kayser-Jones & Koenig, 1994). There is, however, no current proven or practical gold standard to assess capacity for research consent (NIH Bioethics Interest Group, 1998). While interviewing the caregivers of individuals in hospice care, I proposed to invite patients to participate if they were physically able and not confused. The IRB's primary concern was that patients might be heavily medicated for pain, which could cloud their understanding of participation. Because, in fact, most hospice patients at the end of life are medicated to relieve pain, the conclusion following my discussion with the IRB, was that because these same individuals were making decisions about the termination of their medical treatment, they could also determine whether or not to participate in the study.

Rather than one formalized document-signing moment, consent is sometimes a prolonged negotiation between researcher and informant(s) (Kayser-Jones & Koenig, 1994). Participants may initially agree to participate with some reluctance, then become disenchanted or disconcerted by the questions that are asked (Weiss, 1994). Under these circumstances, participants may continue answering questions but with less detailed or informative answers. Social desirability—not wanting to display rudeness or impoliteness—may technically constitute consent, but in reality, the participant is holding back. These situations present a dilemma for the researcher. On the one hand, the interviewer is concerned about getting the data, particularly with a sample that is difficult to generate. On the other hand, it is important to consider whether continued questioning and inattention to the participant's nonverbal behavior actually becomes intrusive.

Diminishing consent can also occur when participants' physical or cognitive abilities begin to waiver or fatigue sets in. The participant may begin to feel poorly or become confused. Aiming to understand the experiences of people who were caregiving for loved ones during the tenuous period of time near death, I established a protocol that involved four stages: (1) notification of hospice family caregivers about the study by letter, (2) verification of the patient's status (that they were still alive) followed by a telephone call within 2 weeks of the patient's admission, (3) contact by phone with a brief description and request for an interview in the home, and (4) if they agreed, a telephone call on the appointed day, to determine if the situation was medically stable enough for an interview before leaving for the in-home interview, and ending finally with completion of a written consent. Many potential participants completed the first three stages, but when the situation worsened the interview was cancelled on the day of the interview. Three situations changed rapidly between the confirmatory phone call and arrival at the home so the interview was cancelled at the door.

Gaining entrée was clearly mixed with elements of informed consent in this fragile situation. Both timing of contact and clarity of the initial brief description (probably the first five sentences), established whether the individual caregiver would consider participation. Given that consent can become a moving target, it seems important for all researchers to heed the guidance provided by the American Anthropological Association (2002): it is the quality of the consent rather than the format that is relevant. Knowing how and when to address continued informed consent is an important issue for both participant well-being and the integrity of the data.

Discussion of informed consent in a chapter on ethics in qualitative research would be incomplete without mention of *Tearoom Trade* (1970), Laud Humphreys' controversial study of men who sought sex with other men in public restrooms. This study raised issues of camouflage and deception within the research community. Camouflaging his role as a researcher, Humphreys acted as a "watch queen" in a park men's room. He observed individuals without asking permission, noted their license plate numbers and then visited them at home posing as a surveyor for the health department. Humphreys articulated that the importance of educating society about how "normals"—married men and pillars of the community—engage in impersonal sexual encounters and further, efforts to destigmatize gayness, justified this questionable research behavior. Humphreys (1970) argued that,

> We are not protecting a harassed population of deviants by refusing to look at them. The greatest harm a social scientist could do to this man would be to ignore him. Our concern about possible research consequences for our fellow "professionals" should take a secondary place to concern for those who may benefit from our research. (p. 169)

Although perhaps not as dramatically as in this controversial study, the question of whether knowledge that propels understanding is worth risks to human privacy and dignity remains a difficult ethical issue.

CONFIDENTIALITY CONCERNS: RESOLUTION IS NOT ALWAYS EASY

The 45 CFR 46 (1991) standard for confidentiality stipulates that the only record linking the subject and the research should be the consent document, the principle risk being potential harm from a breach of confidentiality. One interpretation is that the interviewer will treat the respondent's participation and communication as completely confidential information—sharing it with no one (Weiss, 1994). However, promises must never be made in situations where they cannot be kept (Tutty, et al., 1996), particularly by licensed clinicians (nurses, social workers) whose mandatory reporting responsibilities in the cases of child or elder abuse remain unchanged when they are conducting research and must be noted as such on the consent form. Further, when a researcher hears about violence in relationships, it is crucial to consider the possibility of a participant's expressed wishes to harm another person, which bring to light important questions about the researcher's duty to protect (Appelbaum, 1989).

The format of qualitative data brings additional confidentiality concerns forward. IRB guidelines state that there should be no link between the data and the identity of the individual (confidentiality must be guaranteed even if anonymity is not). Qualitative data are, however, "live," encompassing tapes and transcripts of interviews as well as the researcher's notebooks and journals, all filled with purposefully thick and rich descriptions. Coding does not always remove identifying information, particularly for specific subsets of the population.

Transcription of audiotaped interviews is often performed by someone external to the study and represents additional ethical issues. Upon returning the tapes from one phase of a study, a transcriptionist asked me to make sure

I assigned her the second tape from a particular participant because she had become very interested and wanted to know "how it turned out." Concerned about this undue curiosity, I sought consultation from a colleague who suggested that when she contracts with transcriptionists she requires them to sign a confidentiality statement pledging commitment to protecting the fragile nature of her vulnerable participants.

Ownership of interview tapes and transcripts as well as the use of the data for nonresearch activities are important and sometimes sticky confidentiality issues for consideration. After an in-depth interview, a grandparent caregiver asked me if she could have a copy of the tape to share with her family. Uncertain, I sought advice from the IRB and was told that the individual tape was not her property; I could only provide her with analyzed data in aggregate form. CFR guidelines clearly indicate that a research participant can withdraw from a study and have the data destroyed at any time but they do not stipulate how requests for tapes should be handled.

The IRB at my current university graciously tackled this question and provided five opinions about how they would view such a case. The diversity of perspectives and opinions is best illustrated in their words, here conveyed anonymously:

> When a University mandates that only aggregate data be reported to the participant, they effectively strip away the participant's right to the data.

> The higher priority is the rights of the research participants. And as far as I know, the participant can request, or in fact insist, that she be given the tape. In fact, she can insist that the tape be destroyed. She "owns" the data, not the university. I know that ethical standards in my own field insist that research participants have rights to the product (photos, tapes, videos, etc.) indefinitely, unless they specifically sign them away.

> I am not aware of any regulation that states that the data that is collected in a research study is the property of the participant. Therefore, on that point alone, I would say that they do not have to hand over the tape. However, depending on the circumstances, the PI might decide to send a transcript.

> The information may be potentially hurtful to the caregiver him- or herself. For this reason, the researcher is obligated to protect the confidentiality of the information. If the information were given to the caregiver, and if the information resulted in any damages, I think the university could be liable. This would be true even though the caregiver might be the one to release the information.

> This is a question that would benefit from a meeting and discussion. I would want to know what the PI promised to do, why the participant wanted the tape . . . would need to reason together (with the PI) about whether or not the request should be granted.

Many scenarios could raise the issue of access to and ownership of taped and transcribed qualitative data: a relative requests an interview tape after a participant's death and the tape includes content that demeans her, or a tape is requested for use in a custody battle. Although the guidelines cannot address every potential dilemma, certainly consultation with others provides support while helping to clarify the complexity of the issues and identify the possible courses of action to ensure that no harm is done.

RISK VERSUS BENEFIT: EMOTIONAL REACTIONS AND RESPONSES

With the frail elderly, or those suffering from debilitating illness, even participation in an interview can be potentially harmful. Interviews may need to be modified to avoid fatigue (such as alternating types of questions, or conducting two shorter rather than one longer interview) (Kayser-Jones & Koenig, 1994). Following an in-depth interview, I asked older caregivers to complete both the Brief Symptom Inventory (BSI) and the Ways of Coping scales, which together totaled 125 questions. Fatigue often became a factor. Caregivers would also be simultaneously attending to the needs of a loved one, making concentration difficult. Incorporating their feedback, I modified the process and began taking self-addressed stamped envelopes with me so the participants could complete and mail the written questions later.

What are the benefits for individuals who participate in qualitative research? The contribution to knowledge or improved services motivates some, particularly evidenced by statements such as, "I'm glad to help." Comparing qualitative research to other types is also informative: drug trials, written surveys and interpersonal exchanges in interviews clearly highlight the special benefits of qualitative methods. A colleague remarked that several participants in her study (victims of abuse) made statements such as, "This interview has been helpful, thank you for letting me tell you my story." Other participants remarked, "How quickly do you think your work will make people realize what we go through?" Despite the limited awareness about the length of the data collection to publication process, the point is well taken—the opportunity to discuss a difficult experience with an interested and nonjudgmental researcher can generate positive feelings and hope for change among those who feel disenfranchised.

One of the most common outcomes of in-depth interviews is a participant's unforeseen emotional reaction. Emotions are a natural response to the discussion of an intense experience and crucial for a complete understanding of the participant's perception of the event or issue being studied (Weiss, 1994). Just as cognitive, behavioral, and physical reactions all need to be explored, emotional reactions require equal time in qualitative research. IRBs are, however, often fearful that the expression of intense emotion may lead to a situation that gets out of control. Fears of damage rendered by emotional expression or reactions during an interview generate concern that the organization will be responsible for extending a participant's problems. Perceptions of liability-charged outcomes from emotional responses can motivate extraordinary caution by some IRBs.

Preparation for a qualitative study requires thoughtful consideration of potential participant reactions. A researcher who asks a participant to divulge the details of a difficult or possibly painful experience should be prepared for the possibility that through the research encounter a person could have a first-time recognition of the trauma or potentially reexperience it while telling the story. This possibility should not be avoided, but rather be anticipated and planned for. A list of community resources for support and assistance should be developed and provided for participants who express a need for assistance. Although many IRBs leave it to the discretion of the researcher, others require some version of the following statement within the informed consent document:

> I know that the questions in this interview are about emotions and grief. If I have an intense emotional reaction or feel the urge to harm myself or another person during this interview, telephone contact will be made for assistance. I am aware that counseling is available if I decide I need help after this interview.

Some research projects use methods such as clinical indices or unstructured interviews, which "feel" therapeutic to a participant. In-depth research interviews conducted by mental health professionals should never be construed as professional mental health assistance, a phenomenon known as the "therapeutic misconception" (Appelbaum et al., 1987). The researcher's response to a participant's emotional reaction is important. Researcher's natural responses often include feeling guilty for causing pain and wanting to offer comforting words ("Crying is part of losing someone—everyone needs to cry" or "Don't cry"). Weiss (1994) provides simple wisdom for qualitative researchers in this situation—it is best to just sit quietly and wait.

RESEARCHER AS INSTRUMENT: DANGERS AND OPPORTUNITIES

Students are taught that the use of self as instrument is an important element of qualitative research (Berg, 2001; Moch, 2000; Padgett, 1998a,b; Tutty, et al., 1996, Weiss, 1994). The phrase, however, may have vastly different interpretations depending on the educational background, life experience, personal opinions, and style of the investigator. The researcher's role is further influenced by the field of inquiry and sociopolitical context. Generally interpreted, the use of self includes social behaviors such as chatting (Berg, 2001), reaching out, making people feel comfortable, being nonjudgmental, and building on shared humanity as a basis for greater understanding.

The qualitative researcher, functioning as an instrument for both observation and data collection, can become immersed in the life of the individual, organization, or community shortly after entering the field, (Ely, et al., 1991; Padgett, 1998b; Strauss & Corbin, 1998). During this dynamic and continually evolving process, the participants' unique experiences and the researcher's individual perspectives converge. Knowledge and understanding emerge from what the researcher does, learns, and experiences in this context. Robert Weiss (1994) describes his reactions to the experience of interviewing:

> Occasionally an interview is engaging enough for me not only to feel in tune with the other person's rhythm of speaking and thought but also to see the world through the other person's eyes. At such times I feel myself to be split, with one part functioning professionally, asking questions and monitoring responses, while another part is identified with the respondent. Identification can become so strong that I feel my contact with my own core self has been loosened. I remain aware, of course, that I am with the respondent as an interviewer, but the world in which I live is replaced temporarily, by the respondent's. After . . . I am likely to be a bit disoriented— the way someone is emerging from a movie. (p. 125)

As a professional social worker I learned to trust my gut, which in most circumstances meant paying attention to a hunch that there is more happening in a situation than meets the eye. The same sensation that leads a clinician to pose questions differently can also trigger the researcher to ask probing—but not idle or intrusive—questions (Weiss, 1994). Both danger and opportunity can be found in the use of self as instrument; clinicians who have made the transition to researchers are cautioned not to turn qualitative interviews into psychosocial histories or therapeutic encounters, and researchers without the ability to read situations are encouraged to develop self-awareness and insight about more subtle shades of meaning.

We cannot completely divorce ourselves from who we are or what we know (Strauss & Corbin, 1998). If used correctly and judiciously, personal experience can increase sensitivity by providing a comparable basis for meaning in experiences such as grief and loss (Weiss, 1994). In other situations, for example, a study of girl gangs (Sikes, 1997), there is no basis for comparison. The ethical imperative of doing no harm must be upheld by a researcher who brings self-awareness to the research interaction. An important source of prevention and a safeguard against what could be considered the misuse of self can be found in peer debriefing and support (see Chapter 10).

Being enveloped in qualitative research is a bit like being in a surround-sound theater where you experience a participant's world—graphically and profoundly—with all five senses. When studying intensely emotional situations, researchers can feel flooded and possibly overwhelmed, especially when a story triggers intense feelings or unresolved emotional issues. The researcher can also be personally changed by the experience of hearing a life story in vivid and painful detail as shared by someone who is in an uncertain or fragile situation (Moch, 2000). Both awe and profound respect accompany these personal–professional experiences. Susan Diemert Moch reflects on her reactions to conducting research with breast cancer patients:

> Such lessons about life were good for me. I realized that now is the best time to nurture relationships—to share myself more with family, friends, and others in the world around me I wondered if I, too, could learn to become more perceptive through the wisdom of these women . . . they were teaching me to slow down, reflect on my life and open the boundaries dividing me from the world. (Moch, 2000, p. 131)

Some qualitative researchers have suggested achieving a type of neutralization of intense feelings (Weiss, 1994); others refer to *bracketing*, the conscientious (and constant) effort to suspend our assumptions, beliefs, and feelings to better understand the experience of our respondents (Ely et al., 1991, p. 50). However, neither bracketing nor neutralization imply that feelings and emotions should be shut off. Rather these concepts underscore the importance of working at becoming aware of our own issues so that we can remove or at least contain them.

Repeated exposure to the life-threatening or violent experiences of another person can lead to vicarious traumatization and secondary stress syndrome (Figley, 1995). Primarily found in mental health professionals, it is also germane to a discussion of qualitative research where interviewers encounter intense, long-term exposure to participants' unfiltered descriptions of sometimes difficult and traumatic experiences. Clearly, the potential effects of sharing the lived experience of participants cannot be ignored. Considering the wear and tear that is experienced, peer support, debriefing, and time for reflection are important. Keeping emotional reactions in check has two important ethical implications: (1) protecting our participants from the undue burden of dealing with our reactions, and (2) preserving the integrity and validity of our data.

DUAL RELATIONSHIPS:
MAINTAINING BOUNDARIES

Conflicts of interest occur when personal or financial interests prevent researchers from acting without bias. All professional organizations' codes of ethics caution their members to remain alert to conflicts of interest, prevent conflict, and disclose them. Examples from research include subjects who are also clients, friends, or family members.

Dual relationships that are less clear can lead to potential ethical quandaries. Each of us occupies multiple roles—parent, child, student, teacher, and community member. In the sometimes-awkward initial moments of gaining entrée and building rapport, it is natural and often acceptable for the qualitative researcher to share personal experiences, which might enhance a participant's feelings of trust and understanding.

Expectations are critical components for the researcher to consider before entering the field: the research relationship is a collaboration and partnership rather than a friendship and enduring relationship. Too much self-disclosure can cause misunderstandings and blurred relationships after the research relationship is terminated. What might the participant expect from you after the study is completed? Conducting research in the community where I live, I have developed my own litmus test: "How will I feel about what this person or family knows about me if I meet them in the grocery store?" The answer, different for each researcher, is important to consider before it is put to the test. Similarly, we must be mindful of our participants' own feelings of embarrassment or chagrin upon seeing us in a nonresearch context and ensure that our reactions do not cause further discomfort.

In some situations, investigators study a group to which they belong. Kathleen MacPherson (1988) in "Dilemmas of participant-observation in a menopause collective" wrote about the dilemmas she faced when studying "her own":

> I was led into a series of disconcerting dilemmas: increasing my workload . . . being forced to take sides in conflicts . . . feeling guilty about possibly exploiting the group for my own purposes . . . and wondering if I was exposing my group's weaknesses. There were positive features; I learned how to combine participant and researcher roles . . . I learned that the group felt less concerned about my research than I . . . I probably contributed to the group's survival by sharing my analysis. (p. 193)

Although there are no ethical standards prohibiting studying one's own, it seems crucial to explore the short- and long-term effects of such duality. MacPherson (1988) notes that in some populations (particularly related to aging) we all hold dual roles.

COMPROMISING CIRCUMSTANCES: SUGGESTED GUIDELINES FOR ETHICAL QUALITATIVE RESEARCH

Qualitative researchers may confront unanticipated circumstances where they become aware of threatening information. In these cases, researchers' conduct should be guided by their training, applicable codes of ethics, legal requirements, and, particularly in unsafe circumstances, common sense. A classic example of compromising circumstances is described by Steven J. Taylor, who was conducting ethnographic research in a state institution for the mentally retarded:

> I spent one full year observing one ward characterized as serving 73 "severely and profoundly retarded, ambulatory aggressive, young adult males." . . . I struck . . . a bargain with institutional officials and ward staff.

In exchange for letting me observe, I promised to maintain confidentiality and refrain from interfering in institutional activities. (1987, p. 289)

But Taylor's detachment was sorely tested. "The abuse was morally appalling, yet sociologically interesting. How is it that human beings can routinely abuse other human beings under their care?" (1987, p. 291).

Despite strong inclinations to do something, Taylor considered the possibilities and decided to wait rather than act impulsively. For Taylor, the ethical issue became not whether to do something, but what, how, and when to do it (Padgett, 1998b). He also acknowledged that other researchers might have taken a more proactive stance (and thus jeopardized the study). There are no easy answers. Striking a balance between the pursuit of knowledge and protecting one's informants requires constant vigilance.

Below are a few ethical guidelines for qualitative researchers culled from my own and others' experiences.

1. *Anticipate, anticipate, anticipate.* The importance of thinking through and carefully preparing for qualitative research with at-risk groups cannot be overemphasized. Try to anticipate any ethical dilemmas that could emerge. Plan for dilemmas even if they seem preposterous. Play them out so that you are mentally prepared and ready to handle whatever may occur. Think about the vulnerable population from social, emotional, and moral perspectives prior to entering the field—and your responses should something occur. Consider the standards by which you must act. Your actions are governed by the IRB, professional codes of ethics, and personal morality. They preserve the integrity of your data and analyses, but should be guided by ethical principles of doing no harm. It is ultimately important to go into fieldwork thinking about potential moral and ethical dilemmas before encountering them (Taylor, 1987). Prevention is always the best intervention.

2. *Do your homework.* Do not rush into the field. Spend time learning about the experiences, needs, and vulnerabilities of the population that you are studying. Immerse yourself in policy, program, and social issues that affect the population. Get permission to shadow (Ely, et al., 1991) key informants (if you can), attend meetings, ask to tour facilities, and interview persons who are knowledgeable about the group. Ask them what you might expect to find (including moral or ethical dilemmas) and what you need to know about the group you are studying.

3. *Be aware of spillover, splatter, and surprises.* Be prepared for something to touch you in an unexpected way. Think of ways to control impulsive responses—some people giggle when faced with extreme distress and others flee the scene. Expect to leave the field or an interview feeling drained and sometimes overwhelmed. Make a commitment before you begin that you will keep your reactions in check until you arrive safely home.

4. *Practice self-discipline.* Write or audiotape notes to yourself about your reactions after every interview, meeting, or day in the field. Watch for themes

and patterns over time and be sensitive to changes you observe in yourself—as the research instrument your calibration is critical.

5. *Be a good guest.* "Be alert to proper demands of good citizenship or host-guest relations" (American Anthropological Association [1998], Code of Ethics, Standard 3). Honor the home of the person who has invited you to enter—whether it is the plastic tarp of a homeless individual or a room in a nursing home—and thank them for sharing it with you. Resist any urge to comment on odor or filth. Learn to be friendly to animals—pets are important gatekeepers and a source of entrée to the person's life. Be observant, noting photos on the wall and prized possessions. Comment on them—it is considerate and guest-like (while also documenting observations about the person or environment for later recording in your field notes).

6. *Use self-reflections.* Always cross-examine your interviews—what went well and what went poorly—and learn from them (see Tutty, et al., 1996, pp. 79–82, for helpful suggestions). Use a journal or tape recorder for reflections immediately after you leave an interview or period of observation. Pay particular attention to the parts that made you uneasy.

7. *Practice social responsibility.* If you uncover appalling or dangerous circumstances remember that you have at least four choices: (1) intervene, (2) leave the field, (3) blow the whistle, or (4) continue the study, and use the data to push for macrolevel change when the study is completed (Taylor, 1987). These are not mutually exclusive. When in doubt, consider leaving the field temporarily and then deciding on the next best course of action.

8. *Embrace discomfort.* Whenever you feel the telltale butterflies in your stomach, use the ethical uncertainties and ambiguities as signposts along the journey of discovery. Clearly, exploring the needs and complicated life experiences of vulnerable population groups is accompanied by issues that require care and sensitivity. Carefully working with these issues can bring your understanding of the population to an important and desirable new level.

REFERENCES

American Anthropological Association. (1998). *Code of ethics.* Retrieved June 16, 2002 from http://www.aaanet.org/committees/ethics/ethcode.htm

Appelbaum, P. S. (1989). Tarasoff and the researcher: Does the duty to protect apply in the research setting? *American Psychologist, 44* (6), 885–94.

Appelbaum, P. S., Roth, L. H., Lidz, C. W., Benson, P., & Winslade, W. (1987). False hopes and best data: Consent to research and the therapeutic misconception. *Hastings Center Report, 17* (2), 20–4.

Berg, B. L. (2001). *Qualitative research methods for the social sciences* (4th ed.). Boston: Allyn & Bacon.

Choi, N. G., & Snyder, L. J. (1999). *Homeless families with children: A subjective experience of homelessness.* New York: Springer.

Code of Federal Regulations (CFR). (2001). Title 45 Public Welfare Department of Health and Human

Services Part 46—Protection of Human Subjects (45 CFR 46). Retrieved May 2, 2002 from http://ohrp.osophs.dhhs.gov/human-subjects/guidance/45cfr46.htm#46

Demi, A. S., & Warren, N. A. (1995). Issues in conducting research with vulnerable families. *Western Journal of Nursing Research 17*, 188–202.

Ely, M., Anzul, M., Friedman, T. ,Garner, D., & McCormack-Steinmetz, A. (1991). *Doing qualitative research: Circles within circles*. London: The Falmer Press.

Figley, C. R. (1995). *Compassion fatigue: Coping with secondary traumatic stress disorder in those who treat the traumatized*. New York: Brunner/Mazel.

Gilgun, J. F. (1994). Hand into glove: The grounded theory approach and social work practice research. In E. Sherman and W. J. Reid (Eds.), *Qualitative research in social work* (pp. 115–125). New York: Columbia University Press.

Humphreys, L. (1970). *Tearoom trade*. Chicago: Aldine.

Kayser-Jones, J., & Koenig, B. A. (1994). Ethical issues. In J. F. Gubrium & A. Sankar (Eds.), *Qualitative methods in aging research* (pp. 15–32). Thousand Oaks, CA: Sage.

MacPherson, K. (1988). Dilemmas of participant-observation in a menopause collective. In S. Reinharz & G. D. Rowles (Eds.), *Qualitative gerontology* (pp. 184–96). New York: Springer.

Miles, M. B., & Huberman, A. M. (1984). *Qualitative data analysis*. Beverly Hills, CA: Sage.

Minkler, M., & Roe, K. M. (1993). *Grandmothers as caregivers: Raising children of the crack cocaine epidemic*. Newbury Park, CA: Sage.

Moch, S. D. (2000). The research experience as described in published reports. In S. D. Moch & M. F. Gates (Eds.),

The researcher experience in qualitative research. Thousand Oaks, CA: Sage.

National Commission for the Protection of Human Subjects of Biomedical and Behavioral Research. (1978). *The Belmont report: Ethical principles and guidelines for the protection of human subjects of research*. Washington, DC: Government Printing Office. (DHEW publication no. (OS) 78–0012.)

National Institutes of Health (NIH) Bioethics Interest Group. (1998). Research involving individuals with questionable capacity to consent: Ethical issues and practical considerations for institutional review boards (IRBs). Expert Panel Report to the National Institutes of Health (NIH). Retrieved March 12, 2002 from http://www.nih.gov/sigs/bioethics/reports/topics.htm#xassess

Padgett, D. K. (1998a). Does the glove really fit? Qualitative research and clinical social work practice. *Social Work, 43* (4), 373–81.

Padgett, D. K. (1998b). *Qualitative methods in social work research: Challenges and rewards*. Thousand Oaks, CA: Sage.

Sikes, G. (1997). *8 ball chicks: A year in the violent world of girl gangs*. New York: Anchor Books.

Strauss, A., & Corbin, J. (1998). *Basics of qualitative research: Techniques and procedures for developing grounded theory*. Thousand Oaks, CA: Sage.

Taylor, S. J. (1987). Observing abuse: Professional ethics and personal morality in field research. *Qualitative Sociology, 10*, 288–302.

Tutty, L. M., Rothery, M., & Grinnell, R. M. (1996). *Qualitative research for social workers: Phases, steps, & tasks*. Boston: Allyn & Bacon.

Weiss, R. S. (1994). *Learning from strangers: The art and method of qualitative interview studies*. New York: The Free Press.

12

"Doing" Narrative Analysis

MARGARETA HYDÉN
AND CAROLINA ÖVERLIEN

First-rate qualitative research results from hard work and systematic approaches. That means gathering rich data, synthesizing them, and make analytic sense of them. To implement such an agenda, one needs to rely on some kind of methodology. Research method, for us, connotes a way of knowing. This means we take methodology to be more than sharply marked-off techniques and procedural guidelines. Of course, our understanding of research methods includes a set of strategies, but it is closer to an understanding of methods that implicates perception, comprehension, and representation. Narrative analysis provides us with possibilities to carry out our work in accordance with this understanding.

Narrative analysis covers a large and diverse range of approaches, the result of the rapid expansion of this area of inquiry over the past dozen or so years (Mishler, 1999). Some background on narrative theory places this chapter in context.

Narrative is a fundamental human way of giving meaning to experience. It is one of the first forms of discourse we learn as children (Nelson, 1989). Despite its common occurrence, the precise definition of *personal narrative* remains ambiguous (Riessman, 1993). The term generally refers to a particular kind of text organized around consequential events in the teller's life. Data are usually gathered in an interview process that makes it possible for the interviewee to express themselves in lengthy turns and to organize their replies into long stories. Mishler (1986) concluded as a result of his empirical studies that the standard approach to interviewing was inappropriate for and inadequate to the study of the central questions of the social and behavioral sciences. Namely, how individuals perceive, organize, give meaning to, and express their understandings of themselves, their experiences, and their worlds. Further, Mishler stated, the traditional approach neglects examining how these understandings are related to their social, cultural, and personal circumstances. In the narrative-oriented interview, the researcher invites the interviewer into a past-time world and to recapitulate what happened then to make a point, often a moral one.

We shape our world and ourselves by telling stories. To change, we must bring a new story into being. The interpretation of an event and its metaphorical use is a narrative invention that provides continuity both with the received facts and with the narrator's conception or invention of the event. In both telling and interpreting experiences, narrative mediates between an inner world of thought-feeling and an outer world of observable actions and states of affairs. This is why narrative analysis is of such concern in social science today (e.g., Andrews et al., 2000; Bruner, 2001; Mattingly & Garro, 2000; Mishler, 1995; Riessman, 1993). This is why narrative analysis is of concern to us.

Narrative analysis has opened up new horizons for interpretative investigations that focus on social, discursive and cultural forms of life (Brockmeier & Harré, 2001). In this chapter, we present narrative analysis by introducing three central themes, each representing three kinds of activity. They are *entering the rhetorical domain, conducting the teller-oriented interview*, and *analyzing narrative power*. This is not a complete list of themes in narrative-oriented research, nor is it the only way to characterize narrative analysis, but it captures some important features of the narrative approach. Throughout the chapter, we illustrate these themes using a study involving a particular type of social work practice, namely working with adolescents in compulsory care. The study concerned the difficulties the staff faced when working with girls and young women who had been victims of sexual abuse. We were interested in finding out what kind of work identity the resident assistants developed in the contradictory context of offering support and care involuntarily.

ENTERING THE RHETORICAL DOMAIN

Some years have gone by since our first encounter with our research field. If someone had asked us about it, this would be our story:

1   It was the remoteness and the seclusion that first struck us.

2   The first time we visited the youth detention home for

3   teen-age girls called "The Garden" was a cold winter's day

4   We took the 06.15 westbound train from Stockholm.

5   Three hours later we changed to a rail-car and

6   then to the local bus.

7   The last five miles we walked across snowy fields,

8   stiff with cold and laughing about our inappropriate

9   clothing, perfectly suitable for strolls along the streets

10   of Stockholm, less so for the conditions at hand.

11   As we talked about the insufficiency of our external

12   appearance we started to worry about the internal.

13   So I think the second thing that struck us was the most

14   likely difference between us and the teen-age girls and

15   the staff members we were going to meet.

16   Then we heard two voices shouting "hey, you are on the

17   wrong way," and we saw two teen-age girls, and we said

18   "no, we are on our way to The Garden," and they said

19   "who are you" and we said "researchers," and they said

20   "then you have met the right persons,

21   we know all you need to know."

22   So there we were, not only two women struggling with conditions,

23   determined to carry through the mission of researching a reality little

24   known, but the four of us,

25   and the girls' confidence in us carried us through the snow.

The two women "struggling with the conditions" are the authors of this chapter. As we recall this episode some years later, the facts—although culturally transmitted—are probably right. We can check them against our memory—which of course could be more fallible than reliable—but we know that we were there, that it was far from Stockholm and very cold, and that we met two girls. More important than recalling the facts, however, is that the story contains a variant of the metaphoric theme that constituted a common feature of our experiences at our destination—a youth detention home for girls and young women we will call The Garden. The girls hidden away in the most remote of places and the challenge of entering this distant world was a theme that characterized our research project from the start.

Because sexual abuse was seen as a fundamental component in the complex picture of self-destructive behaviors that were reported—drug abuse, promiscuity, cutting, and suicide attempts—to be able to develop ways of handling experiences of sexual abuse was considered as important. The prevailing therapeutic discourse at The Garden emphasized the importance of verbalizing traumatic experiences. Viewed as a fundamental assignment, the resident assistants' professional self-confidence and positive work identity depended on the capacity and skills to assist the girls in talking about what had happened. A failure in doing so threatened to put their work identity as valid staff members at stake.

In this chapter, both *story* and *narrative* are used. In the understanding reflected in the chapter, the distinguishing elements between the two terms are that *narrative* is telling; a performative event, the *process* of telling a story. A *story* is an *account* that may involve the narration of a series of events, with time as an organizing factor. We further understand a narrative as a distinguishable entity, as possible to discriminate from other forms of discursive practices. We limit the discussion here to *personal narratives*, first-person accounts in interviews of informants' own experience, putting aside other kinds of narratives (e.g., texts from media about events).

WHAT IS A NARRATIVE?

Perhaps because of its common occurrence, the precise definition of a personal narrative remains ambiguous. "It is an umbrella term" Mishler (1999) states and continues,

> which disturbs some proponents and critics, but I am opposed to any effort to police the boundaries of this area of work. It would be misguided and useless. More importantly, the excitement of doing narrative research is owing to, in some degree, the multiplicity of approaches and the clash of different perspectives. (p. 17)

Narrative generally refers to a particular kind of text organized around consequential events in the teller's life. It then includes characters and a plot that evolves over time. The teller takes the listener into a past-time world, and recapitulates what happened then to make a point, often a moral one. No formal model of story actually exists. However, personal narratives depend on certain structures to hold them together.

Labov's (1972, 1982) structural approach has been cited by many investigators and summarized by Riessman (1993). Narratives, he argues, have six formal properties and each has a function. These include an abstract (summary or substance of the narrative), orientation (time, place, situation, participants), complicating action (sequence of events), evaluation (significance and meaning of the action, attitude of the narrator), resolution (what finally happened), and coda (return to the present). With this structure, a teller constructs a story from a primary experience and interprets the significance of events in clauses and embedded evaluation.

The narrative of our first visit to the institution, barely meets the criteria proposed by Labov. It includes an abstract (line 1), an orientation (lines 2–6), two examples of a complicating action (lines 7–12 and lines 23–28), an evaluation of the first part of the narrative (lines 13–15), and a resolution (lines 22–25). So far so good, but what is almost missing is a coda, the part of the narrative that takes us back to the present. Maybe the resolution part could be viewed as including the coda, but we are hesitant to assert this. "Narrative necessarily comprises two features," Bruner suggests and continues,

> One of them is telling what happened to a cast of human beings with a view to the order in which things happened. That part is greatly aided by the devices of flashback, flashforward, and the rest. But a narrative must also answer the question "Why," "Why is it worth telling, what is interesting about it?" Not everything that happened is worth telling about, and it is not always clear why what one tells merits telling. We are bored and offended by such accounts as "I got up in the morning, got out of bed, dressed and tied my shoes, shaved, had

breakfast, went to the office and saw a graduate student who had an idea for a thesis. . . . (2001, p. 29)

We also hesitate to claim that our narrative meets Bruner's criteria and should pass as an account that merits telling. If the two girls had not made their appearance, our narrative would have had probably failed: how interesting is it to hear about two women endlessly traveling by train and walking in the snow? Nevertheless, the metaphoric theme of the narrative constituted a common feature of our experiences at the institution and worked as a context for the stories our respondents gave us. As we will show, these stories indisputably meet Labov's as well as Bruner's criteria.

CONDUCTING A
TELLER-FOCUSED INTERVIEW

An interview can be viewed as a form of discourse (Mishler, 1991). Shaped and organized by asking and answering questions. It is a joint product of what interviewees and interviewers talk about. In our study, the questions were primarily aimed at constructing a framework within which the interviewees would have the opportunity to discuss their thoughts and feelings. What we wanted to get access to was their understanding and inner logic—or possibly their lack of inner logic and understanding. The interviews were preceded by observations, and followed by reflexive interviews. The second author (C.Ö.) stayed at the institution for 2 weeks and observed interactions between the resident assistants and the girls. Special attention was paid to discussion and situations concerning sexual abuse.

When the topic of sexual abuse seemed to create a dilemma or a problem for the staff, interviews with them were conducted the same day or soon thereafter. For each situation, a group interview with the staff at the department was conducted as well as individual interviews with each of staff member involved. The group interview was announced as a "45-minute gathering, aimed at reflection." To encourage free narratives, we chose an open interview style with few questions formulated in advance. We prepared only a few questions: What has happened? How do you understand this situation? Why do you think about it as sexual abuse?

Following Mishler's advice (1986), the first author (M.H.) developed a format for interviewing built on the assumption that the research interview is relational and that places at the informant's disposal a framework for developing his or her understanding. Such an interview form gives the researcher the opportunity to gain richer material than the traditional in-depth interview.

Thus, the questions are primarily aimed at constructing a framework and a relationship within which the informants feel free to discuss their thoughts and feelings. It is their associations, their inner logic and understanding thereof, that the researcher wants to access.

ANALYSING NARRATIVE POWER

Storytelling can be seen as a power relationship between teller and listener. Plummer (1995) formulates this vividly: "For narratives to flourish, there must be a community to hear; for communities to hear, there must be stories which weave together their history, their identity, their politics" (p. 87). Power is not something a person either has or does not have, he states, an "all or nothing phenomena." Rather, it is a "flow of negotiations and shifting outcomes" (p. 26). Sexual stories, he argues, are part of this flow of power. The flow can be negative or positive, giving the narrative either oppressive and repressive powers or creative and constructive powers.

Narratives come in many different forms and may be contradictory, fragmented, personal, or grand. In relation to power, the grand master narratives hold a special position among narrative genres. The master narratives are *grand* in that they connect us to others, to morality, and to the moral self. When a story of sexual abuse is told, in most cases it brings into being a language that reflects the Freudian legacy. For example, the heated debate on the existence of repressed memory would have been impossible without access to the psychoanalytic language of the conscious and the unconscious (for argumentation for the existence of repressed memory, see Bass & Davis, 1988; for an argumentation against it, see Loftus & Ketcham, 1994): the whole way of reasoning is based on the notion of a mind with an ability to bury the entire memory of traumatic experiences so deeply within the unconscious that it can only be recalled in the form of a flashback triggered by a sight, a smell, or a sound. To heal, the traumatized person must enter "the journey out of the darkness of sexual abuse" (Schave, 1993).

Three fundamental questions can now be asked for the analysis of the power-related aspects of the joint enterprise of the teller and listener in producing stories.

1. Concerning the *status of the stories:* Where are the stories located in the institutional world? Are they stories one likes to tell, or stories that must be told, or are they, as O'Connor suggests (2000) stories that cannot be told? Who is privileged by the storytelling: the teller, the listener, the perpetrator, or the families or friends that might appear as protagonists in the story?

2. Concerning the *control of the stories:* Who owns them? Who is in charge of them: the teller, the listener, the perpetrator, the families or friends that might appear as protagonists, or the surrounding society? Is it possible to gain control of them, that is, to move from a powerless to a more powerful position?

3. Concerning the *responsibility for the stories:* These questions are closely connected to the questions concerning control of the stories: If the stories are harmful, who is to blame and who is to shoulder the responsibility?

QUESTIONS FOR ANALYZING
POWER-RELATED ASPECTS
OF STORYTELLING

With these questions in mind, we will now return to our study and see how they can be used to make analytic sense of our data. Due to space limitations, we exclude the phase of the research process that preceded the analysis and followed the gathering of data—transcribing and putting the interview material in order for analysis. We turn directly to our interest in understanding how our informants' work identity as resident assistants was produced and performed in the research interviews.

From our corpus of 5 group and 29 individual interviews, excerpts from 6 were selected for this chapter. They reflect our first round of analysis, focusing on the content of the interviews. From that, we identified four main themes connected with problems, difficulties, and dilemmas the staff faced in hearing sexual abuse stories. The first problem concerned the *tracing of the sexual abuse story*, the second regarding the *danger of telling*, the third dealt with the *reenactments of the abusive event*, and the forth concerned the problem of *talking about something that could not be made right again*. To gain a more profound analytic sense of these themes, we apply a narrative approach to our interview data. We present the four analytic themes in turn.

TRACING THE SEXUAL ABUSE STORY

The abuse story, so constructed that the young woman represented herself as repulsive and worthless, was seen as a fundamental component in the complex picture of self-destructive behavior to which the young women subjected themselves. If a young woman started to verbalize her experiences in that direction, the staff might question her version of the story. She was viewed as being in need of another version of the abuse story—one that cast her as the victim and the perpetrator as the monster. In the right kind of dialogue, this could be done. The resident assistants wanted to create these positive dialogues so that the sexual abuse story could become a healing one. By verbalizing the story and having in come into the open, the healing process was expected to begin. One of the main problems mentioned in connection with this wish was to find a way into the untold story.

In the interview excerpt below, Tina (T.), one of the most experienced female resident assistants, tells interviewer Carolina Överlien (C.Ö.) about this dilemma.

1 **T.:** we had a girl several years ago who absolutely didn't want to tell either and she'd been here for a year and a half and we knew (.) I knew
2 **C.Ö.:** Yes
3 **T.:** that she'd been abused (.) and then she (.) Nina was her name the girls' support person (.) she went to see Sven [the psychologist] (.) a few times for advice (.) because you don't know whether to confront them or not at a time like that

4 **C.Ö.:** But let me just ask you how did you know was it written [anyplace

5 **T.:** [no

6 **C.Ö.:** [had there been a court case

7 **T.:** no [(.) she (.) slept with her clothes on (.) her trainers (.) slept on top of the covers (.) you know had to always be ready to jump out of bed (.) she might sleep under the bedspread but never the covers

8 **C.Ö.:** Mm

9 **T.:** Eh (.) and she had any number of explanations for why she did that her skin peeled so much (.) that she was afraid it was going to fall off if she didn't keep her trainer trousers

10 **C.Ö.:** Aha

11 **T.:** Right there were (pause) you know there were millions of signs like that the way she took showers and (.) well millions of things like that

12 **C.Ö.:** So there were millions of signs that made you sure you knew

13 **T.:** Yes (.) and then of course in the social worker's report it said that(.) well that she refused to do as her parents said and she had run away from home (.) she and several other girls were in one of those apartments that (.) some dirty old man had no but you know a man like that (.) a man you might suspect of something maybe doing something with the girls but there was never any evidence

14 **C.Ö.:** No

15 **T.:** But they were in his apartment all the time because they were allowed to booze up there and he gave them (.) drinks and stuff you know (.) and the people who hung around there were the problem people in town and that kind of thing you know (.) so you get to imagining when I read that kind of thing I get to thinking and I have my thoughts about that kind of stuff

16 **C.Ö.:** Right

17 **T.:** but we did ask her (.) or rather we said we realized (.) like that the girls' contact person she was like in her black books for two months after that and so was I you know

18 **C.Ö.:** Aha

19 **T.:** because I was with her that time

20 **C.Ö.:** You told her you suspected it

21 **T.:** Yes and then she wanted to do us (.) from a psychological point of view she wanted to murder us then (.) when we said we knew

22 **C.Ö.:** Mm

23 **T.:** Eh (.) but after some time more and more began to come out she told us more and more

24 **C.Ö.:** Mm

25 **T.:** and then (.) but she was never really outright almost you know (.) but she got very secure with us later when she knew we knew then

This young woman in Tina's department showed symptoms of sexual abuse. Nina, the female "contact person" was unsure about whether to confront her and talk to her about it. Nina went to the psychologist at the center, Sven, for guidance. The reason they suspected sexual abuse was because the young woman "slept with her clothes on" and "slept on top of the covers" (turn 7). She also acted oddly and had spent time together with a man whom Tina suspected was a sexual abuser of young women. Finally, they confronted the young woman with what they suspected and the result was that Nina, the contact person, "was in her black books for two months." But, after a while, the young woman told them more and more and the resolution was that she finally felt secure with the staff "when she knew we knew" (turn 25).

The story of sexual abuse in this narrative can be seen as a story that must be told, even though the decision to encourage the storytelling involved danger for the listener. Tina and Nina were "in her black books for two months" after they confronted the young woman with their suspicion, and "from a psychological point of view she wanted to murder us then" (turn 21). In spite of this, the resolution of the narrative shows that Tina believed that the story had to be told for the young woman to heal. It was only "when she knew we knew" that she became secure.

Part of the task of the resident assistants is to use their intuition and work experience to know whether or not to confront a young woman with suspicions of abuse and thereby encourage her to tell her story of sexual abuse. The staff are responsible for letting the story come into the open. However, this responsibility is a heavy burden to carry; the telling of sexual abuse stories is risky business. Once the story is told, both teller and listener lose control of the story. The message of the resolution section (turn 25) is that the decision to confront was right, but up to the point of turn 25, this was not certain. The story of sexual abuse in this excerpt is believed to have had the power to heal but neither teller nor listener had the control to prevent the story from causing harm.

THE DANGER OF TELLING SEXUAL ABUSE STORIES: THE POWER OF THE LISTENER

Once told, there was no guarantee that the story would be accompanied by a positive flow of power. It could have become a weapon in the hands of the wrong listener, causing a flow of negative power that could be oppressive or even fatal. To be furnished with a healing capacity, it needed to be taken care of in constructive conversations. Neither the resident assistants nor the girl could guarantee that this would happen.

In the excerpt below, we meet Tina again, in an individual interview that followed a group interview. The situation that prompted this series of interviews was the return to The Garden of a young woman who, after threatening the staff with a hammer, escaped and stayed away for several weeks. The staff were worried that she offered sexual favors for drugs while on the run, something they labeled as sexual abuse, focusing on the men who took advantage of the young woman's vulnerable position. The main issue in the joint interview was the difficulties in finding a way into the assumed sexual abuse story, because the young woman was perceived as very aggressive and so far had turned down every effort to contact her. In her individual interview, Tina problematized these efforts further, recollecting one incident when a girl was confronted with suspicions of sexual abuse thereby allowing the sexual abuse story to come out. For this young woman, Tina explains, the telling of sexual abuse turned out to be fatal:

1 **T.:** Yes it's really difficult (.) you know there's a girl (.) and the staff did so to speak what they thought was right (.) when she told
2 **C.Ö.:** Mm
3 **T.:** Because she laid it out (.) signs and sort of saying things when she got back from from (.) when she'd been home to visit you know (.) so she she really wanted to be asked
4 **C.Ö.:** Mm
5 **T.:** And it's really difficult then when it all comes out
6 **C.Ö.:** Mm
7 **T.:** But she said things like in the end she wanted to have a pregnancy test after she'd been at home (.) and we knew she'd just been home with mom and dad and not gone out or anything (.) so it was well it was like that (.) when she got home (.) her dad would send her mom out to walk the dog (.) and he'd take her down into the root cellar (.) and abuse her sexually (.) so it was under pretty grotesque conditions you know (.) and of course it had been going on for any number of years and (.) all that kind of stuff yeah (.) so I think (.) when she told and there was a trial and all that but then she got (.) she got completely you know (.) disowned by her family of course you know her brothers and sisters refused to have any (.) any contact and ended up in the mental hospital and I think now she's committed suicide (pause) so that (pause) it's really difficult (pause) it's really difficult

The young woman was interpreted as "showing signs of sexual abuse" and was "sort of saying things" that made Tina conclude, "she really wanted to be asked." Believing that talking is the right thing to do, the staff encouraged the young woman to talk about what had happened while she was on leave. The young woman told a story about how her father had sexually abused her in a "root cellar" while her mother was out with the dog. Tina believes this had been going on "for any number of years." The story of sexual abuse led to a trial, abandonment, mental hospitalization, and, finally, (presumed) suicide.

The staff members invite the young woman to talk and thereby to expose her father and the abuse that took place in her home. Because they are not present, the staff has no control of how the story will be received by the family. However, even though they do not have control, they do have responsibility. It is interesting to note the use of *one* instead of *we* or *I*. One possible interpretation of the use of *one* is that the narrator wants to spread the responsibility and thereby the blame for what happened beyond herself, the department, and possibly also the detention home. However, she is also questioning the actions of the staff. They did what they thought was right, she explains in turn 1, but in retrospect, was encouraging this girl to talk the right thing to do when a story of sexual abuse can be powerful enough to kill a young woman? Here Tina begins to question the Freudian grand master narrative of the healing function of talk. Furthermore, Tina claims that the young woman "wanted to be asked." The responsibility for the telling of the story and the tragic outcome of this action is placed not only with the staff who encouraged her to talk, but also with the young woman herself.

At the same time as the sexual abuse stories are seen as powerful in the sense that they can heal, they also have the power to harm the listener. They take on a life of their own once told; neither the teller nor the listener owns or controls the story once it comes into the open. The stories can be told without the young woman being prepared for it or even wanting it, and when a story of sexual abuse is told without control it can become dangerous. The shared understanding is that the harm comes from the young woman not being prepared to receive her own story—she does not have the agency to carry it. The stories that must be told then turn into stories that cannot be told.

The responsibility to decide whether or not a story of sexual abuse is a must-be-told story or a cannot-be-told story is the impossible task of the resident assistants. Responsibility in these cases is also placed with the young women themselves who "want to be asked." Consequently, the power of sexual abuse stories and the dilemma of separating the must-be-told stories from the cannot-be-told stories make both the telling and not telling dangerous. Although The Garden resident is the main character in her story, her position is not powerful enough to prevent her from being harmed. Neither is the position of the staff members.

In the two narratives, the teller has the position of being the reteller of the story. This has direct relevance in the sense that the teller is supposed to take action. We now turn to the two more narratives, where the teller has the position of an agent or counteragent, and the story therefore becomes a narrative of personal experience.

THE UNCERTAIN POSITION
OF MALE STAFF: REENACTMENT
OF THE ABUSIVE EVENT

The daily activities at The Garden are focused on the group rather than on the individual. Each young woman has her own room, but she spends the majority of the day with a group. However, the staff members have the right to place a young woman in solitary confinement. When a young woman is put into solitary confinement as a result of her unruly behavior, she is put into an isolated room with bare walls and floor. The confinement practice is, however, not to be used as a punishment. It can last from minutes to hours depending on how long it takes for her to calm down, but has a maximum length of 24 hours. The staff say that they feel forced to use isolation because of the behavior of the young woman. She is the one who provokes the confinement, and is at times said to have "asked for it."

The justification arguments are psychological, stating that the young women, due to their weak egos, cannot set limits on their own behavior, and this is especially argued in regard to aggression and sexuality. The young woman's behavior can therefore be harmful to herself or to the group; the resident assistants must help her set limits by placing her in confinement. This accountability is necessary in the institutional world where issues of force and resistance must constantly be justified. All incidents of solitary confinement are to be reported to the state department in charge of youth detention homes, The National Board of Institutional Care (NBIC). The practice is seen as a last resort, to be used when all other possible solutions have failed. Frequent occurrences of solitary confinements at a detention home are seen by the NBIC as possible signs of a malfunctioning institution.

The solitary confinement practice was a common topic of conversation at The Garden. Our impression was that the staff members felt obliged to comment on the practice and were anxious to have it understood not as another deprivation of liberty in compulsory care, but rather as a tool used restrictively within the framework of treatment. The comments included statements such as, "our solitary confinement statistics are no higher than at other institutions," or, "it is enough to get one girl who needs to be placed in confinement all the time for the numbers to increase drastically," or, "some girls want solitary confinement and repeatedly create situations they know will result in confinement."

A discourse about sexual abuse that takes its starting point in the positions of victim (the girl) and perpetrator (the man) challenges the discourse about "girls with weak egos who need limits." This was especially obvious when the male resident assistants talked about how it was their job to place the young women in solitary confinement and how uncomfortable this made them feel.

In an individual interview, one of the young male staff members, Patrick (P.) was asked about the views of the male staff concerning physical closeness, especially with young women who have been victims of abuse. He explained that male resident assistants avoid physical closeness with the young women generally, but that male physical strength is often needed and used in solitary confinement practices. Patrick then tells about a confinement situation with a young woman who had previously been sexually abused.

1 **P.:** we had a girl here before who got taken to court because she kept on threatening so much (.) she'd been terribly abused that (.) was the worst thing I've been through she'd been (pause) I she's I don't know what she's doing now but she was sentenced to in-patient psychiatric care but she had been (.) raped by her brothers and guys and all kinds of people ever since she was little like

2 **C.Ö.:** Mm

3 **P.:** and we just kept constantly having to put her in solitary and solitary and solitary

4   **C.Ö.:** Mm
5   **P.:** it was as if she went on repeating the things she had gone through by making us men you know (.) lie down on her and
6   **C.Ö.:** Mm
7   **P.:** hold her and (.) that kind of thing
8   **C.Ö.:** Mm
9   **P.:** it was kind of creepy
10 **C.Ö.:** Yes
11 **P.:** Really
12 **C.Ö.:** I'm sure
13 **P.:** Yeah (.) but you don't realize it until it's (.) I was pretty new then and you didn't realize until you got some distance to it that she was reexperiencing those things

The discourse of reenactment and reexperiencing were frequently used in connection with telling about sexual abuse. In this excerpt, Patrick explains that "it was kind of creepy" to be positioned as one of the actors in a play reenacting an abusive situation. A young woman Patrick used to work with has been "terribly abused" by "her brothers and guys and all kinds of people ever since she was little" (turn 1). She threatens the staff to the extent that she ends up being taken to court and she is sentenced to in-patient psychiatric care. While she was at The Garden, the staff repeatedly put her into solitary confinement. When staff members put a young woman in confinement, the action itself can be rather violent and involve a great amount of physical contact. If she resists the isolation and refuses to walk by herself, she may be pinned to the floor by staff members to avoid violence. Contrary to instructions that male staff should avoid physical closeness with the young women, the confinement practice is mainly carried out by male staff members because they are physically stronger. The importance of gender in regard to the position of the listener is therefore left unexamined.

Patrick understands the situation as *her* repeatedly *making them* put her into solitary confinement as a way of repeating the experience of abuse by having men lying on top of her holding her down. He is extremely uncomfortable with this situation. In turn 13, he expresses how he realized that "she was using" the situation and him as a male staff member for her own purposes of repeating the abuse she had previously experienced. However, it was not until later when he "got some distance to it" and had more experience as a resident assistant that he understood what he had been through.

The next example shows that the sexual abuse story not only has the power to heal or to harm, but also to be repeated without those involved having control. The only actor who could potentially have control would be the young woman, but the staff members are, as we show below, cast in a role without even being aware of it. When a young woman relives her experience of sexual abuse, the story has the power to locate new persons in the different roles of the old story. A staff member can thereby find him or herself in the role of a perpetrator. This is what is happening to Patrick, who without being aware of it is cast in the role of abuser. He does not have control of the story being played out, and it is not until later that he understands what has occurred.

Patrick does not place the responsibility for his victimization either with the young woman or with himself, but rather with her life history. It is what others have previously forced her to endure that is now "forcing" her to stage the abuse situation and him to victimize. By placing the blame outside the young woman, he also avoids the idea of her as a perpetrator, as someone who is forcing him into this position. His reluctance to situate the responsibility for what occurred with something or someone other than himself can also be seen in turn 5 where he uses *us* before switching to *one*, then to *I*, and again back to *one* (turn 13). The use of *us* in turn 5 can be seen as a way to shift blame from him as a person to male staff in general or to all the male staff involved in the isolation incident. The shift from *one* to *I* in his final turn can be seen as a way for him to explain the situation not to the interviewer, but to himself. The shift between the pronouns *one* and *I* emphasizes that although he, as a person, was new at the job, he was not alone in the isolation situation. The shift to *one* indicated the controversy of the isolation practice and his concern about the action taken.

An alternative narrative that is not brought up here is one about her having been repeatedly subjected two-fold or five-fold as a victim of sexual abuse, as placed in compulsory care after a long period of self-destructiveness and now, against her will, being placed in solitary confinement. Another possible narrative is one where Patrick ascribes to himself more leeway and tries to change his own behavior to minimize the risk of being cast as a perpetrator.

A sexual abuse story that is played out by the victim placing the person who is supposed to be her caregiver in the role of perpetrator is an example of a sexual abuse story that cannot be told. Patrick's work identity and his identity as a male are seriously threatened by the incident. As a staff member, he is expected to act and the action results in the solitary confinement, but in the process he feels victimized by the young woman in question, who assigns him the role of perpetrator. In turn 13 Patrick tells us that this incident was a turning point, an incident that led him to restore his work identity. When he "got some distance" from the incident he changed, although he does not tell us how.

In a group interview conducted by M.H. some weeks later, Patrick presented a similar narrative about a young woman who came back to The Garden after a run-away period. The issue that is discussed in the group interview is how *sexual abuse* can actually be defined. Patrick says he wants to contribute to the discussion by giving a really good example of what he thinks it is like to be a victim.

> **P.:** I can tell you about another situation because it's a pretty good example now with her in particular (.) when she came back once after running away and there was me and another person on duty (.) just male staff (.) at night (.) and the person on call was a man too so there were three of us on duty (.) and (.) she was drunk and like that she'd been down (.) doing some streetwalking and walking the streets so they had

lots of cash (pause) and she (.) got put to bed in the infirmary and she kept puking on her sheets like this putting her fingers down her throat you know (.) but then later (.) she took off all her clothes and lay in there naked and parting her legs and saying come on over here and have a fuck (.) as long as you pay

M.H.: Mm

P.: and so we had to (.) we had to (.) we didn't have any (laughter) we had to force her into her clothes and put her in solitary confinement (.) and she just kept on at it all night (.) but that was a kind of repeating too

When the young woman comes back to The Garden after being on the streets of the city for weeks, she is drunk and in bad psychological and physical condition. The night she comes back, there are only male staff working at her department and only male staff on call. After repeatedly vomiting, she takes her clothes off and offers her body to the male staff in exchange for money. The staff members have to "force her into her clothes" and "carry her into solitary confinement." The young woman relives her abuse, Patrick explains, by placing him in the role of a perpetrator.

Patrick's laughter in turn 3 could be interpreted as his being clearly uncomfortable with the role and with having his identity as caregiver threatened, but he rescues the situation by establishing that this too was a situation of reexperienced abuse. It had nothing to do with him as a male resident assistant but rather with the abuse she has previously experienced. The argument that the young women relive or reexperience their sexual abuse by casting the male resident assistants in a role is an argument used not only by Patrick, but supported by all of the resident assistants in the group interview. This argument can be seen as one of the grand narratives at The Garden, and as a frequently used explanation of isolation practices that become difficult in one way or another for the male resident assistants. The next two examples are dangerously charged with a story that has the power to harm the teller by placing him in the role of agent, thereby threatening his work identity.

"I CAN'T TALK ABOUT WHAT I CAN'T MAKE RIGHT"

Talking about sexual abuse can be dangerous because the story is attributed the power to heal and to harm, and to cast the caregiver in an unfavorable role. How do the staff members cope with such problems? A number of staff members argue that although it is important for the young women to talk, they should talk to someone else, preferably one of the psychologists or the nurse because they are better trained and do not interact with the young women on a daily basis. Other staff members argue that talking should not be a priority at all, because of the resident assistants' limited knowledge of how to deal with complex subjects, especially sexual abuse. "I am not one of those great talkers," said Pia, a recently employed resident assistant, who explained why she did not invite conversations about abuse.

In one of her individual interviews, Birgitta (B.), an older resident assistant with many years of experience, gives the following response to a question concerning whether or not it is good for the young women to talk about abuse they have experienced.

1　**B.:** and I think when you talk to the girls (.) (x) but it's always a little risky because you don't want to go too far into things with them and talk because I don't think that's a good idea when I work with them on a daily basis to go too far into things with them

2　**C.Ö.:** Because

3　**B.:** Because I think I upset them too much then

4　**C.Ö.:** Mm

5　**B.:** in ways I'm not equipped to take on (.) make everything all right

Birgitta explains that her reluctance to talk about sexual abuse has to do with her role as a resident assistant in which she is expected to give care. Caregivers are expected not only to receive talk, but be able to "make everything all right." They are also expected to "take on" painful stories. Because Birgitta feels she is unable to do this, she avoids eliciting the sexual abuse stories.

The topic of discussion in the interview, from which the next excerpt was taken, is what happens to the young women when they are on the run from The Garden. Mimi (M.), one of the most experienced resident assistants, talks about a young woman who has been missing for a few days. She is heavily addicted to drugs and the staff are convinced that she is offering sexual favors in return for drugs while away (which they label as sexual abuse). When the police bring her back after being reported missing by the institution, she is in a terrible state psychologically and the staff feel anxious about her mental health. They have been able to make her talk about where she has been while on the run and what drugs she has been taking, but not about sexual abuse.

1　**M.H.:** Do you think it would be good for her if she could talk

2　**M.:** Not necessarily

3　**M.H.:** No

4　**M.:** when you see what happens just with a little thing like this that isn't really anything

5　**M.H.:** Mm

6　**M.:** because all she told us was where she had been and what drugs she had taken

7　**M.H.:** Mm

8　**M.:** that's all she's told

9　**M.H.:** and it gets

10　**M.:** it gets to be too much for her

11　**M.H.:** Mm mm

12　**M.:** Plus her having asked for help kind of with her homework for us to help her (.) and it really makes you realize how hard it is to how to behave with men then

13　**C.Ö.:** So you think it might be better to talk with someone else

14 **M.:** Yes
15 **C.Ö.:** who doesn't work with her on a daily basis
16 **M.:** Yes
17 **M.H.:** Or no one at all
18 **M.:** Maybe (.) though (.) if we lifted the lid off completely I think the kid might explode

According to Mimi, talk about the sexual abuse is more likely to harm than to heal. To "explode" could mean to have an outburst of severe aggression, to go crazy, or to commit suicide, as was the outcome in the earlier example.

The great responsibility for controlling these powerful stories, the dilemma of knowing what is a must-be-told story and a cannot-be-told story, and the feeling of being unable to contain them and to "make everything all right" leads the staff to avoid eliciting sexual abuse stories. Not initiating talk about sexual abuse is one way of dealing with this dilemma; it is built into the structure of the institutional world. Instead, somewhat contradictorily, the staff members assure the young women that if they want to talk, they will listen. The young women should come to them if they feel a need to talk, rather than the staff members coming to the young women. A large part of the responsibility of letting the story out is thereby shifted to the young woman. The young woman is left with the decision of when this powerful and possibly dangerous story should be told.

NARRATIVE—A FUNDAMENTAL WAY OF GIVING MEANING TO EXPERIENCE

We shape our world and ourselves by telling stories. In both telling and interpreting experiences, narrative mediates between an inner world of thought-feeling and an outer world of observable actions. This is why we found narrative analysis applicable as a procedure for exploring the difficulties the staff at The Garden faced when working with young women who had been victims of sexual abuse and how this affected the type of work identity the resident assistants developed.

In this chapter, we presented three basic themes for a narrative approach. First, we talked about how we entered the rhetorical domain of the detention home. Our informants entered into the therapeutic discourse that was valued at the institution and used the resources it provided to construct their concrete social reality. Realities so produced are reflexive, because the discourse that we enter to describe social realities also constitute those realities.

The outcome was quite disheartening. The staff were supposed to be active agents in the highly valued construction of a sexual abuse story that could form the basis for healing the wounds the traumatic events had caused. The main plot in story after story they gave us referenced how they were exceeded by narrative power and positioned powerless to such an extent that their work identity was at stake. Second, we described the teller-focused interview, aiming at facilitating a form of interview that encouraged free narratives. In this form of interviewing, the questions are primarily aimed at constructing a framework and a relationship within which the informants could feel free and have the opportunity to discuss their thoughts and feelings.

This chapter demonstrated some of the technique of narrative analysis and what can be gained from it. As a resource, we used a series of analytic questions focusing on the power related aspects of storytelling following Plummer's (1994) argument that sexual stories are part of a "flow of power."

As resident assistants at a detention home, our respondents were working in the contradictory context of offering support and care involuntarily. The resident assistants must operate under guidelines that are diffuse, with treatment goals such as "strengthening the individual" and "setting limits for deviant behavior." With limited or inadequate qualifications, they are expected to prevent the sexual abuse story from causing harm by using tools such as intuition and work experience. Although they do not have sufficient guidelines, tools, or education, they have a key role in the telling of stories they perceive as having the power to harm as well as heal.

ACKNOWLEDGMENTS

The narrative excerpts in this chapter were taken from a study entitled "To Talk about Sexual Abuse and Other Difficult Experiences" financed by the National Board of Institutional Care of Sweden. The authors thank Catherine Kohler Riessman and Elliot Mishler for their valuable comments.

REFERENCES

Andrews, M., Day Sclater, S., Squire, C., & Treachter, A. (2000). *Lines of narratives. Psychological perspectives.* London and New York: Routledge.

Bass, E., & Davis, L. (1988). *The courage to heal: A guide for women survivors of sexual abuse.* New York: Harper & Row.

Brockmeier, J., & Harré, R. (2001). Narrative: Problems and promises of an alternative paradigm. In J. Brockmeier & D. Carbaugh (Eds.), *Narratives and identity. Studies in autobiography, self and culture.* Amsterdam: John Benjamins.

Bruner, J. (2001). Self-making and world-making. In J. Brockmeier & D. Carbaugh (Eds.), *Narratives and identity. Studies in autobiography, self and culture.* Amsterdam: John Benjamins.

Labov, W. (1972). The transformation of experience in narrative syntax. In W. Labov (Ed.), *Language in the inner city. Studies in the Black English vernacular* (pp. 354–96). Philadelphia: University of Pennsylvania Press.

Labov, W. (1982). Speech actions and reactions in personal narrative. In D. Tannen (Ed.), *Analyzing discourse: Text and talk* (pp. 219–47). Washington, DC: Georgetown University Press.

Loftus, E., & Ketcham, K. (1994). *The myth of repressed memory. False memories and allegations of sexual abuse.* New York: St. Martin's Press.

Mattingly, C., & Garro, L.C. (2000). *Narrative and the cultural construction of Illness and healing.* Berkeley: University of California Press.

Mishler, E. (1986). *Research interviewing. Context and narrative.* Cambridge, MA: Harvard University Press.

Mishler, E. (1999). *Storylines. Craft artists' narratives of identity.* Cambridge, MA: Harvard University Press.

Nelson, K. (1989). *Narratives from the crib.* Cambridge, MA: Harvard University Press.

O'Connor, P. E. (2000). *Speaking of Crime: Narratives of Prisoners.* Lincoln, NE: University of Nebraska Press.

Plummer, K. (1994). *Telling sexual stories: Power, change and social worlds.* New York: Routledge.

Riessman, C. K. (1993). *Narrative Analysis.* Newbury Park, CA: Sage

Schave, B. (1993). *Forgotten memories. A journey out of the darkness of sexual abuse.* Westport, CT: Praeger.

13

Mixed Methods, Serendipity, and Concatenation

DEBORAH K. PADGETT

The used of mixed (quantitative–qualitative) methods has received much attention in the literatures of practice-based professions such as nursing, social work, and medicine. Such studies are attractive because they offer an opportunity to compare and contrast findings from the two methods and to engage quantitative and qualitative researchers in the kinds of cross-disciplinary collaboration that increasingly characterize the research enterprise (Weaver et al., 1996).

This chapter is designed to probe the realm of mixed-methods studies and to offer some suggestions for how their synergy can be put to optimal use. I briefly review mixed-methods research, then discuss the role of a primary strength of qualitative research—serendipity—and how serendipitous findings are especially valuable in the context of mixed-methods studies. Next, I argue that findings from either or both sides of a mixed-methods study can be used to propel knowledge beyond the bounds of a single study (a process of concatenation). Both of these concepts—serendipity and concatenation—are illustrated drawing upon a mixed-methods study in which I participated as co-principal investigator.

MIXING METHODS

Combining quantitative and qualitative methods has had powerful backing over the years, beginning with Donald Campbell and his colleagues (Campbell & Fiske, 1959; Webb et al., 1966). Their earliest rationale for mixing methods was largely confirmatory, that is, to cross-validate findings. However, discrepancies were viewed as a problem of interpretation mostly on the qualitative side (Morgan, 1998).

A number of leading researchers carried the banner of mixed-methods research forward into the 1990s, including Mark and Shotland (1987), Brewer and Hunter (1989), Brannen, (1992), Reichardt and Rallis (1994), Creswell (1994), Greene and Caracelli (1997), Tashakkori and Teddlie, (1998) and Barbour (1999). In the social sciences, similar ideas were cloaked in more vivid descriptions such as "dialectical tacking" (Geertz, 1979) and "double hermeneutics" (Giddens, 1976). No doubt influenced by this momentum, Campbell and Russo (1999) later offered a more balanced justification for mixing methods, insisting that because all methods are imperfect, combining them greatly enhances a study's capacity for generating and testing theory.

Because the mix-and-match possibilities are many (given the diversity of qualitative approaches as well as of quantitative designs), some researchers developed typologies of mixed-methods designs based on dominance (of one side versus the other) and temporal sequencing (one method is used first or both simultaneously) (Creswell, 1994; Morgan, 1998). Of these types, the most difficult to carry out is the fully integrated design in which the study's two parts (quantitative and qualitative) are implemented simultaneously with neither side dominant (Padgett, 1998). The challenges are largely due to the demands posed by differing timelines and expertise as well as higher personnel and resource costs (Morgan, 1998).

Are any of these designs more or less likely to generate discrepancies (as opposed to convergence or complementarity)? If one of the sides of a mixed-methods study is subordinate or nested, it is likely to be used for convergence (validation) or to generate complementary (different but nonconflicting) findings. When each side has a critical mass of data (generated by breadth for the quantitative data and depth for the qualitative data), the study has a stronger foundation for yielding independent findings that can turn out to be discrepant. Having both sides achieve stand-alone status is time and resource consuming, but it is worth the effort if we want to make optimal use of mixed methodologies.

Mixed-methods studies that are dominantly quantitative or qualitative (e.g., a quantitative survey that includes a few open-ended questions or a qualitative study that uses a scaled measure) do not yield the same benefits because one method is too weak to make a stand-alone contribution. Regrettably, mixed-methods studies that give the quantitative side dominance are more likely to be favored by funders and publishers. This is an improvement over the days when *only* quantitative studies were accepted—perhaps the pendulum will swing further toward supporting truly integrated methodologies.[1]

Mixing methods does not mean that they have to be completely blended (like paint). A mixed-methods study applies the lenses of quantitative and qualitative methods to the same subject of inquiry, same setting, and to roughly the same group of respondents (even if that group is subsampled for the qualitative portion of the study). It is in this context that the promise of serendipity is realized (if it is to occur at all).

THE RISE AND FALL (AND RISE?) OF SERENDIPITY IN QUALITATIVE RESEARCH

The element of surprise, and the capacity to be surprised, have always been present in qualitative research. Serendipity was an unstated raison d'être of anthropological fieldwork in non-Western societies in the early twentieth Century—it also inspired some of the classics in urban sociology. Whether it was the sexual freedom of Samoan adolescents or the work ethic of street-corner men in Washington, DC, a key contribution of qualitative studies was their capacity for discoveries that challenged conventional notions of human behavior. The enduring popularity of works by Margaret Mead, Elliott Liebow, Irving Goffman, and Carol Stack attest to the staying power of these authors' insights. The successful qualitative study was (and is) one that challenges us to see and think differently and to arrive at a deeper understanding than we had before.

Serendipitous discoveries can also come from quantitative studies—otherwise why collect data in the first place? Sociologist David Mechanic recently offered an example by pointing to the surprising lack of evidence that managed care has led to reduced time spent with physicians (2001). Similarly, it was only by conducting widespread surveys (including diagnostic assessments) of homeless Americans in the 1980s that we learned that a minority—not the majority—were suffering from mental illness. But the parameters of a quantitative study are constricted by its reliance on predetermined hypotheses and questions.

The power of a serendipitous finding lies in its counterintuitiveness and its juxtaposition. The fact that managed care physicians were spending the same or more time with their patients has meaning only in the context of popular perceptions that the opposite was true. In Talley's Corner (1967), Elliott Liebow's observations of a strong work ethic among poor African-American men flew in the face of popular stereotypes. Similarly, Erving Goffman (1961) probed beneath the surface of everyday life to describe how we manage stigma and create our public selves in the process.

In an era of multiple realities, surprises and juxtaposition become more difficult to pull off—it is hard to get traction when the ground is shifting. Thus, the shocking 1970s-era assertion that Margaret Mead's reports of libertine Samoan sexuality revealed more about her own biases than any "facts on the ground" would hardly raise an eyebrow today.

The terrain of qualitative methods has become so expansive and contested that the value of serendipity has been lost, or at least discounted. But that does not mean that we should give up on it. If one accepts that qualitative research is a "journey of discovery" to an unknown destination (Padgett, 1998, p. 1), then surprises are a fortuitous byproduct of that journey.

The metaphor of discovery implies an external reality awaiting our patient search, an assumption that is unacceptable if one assumes that reality is something that is invented (or contrived). But I would argue that the boundary between invention and discovery is not clear in qualitative research, nor should it have to be. Discoveries need not have to uncover facts to be of value, they can entail observations and insights, for example, pointing out connections, patterns, or relationships in the brilliant manner of Irving Goffman's observations about stigma management.

Of the various types of qualitative approaches, *ethnography* and *grounded theory* are better positioned for serendipitous findings than later arrivals on the qualitative scene that are influenced by philosophy, linguistics, and critical theory. For example, *phenomenological methods* emphasize textual immersion and introspection (Giorgi, 1985) and *narrative analyses* involve interpretation of the linguistic and content structures of stories and the point of view of narrators (Mishler, 1986). Although tending toward "burrowing inward" (thereby elevating text over context), phenomenological and narrative studies can also be situated within larger historic, economic, and social structural realms, thereby making juxtaposition possible.

Regardless of one's epistemological proclivities, serendipitous findings ultimately depend on an awareness of context (both proximal and distant) and on creative insight. As always, the instrument of discovery (*or invention*) is the researcher. If the qualitative researcher lacks the capacity to think creatively as well as groundedly, then no amount of interpretive latitude will suffice.

Henceforth, I will work from the assumption that serendipitous discovery is a valuable asset in qualitative research. Although not guaranteed to occur, surprises are far more likely to happen within the fluid, creative flow of a qualitative study compared to the structured confines of quantitative research. In this regard, mixed-method studies have a distinct advantage. By offering opportunities for internal and external juxtaposition, they increase our chances of serendipity. And when it comes to external juxtapositions, mixed method studies are fertile ground for concatenation.

INTRODUCING CONCATENATION: A TEMPORAL SEQUENCING OF CRITICAL JUNCTURES IN KNOWLEDGE DEVELOPMENT

The above heading represents an attempt on my part to make sense of the varied ways that qualitative and mixed methods studies can give rise to unusual convergences of ideas—a *concatenation*. I arrived at this awkwardly worded endpoint while contemplating the all-too-frequent outcome of a mixed-methods study in which I participated: what to do if the qualitative and quantitative findings are discrepant.

When the two sets of findings are complementary, interpretation is relatively easy (and the qualitative data are typically accorded legitimacy because they affirm the quantitative gold standard). But when findings are contradictory, we face the prospect of interpreting the differences—and the risk that the qualitative data will get short shrift. As noted by Green and Caracelli (1997), "Compared with knowledge claims produced in a single-method study, this . . . mixed method set of knowledge claims is likely to be more pragmatically relevant and useful, and more dialectically insightful and generative, even if accompanied by unresolved tensions" (p. 13).

A classic article by M. G. Trend (1978) documents this dilemma. Trend's research firm (ABT Associates) was brought in to mediate a dispute that arose during a social experiment in which low-income families were given cash allowances to obtain housing on the open market. Quantitative outcomes were measured (e.g., success in obtaining housing, program and housing costs) and a field worker was assigned to observe the participating agencies' activities during the experiment. Complications arose when the initial data analyses showed the quantitative and qualitative findings to be sharply discrepant, the former showing success in terms of cost savings and the latter revealing failure in terms of deep discord and tension within the agency.

As the evaluators struggled with these differences, the credibility of the qualitative data was called into question and the field worker was "suspected of having been caught up in office politics and of having lost his scientific objectivity" (Trend, 1978, p. 349). A second analyst was hired to review the field notes and some reconciliation was achieved by noting that one side in the debate had focused only on quantity and the other only on quality. Thus, success in quantitative terms (i.e., in cost efficiency) was achieved at the expense of staff morale. Ultimately, however, the damaging observations about staff discord created havoc within the evaluation team and the field worker was dismissed.

Trend's investigation found that both sides were correct in their observations—they were looking through different lenses. But he also uncovered a disturbing fact—part of the cost savings generated by the program's success had come from the salaries of discouraged staff members who had quit! Trend concluded:

> The difficulty lay in conflicting explanations or accounts, each based largely upon a different kind of data. The problems we faced involved not only the nature of observational versus statistical inference, but two sets of preferences and biases within the entire research team. . . . (1978, p. 352).

Commenting on the Trend study, Kidder and Fine (1987) argued that qualitative findings are neither inferior nor soft, but have a unique form of credibility because of their phenomenological nature; that is, they capture the perspectives and voices of participants in ways that experiments and standardized measures cannot. A study of incest by Phelan (1987) illustrates this perfectly. Phelan contrasted two types of incest perpetrators (fathers and stepfathers) using both quantitative data and in-depth interviewing in a sample of 102 cases. The quantitative data revealed a striking difference: biological fathers were more likely to have full intercourse and involve multiple daughters. Only by reviewing the qualitative data was Phelan able to interpret the meaning of this almost counterintuitive finding: stepfathers viewed their stepdaughters as "love affairs," necessitating gradual intimacy but biological fathers considered their daughters objects to be used for their own gratification.

But even if both types of findings are accepted (which is increasingly the case), we are faced with the conundrum: how do we write about them without risking having the qualitative findings delegitimized? The usual solution is to present them in parallel but separate fashion and then fall back on the mantra of "more research is needed," which can give an anticlimactic feel to a mixed-method research report. Why not view such an outcome as an opportunity, a springboard for new directions of inquiry (Bryman, 1988; Rank, 1992)? Rather than struggle with reconciliation—wrapping everything up in a tidy package to achieve closure—we can view each study (and each part of a multimethod study) as a link in a chain (i.e., concatenation). In this manner, a study's findings are viewed not as ends in themselves but as a potential source of cross-fertilization. In this context, discrepancies point to interesting new paths of inquiry rather than problems of interpretation.

Concatenation could well be seen as putting old wine in a new bottle. We use a form of concatenation when writing literature reviews and formulating our research problems—scholarly research does not take place in a knowledge vacuum. Concatenation also occurs when we write the discussion section of our report and return to the literature to contextualize the import of our study. Clifford Geertz refers to something like this when he writes about ethnographic accounts that extend outward to intersect with others, thereby widening their implications and deepening their hold (1995, p. 19). In these instances, we seek connections, our place, in the web of ideas that constitute a body of knowledge.

However, what I am referring to is much more than what typically happens when we review our findings and state that they are consistent (or not) with the extant literature. I am referring to something more proactive, a level of outreach made possible by the recent explosive growth of Internet databases capturing virtually all published knowledge of the last several decades. Sitting at home on my PC, I can type in a few key words and retrieve a world of information from powerful search engines linked to respected peer-reviewed journals, government reports, and a host of other resources. The advent of e-journals (full-text articles on-line) has been an incredible boon to this enterprise of instant information retrieval.

If one can visualize what concatenation looks like as a form of knowledge development, it is a branching out, a chain with links or nodes representing convergences of findings from disparate studies that, in turn, propel us forward to new ideas for inquiry. This growth need not be linear or unidirectional—it can loop back recursively if we come across ideas that send us back to revisit (and reformulate) our earlier questions and/or findings.

Some studies are fertile sources of these convergences, sending out tendrils that connect in some meaningful way; others are, in terms of concatenation, dead ends. Because empirical studies do not provide answers until the data are analyzed and interpreted, it is usually impossible to know in advance how fertile a particular study will be.

There are a few ways to hedge our bets. Studies that have such traction out in the world dig deeper and are driven by an abiding intellectual curiosity. This means grounding one's self in what is known before, during, and (especially) after the study is completed. Mixed-methods studies increase our chances of concatenation because we can take two sets of findings out into the world and see how they resonate with those from other qualitative and quantitative studies. I will at last illustrate serendipity and concatenation with examples from my own research.

THE HARLEM MAMMOGRAM STUDY

The Harlem Mammogram Study was a 4-year mixed-methods study (1995 to 1999) funded by the National Cancer Institute to examine factors that influence delay in response to an abnormal mammogram among African-American women living in New York City. The primary dependent variable in the study was length of time until diagnostic resolution, that is, how long it took the women in our study to complete all diagnostic tests needed to establish if they did (or did not) have breast cancer (Kerner et al., 1999).

The interview, which took place approximately 7 months after the index abnormal mammogram, consisted of two parts: (1) quantitative—a structured set of questions designed to elicit data on several domains of predictors (which took about 45 minutes) and (2) qualitative—open-ended questions designed to allow the woman to talk freely about her health care and life experiences. Due to budgetary and time limitations, we subsampled for the qualitative interviews and ended up with transcripts for 45 women. The sample size for the quantitative analyses was 212.

Our quantitative model tested hypotheses regarding the influence of socioeconomic status versus an array of other possible predictors of delay. These included demographic characteristics such as age, marital status, and place of birth; clinical variables such as severity of the abnormal mammogram, presence of symptoms, family history of breast cancer and other health problems; system variables such as satisfaction with the mammogram experience, whether they had a regular source of medical care and so on; and, finally, psychological status variables, such as breast cancer fears, psychological distress, alienation, and health locus of control.

In the qualitative portion of the interview we asked the women to talk about their experiences with the mammogram, their opinions about breast cancer treatment, how they took care of their health, and whether any aspects of their lives interfered with their ability to stay healthy. For those who had had a diagnosis of breast cancer ($n = 5$), we asked about experiences with the cancer treatment and its aftermath.

Juxtaposing the Quantitative and Qualitative Findings
Within the Mammogram Study

For the quantitative analyses, we dichotomized the outcome variable into before versus after 90 days (a clinically meaningful definition of timely follow up) and found that about two thirds of the women were adherent within this time span. We then performed logistic regression analyses to determine which predictors were significant. To our surprise and dismay, virtually all of the log odds ratios were not statistically significant and extremely modest. Contrary to our original hypotheses, neither socioeconomic status nor any of the psychological or attitudinal variables proved significant

The strongest predictor was the least surprising—severity of the abnormal mammogram. Women who had a score of 5 (highly suggestive of breast cancer) were 24 times more likely to have timely follow up (within 90 days) than women with mammogram rating scores of 3 or 4 (indicating suspicion and a need for follow-up tests, but not strongly suggestive of cancer). Given the investment made by radiologists and primary care physicians to get such women properly diagnosed and treated, this finding was hardly earthshaking. Clearly, women's decisions about diagnostic follow up were driven by factors not captured in our quantitative model even though it was firmly grounded in the literature as well as clinical judgment.

Meanwhile, our analyses of the qualitative data yielded findings that were interesting but only peripherally related to the main study hypotheses. In some instances, we were surprised by what we did *not* find. For example, we entered the study expecting to hear expressions of fatalism and had a specific question about it. Representatives of the cancer establishment had made frequent references to religious beliefs and fatalism in the African-American community and we accepted this as received wisdom.

To the contrary, none of the women in our study agreed with the statement "There are times when an older woman might forego cancer treatment if she thought it was God's will to accept her fate." One of our interviewees, an active woman in her 80s, argued vigorously that age and religion should have nothing to do with the need to pursue all available medical treatment.

In sum, the themes that emerged from the qualitative data seemed less important in terms of juxtaposition with our hard outcomes than in shedding light on more subtle aspects of women's lives vis-à-vis cancer screening and follow up. It was here that serendipity entered the picture via concatenation.

Juxtaposing "Outside": Qualitative Findings
in the Context of Other Studies

Two themes emerged from the qualitative analyses that had the potential for concatenation: (1) the emotional and physical toll of repeated abnormal mammograms and (2) the *air theory* of cancer.

The Emotional Toll of Repeated False-Positive
Mammograms: Adding Fuel to the Fire?

With regard to the first theme, quantitative research had focused on disproportionately high levels of anxiety up to 6 months after an abnormal mammogram (Lerman et al., 1991) and our qualitative analyses revealed the fears and frustrations of enduring painful tests and waiting for the results in the women's own words (Padgett et al., 2001).

But we also found another dimension to this problem: the angst of women who had experienced repeated abnormal findings. These repeat respondents told us that they feared harmful effects of multiple exposures to radiation and they grew weary of the psychological toll of being called back for another cycle of waiting and wondering. They also talked about the physical effects of the follow-up tests, including pain, infections, and scarring. One interviewee spoke of the ordeal of watching a frustrated surgeon searching for an area of unscarred tissue for yet another needle biopsy.

Intrigued, we returned to the quantitative data and found that women who had a history of repeated abnormal mammograms (29% of the total sample) were 2.5 times more likely to delay follow up. If we had not heard a possible explanation for this in the qualitative interviews, this odds ratio would have seemed counterintuitive. After all, such women are assumed to be at higher risk and thus more compliant with recommendations.

Upon closer examination of the literature (especially medical journals), we found that the United States has one of the highest false-positive rates in the world for mammography and that American physicians staunchly defend erring on the side of caution (no doubt due to fears of malpractice lawsuits). Over 90% of women with abnormal mammograms do not have breast cancer (the rate is 85% of women who undergo biopsies). Sweden, a country not known for low-quality health care, had a significantly lower rate of false-positives (and therefore of follow-up testing). Discovering that a high rate of false-positives was not a universal byproduct of breast cancer screening practices added meaning to our qualitative findings about the psychological toll associated with this phenomenon.

The concatenation began almost simultaneously. While our article was under review, a study was published by Mary Barton and colleagues at Harvard Medical School showing that women with false-positive mammograms incur significantly more non–cancer-related medical costs in the period afterward compared to a matched sample of women with normal mammogram results. The authors suggested that psychological reactions were partly responsible for the additional use of medical services (Barton et al., 2001).

Not long afterward, a heated controversy erupted in the national media regarding a study that questioned the effectiveness of mammograms in saving lives (Olsen & Gotzsche, 2002). The Danish authors cited serious methodological flaws in previous research that had shown mammograms to reduce deaths from breast cancer (albeit by a relatively modest 30%).

Although doubts about mammograms had been percolating within the cancer establishment for years, the Danish study set off a furious debate about whether their burgeoning costs—physical, financial, and psychological—were justified. If additional lives are not saved and women are subjected to potentially dangerous tests and surgeries (for tumors that are benign or too slow growing to affect their life span), why expend millions of scarce health care dollars when they could be diverted to more effective treatments or screening techniques? Our findings of psychological distress exacerbated by high false-positive rates did not directly challenge the effectiveness of mammograms, but they could add fuel to the fires of skepticism.

The position taken in the debate by prominent American physicians was swift and strong—but also divided. Defense of the status quo involved questioning the Danish researchers' methods and insisting that, however flawed, mammograms were the best (and only) hope for early detection of breast cancer. Many breast cancer survivors stepped forward to argue that mammograms had saved their lives. With a lack of consensus among national experts, women were (and continue to be at this writing) left to decide for themselves. Although only time will tell, we would like to think that our qualitative analyses illuminated one small corner of the debate by reporting on the emotional fallout of repeated calls for follow-up tests.

The Air Theory of Cancer: From Misguided
Folklore to Medical "Fact"?

Our second thematic finding was *emic* rather than *etic*—it came spontaneously from our respondents, not from our coding and data analysis. One of the questions in our qualitative interview was "What do you think makes breast cancer spread in the body?" We anticipated hearing some version of the medical explanation (e.g., untreated cancer cells spread via the lymph nodes) or perhaps one based on popular attributions (e.g., stress). In truth, we were not entirely sure of what response we would receive, we only thought that the question was worth asking.

We were not prepared to hear about air. Here is a typical answer from an air theory adherent: "When they open you up . . . when the air hits . . . then the cancer spreads. . . ." The dangers of air exposure were mentioned in one third of the qualitative interviews, almost certainly an undercount because we did not inquire directly about it. Probing further revealed a concern that surgery exposes tissue to the air that, in turn, causes cancer cells to spread, like wildfire, throughout the body. Some women noted that this was a widely held belief, but none could vouch for its origins.

We were thus confronted with a belief that might inhibit a woman from adhering to recommendations that could lead to surgical intervention, especially if she was asymptomatic. The logic was self-evident: if there are no symptoms such as pain or a palpable lump, why endure a painful procedure such as a biopsy when it could lead to an even more painful procedure (surgery) that could actually cause a cancer to grow?

Coincidental with this discovery, we retrieved an article published by anthropologist Holly Mathews and her colleagues about rural African-American women in North Carolina with late-stage breast cancer who made similar references to the dangers of exposing breast tissue to air (Mathews, Lannin, & Mitchell, 1992). Many of these women had delayed seeking treatment until the cancer had spread throughout their bodies.

Tracking down the origins of air theory beliefs was a challenge. It appeared to have no obvious links to indigenous theories of disease such as the hot/cold system of beliefs in Latin America, although it was reminiscent of medieval European fears of malaria (literally, *bad air*). Air theory may have been a protective factor dating back to the days of leeches, barber-surgeons, and nonsterile surgery.

The air theory belief was the type of qualitative finding guaranteed to get attention from the medical establishment—my conversations with physicians about it produced a sort of irritated condescension and bemusement. Here was another example of a quaint but potentially dangerous folk belief that stood in the way of patients' appreciation of the benefits of modern medicine. How could air theory believers blame the act of surgery when it was the best hope for saving lives?

Then the chain of inquiry led me in an unexpected direction. In early January 2002, I came across a magazine article on the rising popularity of minimally invasive, or laparoscopic, surgery (where incisions are small and the actual cutting takes place within the body cavity using a scope). Proponents of this high-tech approach began with gynecological procedures, graduated to removing gall bladders, and then expanded to areas of the body formerly reserved for open (large incision) surgery—kidneys, spleen, colon, and heart.

Medical researchers found that cancer patients who undergo open incision surgery were ⅓ to ½ times more likely to have recurrences of cancer compared to those who had laparoscopic surgery. One explanation for this arises from the fact that the body's immune response is weakened by surgery. Presumably, a longer period of immune suppression is the result of damage to muscle and skin tissues caused by long, deep incisions, and open-wound surgeries.

But in addition to incision length, there was also medical speculation about—air! I quote Dr. Richard Whelan, colorectal surgeon at Columbia-Presbyterian Hospital in New York City ". . . if the surgery is performed closed, you're better able to deal with tumor cells left over in a cancer patient . . . in open surgery, those cells are given a chance to run rampant right after the surgery" (Dominus, 2002). Whelan speculated about the harmful effects of exposing cancerous body organs to microbes in the open air. A quick search of Medline revealed a journal article authored by Dr. Whelan and his colleagues that framed air theory in medical terminology: "The effect of peritoneal air exposure on postoperative tumor growth" (Southall et al., 1998).

Although the culpability of air (versus some other harmful agent) remains unresolved, even the mention of such a theory puts a seemingly erroneous folk belief in an entirely different light. Regardless of their provenance, air theory beliefs were given a degree of vindication by the ultimate arbiter of scientific truth—the medical establishment. If such beliefs resulted in the avoidance of all medical care, they would be maladaptive for women with breast cancer (to say the least). But adherents of air theory could surely take comfort in the growing popularity and availability of minimally invasive surgery.

MIXED-METHODS DESIGNS: OPPORTUNITIES FOR CONCATENATION

Our serendipitous findings emerged from the qualitative side of a mixed-methods study. None of this could have been foreseen at the outset of the study and we are gratified that a qualitative component was included.

Another example of the advantage of using mixed methods comes from the New York Housing Study (the setting for Amy Barr's study described in

Chapter 6). In the Housing Study, the best efforts of investigators were put forth to ensure a rigorous randomized trial—many quantitative outcomes were measured at 12, 18, 24, and 48 months. The goal was to evaluate an innovative program for housing the homeless mentally ill (Pathways to Housing, Inc. [PTH]) to see if it was more effective in terms of housing stability, reduced dependency upon alcohol and drugs, and improved quality of life.

The quantitative findings measured at 12 months postrandomization were rather disappointing. Not very surprisingly, subjects in the experimental (PTH) condition manifested greater housing stability than subjects in the control group (PTH participants were offered guaranteed housing and control group participants the "usual arrangements" of residential treatment centers, homeless shelters, and so on). But PTH tenants fared little better than controls in key quantitative outcomes of quality of life and substance abuse reduction (Shinn & Tsemberis, 2002). The Housing Study interviewers firmly believed (and had observed) that PTH tenants were doing much better living independently in their own apartments and were frustrated that the quantitative measures were not capturing this.

The quantitative analyses were based upon the "safe" assumption that random assignment produced equivalence between the two groups and that any differences at the study's end could be safely attributed to the experimental program. But what if the real differences are not detectable this way; available instruments are too blunt to capture the elusive and sensitive aspects of this "new" life after years of homelessness and despair? Here the qualitative data provided much-needed insights—they also gave us pause with regard to our earlier assumptions.

Indeed, "group equivalence" may have broken down due to the "success" of the experimental program in raising the bar. Entry into PTH appears to have induced an unanticipated (but common) human yearning: wanting more out of life. PTH's founder and executive director, Dr. Sam Tsemberis, cites Maslow's hierarchy of needs, saying PTH tenants have their basic need for housing and shelter satisfied and thus set their sights to higher goals such as self-actualization (Dr. Tsemberis, personal communication). Having an apartment, once an impossible dream, was now an everyday reality that enabled the tenants to imagine a life with much greater possibilities.

Thus, PTH tenants spoke during the qualitative interviews about the intangibles of their improved quality of life, for example, having a pet, entertaining friends, or staying out late without a curfew. They wanted to go back to college, learn a trade, get a job—get back what they had lost in the intervening years and find some semblance of their earlier aspirations to be teachers, truck drivers, or artists.

These yearnings, reminiscent of Debbie Gioia's findings in Chapter 5, contrasted sharply with those of control group members, who were gratified when they could find a residential placement of any kind, even one where their behavior was under strict control and constant monitoring. For them, the day-to-day pursuit of shelter, personal hygiene, and food rendered other hopes beyond their grasp. These are the sort of contextual factors that are difficult to anticipate and measure in the closed system of quantitative research.

We have all seen or participated in quantitative studies that yielded ambiguous (or unexciting) findings despite our best efforts. There is no shame in nonstatistically significant findings (although journals do tend to shun them). But the value of a mixed-methods study allows us to hedge our bets—qualitative analyses rarely fail us in the same way as quantitative analyses, and sometimes they provide us with our best insights.

Imagine if early research on the "gay men's disease" in the early 1980s had been confined to quantitative designs using records (hospital charts, death certificates, and autopsy reports) and structured (close-ended) surveys and interviews. How much longer would it have taken for epidemiologists to identify the culprit? Granted, the identification of the pathogen—the HIV virus—was done through old-fashioned laboratory research, but this came well after the mode of transmission was identified and preventive measures (i.e., safe sex) implemented. All of this was made possible by countless hours of in-depth, flexible questioning to find the patterns of behavior that accelerated the epidemic of HIV infections and AIDS.

CONCLUSION

In this chapter, we have seen how qualitative findings can redeem a mixed-methods study by offering more flexible opportunities for serendipity and concatenation. In the Harlem Mammogram Study, the disappointing lack of variance explained by the quantitatively derived model was offset by qualitative findings that juxtaposed in interesting ways with those of other studies (all quantitative) on the effectiveness of mammography and the potential dangers of open-incision surgery. In the New York Housing Study, measured variables were not capturing the differences that mattered. These insights gain their meaning from the synergy of mixed-methods designs. Although always subject to nullification, they nevertheless represent discoveries, something new and unforeseen.

Not all qualitative studies yield serendipitous findings and lead to concatenation, but the occurrence of these two phenomena is no accident either. Serendipity thrives in an atmosphere of creativity mixed with rigor. Only by maintaining vigilance—using the vast resources of database searching to the fullest—can we hope to see our findings succeed out in the world. Like delicate tendrils from a vine, they may find solid ground but they can also wither and die.

There are still paradigm purists who find mixing methods (and epistemologies) distasteful. The widely heralded second edition of Denzin and Lincoln's *Handbook of Qualitative Research* (2000) barely mentions mixed methods within its massive (1065 pages) expanse. But avoidance or outright objections are unlikely to stem the tide of interest among researchers in the practice-based professions.

The growth of knowledge through concatenation facilitates development of grounded theories as well as refinement of existing ones. When derived from mixed-methods designs—where internal and external juxtapositioning are possible—this growth is enhanced considerably. Many of us are already pursuing concatenation. This wordy phrase signifies a rather old-fashioned combination of hard work and openness of mind.

ENDNOTES

1. To make matters complicated, qualitative researchers mix qualitative approaches *within* a study (e.g., focus groups, observation, in-depth interviews). Although often encouraged as a form of triangulation, this mixing is considered risky by some who argue that epistemological assumptions vary widely across these approaches (Barbour, 1998).

ACKNOWLEDGMENTS

This chapter is based upon a symposium paper presented at the Society for Social Work and Research (SSWR) annual meeting in San Diego, California, January, 2002. I wish to thank Roberta (Bobbie) Sands, Julianne Oktay, Jim Drisko, and Gary Holden for their helpful suggestions on the earlier drafts (some of which I ignored at my own risk). I also wish to acknowledge and thank the esteemed qualitative researcher Norman Denzin for graciously agreeing to read an earlier draft—which he labeled "late post-positivist."

REFERENCES

Barbour, R. S. (1998). Mixing qualitative methods: Quality assurance or qualitative quagmire? *Qualitative Health Research, 8,* 352–61.

Barbour, R. S. (1999). The case for combining qualitative and quantitative approaches in health services research. *Journal of Health Services Research & Policy, 4,* 39–43.

Barton, M.B., Moore, S., Polk, S., Shtatland, E., Elmore, J.G., & Fletcher, S.W. (2001). Increased patient concern after false positive mammograms: Clinician documentation and subsequent ambulatory visits. *Journal of General Internal Medicine, 16,* 150–6.

Brannen, J. (Ed.). (1992). *Mixing methods: qualitative and quantitative research.*

Aldershot, Great Britain: Avebury Press.

Brewer, J. & Hunter, A. (1989). *Multimethod research: A synthesis of styles.* Newbury Park, CA: Sage.

Bryman, A. (1988). *Quality and quantity in social research.* London: Unwin Hyman.

Campbell, D. T., & Fiske, D. W. (1959). Convergent and discriminant validity in the multitrait-multimethod matrix. *Psychological Bulletin, 56,* 81–105.

Campbell, D. T., & Russo, M. J. (1999). *Social experimentation.* Thousand Oaks, CA: Sage.

Creswell, J. W. (1994). *Research design: Quantitative and qualitative approaches.* Thousand Oaks, CA: Sage.

Denzin, N.K. & Lincoln, Y.S. (2000). *Handbook of qualitative research*. (2nd ed.) Thousand Oaks, CA: Sage.

Dominus, S. (2002, January 14). The kindest cut. *New York Magazine*.

Geertz, C. (1979). From the native's point of view: On the nature of anthropological understanding. In P. Rabinow & W. Sullivan (Eds.), *Interpretive social science*. (pp. 102–27). Berkeley: University of California Press.

Geertz, C. (1995). *After the fact: Two countries, four decades, one anthropologist*. Cambridge, MA: Harvard University Press.

Giddens, G. (1976). *New rules of sociological method*. New York: Basic Books.

Giorgi, A. (Ed.). (1985). *Phenomenology and psychological research*. Pittsburgh, PA: Duquesne University Press.

Goffman, E. (1961). *Asylums: Essays on the social situation of mental patients and other inmates*. Garden City, NY: Anchor.

Greene, J. C., & Caracelli, V. J. (Eds.). (1997). *Advances in mixed-method evaluation: The challenges and benefits of integrating diverse paradigms. New directions for program evaluation,* no.74. San Francisco: Jossey-Bass.

Kerner, J. F., Yedidia, M., Padgett, D. K., & Mandelblatt J. M. (1999, June 20). *Barriers to abnormal mammogram follow-up among Black women*. Report to the National Cancer Institute.

Kidder, L. H., & Fine, M. (1987). Qualitative and quantitative methods: When stories converge. In M. M. Mark & R. L. Shotland (Eds.), *Multiple methods in program evaluation. New directions for program evaluation*, no. 35 (pp. 57–75). San Francisco: Jossey-Bass.

Liebow, E. (1967). *Talley's Corner*. Boston: Little Brown & Company.

Lerman, C., Trock, B., Rimer, B.K., Boyce, A., Jepson, C., & Engstrom, P.G. (1991). Psychological and behavioral implications of abnormal mammograms. *Annals of Internal Medicine, 114,* 657–61.

Mark, M. M., & Shotland, R. L. (Eds.). (1987). *Multiple methods in program evaluation. New directions for program evaluation*, no. 35. San Francisco: Jossey-Bass.

Mathews, H., Lannin, D. R., & Mitchell, J. P. (1992). Coming to terms with advanced breast cancer: Black women's narratives from eastern North Carolina. *Social Science and Medicine, 38,* 789–800.

Mechanic, D. (2001). Lessons from the unexpected: The importance of data infrastructure, conceptual models and serendipity in health services research. *Milbank Quarterly, 79* (3), 459–77.

Mishler, E. (1986). *Research interviewing: Context and narrative*. Cambridge, MA: Harvard University Press.

Morgan, D. (1998). Practical strategies for combining qualitative and quantitative methods: Applications to health research. *Qualitative Health Research, 8,* 362–76.

Olsen O., & Gøtzsche, P. C. (2002). Screening for breast cancer with mammography (Cochrane Review). *The Cochrane Library, 3*. Oxford: Update Software.

Padgett, D. K. (1998). *Qualitative methods in social work research*. Thousand Oaks, CA: Sage.

Padgett, D. K., Yedidia, M., Kerner, J., & Mandelblatt, J. (2001). The emotional consequences of false positive mammography: African-American women's reactions in their own words. *Women and Health, 33,* 1–14.

Phelan, P. (1987). Compatibility of quantitative and qualitative methods: Studying child sexual abuse in America. *Education and Urban Society, 20* (1), 35–41.

Rank, M. (1992). The blending of qualitative and quantitative methods in understanding childbearing among welfare recipients. In J. F., Gilgun, K. Daly, & G. Handel (Eds.), *Qualitative methods in family research* (pp. 281–300). Newbury Park, CA: Sage.

Reichardt, C. S., & Rallis, S. F. (Eds.). (1994). *The qualitative-quantitative debate: New perspectives. New directions for program evaluation,* no.61. San Francisco: Jossey-Bass.

Shinn, M. B., & Tsemberis, S. (2002). Comparing housing first and continuum of care programs for homeless individuals with co-occurring psychiatric and substance abuse diagnoses: An experimental evaluation. Under review.

Southall, J.C., Lee, S.W., Bessler, M., Allendorf, J.D., & Whelan, R.L. (1998). The effect of peritoneal air exposure on postoperative tumor growth. *Surgical Endoscopy, 12,* 348–50.

Tashakkori, A., & Teddlie, C. (1998). *Mixed methodology: Combining qualitative and quantitative approaches.* Thousand Oaks, CA: Sage.

Trend, M. G. (1978). On the reconciliation of quantitative and qualitative analysis: A case study. *Human Organization, 37,* 345–54.

Weaver, T., Renton, A., Tyrer, P., & Ritchie, J. (1996). Combining qualitative studies with randomised controlled trials. *British Medical Journal, 313,* 629.

Webb, E. J., Campbell, D. T., Schwarts, R. D., & Sechrest, L. (1966). *Unobtrusive measures: Nonreactive research in the social sciences.* Chicago: Rand McNally.

14

Spreading the Word

Writing Up and Disseminating Qualitative Research

DEBORAH K. PADGETT

We now come to the last stage of the qualitative research experience—the all-important task of writing up and disseminating qualitative studies. When it comes to guidance on writing a qualitative research report, there is no need to reinvent the wheel—virtually all textbooks contain chapters on writing qualitative reports and there are a number of books devoted solely to this topic (see, for example, Ely et al., 1997 and Wolcott, 1990). Therefore, I will only briefly summarize the highlights of how-to guidelines, then move on to discuss recent developments in writing and disseminating, especially publishing, qualitative reports. The usual caution regarding standpoint—in this case my own—applies to what lies ahead.

ADVICE ON WRITING UP
QUALITATIVE RESEARCH

Some things do not change. When it comes to qualitative research, the craft of writing—the ability to stay grounded in the data but still weave a spell of creative provocation—is paramount. A quantitative study can survive a poorly written report—the numbers and tables carry the essential message—but a qualitative study cannot. The write up is the capstone, the make-or-break end of the road.

Form matters almost as much as substance. Perhaps it is better to say that form *is* substance, because both are interwoven in a qualitative report. The web of ideas that convey the study's findings—the structure of the narrative—translates (and transcends) all of the work that has gone before. Although teamwork has become increasingly common in qualitative studies, the writing up task usually falls on one person for a very important reason—it is difficult to apportion writing responsibilities and have the report end up integrated and coherent. (By comparison, it is much easier to task out portions of a quantitative report and then assemble them.) This is not to say that others cannot be involved in the final report, but their input is usually more helpful if it comes after the first draft has been written.

The structure and format of the report vary depending on the choice of method. Qualitative approaches based largely on interviews tend to fall into two distinct categories when it comes to presentation of findings: (1) narrative analyses (long, annotated portions of narrative) and (2) grounded theory (codes, clusters, themes, etc.). Ethnographic studies blend observational and interview data to produce a monograph that holistically describes a social group, culture, or setting.

Although journals have more restrictions on space and format than book publishers, there are common dimensions to writing successfully regardless of the length of the manuscript. The ultimate goal is to maintain a balance between description and interpretation. Michael Patton describes this as well as I can imagine:

> . . . qualitative inquiry (is) both science and art, especially qualitative analysis. The scientific part demands systematic and disciplined intellectual work, rigorous attention to details within a holistic context, and a critical perspective in questioning emergent patterns even while bringing evidence to bear in support of them. The artistic part invites exploration, metaphorical flourishes, risk taking, insightful sense-making, and creative connection-making. (Patton, 2002, p. 513)

Decide on, and know, your audience. This piece of advice is intricately related to the original reason for doing the study as well as the chosen outlet of dissemination—dissertation, book, journal, conference, and so on. For example, program evaluation findings need to be written succinctly and be accessible to a variety of stakeholders; practice-relevant studies should lead to implications that are meaningful to practitioners.

Knowledge-building studies, especially dissertations, have somewhat different demands (although they obviously overlap with policy and practice-oriented research). Doctoral students often become so immersed in their study that they forget they are writing for dissertation committee members who might have peripheral knowledge of their topic. In any case, the use of arcane terms or trendy jargon should not displace clear, direct prose.

One of the enduring challenges in empirical research is to write with authority but not arrogance (Coles, 1989). This balance between reaching intellectual heights and maintaining a healthy sense of skepticism about one's own work is the best route to reaching and impressing your audience (note my authoritative tone here). For doctoral students writing their dissertation proposal, this means shrugging off their subordinated status as learner to become a teacher, that is, an expert in their chosen topic. It also means casting aside those nagging doubts and anxieties about measuring up (and letting a dissertation advisor be the judge for a while).

TEN SUGGESTIONS FOR
WRITING UP THE STUDY

The following suggestions are neither exhaustive nor mutually exclusive, but do represent some tips that I have found useful.

1. *Set aside scheduled times to write and stick to them.* Large blocks of time—at least 2 hours—are necessary to dive into and climb out of the writing mode. In qualitative reports, we submerge ourselves even further because we make meaning even as we inscribe it.

2. *Give a detailed description of your methods, including the strategies for rigor used.* Aim for transparency of methods no matter how tempted you are to gloss over this and jump to the most interesting part of the report—the findings.

3. *Organize your analyses and findings, then develop a detailed outline and write from it.* Your choice in how to do this is a matter of personal style. When it comes to analysis and write up, qualitative researchers range from old-fashioned paper sorters (who use the computer only for drafting the final report) to computer techs (who use computers and software for analysis as well as write up).

As a member of the former group, I was deeply gratified by an essay in *The New Yorker* magazine (March 25, 2002) in which Malcolm Gladwell reviewed a book about the myth of the paperless office (Sellen & Harper, 2001). The book begins with a counterintuitive observation and question: paper consumption has actually increased since the advent of personal computers . . . why? According to the book's authors, paper has several advantages: it is spatially flexible (we can spread it out however we wish), it makes ad hoc scribbling easy (how often do we enjoy writing in the margins!), and it can be arrayed across a wide field (or plane) of vision. All of this is particularly helpful if the work is being conducted by a team, but it is also useful for the solo writer.

Even more gratifying was Gladwell's assertion—supported by ergonomic and psychological research—that paper is most valuable when it is piled, not filed. Far from reflecting wasteful disorganization, piles of paper represent living archives that can be resorted to represent the researchers' latest ideas or needs. In contrast, filed papers tend to be neglected, even forgotten. Here PCs *have* made a difference—they are ideal for space-saving storage. Even so, messy desks are not a sign of messy minds; quite the opposite!

Anthropologists have been practicing the sort-and-pile technique to analysis and write up for decades, sifting through stacks of field notes, interviews, photographs, memos, letters, and documents until they arrive at some semblance of coherent organization. My dining room table (and later the floor) did not see daylight for most of 1978 and 1979 when I was working on a dissertation in urban anthropology. Nowadays, I find my desktop and an adjacent table do the trick if supplemented by my living room footstool (where the most current piles of work lie waiting for attention).

My feeble nod to modernity involves carrying sticky notepads at all times, writing down ideas or notes from readings, then organizing and affixing them to sheets of paper. For a previous book, I had one sheet represent each chapter. The chapter outline was entered (spaciously) on the page and the notes that fit each topic were stuck underneath that heading. These sheets of paper, all aflutter with sticky notes, were in front of me when I sat down to write. This is one of those "don't try this in your own home" systems of writing. It also illustrates how idiosyncratic each writer's needs can be.

4. *Balance writing with editing, but don't get bogged down in the latter.* One of the major pitfalls for the self-doubting writer is to fall into a mode of writing a little and editing a lot. It is better to write for awhile, *then* edit. Push ahead and get it all down; you can always pare down later (see tip 7). Use colleagues for feedback, but remember that you are the ultimate arbiter of what and how the story will be told.

5. *Decide on use of self in the report.* Your decision on discussing your role in the write up will be driven by the type of approach as well as your audience. For example, a brief report may have to forego all but the basic details of methods and rigor, but a longer monograph or dissertation affords an opportunity to discuss the researcher as instrument. Such discussions are often presented in a separate appendix to avoid distracting the reader from the story itself.

6. *Focus on style as well as content.* The message—no matter how insightful—will get lost if it is not conveyed via an engaging writing style. Remember that the structure of a qualitative report is usually revealed in its headings and subheadings and in transition sentences that follow a progression in tracing the narrative arc(s) and arguments of your story. Headings act as signposts, informing and leading the reader along the way.

Quantitative reports can be off-putting and tedious but still make their point—qualitative reports that suffer from lethargy and a lack of focus are doomed to fail.

The acceptance of a more informal tone (e.g., use of first-person pronouns) has become widespread in recent years, even in quantitative reports, but the boundaries of creativity are widest for qualitative researchers. Metaphors, for example, are wonderful devices for capturing and conveying phenomena. Narratives can verge into poetry; prose can be colorful and full of sensory description.

At the same time, try to avoid jargon and showy verbiage. When asked to speak before an elite audience in London, the philosopher Bertrand Russell gave his talk the deceptively simple title: "Words and Things." Met with disappointment by the organizers of the lecture, he changed the title to "Linguistic Correlates of Epistemological Constructs" and got enthusiastic approval. There may be occasions (or audiences) that favor this kind of language, but simpler wording is almost always preferable.

7. *Be parsimonious and avoid repetition.* This is where skillful editing can make a difference. All too often, we have difficulty seeing that we are belaboring points and repeating them unnecessarily. Qualitative reports typically need greater length to make their point, but this is no excuse for attenuation and redundancy.

8. *Use citations and references generously, especially in the Methods section of the report.* Qualitative reports with too few citations are most vulnerable to charges of "this stuff is just made up" or "we knew this already—why repeat the obvious?" The Methods section in particular needs to have not only specification of the type of methodology but appropriate citations. Grounded theory studies, for example, should cite Barney Glaser, Anselm Strauss, and/or Juliet Corbin. Similarly, narrative analyses usually cite the work of William Labov, Elliott Mishler, and Catherine Riessman. Be sure to use citations to back up your decisions about sampling, rigor, and so on. If you used computer software, name the program (and cite its source). In short, have no fear of over-referencing. Your report will appear more (not less) authoritative.

9. *Be creative but persuasive.* In Chapter 13, I wrote about the pleasures of serendipitous findings and concatenation. The difficulty with this exhortation is that creativity does not come easily to anyone and especially to a researcher trained to avoid "infidelity" to the scientific method. Imagine trying to be creative with the experimental treatment in a randomized clinical trial!

Creativity also suffers when compressed under the weight of theory. Richardson's (1990, p. 18) metaphor of a theory as a building implies that theories imprison a study, a notion that can be countered by the "theory is a feather" metaphor (Smaling, 2002). On the other hand, creativity alone leads to research reports that are artistic creations. Although some qualitative researchers argue in favor of creative performances (Richardson, 2000), very few actually present their findings as fiction, pictures, or poetry (it is difficult to defend this approach for most audiences). Artful, but unverifiable, qualitative reports place practiced-based researchers in an especially precarious position; we risk marginalization as it is, simply by living and working in a quantitative world (Padgett, 1998).

In a qualitative research report, creativity is balanced with logical persuasiveness, that is, arguments draw their strength from reason and coherence. Smaling (2002) points to nonlogical forms of persuasion such as *ethos* (based on power and authority) and *pathos* (based on appeals to emotion), which are nonfalsifiable. Logical arguments, on the other hand, are embedded in critical thinking and awareness of the fallibility of research findings.

Some have argued that critical thinking and creativity do not mix. Michael Patton bluntly states that critical thinkers do not tend to be creative thinkers (2002). Citing earlier work by Anderson (1980), Patton argues that the skeptic's diligent pursuit of inadequacies narrows the focus and undermines innovation and new insights. Thus, just as creativity to the extreme results in art, critical thinking to the extreme comes across as an obsession with methodological correctness.

This risky business of balancing creativity and persuasion is hardest for action or advocate researchers. On the one hand, creativity risks being stifled not by skepticism but by passionate adherence to a cause. On the other hand, logic can be cast aside in favor of arguments by pathos (appeals to emotion rather than reason). Social workers and other helping professionals often find it difficult to integrate a critical thinking self with an advocate self. This conflict, simplistically portrayed as head versus heart, fuels the continuing debate about the gap between practice and research.

10. *Don't be shy about using tables, diagrams, charts, and typologies.* Many qualitative reports focus solely on a narrative format and eschew tables, diagrams, and charts. These visual devices need not be avoided. They are especially useful when compressing qualitative findings to fit a journal format or for an executive summary written for policymakers and others with short attention spans. Similarly, conceptual typologies can convey a lot of information in an accessible, logical manner.

PUBLISHING QUALITATIVE REPORTS: THE BOTTLENECK CREATED BY A LACK OF AGREEMENT ON STANDARDS, MULTIPLE QUALITATIVE APPROACHES, AND THE SHORTAGE OF PEER REVIEWERS

Interest in qualitative methods has reached a point where even diehard quantitative researchers are looking for ways to get on the bandwagon. This growth has far outpaced the evaluative infrastructure of the methods. Doctoral programs in particular must struggle to meet the demand of students seeking coursework and mentorship in qualitative methods. Meanwhile, journal editors are stymied by the severe shortage of peer reviewers.

The lack of consensual standards in qualitative research has been the subject of much hand wringing (or rejoicing, depending on where you stand on the epistemological continuum). Because this issue has already taken up several trees' worth of paper, let me only state that qualitative methods continue to have diverse criteria for quality emanating from the many approaches within the family of these methods. Even a partial listing reveals the hodgepodge of theories, methods, and philosophies that comprise the family's members: ethnography, grounded theory, narrative, phenomenology, hermeneutic, heuristic, ecological, symbolic interaction, realist, ethnomethodology, feminist, and chaos theory.

How do we judge the publishability of a qualitative study? Consider the difference between ice hockey and figure skating. Whereas winning in ice hockey is determined by the game score, figure skating depends on ratings by expert judges (a sorely tested and possibly corrupt system in the 2002 Winter Olympics). Yet it is the subjective sport that is the most popular of all winter sports. After all, subjectivity guides many determinations of excellence—the Nobel and Pulitzer Prizes, literary awards, dance competitions—even though it is considered anathema in research.

Given the multitude of qualitative approaches (and epistemological leanings), it is virtually impossible to get (or expect) agreement on what constitutes an exemplary study. We are often in the position of the Supreme Court Justice who said (of pornography) "I can't define it but I know it when I see it." Of course, judging quantitative studies is rarely a simple matter of keeping score (the quantitative scorecard involves subjectivity as well). Nor should we assume that an absence of consensual standards in qualitative methods consigns us forever to the realm of personal taste. (Although we might wonder about this when we receive reviewers' comments from some journals—comments that appear even more capricious when delivered anonymously).

As mentioned in Chapter 1, we have six strategies for enhancing rigor available to us (Padgett, 1998). These strategies—prolonged engagement, triangulation, peer debriefing and support, member checking, negative case analysis, and auditing—could be used as a list of guidelines for authors to check all that apply (assuming that not all six strategies would or should apply to a particular study). To my knowledge, neither these nor any other helpful guidelines (see, for example, Drisko, 1997) are applied systematically and routinely by reviewers of qualitative reports whether they are reviewers for journals, research grants, or conference presentations. For that matter, they are not widely used by qualitative researchers either!

The shortage of qualitative methods expertise (and, therefore, peer reviewers) exacerbates the standards problem. Within academia, this bottleneck becomes evident at the middle- and upper-level rungs of the academic ladder where few senior faculty have the expertise and knowledge to judge the quality of a job (or tenure) candidate's scholarly work. Given the pressures of tenure review and the fact that it takes 1 to 2 years to publish even one quantitative study, many junior faculty understandably avoid publishing qualitative studies. That is a pity.

The lack of peer reviewers often leads to rejection of qualitative manuscripts simply for being unreviewable. A worse scenario occurs when the manuscript is sent out for review anyway and is returned (4 months later) with comments like "there's nothing new here" or "this author lacks objectivity." Authors of mixed-methods studies run the risk of being advised to jettison the qualitative portions in favor of a straightforward presentation of quantitative findings, thus losing the synergy from triangulating the two sets of findings. (This happened to me recently.)

Qualitative methods contribute their own vulnerabilities to the publishing and dissemination problem. Abbreviating lengthy reports for journal publication is always a struggle. Quantitative findings can usually be sliced into a few different articles (although the slicing can get pretty thin), but qualitative findings typically need to hang together to make sense—shoehorning them into a journal format may squeeze the life out.

Additionally, blind review of manuscripts works against qualitative studies because the competence and experience of the researcher is an integral part of the study's credibility. (This makes it all the more imperative that the study's methods be fully described and all possible strategies for rigor pursued). It is no accident that grant proposal review committees closely examine the researcher's credentials—whether quantitative *or* qualitative—as well as the study's methods and feasibility.

In the world of book publishing, competition has become fierce and qualitative studies must compete with works by journalists, popular science writers, and the latest intellectual stars at elite universities. Consider, for example, the popularity of works by writers such as Jonathan Kozol and Barbara Ehrenreich. Their books have enough participant observation and rich description to compete with (or displace) traditional qualitative studies. Writer Ann Fadiman's *The Spirit Catches You and You Fall Down* (1997), a book describing the cross-cultural travails of a California Hmong family and their severely epileptic daughter, has achieved cult-like status on some college campuses. Fadiman wrote this moving portrayal not as a social scientist or trained researcher but as a skillful, deeply engaged writer.

A few recent qualitative studies by social scientists have succeeded in the marketplace as well as the classroom. Mitchell Duneier's *Sidewalk* (1999), a participant-observation study of homeless sidewalk booksellers in Manhattan's Greenwich Village, has had a cross-over effect as has Katherine Newman's *No Shame in My Game: The Working Poor in the Inner City* (1999). To make the transition from research report to published book, a qualitative study needs to hit on all cylinders, that is, it must be rigorously conducted, yield important findings, have widespread classroom appeal, and resonate with current intellectual trends.

This is a tall order, but not an impossible one. None of these challenges should deter the qualitative researcher from seeking outlets for disseminating the findings. A dissertation or report can be followed up with a book or article and a presentation at professional conferences. Even findings that are less than spectacular have a place. If the study was well conceived and executed, it will have the unique quality of presenting observations for one group of individuals at one point in time and in one place—findings that stand as part of the record. Of course, it is less likely to get a favorable review for publication in the more prestigious journals, but there are often niche or specialty journals that value such manuscripts.

Although the social sciences and humanities have witnessed a dramatic increase in the blurring of genres (Denzin & Lincoln, 2000, p. 15), the burgeoning literature in qualitative research still manifests a tendency to cluster by discipline within the practice professions; nursing researchers tend to cite other nursing researchers and the same can be said for the fields of social work, medicine, and education. Given the plethora of intradiscipline topics and the perceived need to legitimize ourselves by developing a discipline-specific knowledge base, the genre blurring will take a longer time to gain traction outside of the social sciences. This dramatic tension between the need to bolster theories and research from within the practice-based professions and the desire to join the party—the trend toward interdisciplinary cross-fertilization of ideas—will continue to characterize our work for the foreseeable future.

This allows us to segue into mentioning journals that specialize in publishing qualitative studies: *Social Science and Medicine, Human Organization, Qualitative Sociology, Qualitative Health Research, Qualitative Inquiry,* and *The Qualitative Report* (online at www.nova.edu/ssss/QR). In addition to these venerable journals, new arrivals have entered the picture, including the *International Journal of Qualitative Methods* (online at www.ualberta.ca/~ijqm), *Qualitative Research,* and *Qualitative Social Work.* If one examines the vast array of journal offerings by discipline, anthropology (for obvious reasons) and nursing are the most receptive to (and unequivocal about) qualitative research.

SOME TIPS FOR PUBLISHING QUALITATIVE REPORTS

1. Investigate the journal you are interested in and shape your manuscript according to the Guidelines for Authors as well as the journal's audience. Make sure that the journal has a track record in publishing qualitative studies. If in doubt, contact the editor and ask if these methods are welcome for review.

2. Make a compelling argument for the study's significance and the need for qualitative methods. Position yourself as a skeptic when you are writing. All studies need this, but qualitative studies even more so.

3. Be explicit and detailed in the Methods section, especially in describing the sampling strategies and how data were analyzed. Cite appropriate sources for your choice of methods (e.g., Glaser and Strauss for grounded theory) and be sure to address which strategies for rigor you deployed. You may also wish to cite published guidelines for qualitative research to show reviewers that you are aware such things exist (see, for example, Drisko, 1997; Patton, 2002; Padgett, 1998).

4. When using excerpts and/or brief vignettes in the Results section, be judicious. As mentioned, typologies are good for conceptual condensing and tables, diagrams, and other devices can help organize and display findings visually.

5. Be candid about the study's limitations and strengths. There is no need to apologize for small samples and a lack of external validity (although it does not hurt to explain why apologies are not in order). If you have followed one or more strategies for rigor, these can be reintroduced as strengths enhancing the trustworthiness of the findings.

6. Be cautious in interpreting the findings and their implications. Good studies do not venture beyond what has been presented. They also point the way to future directions in research, policy, and practice.

7. Do not give up if rejected! Almost all manuscripts are rejected in the first round of review—usually the most favorable outcome is to be invited to resubmit after minor revisions. Outright rejections usually come with a firm admonition not to resubmit. If this occurs, there are always other journals to consider. I tend to have a Plan B ready when this occurs (and have had occasions to dip into Plans C and D). For novice researchers, this toughening up takes some getting used to. Journal editors use cautious, noncommittal language but after awhile one can discern when they really mean it.

8. Put *qualitative* in your title and/or key words. This will enhance the retrievability of your study and its dissemination (particularly for anyone interested in conducting methodological reviews of the literature). Database searching is only as effective as the search techniques available and even randomized clinical trials (RCTs) are not fully retrievable using key word searches on MEDLINE (Evans, 2002).

Qualitative studies with whimsical, creative titles are lost to database searching. If, for example, you are embarking on a qualitative study of older men living with AIDS, you might want to conduct a literature search using *qualitative* cross-indexed with *aging* and *AIDS* to see what prior studies have been done on this topic using qualitative methods. (Otherwise, you will get hundreds of quantitative references to sift through.) As an extra bonus, including *qualitative* in your title and abstract will make it easier for journal and book editors to assign your manuscript to peer reviewers with appropriate expertise.

Some qualitative researchers prefer to reference specific methods in the title (e.g., grounded theory, phenomenology) and this is understandable. Hopefully, more databases (e.g., MEDLINE) will be configured to be sensitive (and specific) in searching these terms. Methodological search filters have become essential as systematic reviews become the basis for decisions about evidence-based practice (www.cochrane.org).

Other researchers seem to reject retrievability in the customary sense. For example, a recent issue of *Qualitative Inquiry* (June 2002) contained the following titles:

- "What kind of mother . . . ? An ethnographic short story"
- "Poetry"
- "Happy"
- "9/11, who are we?"
- "Dominance theater, slam-a-thon, and cargo cults: Three illustrations of how using conceptual metaphors in qualitative research works"
- "Stories and silences: Disclosures and self in chronic illness"

Clearly, these authors are aligning themselves with literary tradition in their choice of titles. Of the above, only the next-to-last article would have been available in a key word search for *qualitative* studies.

PRESENTING QUALITATIVE FINDINGS
AT PROFESSIONAL CONFERENCES

This outlet for dissemination gets surprisingly little attention in the literature and seems to be relegated to taken-for-granted status. In tenure and promotion reviews, presentations are given less weight than publications but they are still a win–win situation. For the presenter, the conference is an ideal venue for meaningful interaction and obtaining immediate feedback from the audience. It is also an excellent way to browse the web of knowledge in person and network with colleagues both junior and senior.

For qualitative researchers, there are a few conferences that are methods specific, the foremost being the international conference held each spring at the University of Alberta under the leadership of Dr. Janice Morse (www.iqmc.ualberta.ca). Another conference organized by the Student Qualitative Research Interest Group (SQUIG) is held each January at the University of Georgia (www.uga.edu/squig/).

Most of us are oriented to our own professional meetings and here (again) concerns arise about receptivity to qualitative methods. One of the greatest challenges comes from compressing a qualitative study into an abstract of a few hundred words and still receiving an equitable review in comparison to quantitative studies (which can be condensed more easily for abstracts). As with journal publication, the same problems with lack of reviewer expertise emerge, but the word limits for conference submissions present a disproportionate hazard for qualitative researchers.

As program chair for the Society for Social Work and Research (SSWR) for 2 years (2001 and 2002), I struggled with locating expert peer reviewers for the burgeoning number of qualitative studies submitted. And I agonized when submitters and reviewers alike complained that too little information was available for the qualitative studies to receive adequate reviews of their merits. To help ameliorate this problem—and to assist all submitters in learning how to improve their abstracting skills—we placed exemplar abstracts for quantitative and qualitative studies on the SSWR Website for consultation (www.sswr.org). This hardly resolves the problem, but solutions are difficult to come by. Because no professional organization is willing to tolerate a double standard, that is, longer word limits for qualitative studies, we are left with doing the best that we can.

In the meantime, we are producing a boomlet of new qualitative researchers who can provide much-needed expertise in the future, whether as mentors, peer reviewers, or simply role models. When it comes to the future, our concerns are less about quantity than quality.

CONCLUSION

This chapter addressed the last step in a qualitative study—writing the report and disseminating it as widely as possible. Actually, I prefer to call this the next to last step or, perhaps, the first step in a new direction entirely. As discussed in Chapter 13, there are always new paths to follow, new forks in the road, and (hopefully) new avenues for concatenation. The fun does not have to end just because we have completed our report and spread the word. Once we start our journey of discovery, staying home will never feel the same.

REFERENCES

Anderson, B. (1980). *The complete thinker.* Englewood Cliffs, NJ: Prentice-Hall.

Coles, R. (1989). *The call of stories: Teaching and the moral imagination.* Boston: Houghton Mifflin.

Denzin, N.K. & Lincoln, Y.S. (2000). *Handbook of qualitative research.* (2nd ed.) Thousand Oaks, CA: Sage.

Drisko, J. (1997). Strengthening qualitative studies and reports: Standards to enhance academic integrity. *Journal of Social Work Education, 33,* 187–97.

Duneier, M. (1999). *Sidewalk.* New York: Farrar, Straus, & Giroux.

Ely, M. (1997). *On writing qualitative research: Living by words.* London: Falmer Press.

Evans, D. (2002). Database searches for qualitative research. *Journal of the Medical Library Association, 90* (3), 290–3.

Fadiman, A. (1997). *The spirit catches you and you fall down: A Hmong child, her American doctors, and the collision of two cultures.* New York: Farrar, Straus, & Giroux.

Gladwell, M. (2002, March 25). The social life of paper: looking for method in the mess. *The New Yorker,* pp. 92–96.

Newman, K. (1999). *No shame in my game: The working poor in the inner city.* New York: Russell Sage Foundation and Knopf.

Padgett, D. K. (1998). *Qualitative methods in social work research: Challenges and rewards.* Thousand Oaks, CA: Sage.

Patton, M. Q. (2002). *Qualitative research and evaluation methods* (3rd ed.). Thousand Oaks, CA: Sage.

Richardson, L. (1990). *Writing strategies: Reaching diverse audiences.* London: Sage.

Richardson, L. (2000). Writing: A method of inquiry. In N. K. Denzin & Y. S. Lincoln (Eds.), *Handbook of qualitative research* (2nd ed., pp. 923–48). Thousand Oaks, CA: Sage.

Sellen, A., & Harper, R. (2001). *The myth of the paperless office.* Cambridge, MA: MIT Press.

Smaling, A. (2002). The argumentative quality of the qualitative report. *International Journal of Qualitative Methods, 1* (3), Article 4. Retrieved October 8, 2002 from http://www.ualberta.ca/~ijqm.

Wolcott, H. (1990). *Writing up qualitative research.* Newbury Park, CA: Sage.

15

Coming of Age

Theoretical Thinking, Social Responsibility, and a Global Perspective in Qualitative Research

DEBORAH K. PADGETT

With increasing awareness and appreciation that qualitative methods go where other methods cannot comes the luxury—and the responsibility—to ponder future directions. The stakes become higher as acceptance—and expectations—grow.

As this book has demonstrated, qualitative research embodies many approaches. Unlike quantitative methods, where standardization is the goal, diversity in qualitative methods is celebrated. There are, however, issues that that affect all members of the qualitative family as we face the future. In this final chapter, I would like to address three of these in the context of qualitative research in a practice-based profession. They are (1) balancing theoretical thinking with attention to methodological rigor; (2) maintaining social responsibility and practice relevance regardless of one's paradigm allegiance (or lack thereof); and (3) moving toward a global perspective while still taking care of the home front.

This is not meant to be a definitive or authoritative list—qualitative researchers are not known for such things—but only an avenue for discussing what appear to be pressing concerns in a time of unprecedented growth. Not surprisingly, each segues into the other as well as to related concerns. Together, these three topics throw into relief a defining characteristic of qualitative research: its heterogeneity and multivocality across national boundaries as well as within them.

RAW EMPIRICISM VERSUS
THEORETICAL THINKING

Theoretical thinking, that is, an interest in interpretation and mid- to high-level abstraction, has gained considerable attention in recent years, both pro and con. Proponents of the "more theory is needed" argument see renewed emphasis on theory as a necessary corrective to the proliferation of qualitative studies that begin—and end—with description. Anthropologists and sociologists alike have criticized fellow qualitative researchers for having an obsession with raw empiricism and refinement of methods (Glaser, 2002; Hammersley & Atkinson, 1983; Morse, 1994; Silverman, 1989; Wacquant, 2002).

Although an intense focus on improving methodology hardly precludes attention to theory building (and could be seen as the best route to developing and testing theories), the concern is that the balance has tipped too far, resulting in qualitative studies that are overly cautious, method driven, and idea impoverished. Thus, description becomes an end in itself, drawing attention away from comparative methods and penetrating social, cultural, and political analyses.

French social scientist Loic Wacquant argues that getting too close to one's respondents produces findings that parrot their point of view without making the necessary linkages to the broader sociopolitical frameworks that give them meaning and relevance. He asserts

> . . . there is no such thing as ethnography that is not guided by theory (albeit vague and lay) . . . every microcosm presupposes a macrocosm that assigns it its place and boundaries and implies a dense web of social relations beyond the local site. . . . To fail to exercise theoretical control at every step in the design and implementation of an ethnographic study—as with every other method of social observation and analysis—is to open the door to theoretical simple-mindedness. . . . (2002, p. 35)

Ambivalence and uncertainty about theory have characterized qualitative research from the beginning. Throughout the twentieth century, anthropologists debated the merits of universal theories of culture (the *nomothetic* approach) versus rich, local description of specific cultures (the *idiographic* approach). Among sociologists, the rise of grounded theory after the 1960s (Glaser & Strauss, 1967) hardly produced unanimity about theorizing, even among its early proponents. Sociologist Howard Becker, citing the influence of his mentor, University of Chicago sociologist Everett C. Hughes, offered the following opinion:

> Like Hughes, I have a deep suspicion of abstract sociological theorizing; I regard it as at best a necessary evil, something we need in order to get our work done, but at the same time, a tool that is likely to get out of hand, leading to a generalized discourse largely divorced from . . . day-to-day digging into social life. . . . (1998, p. 4)

A graduate of the famous Chicago School, Becker views theory as a force that must be "tamed" by thinking of it as a collection of "tricks" (1998, p. 4).

He adds that theoretical thinking is useful only when it suggests ways to see the world differently and creates new problems for study.

Evaluation and practice-based researchers have their own rationale for avoiding theory building: practitioners tend to view theorizing as impractical and out of touch with clinical reality (Morse, 1994). For example, an expert on qualitative evaluation, Michael Q. Patton, states "one need not even be concerned about theory" (2002, p. 136).

The unfortunate split between the founders of grounded theory (Anselm Strauss and Barney Glaser) centered on charges by Glaser that his former colleague had betrayed its original premise of generating theory (Stern, 1994). Glaser objected to moves by Strauss and co-author Juliet Corbin (1998) to codify grounded theory methodology, accusing them of staying too closely tethered to the data and to "pure" description rather than seeking transcendence of time and place through conceptualization and theory generation (Glaser, 2002).

> While concepts are "everything" in GT [grounded theory], many researchers find it hard to stay on that level to relate them to each other. They relate the concept to a description and go on and on with description. (p. 8)

Theories do not come from respondents, asserts Glaser. Respondents provide us with the data, but only the researcher can fashion a theory from it. Despite his reasoned (albeit strident) objections, Glaser's stance has not held sway. This may be due in part to his audience (or lack thereof). Strauss' life-long visibility in academia, his scholarly productivity, and his influence on generations of students contrasted with Glaser's decision to leave academia to go into the business world.

The strong emphasis on naturalism and locality that dominated qualitative research over the past three decades helped to solidify the claim that qualitative approaches are not distant and objectifying like quantitative designs (Lincoln & Guba, 1985). A concern with the particular was also seen as an antidote to the universalizing drive toward a science of culture and society that characterized the social sciences throughout much of the twentieth century (Angrosino & Mays de Perez, 2000; Geertz, 1973). Whereas pro-theory advocates do not dismiss the importance of naturalism, they argue that staying close to the setting and the data has come at the expense of higher-level conceptualizing.

THEORIES, THEORETICAL FRAMEWORKS, AND CONCEPTUALIZATION

The reticence shown by Howard Becker and others was a reaction to the overreach and failed determinism of many psychological and sociological theories of the twentieth century, particularly because these "grand" theories conflicted with the inductive approaches favored by qualitative researchers.

However, the fact that most theories are not grand leaves plenty of room for middle-level abstraction in qualitative research. Thus, ideas or hunches that emerge in early stages of analysis are confirmed (or refuted) as the analyses proceed via use of negative case analysis. This iterative process often generates a cascade of new ideas that motivate the researcher to go back and forth until a *conceptual framework* is created.

Conceptual frameworks fall short of a tightly woven predictive theory. Although less ambitious in scope and explanatory power, they nevertheless offer a schema for understanding a phenomenon. As such, they rise above raw description and form vital links to the web of knowledge.

Although conceptual frameworks emerge from the data rather than drive the analysis (as in quantitative research), procedures for inductive analysis vary considerably. For example, anthropologists have traditionally analyzed their data by sweeping across diverse sources of data—field notes, interview transcripts, analytic memos, and documents—and shaping their insights through repetitive readings and thoughtful contemplation.

Sociologists tend to be more procedure oriented. Some use a method known as *analytic induction* (Cressey, 1953; Manning, 1991) in which a theory is developed from a few cases and then tested with subsequent data until a negative (deviant) case arises. Similar to *constant comparative analysis* in grounded theory, analytic induction adopts a step-by-step approach using an inductive–deductive–inductive iteration. This disciplined pursuit of falsification lends a study rigor and credibility.

Conceptualizing is hard work—it does not just magically happen. (In quantitative research, it is more a matter of locating a priori concepts and measuring them than of creating and defending them.) It begins with close and repeated readings of the data and continues with thematic development as the researcher balances abstraction with attention to detail and context. This back and forth of conjecture and confirmation yields the constituent parts of a conceptual framework. The threshold of mid-range theory is crossed when a conceptual model coheres enough to be weight bearing, a function of the investigator's ability to fit it to the broadest expanse of data.

There are several advantages to such mid-level abstraction. First, concepts have greater staying power than pure description, that is, they are less likely to become stale and outdated (Glaser, 2002). Glaser cites as an example Arlie Hochschild's description of flight attendants' jobs as "emotional work" (Hochschild, 1983). A more recent example is Malcolm Gladwell's "tipping point" (2000), a concept that explained phenomena where change was not gradual and progressive (as was previously assumed), but abrupt and overwhelming (rates of infectious disease, crime, etc.).

Second, concepts often outlast (and transcend) the theories in which they were originally embedded (King, Keohane, & Verba, 1994), their descriptive appeal extending their usage far beyond the original theoretical definition. "Division of labor," "ego," and "survival of the fittest" come to mind as a few examples.

Finally, powerful concepts from diverse fields emerge and form bridges for cross-disciplinary thinking that pure description cannot offer. For example, Thomas Kuhn's "paradigm shift" in the history of science (1970) profoundly influenced the development of "punctuated equilibrium" in evolutionary theory. "Quantum leap" in physics and "tipping point" in epidemiology capture similar phenomena. In sum, conceptual and theoretical frameworks offer an opportunity to search for relationships without having to produce all-encompassing explanation.

A PRIORI VERSUS "FRESH"
CONCEPTS AND THEORIES

Inductive thinking need not preclude use of a priori theories and concepts, but flexible frameworks work better than one-cause-fits-all ones. An excellent example of the former is *symbolic interactionism* (Blumer, 1969). Symbolic interactionism provides a model for understanding how beliefs and behaviors are influenced by the symbolic meanings attached to social interactions (think, for example, of how much the behavior of a person with schizophrenia is shaped by a history of stigma-laced encounters). Grounded theory and social constructivism alike were strongly influenced by Blumer's writings on symbolic interaction and many a qualitative study manifests this approach.

Although opinions vary on the subject (as they often do in qualitative inquiry), a priori theories work best when they inform, not deform, the study. Grand theories, with their expansive reach, run the risk of intruding on the researcher's interaction with the data by offering preset concepts into which the data are shoehorned.

We may frame our research questions and analyses drawing on *sensitizing concepts* (Blumer, 1969; Glaser, 1978). Sensitizing concepts orient us in that awkward moment when we begin a qualitative study. For example, a study of adolescents who have lost a close friend to suicide might invoke the concept of *contagion* to refer to the possibility that participants will voice worries about additional suicides in their peer group. We can also apply familiar concepts in new sensitizing ways, for example, a study of parents who care for a severely autistic child might deploy the concept of *grief* to explore how they feel when contemplating the child's difficult future.

Sensitizing concepts are interpretive devices and a starting point. Their ultimate survival depends on where the data take us; emergent concepts may supplement or displace them altogether. For example, I may be interested in exploring the role of *spirituality* in a group of AIDS patients but find that they prefer a secular, existential view of life and death. Or perhaps *contagion* fails to make an appearance in our hypothetical study of adolescent suicide. As is the case with a priori theories, sensitizing concepts should not channel our observations and analyses into the narrow, hermetic passageways of preordained findings.

It is difficult to overestimate the importance of fresh conceptualization in qualitative research. Formulating emergent concepts requires immersion in the study and the data—one of the most challenging tasks for novices *or* experienced researchers. When viewing students' initial attempts at coding transcripts, I am often struck by their tendency to provide running commentary rather than meaning units. Whether the meaning units are *emic* (respondent initiated) or *etic* (investigator initiated), they must capture what is important for the inquiry. A student has achieved progress when he can look at a transcript and distinguish nonrelevant material from meaningful codeworthy information.

Contextualizing is an important counterpart of conceptualizing. By this I refer to conducting the study where respondents live, work, and play and capturing this in situ quality in the analyses and interpretations. Some qualitative approaches such as ethnography entail participant observation to varying degrees and others such as phenomenology contextualize by portraying the lived experience as told by study participants.

These two activities—conceptualizing and contextualizing—coexist in dramatic tension in a qualitative study. Balance is not always easy to achieve. If we become too enamored of our codes and concepts, we risk losing the context. Similarly, over-attention to context leaves the study devoid of ideas and seriously reduces its capacity to have an impact.

SOCIAL RESPONSIBILITY
AND POSTMODERN CRITICISM
IN QUALITATIVE RESEARCH

For anyone committed to socially responsible research, concerns about context need to extend beyond the local to larger social, economic, and political milieus. For researchers in social work, such attention invokes a sense of responsibility for improving social and economic conditions resulting from inequality and discrimination. We know how to talk the talk, but the crux of the matter comes when deciding how, when, and where to walk the walk.

By the late 1980s, discussions of socially responsible research got caught up in the paradigm debates causing upheavals throughout the social sciences. Postmodern writers incorporated neo-Marxist, feminist, Third World liberation theology, and other 1960s-style activisms into their critiques of science and logical positivism. In anthropology, ethnographies were singled out for their claims to scientific and moral authority and the invisible "God's-eye" omniscience of their authors (Clifford & Marcus, 1986; Geertz, 1973; van Maanen, 1988).

Indeed, the act of writing—as well as the products that resulted—became the focus of attention by postmodern critics. Texts (philosophical, historical, scientific, etc.) were viewed as steeped in Western hegemony and patriarchy, reflecting a naïve faith in reason and reality. Thus, soul searching in anthropology in the 1970s and 1980s took place amidst postmodern critiques emanating mostly from European social philosophy (Foucault, Latour, Derrida) and from feminist philosophy (Sandra Harding).

Disavowing value neutrality, postmodern epistemologies staked out a moral high ground by declaring a commitment to hearing the voices of (and collaborating with) the disenfranchised—women, the poor, ethnic minority groups, gays, lesbians, and others—and by denouncing postpositivism as "social engineering" (LeCompte, 1990, p. 229). A methodology from the 1960s (e.g., participatory action research) was taken out, dusted off, and extolled as the ideal way to wed research to the goals of individual and community empowerment (Stringer, 1996; Reason & Bradbury, 2000).

The foregrounding of a "radical politics of action" (Denzin & Lincoln, 2000, p. xvi) has been criticized as lacking credibility given postmodernism's propensity for "navel gazing." Indeed, Snow and Morrill (1995) warn that ". . . this performance turn, like the preoccupation with discourse and storytelling, will take us further from the field of social action and the real dramas of everyday life . . ." (p. 361).

The paradoxical nature of claims that postmodern epistemology and hermeneutic analyses produce "moral tales" and social action was noted by Schwandt (2000) who asked, ". . . does not the creation of moral tales assume that there is a (moral) truth to the matter of interpretation. . . . Does not such a move speak to the need for some criteria whereby we clarify and justify genuine moral truths, thereby distinguishing them from mere illusion or belief?" (p. 200). Schwandt's questions touch on a continuing dilemma for postmodernism: if there is no single reality that is privileged, how can one get traction long enough to adopt a moral stance?

Allusions to action research highlight contradictory impulses within postmodernism—radical action is a far cry from deconstructing and problematizing texts, the latter require Talmudic-like scrutiny of the written word to dismantle its hegemonic claims to power. In philosophy, the humanities, and literature, this kind of activity conforms to extant traditions of scholarship. But for social scientists, the reaction has understandably been mixed (Atkinson, 1997; Denzin & Lincoln, 2000; Hammersley, 1995; Silverman, 1989).

Anthropologists, the most visible proponents (or victims?) of Western delusions of grandeur, have been generally favorable even though this soul searching has created internal frictions and public concern about the discipline's credibility. Sociology, on the other hand, already had a strong commitment to quantitative methods yet still maintained its proud tradition of grounded theory. Psychologists, leaders in quantitative measurement and theories that reflect Western conceptions of the psyche, have been resistant, but there are notable exceptions (e.g., Mary and Kenneth Gergen's work [1991] on feminist constructionist approaches).

TALKING AND ENACTING: THE PURSUIT
OF SOCIAL RESPONSIBILITY

Reams of print have been devoted to the topic of socially responsible research. These discussions predate postmodernist thought (e.g., Piven & Cloward, 1971) and continue independently of it in the works of liberal/leftist thinkers from a variety of disciplines. Although unable to claim a monopoly on the subject, postmodern criticism has nonetheless called attention to how Western values and oppression pervade much of what we know (or think we know) about the world's peoples, their history, political economy, social structure, cultural values, and so on. Beneath the trendy jargon and quasi-mystical evocations[1] lies a well-intentioned argument.

Regardless of our epistemological leanings, a continuum of commitment confronts researchers from the outset. Thus, it is one thing to *talk and write* about social responsibility in the abstract, another to *incorporate* it into an empirical study in the topics that we choose and the audiences that we seek for our findings, and still another to *enact* this commitment by engaging in social action and advocacy to ameliorate oppression. Within the enactment mode, the stakes become higher (and the challenges greater) if we follow a participatory action model in which respondents and their communities become partners in carrying out the research from start to finish.

Here is a hypothetical example inspired by a recent controversy set off when New York City Mayor Michael Bloomberg terminated a longstanding eviction lawsuit against a group of squatters in the East Village and offered to sell the buildings to them for a token sum. The squatters were predominantly working class families (with a sprinkling of artists and anarchists).

A researcher in the *incorporate* mode might choose to study this neighborhood as a naturally occurring example of grassroots self-empowerment. She would likely conduct traditional participant observation and in-depth interviewing and would seek audiences for the findings that are not likely to misappropriate them for conservative causes (although there are never any guarantees). An *enacting* researcher would identify herself as a researcher-advocate and ensure that community input is sought in decisions about the interpretation and dissemination of findings. She would also find ways to advocate with and for the squatters as they fight eviction by the city authorities. A participatory action enactment project would involve meeting with community leaders at the outset to solicit their ideas about how the research should be conducted, to fully involve them in the study, and to pursue activism jointly (e.g., organize a protest, testify at city council hearings, etc.).

These rank-order categories—talking about, incorporating, enacting, and participant enacting—are descriptive devices that admittedly obscure a dynamic situation in which the researcher's involvement can ebb and flow depending on the circumstances. They are, however, useful in thinking about possible tradeoffs between methodological rigor and social commitment.

As the balance tips toward overt action and advocacy, the risk of bias and loss of credibility grows. For example, an incorporating researcher would be less likely than a participatory-enacting researcher to romanticize the community's residents or gloss over bad news (e.g., internal strife due to racial or class tensions, a community leader who deals drugs, etc.). He could still strive to present an even handed but nuanced portrayal and call attention to good news, for example, how the squatters had improved neighborhood safety and created a sense of cohesion with poor families living nearby. As a researcher increases his identification with social action and advocacy, his allegiance to methodological rigor is tested and risks serious erosion.

This observation brings us back full circle to a point made in the Introduction regarding the threshold of research. It also raises (again) the question of whether we need to apply this term to something worthwhile—whether it is serving clients or community activism—when the terms of engagement are so costly. There are hardy souls capable of doing it all, but for most of us, simultaneous blending of qualitative research and social activism risks distorting the research beyond recognition or introducing an ethical bind caused by dual relationships and loyalties. The more activist the effort, the more difficult it becomes to stay with the data and maintain one's integrity and identity as a researcher.

My own experience with this dilemma occurred in 1993 when a Croatian friend took me to meet the first small group of Bosnian Muslim refugees arriving in New York. An initial urge to study these severely traumatized individuals (a coup for anyone interested in refugee studies) was quickly set aside in favor of advocacy to help them get the medical, dental, and psychological services they desperately needed. This was a natural segue for me because I had knowledge of the culture and language dating back to my graduate school days in anthropology and I wanted to do something to help.

Six years later, a nascent desire to honor the survivors' voices combined with deepening friendship to give rise to a project with a young Bosnian man who agreed to have his story—including his internment and torture at the hands of a childhood friend (a Bosnian Serb)—recorded on audiotape for posterity. Not long after arriving in New York, Sead had been befriended, then abandoned, by a wealthy American with friends in the publishing industry, and he still harbored hopes of having his story reach a wider audience. We agreed that a book would serve both of our interests.

Despite having a strong identity as a researcher, I was never able to deploy a research agenda in any usual sense of the word. I did collect data—Sead and I had 28 in-depth interview sessions supplemented by many informal interviews with his mother, brothers, and wife. And there were innumerable occasions spent with the family celebrating (Sead's swearing-in ceremony as an American citizen) as well as mourning (the death of Sead's infant daughter).

The manuscript is still in progress, and the royalties (if we should be so fortunate) would accrue to Sead. Meanwhile, my role as self-appointed advocate has long since shifted into that of a family friend. Although exploitation can occur in any relationship, imposing a research agenda on this situation—no matter how egalitarian—would have seemed gratuitous. And it almost certainly would have come off as opportunistic within the Bosnian community (where many suspect that journalists, academics, and various agency helpers do not understand them or care about their interests.)

Confusion about roles pervades discussions of socially responsible research and obscures an important distinction between the research (which is more effective if kept methodologically rigorous) and the researcher (who can and should get involved). The fusion of social activism and research is particularly risky for qualitative researchers. It raises questions about the limits of researchers' capacities (and roles) and whose agenda is being served, and it sets the stage for unrealistic expectations leading to disappointment and disillusionment. Given the nature of qualitative research, activist involvement can stretch the methods beyond their carrying capacity.

This poses a fundamental dilemma for postmodern qualitative researchers whose credibility depends on matching action with exhortations. Unlike top-down theorizing in the tradition of Foucault, empirical researchers work at ground level with real methods and findings. This has been done by a few scholars working within postmodern feminist traditions. For example, Michelle Fine and colleagues demonstrated how researchers can collect the stories of young adults coping with poverty but also organize support groups and testify at state budget hearings (Fine & Weis, 1998; Fine et al., 2000).

Within the qualitative methods family, those who argue that qualitative methods are the shortest (or only) route to social utility often point to how the personal can be political. Feminist and action researchers, for example, assert that an egalitarian and empowering relationship between the researcher and the researched represents a microcosm of the larger social change they envision (Reinharz, 1992). Others imply that the user-friendly, quasi-therapeutic aspect of this relationship is so superior to the objectification of experimental subjects that *any* qualitative study is more socially responsible than a quantitative one.

Socially responsible in an immediate sense, perhaps, but the benefits of participating in a qualitative study do not equal social change. In the rough-and-tumble arenas of political, social, and economic policy-making, qualitative methods have not shown (or been allowed to show) much of an impact. Because the vast bulk of social science research, publications, and funding is exclusively quantitative, it would be naïve to think otherwise.

Our unique strength as qualitative researchers—the ability to peel back the surface layers to reveal interstitial meanings—is seriously compromised if we give in to either of two natural impulses—to victimize or valorize our respondents. Victim stories raise consciousness but they also downplay human agency. "Portraits of courage" can be used to further a right-wing agenda to restrict social spending.

Because even the most conscientious researchers cannot fully control how their findings are interpreted and exploited by others, we seek to situate our findings where they will do the most good. Alas, there are limits on what we can expect because research of any type is often ignored by the powers that be (Hammersley, 1995). But it is still better to arm one's self with evidence than with anecdotes.

PRAGMATISM AND THE RESEARCH–PRACTICE DIVIDE—UTILITY FOR WHOM OR WHAT?

Philosophical pragmatism places a premium on knowledge that is useful, that is, *utility* is seen as a major criterion for evaluating the worth of a study in contrast to knowledge for its own sake. As such, pragmatism is a sound foundation for forging links between theory, research, and practice (Diggins, 1994).

Practice-based researchers tend to define *social utility* in terms of a study's capacity to improve the human condition—a vague but worthwhile goal. In this context, success requires action beyond the immediate context of the researcher–researched relationship. Some postmodernist qualitative researchers (e.g., Michelle Fine and colleagues) make the leap from micro to macro effectively. By and large, however, postmodern qualitative research has been more talking about enacting than actually enacting.

In the vast and varied landscape of qualitative inquiry, some types of studies have a shorter distance to cover than others when it comes to social utility. Thus, a study of childhood asthma in a poor neighborhood has more translational potential than one of eating disorders among adolescents girls.[2]

The chosen topic of inquiry within an oppressed community can be more or less useful to the goal of social reform. For example, a study of women on welfare could focus on their struggle to balance a low-wage job and child care or it could focus on the experience of anxiety and depression for those so afflicted. Although implications for the first study lead to questions about welfare policies, the latter would most likely direct us to thinking about outreach, screening, and mental health treatment. Nor can we automatically assign high social utility to all practice-based qualitative research because it can be local in scope (e.g., a case study of a single agency) or intent (e.g., life history interviews with dying patients).

A social worker is ethically obliged to pursue social justice as part of his or her mandate to help individuals and families in need—and social work researchers aspire to this when formulating and carrying out their studies. But even the most well-intentioned researchers can unwittingly aid and abet sociopolitical agendas that are far from emancipatory.

Practice-based researchers may perpetuate or reinforce the more restrictive aspects of their professional counterparts' roles—doctors, nurses, teachers, and social workers have all been accused of wittingly or unwittingly promoting social control. The movie "One Flew Over the Cuckoo's Nest" and the notorious Rosenhan experiment[3] gained national attention because they confirmed a public perception of what many advocates for the mentally ill had been arguing since the days of Dorothea Dix—society seeks to control, not heal.

The voices of patients and clients are not easily heard or honored in agencies, hospitals, and clinics. Chronic shortages of time and resources limit meaningful contact with clients, and staff burnout can produce resistance due to fatigue and low morale. Even the most sympathetic (or radicalized) practitioner must be mindful of her status (and salaried employment) within a powerful social hierarchy that ultimately values control more than empowerment. And although practice-based researchers employed in academia have more latitude to engage in social action, their necessary partnerships with gatekeeping agencies and other practice settings place inevitable constraints because rocking the boat could jeopardize the agency's service delivery (and funding).

Invoking the reality principle a step further, there is also the question of what our participants really want from us—and if social change is more our agenda than theirs. Although all research participants can appreciate being treated in an empathic, egalitarian manner, this does not mean that they want to become partners in the joint pursuit of activist research. Indeed, they might respond to such an invitation with, "Why should we help you researchers do your job? You're the ones with the time, the money, and the power to make things happen!"

Nor (alas) should we even assume that potential research participants are more enamored of qualitative than of quantitative research. As a member of the Pathways to Housing Human Subjects Committee (a program for the homeless mentally ill described in greater detail in Chapter 6), I always learn something new from its consumer members when they express lively opinions about the various studies put before them. For example, the relative tedium of a brief quantitative interview may be preferable to the open-ended commitment sought in qualitative research. Quantitative designs may also be preferred because they are a fast track to obtaining data on program effectiveness and thus assembling a case for funding and support (Padgett, 2000).

The dimensions of qualitative research that we celebrate—rapport, deep involvement, and collaboration—may seem like an intrusion and emotional roller coaster to prospective participants. Although I would like the think that any population is reachable no matter how alienated (neo-Nazis), secretive (pedophiles), or arrogant (corporate chief executives), there are limits to rapport building and to a qualitative researcher's capabilities. And there are ethical guidelines strictly limiting even the semblance of coercion as we approach potential respondents.

The bottom line on socially responsible research is a pragmatic one: the proof is in the pudding rather than in the untested recipe. Any epistemology or methodology can aspire to the goal of socially responsible research—and those that do so should be commended—but its attainment depends on tangible activity.

A GLOBAL PERSPECTIVE IN QUALITATIVE RESEARCH: CRISS-CROSSING BOUNDARIES AND PARADIGMS

In this final section of the chapter (and of the book), I turn to a topic that is front and center these days—a global or transnational perspective—with a focus on what this means for social work research in general and qualitative social work research in particular. *Globalization*, that ubiquitous term for the gradual dissolution (or meaninglessness) of national borders, has been cast as the savior or villain of the new millennium, depending on one's political leanings. For governments and multinational corporations, globalization means unfettered economic expansion, free trade, and the spread of Western industry and technology. But for diverse constituencies concerned about economic inequality, globalization means capitalism run amuck and a massive transfer of wealth to the West that will destabilize Third World economies, degrade the environment, and accelerate the decline of local cultures.

However, another trend flies in the face of the one world envisioned by globalism's celebrants—ethnic and religious conflicts steeped in intolerance and violence (Slouka, 2002). Sadly, the past decade has produced ample evidence of such conflicts and the massive suffering that they engender: the genocidal murders in Rwanda and Bosnia, Muslim-Hindu strife in India, the Taliban's brutal oppression of women in Afghanistan, fundamentalist Islamic terrorism against the West, and the rise of an anti-immigrant right wing across Western Europe, to name just a few. These are troubling signs of how intolerance can defy national borders and thrive amidst economic inequality. Intragroup conflicts become international when anti-West sentiments are inflamed by the insensitivity of a resource-guzzling West (with the United States at the forefront).

For the profession of social work, globalization and ethnoreligious conflicts can seem distant both geographically and psychologically from the pressing local concerns of clients struggling with poverty, child abuse, HIV/AIDS, drug abuse, violence, and other problems. Making the connection between local and transnational has been the goal of the International Federation of Social Workers (IFSW) since its establishment in 1956. IFSW has a strong commitment to addressing the role of social work in global problems such as war, terrorism, and poverty. Its activities understandably tilt toward education, advocacy, and international cooperation (www.ifsw.org). (The reality of geopolitics hit home in 2002 when the IFSW World Conference in Zimbabwe had to be cancelled due to political instability in that country.)

Although clearly sympathetic with national and international advocacy, empirical researchers must also attend to the local because we are expected to carry out studies that have relevance for our target audiences (practitioners and service users). How do we attend to these mandatory aspects of context—local, state, and national policies governing welfare and social services—as well as global events? This is especially daunting for qualitative researchers whose raison d'être is deep immersion in a local context that, in turn, tugs us away from the bigger picture.

From the standpoint of some of our colleagues abroad, neglect of the bigger picture is especially characteristic of researchers in the United States where American exceptionalism has been (and remains) a troublesome thread running through modern history. In qualitative research, this criticism often takes the form of accusations of uncritical positivism and blatant disregard of research from Third World and developing countries (Wacquant, 2002).

Similar to our colleagues in the social and behavioral sciences, U.S.-based social work researchers are overwhelmingly postpositivist and quantitative (although few would welcome such a label because its derivation and usage have been largely in the hands of constructivist and postmodern critics who view postpositivism as a desperate attempt to rescue positivism from a well-deserved extinction). Quantitative data and sophisticated statistical analyses dominate the programs of the annual meetings of major U.S. professional organizations—the American Sociological Association, American Psychological Association, American Public Health Association, and so on. Similarly, the Society for Social Work and Research (SSWR) has grown by leaps and bounds (quadrupling its membership in 7 years of existence) by featuring (predominantly quantitative) research at its annual conference (see www.sswr.org for details). Doctoral dissertations and peer-reviewed journals in U.S. social work have also been overwhelmingly quantitative (Fraser, 1993; Glisson, 1995).

The exact opposite is true in Sweden, where only a small percentage of social work doctoral dissertations are quantitative (Dellgran & Hojer, 2001). Indeed, social work research in Europe, Canada, Israel, Australia, and other nations with strong academic social work programs tends to be more eclectic and less dominated by a need to be numerical.

Part of this difference can be attributed to the bigger picture—an historic tradition of American geopolitical isolation that contrasts with the close economic and social ties within the European Community as well as with its former colonies (Australia, Hong Kong, India, etc.). In addition, U.S.-based research has been more in the thrall of science and technology with strong government support for hard science ranging from NASA's space programs to the recent Genome project.

However, closer examination of research conducted on both sides of the Atlantic reveals that epistemological and methodological stereotyping does not hold up completely and the quantitative versus qualitative divide is not so clear cut after all. For example, Great Britain is the home of the Cochrane and Campbell Collaborations, international consortia of researchers dedicated to advancing evidence-based practice in medicine and social welfare, respectively. Although both groups have not ruled out inclusion of qualitative studies, the reviews thus far have been the result of meta-analytic number crunching using advanced statistical analyses of aggregated clinical trials.

In the realm of qualitative research, we need not reiterate that critics of quantification and positivism (e.g., Guba and Lincoln) are just as likely to be American as European. Although still rooted in pragmatism rather than paradigm purism, researchers across an array of disciplines in the United States have become more receptive to qualitative approaches (as noted in the introductory chapter of this book).

Another promising recent trend—increased interdisciplinary and international cooperation—opens doors to new approaches to thinking about and doing research that transcend national boundaries and undermine paradigm purism. The University of Calgary sponsors an international qualitative methods conference each year (see www.ualberta.ca/~iiqm/) in which a variety of disciplines is represented and has recently started publishing an international journal using multiple languages (see www.ualberta.ca/~ijqm/). The recent debut of yet another journal (*Qualitative Research*) contained an editorial urging contributors from a variety of disciplines to engage "orthodox with heterodox" and "modern with postmodern" (Atkinson, Coffey, & Delamont, 2001, p. 5)

Although still thoroughly underrepresented, the voices of Third World practitioners and researchers (not to mention their clients) are beginning to be heard (Smith, 1999). Not surprisingly, our colleagues in developing nations have more to contend with than epistemological debates, not the least of which is the legacy of colonialism and the economic dislocations of globalization (Chan, 2000; Midgley, 2000; Smith, 1999). Here, adopting a global perspective is an absolute necessity because Western economic policies permeate almost every aspect of life (Mercado–Martinez, 2002).

ADOPTING A GLOBAL PERSPECTIVE: CONSTRAINTS AND OPPORTUNITIES

In any country, social work research follows the lead of its parent profession in addressing the urgent needs of poor children and families, the elderly, and the sick. Documenting the extent of these needs, testing new models of intervention, and analyzing the impact of social policies are all enormously complex tasks.

Our studies and advocacy are necessarily directed toward institutions and policies that have the most immediate impact on clients' lives. Because each nation has its own social welfare programs (some far more generous than others), international differences in social work practice and research are inevitable. In the United States, this means staying abreast of programs funded by states and the Federal government: Medicaid, Medicare, Social Security Disability Income (SSI), and Temporary Assistance for Needy Families (TANF), to name only a few.

Still, the need to be mindful of state and Federal policies that impinge on the poor should not preclude thinking beyond our borders. So many problems we confront at home have international repercussions (the HIV/AIDS epidemic, drug abuse and drug trade interdiction, female circumcision and other forms of gender oppression, acts of terrorism, etc.). And even those problems that seem inherently bounded to the local context (e.g., violent crimes, child abuse, homelessness) can be the source of cross-national comparisons that highlight the commonalities of home-grown causes.

Social work researchers can infuse a transnational context into their studies in various ways and to varying degrees. For example, we could adopt a big picture standpoint and select a topic (e.g., child labor laws) for cross-national policy analysis using documents and archival data. Or we may focus on globalization's impact in our own backyard by studying migrants and refugees making a new life after being dislocated by poverty, war, and/or ethnic cleansing. Indeed, virtually any study of an ethnic group in the United States must refer to old country cultural values and norms that influence their sojourn in an adopted homeland.

If we want to use qualitative methods to study a topic in depth and transnationally, we can work with colleagues abroad to conduct interviews on site and set the stage for direct cross-national comparisons (see, for example, Chapters 2 and 7). At other times, we may carry out a study in one location and refer to findings from similar research from other cultures or nations (see the Mammogram Study example described in Chapter 13).

There are many other ways to think globally and act locally as researchers, and every one of these can (and should) involve the pursuit of social responsibility. Indeed, the web of economic, political, and social ties that bind the world's citizens—combined with the chasm of inequality that separates the West from the rest (of the world)—demand no less.

A PRAGMATIC, OPTIMISTIC VIEW
OF THE FUTURE

In this final chapter, I have argued in favor of (1) conceptualization even when theory eludes our grasp, (2) socially responsible research regardless of epistemology, and (3) a global perspective that takes into consideration local as well as national and transnational contexts. The dramatic tensions that enliven the qualitative family debate are a source of energy that will propel us forward in the years ahead. The main house still belongs to quantitative research, but the front door has never been wider for qualitative research (we are no longer directed to the service entrance). Besides, sole ownership need not last forever.

Because the qualitative family is a rather unruly bunch, there are serious differences of opinion on what to do about the main house (permit me to stretch the metaphor of construction a bit further). Some qualitative researchers refuse to get near the house, insisting that its foundation is decrepit and crumbling. They argue forcefully in favor of building a more habitable dwelling in a more idyllic location (Qualtopia?)—but they never seem to get beyond digging the foundation. Others argue that there are really many houses—but get lost in a hall of mirrors of their own construction—what Martyn Hammersley calls "the self-refuting character of relativism" (1995, p. 107). Pragmatists accept that the main house will dominate the landscape for the foreseeable future but assert their right to enter and leave it as they see fit.

Whether situated in academia or an agency, we social work researchers get daily reminders that we still live in a quantitative world. To survive, programs must articulate goals and measurable objectives and offer up evidence of their effectiveness. If anything, the decline in spending on social services has led to a Darwinian-style competition based not on good intentions but on hard outcomes.

We know that science and quantification have limits when it comes to understanding human factors—the sine qua non of practice and practice-based research. But ignoring the elephant in the room (quantitative methods) will only increase the marginalization of the social work profession and its researchers. Social work values invariably inflame conservative passions with hot-button issues like welfare reform, human rights, and equal access to health and mental health care. No other practicing profession puts such goals front and center; not education, medicine, nursing, law, or engineering. Nor does any other profession work so consistently and exclusively with society's most troubled and stigmatized.

Already put on the defensive in an era of anti-progressive values and scarce resources, social workers and researchers must accept the reality principle when pondering the merits of quantitative versus qualitative research. Our ultimate stakeholders—practitioners and services users—deserve to have research that is understood and respected beyond a small circle of believers and friends.

CONCLUSION

This book began with observations about the limits of science and technology and the not-unrelated fact that qualitative methods were enjoying popularity as never before. Not willing to rest on their laurels, the contributors provided chapters showcasing exemplar studies and offering methodological guidance on topics new and old.

Our overarching goal was to offer role modeling and vicarious experiences that could put the reader as closely as possible to the reality of doing qualitative research. We caution that this effort cannot substitute for hands-on learning, but the closer an advanced text can approximate it, the better (at least until the much-desired state of fully supportive infrastructures is achieved and mentoring and other forms of expertise are in abundance). If this book has in some way enhanced your ability to conduct qualitative research that manifests high standards and creative thinking, our goal has been attained.

ENDNOTES

1. The latest edition of the *Handbook of Qualitative Research* appears to have gone over the edge toward the quasi-mystical as evidenced in the following quote about the future: "The dividing line between science and morality will continue to be erased. A postmodern, feminist, poststructural, communitarian science will move closer to a sacred science of the moral universe" (Denzin & Lincoln, 2000, p. 1022). Has rejection of science now shape shifted into a spiritual quest?

2. This does not mean that studies of personal problems cannot also be political—eating disorders can be viewed as the product of gender oppression in society. But the burden of demonstrating social responsibility is greater for researchers who choose these topics as part of an activist agenda.

3. Rosenhan and his psychologist colleagues (1973) were severely criticized for this deception in which graduate students, who feigned vaguely psychotic symptoms, were immediately admitted to an inpatient psychiatric unit where they were kept on locked wards and treated despite insisting that they felt back to normal. Not surprisingly, the study gained notoriety and stirred controversy for years to come.

REFERENCES

Angrosino, M. V., & Mays de Perez, K. A. (2000). Rethinking observation: From methods to context. In N. K. Denzin & Y. S. Lincoln (Eds.), *Handbook of qualitative research* (2nd ed., pp. 673–702). Thousand Oaks, CA: Sage.

Atkinson, P. (1997). Narrative turn or blind alley? *Qualitative Health Research, 7,* 325–44.

Atkinson, P., Coffey, A., & Delamont, S. (2001). A debate about our canon. *Qualitative Research, 1* (1), 5–21.

Becker, H. S. (1998). *Tricks of the trade: How to think about your research while you're doing it.* Chicago: University of Chicago Press.

Blumer, H. (1969). *Symbolic interactionism.* Englewood Cliffs, NJ: Prentice-Hall.

Chan, C. (2000). Chinese culture and values in social work intervention. In N. T. Tan and E. Envall (Eds.), *Social work around the world.* Geneva: International Federation of Social Workers.

Clifford, J., & Marcus, G.E. (Eds.). (1986). *Writing culture: The poetics and politics of ethnography.* Berkeley: University of California Press.

Cressey, D. R. (1953). *Other people's money: A study in the social psychology of embezzlement.* Glencoe, IL: Free Press.

Dellgran, P., & Hojer, S. (2001). Mainstream is contextual: Swedish social work dissertations and theses. *Social Work Research, 25,* 243–52.

Denzin, N. K., & Lincoln, Y. S. (Eds.) (2000). *Handbook of qualitative research* (2nd ed.). Thousand Oaks, CA: Sage.

Diggins, J. P. (1994). *The promise of pragmatism.* Chicago: University of Chicago Press.

Fine, M., & Weis, L. (1998). *The unknown city: The lives of poor and working-class young adults.* Boston: Beacon.

Fine, M., Weis, L., Weseen, S., & Wong. L. (2000). For whom? Qualitative research, representations, and social responsibilities. In

N. K. Denzin & Y. Lincoln (Eds.), *Handbook of Qualitative Research* (2nd ed., pp. 107–31). Thousand Oaks, CA: Sage.

Fraser, M. (1993). Social work and science: What can we conclude about the status of research in social work? *Social Work Research & Abstracts, 29* (2), 40–4.

Geertz, C. (1973). *The interpretation of cultures: Selected essays.* New York: Basic Books.

Gergen, K. J., & Gergen, M. M. (1991). From theory to reflexivity in research practice. In F. Steier (Ed.), *Method and reflexivity: Knowing as systemic social construction* (pp. 76–95). London: Sage.

Gladwell, M. (2000). *The tipping point: How little things can make a big difference.* Boston: Little, Brown & Co.

Glaser, B. G. (1978). *Theoretical sensitivity: Advances in the methodology of grounded theory.* Mill Valley, CA: Sociology Press.

Glaser, B. G. (2002). Conceptualization: On theory and theorizing using grounded theory. *International Journal of Qualitative Methods, 1* (2). Article 3. Retrieved July 14, 2002, from http://www.ualberta.ca/~ijqm/

Glaser, B. G., & Strauss, A. L. (1967). *The discovery of grounded theory.* Hawthorne, NY: Aldine.

Glisson, C. (1995). The state of the art of social work research—Implications for mental health. *Research on Social Work Practice, 5,* 205–33.

Hammersley, M., & Atkinson, P. (1983). *Ethnography: principles and practice.* New York: Tavistock.

Hammersley, M. (1995). *The politics of social research.* London: Sage.

Hochschild, A. R. (1983). *The managed heart: Commercialization of human feeling.* Berkeley: University of California Press.

King, G., Keohane, R. O., & Verba, S. (1994). *Designing social inquiry: Scientific inference in qualitative research.* Princeton, NJ: Princeton University Press.

Kuhn, T. (1970). *The structure of scientific revolutions.* Chicago: University of Chicago Press.

LeCompte, M. D. (1990). Emergent paradigms. How new? How necessary? In Egon G. Guba (Ed.), *The paradigm dialog* (pp. 227–45). Newbury Park, CA: Sage.

Lincoln, Y. S., & Guba, E. G. (1985). *Naturalistic inquiry.* Beverly Hills, CA: Sage.

Manning, P. K. (1991). Analytic induction. In K. Plummer (Ed.), *Symbolic interactionism: Contemporary issues* (Vol. 2, pp. 401–30). Brookfield, VT: Edward Elgar.

Mercado-Martinez, F. (2002). Qualitative research in Latin America: Critical perspectives in health. *International Journal of Qualitative Methods,* Vol. 1, Article 4. Retrieved February 12, 2002 from http://www.ualberta.ca/~ijqm/

Midgley, J. (2000). Globalization, postmodernity and international social work. In N. T. Tan and E. Envall (Eds.), *Social work around the world.* Geneva: International Federation of Social Workers.

Morse, J. (1994). Cognitive processes of analysis. In J. Morse (Ed.), *Critical issues in qualitative research methods* (pp. 23–43). Thousand Oaks, CA: Sage.

Padgett, D. K. (2000). Qualitative evaluation: Coming of age. In D. Royse, B. T. Thyer, D. K. Padgett, and T. K. Logan (Eds.), *Program Evaluation* (3rd ed., pp. 148–69). Pacific Grove, CA: Wadsworth.

Patton, M. Q. (2002). *Qualitative research and evaluation methods* (3rd ed.). Thousand Oaks, CA: Sage.

Piven, F. F., & Cloward, R. A. (1971). *Regulating the poor: The functions of public welfare.* New York: Pantheon.

Reason, P., & Bradbury, H. (2000). *Handbook of action research: Participative inquiry and practice.* Thousand Oaks, CA: Sage.

Reinharz, S. (1992). *Feminist methods in social research.* New York: Oxford University Press.

Rosenhan, D. L. (1973). On being sane in insane places. *Science, 179,* 250–8.

Schwandt, T. A. (2000). Three epistemological stances for qualitative inquiry: Interpretivism, hermeneutics, and social constructionism. In N. K. Denzin & Y. S. Lincoln (Eds.), *Handbook of qualitative research* (2nd ed., pp. 189–213). Thousand Oaks, CA: Sage.

Silverman, D. (1989). Telling convincing stories: A plea for cautious positivism in case studies. In B. Glassner & J. D. Moreno (Eds.), *Qualitative-quantitative distinctions in the social sciences* (pp. 55–77). Dordrecht: Kluwer.

Slouka, M. (2002, September). A year later: Notes on America's intimations of mortality. *Harper's Magazine,* 35–43.

Smith, L. T. (1999). *Decolonizing methodologies: Research and indigenous peoples.* New York: St. Martin's Press.

Snow, D., & Morrill, C. (1995). Ironies, puzzles, and contradictions in Denzin and Lincoln's vision of qualitative research. *Journal of Contemporary Ethnography, 22,* 358–62.

Stern, P. N. (1994). Eroding grounded theory. In J. M. Morse (Ed.), *Critical issues in qualitative research* (pp. 212–23). Thousand Oaks, CA: Sage.

Strauss, A. L., & Corbin, J. (1998). *Basics of qualitative research: Techniques and procedures for developing grounded theory* (2nd ed.). Thousand Oaks, CA: Sage.

Stringer, E. (1996). *Action research: A handbook for practitioners.* Thousand Oaks, CA: Sage.

van Maanen, J. (1988). *Tales of the field: on writing ethnography.* Chicago: University of Chicago Press.

Wacquant, L. (2002). Scrutinizing the street: poverty, morality and the pitfalls of urban ethnography. *American Journal of Sociology, 107* (6), 1468–534.

Coda

A Few Observations for Students

Theses and dissertation are ideal occasions for doing qualitative research. Completing a doctorate is one of the few times in life when we have the "luxury" (and the duty) to design and carry out a study that is our own and to engage in theoretical thinking ad infinitum (or is it ad nauseum?). And thesis or dissertation advisement presents a rare and special opportunity for mentoring (even though it doesn't happen often).

There are students who have neither the time nor temperament for qualitative study. These are the students who say, "I just want to get it over with." The alarm bells also go off when I hear that "a qualitative study is best for me because I hate statistics and numbers." It is much better to embark upon a qualitative study because(1) it suits your topic of interest and (2) you have enough (lots of) time, self-discipline, and intellectual curiosity (not necessarily in that order).

Qualitative methods have one noteworthy drawback for students—the researcher credibility issue. This is a dilemma for anyone new to qualitative methods—how can one establish such credibility before conducting a study? Any study fares better when conducted by an experienced investigator, but qualitative studies are even more dependent on this because the researcher-as-instrument factor is so critical.

How do we address this Catch 22? In addition to the obvious (i.e., taking coursework in the methodology and seeking out expert mentors), the research proposal should be designed with ample attention to rigor to convey the important message that you, the novice, know whereof you speak. Graduate programs that have infrastructure supports such as faculty mentors and peer support groups (see Chapters 9 and 10) offer a nurturing environment for the emotional and methodological challenges that come with the immersion and lack of structure of a qualitative study.

CHOOSING THE TYPE
OF QUALITATIVE APPROACH

The qualitative methods family continues to be diverse and vibrant. Even a partial listing of approaches offers a dizzying array of possibilities: ethnography, grounded theory, narrative, phenomenology, case study, hermeneutic, ecological, symbolic interaction, feminist, ethnomethodology, historiography, and discourse analysis. Although some are a closer fit with a particular discipline than others (e.g., ethnography is the sine qua non of anthropology), these approaches are relatively portable and accessible to researchers from a variety of backgrounds (assuming they are willing to expend the time and energy necessary to attain mastery).

The question still remains: how to choose which one(s) to deploy? Sometimes a student is influenced by the graduate program's overall mission or by a mentor's work. At other times, the student's topic cries out for a particular approach and he or she wends his or her way to it. Often, the student must blend several methods or approaches together to get the right combination. In a study of self-harm (cutting) among young women, for example, a doctoral student in my program adopted feminist, ecological, and family systems perspectives.

TOPICS FOR QUALITATIVE STUDY: SOME ARE A BETTER FIT THAN OTHERS

Considering which topics are optimal for a qualitative methods dissertation has led me to categorize some as "self-evident," other as "has possibilities," and still others as "are you sure you want to study this with qualitative methods?" With self-evident studies, there is a sense that *only* qualitative methods will work. These are usually (although not always) studies of populations or topics that are unfamiliar to the researcher as well as to a large segment of society. Here are a few examples from students who are familiar to me. They are studying

- Late adolescent women who have engaged in repeated acts of "cutting," or self-mutilation
- Young South Asian Americans' beliefs and practices regarding the tradition of arranged marriages
- Runaway youths ("street kids") in the Orthodox Jewish community (yes, they do exist)
- Transgender adults contemplating sexual reassignment surgery

These studies are valuable because they offer the benefit of hearing about the experience of "hidden" populations in their own words rather than filtered through psychologizing language (or any other perspective that can cloud or distort). Such topics require methods of inquiry in which rapport and prolonged engagement are central. Although often challenging, self-evident studies confer an advantage on the qualitative researcher because virtually any findings will make a contribution.

Studies that fit the "has possibilities" category tend to involve groups or setting that are better known (although not necessarily in depth). Consequently, they tend to be driven more by innovative ideas than by exploratory impulses. There are far more "has possibilities" than "self-evident" studies out there waiting to be conducted. Examples include studies of hospices, homeless shelters, or health clinics for migrant workers. Participants might include Alzheimer's caregivers, Vietnam veterans, or women firefighters.

Finally, there are the "are you sure you want to use qualitative methods?" studies. These include virtually all studies where the researcher has a strong interest or investment in knowing whether something "works" (or doesn't work). Of course, qualitative methods give added value to quantitative evaluations by exploring how or why something works, but their investment of time and resources is questionable otherwise.

"Are you sure . . ." studies include research on populations that do not have enough life experience or verbal capacity to make them "interview worthy" (e.g., very young children or the severely cognitively impaired). Observational data are a possibility here, but in the case of the severely ill or impaired, a qualitative study may not be worth the risks to them as human "subjects."

There is one more "are you sure . . ." category: studies of one's fellow professionals. The desire to study one's own is understandable and the inherent biases of doing so are not insurmountable—many students who are also social workers, teachers, nurses, and physicians have studied their co-professionals successfully. But it takes an exceptionally talented and skilled researcher to make such a study work. Too often, it is driven less by intellectual curiosity than by powerful feelings and hunches generated by personal experience. It is very hard to rid one's self of preconceptions and not-so-hidden agendas.

These three categories of topic worthiness are admittedly subjective. The most contested boundary would probably be between "has possibilities" and "are you sure . . ." studies (although some self-evident studies may not be obvious to everyone). The risk of ending up with mundane, ho-hum findings seems lowest for self-evident studies, although even these can be mishandled and yield little of substance. Methods matter, regardless of the topic. Although the researcher credibility issue looms large for novices in qualitative research, this book and a plethora of others—along with coursework, mentors, support groups, and hands-on experience—can provide a solid foundation for building a scholarly career.

Name Index

Subject Index

TO THE OWNER OF THIS BOOK:

I hope that you have found *The Qualitative Research Experience* useful. So that this book can be improved in a future edition, would you take the time to complete this sheet and return it? Thank you.

School and address: _____

_____

Department: _____

Instructor's name: _____

1. What I like most about this book is: _____

_____

_____

2. What I like least about this book is: _____

_____

_____

3. My general reaction to this book is: _____

_____

_____

4. The name of the course in which I used this book is: _____

_____

5. Were all of the chapters of the book assigned for you to read?_____

   If not, which ones weren't? _____

6. In the space below, or on a separate sheet of paper, please write specific suggestions for improving this book and anything else you'd care to share about your experience in using this book.

_____

_____

_____

_____

OPTIONAL:

Your name: _____ Date: _____

May we quote you, either in promotion for *The Qualitative Research Experience*, or in future publishing ventures?

Yes: _____ No: _____

Sincerely yours,

William Nugent and Jackie Sieppert

FOLD HERE

FOLD HERE